BUSINESS ETHICS

BUSINESS ETHICS

WHAT EVERYONE NEEDS TO KNOW®

J.S. NELSON AND LYNN A. STOUT

OXFORD
UNIVERSITY PRESS

OXFORD
UNIVERSITY PRESS

Oxford University Press is a department of the University of Oxford. It furthers
the University's objective of excellence in research, scholarship, and education
by publishing worldwide. Oxford is a registered trade mark of Oxford University
Press in the UK and certain other countries.

"What Everyone Needs to Know" is a registered trademark
of Oxford University Press.

Published in the United States of America by Oxford University Press
198 Madison Avenue, New York, NY 10016, United States of America.

CIP data is on file at the Library of Congress
ISBN 978-0-19-061026-5 (pbk.)
ISBN 978-0-19-061027-2 (hbk.)

1 3 5 7 9 8 6 4 2

Paperback printed by LSC communications, United States of America
Hardback printed by Bridgeport National Bindery, Inc., United States of America

CONTENTS

12 Specific Liability Questions and Whistleblowing Options   218

13 How to Institute Best Practices   256

14 Designing an Ethical Culture   291

PREFACE

This book was a labor of love. Lynn Stout, who had been my Corporations professor at Harvard Law School, and who had kept in touch with me for nearly twenty years afterwards as I taught in business schools, asked me whether I would like to co-author a book on business ethics with her. The original idea for the book had been legendary Oxford University Press (OUP) editor Scott Parris's. He had brought the proposal to Lynn, and Lynn wanted my perspective from teaching in business schools.

We were together excited to create the first book we knew of its kind that would survey not only moral philosophy, behavioral science, economic principles, and other contributions, but to make business-law concepts accessible and understandable to businesspeople and students of law, business, and ethics. We thought it would be particularly important to talk about compliance, investigations, whistleblowing, and prosecutions as well. We wanted to end with an appendix of people and resources that anyone with questions could reach out to.

Lynn and I shaped the table of contents and its questions together. The plan was that we would each write half of the book. Lynn wrote the first chapter, and she was able to outline her ideas for the second before getting sick. She eventually succumbed after a long battle to the cancer that took her life. Her dying wish was that the Press list me on the book as first author. The Press's response was moving: "that would be the ethical thing to do."

I have continued to labor since Lynn's passing to bring to life this book that was her vision and a natural extension of her work. Lynn was deeply committed to popularizing business law and ethics. It is my humble honor and pleasure to be able to get this manuscript into your hands as Lynn's last book, published after she has passed. She may be gone, but she will never be forgotten, and the passion of her words and educational mission live on in this book, as well as in the rest of her work.

I was helped in the completion of this work by the incredible support of my husband and children, who, particularly during the pandemic, had to contend with the book as another child demanding attention in the house. I am grateful to my mother, an English professor for some fifty years, who patiently reviewed early drafts. Christina Collins reviewed manuscripts as an editor, as well as my friend. Rosalind Wang patiently served as a sounding board and source of encouragement. The spectacular Emily Lavelle, of Lavelle Communications, helped navigate the book-publishing process, and so much more. I was cheered on in the project by my ComplianceNet co-conveners Benjamin van Rooij, Yuval Feldman, Melissa Rorie, Adam Fine, and Colin Provost. Professors in their areas of specialty, and particularly Steve Chanenson, Brett Frischmann, Andrew Lund, Jennifer O'Hare, Linda Treviño, Mary Gentile, Robert Prentice, Elizabeth Pollman, Ed Freeman, Marty Lipton, Miriam Baer, Don Langevoort, Usha Rodrigues, Colin Mayer, Veronica Root Martinez, Marc Cohen, Cynthia Williams, Claire Hill, Charles O'Kelley, Bill Bratton, Jill Fisch, Jeffrey Gordon, and so many others to whom I am indebted, gave graciously of their time and energy at different points. In addition to the support that I received from OUP, I benefitted from the aid of faculty assistants Carla Edwards, Patty Trask, and Victoria Durand; and students who touched chapters at points, including (in alphabetical order) Erica Atkin, Juliana Clifton, Lauren

DeBona, Zachary Epstein, Erin Fontaine, Meaghan Geatens, Paige Gross, Rachel Hanscom, Ryan Kelly, Yuliya Khromyak, Kaitlyn Krall, Andrew Mark, Louis Masi, Victoria Mazzola, John Morgan, Eric Nascone, Michael Neminski, Shawna Riley, Abraham Schneider, Nathaniel Stanger, Matthew Venuti, Stephanie Wood, and Melissa Zillhardt.

Most of all, now that this labor of love has come to completion, I am delighted that it is in your hands. That's where it should be—to guide you, to engage you, and to help you think more deeply about topics fundamental to our lives and the society to which we contribute around us. Lynn, as an educator, would be proud. She would want you to have these tools, and to go forth to make the world a better place—the cause she fought for and spent her life on, right up until her last breath. May her passion now be yours.

J.S. Nelson
Visiting Associate Professor
Harvard Business School, 2021-22

1

AN OVERVIEW OF
BUSINESS ETHICS

What are business ethics?

Business ethics are the set of moral principles that govern behavior in a specific sphere of life: the world of business. Some people think of the business environment as a cutthroat place in which people will do whatever they can get away with, including violating the law and misleading and harming others, in order to get ahead. This view, however, is misleading and inaccurate. Certainly, you can see instances of bad behavior in the business world (as in other areas of life), but most people with real experience in business will tell you that sound ethics are integral to a successful business career.

Business ethics embrace the idea of values and the importance of being willing to make moral judgments about right and wrong conduct. People often feel uncomfortable with the idea of exercising moral judgment. As you will see in this book, however, it is impossible to avoid this responsibility in business life and, indeed, in life generally. Moreover, although sometimes it can be difficult to figure out what the morally correct course of action might be, much of the time this becomes surprisingly obvious with a little guidance and forethought. Of course, this does not mean that following the morally correct course of action will always be easy. We hope this book will make it easier, in part by showing how ethical behavior usually works out best in the long run.

Like the idea of exercising moral judgment, the word "morality" makes some people feel squeamish. This is probably because the phrase is so often used in a religious or cultural context to defend idiosyncratic rules governing diet, dress, or sexual behavior. Business ethics take a more universal approach to moral rules. They are concerned with the basic principles that regulate our behavior in dealing with others in business, whether they are employees, customers, suppliers, or the general public.

Finally, business ethics are pragmatic. They offer concrete guidance for how to behave in business dealings, including advice for difficult situations. They also give practical guidance for daily decision-making.

What do ethics have to do with making money?

It's nice to make money, and sometimes it's a necessity. Business ethics teach, however, that we have a moral responsibility to pay attention to *how* we make money. Some ways of earning a living are ethically better than others, and some ways of making money are simply ethically unacceptable— not to mention possibly illegal.

Let's start with the positive story of how making money can be good not only for the person who makes money, but for society as a whole. You might be familiar with the eighteenth-century economist Adam Smith's parable of the market being an "invisible hand" that moves goods and services to those individuals who value them more. A farmer who has harvested more corn than she can possibly eat sells some of the corn for money that she then uses to buy a much-needed pair of shoes; while the shoemaker, who has manufactured more shoes that he can possibly wear, sells a pair to the farmer for money he can then use to buy some of the farmer's corn for dinner. Both the farmer and the shoemaker have made money, and both feel they have been left better off. The world is a better place for their self-interested exchange. Each party has not only benefited him or herself, but someone else as well.

Unfortunately, it is also possible to make money without leaving the world a better place. This possibility is one of the principal concerns of business ethics. To use an obvious example, a burglar who makes money by breaking into others' houses and stealing has not made the world a better place. Nor has the contract killer who commits murder for hire. Nor has the con artist who makes money by defrauding people.

These obvious examples illustrate an important point: as a general rule, it is unethical to make money by damaging others' persons and property (which economists call "imposing external costs") or misleading others. But what should we do when the situation is less obvious? When is it acceptable to profit from selling a product that provides clear benefits to some people, but also imposes some external costs on others—for example, mining a much-needed mineral, but using techniques that pollute the local water supply? When is it acceptable to sell something to a buyer whom you have not misled, but who believes something about the product that you know is not true?

Business ethics help us deal with these sorts of questions. They help us ensure that we are doing well by doing good, rather than doing well by doing harm.

How are business ethics different from general ethics?

Most people follow at least some ethical rules in their daily lives. (The small percentage of individuals who do not are called psychopaths; we discuss them more in Chapters 2 and 10.) The world of business, however, presents some unique issues, which is why they have evolved as a specialized field of ethics.

One of those unique issues is the sheer size and frequency of the ethical challenges that businesspeople must face. It is not unusual for those in business to be presented, almost daily, with opportunities to personally profit by violating the law or by harming or misleading others. The stakes can be enormous, especially when a big transaction or career-making decision is involved. This means people in business often face much larger temptations in the office than on the street. (Although it is usually not very tempting to shoplift a small item, the opportunity to make millions of dollars by insider trading or cheating on a large contract is far more enticing.) As a result, businesspeople must always remain aware of and sensitive to their ethical obligations. If they do not, they risk joining the long and sad parade of once-virtuous—but now notorious—white collar criminals like Enron Chair Kenneth Lay, Goldman Sachs director Rajat Gupta, and business maven Martha Stewart.

A second unique aspect of business ethics is that they operate in a social environment—business dealings—in which people, to some extent, often tolerate, expect, or even praise the selfish pursuit of personal gain. This makes the business environment quite different from many other social environments in which we interact with other people. Few of us want to be perceived as selfish at a wedding reception or a bar mitzvah. But when we are negotiating a contract or trying to sell a product, a certain degree of material self-interest is expected. The key phrase here is the qualifier, "a certain degree of." Business ethics help to keep us from crossing the line from legitimately self-interested behavior, over to unethical and/or illegal behavior.

Third, business ethics emphasize the obligations we owe not only to our friends and family, but also the obligations we owe to people with whom we have only an "arm's-length" business relationship, and even obligations owed to total strangers. Indeed, sometimes business ethics go further still, and teach that we have obligations to intangible legal entities like corporations. This aspect of business ethics can raise some practical difficulties. It is relatively easy and natural for a person to remember the interests of friends and family who she likes, and with whom she interacts on a daily basis. However, as we discuss more in Chapters 8 and 9, it is often more difficult for us to stay aware of, and respect, duties owed to people whom we don't know well or even may have never met—much less duties owed to intangible legal entities. Business ethics help us find our way through this minefield.

Finally, a fourth distinguishing characteristic of business ethics is that ethical problems in this context tend to involve unique concepts and rules specific to the business world. Many of these concepts and rules are based on, or draw upon, legal rules that apply primarily to business institutions and business dealings. For example, in this book we will discuss fiduciary duties, rules against fraud, duties owed to corporations and other legal entities, and the resources and legal protections available to "whistleblowers." Business ethics and the law are deeply intertwined.

What does it mean to have an ethical duty?

An ethical duty is an obligation or responsibility that must be met without regard to one's immediate self-interest. In other words, ethics require us to do our best to meet our obligations, even when we don't particularly want to. In Chapter 2, we explore why, in the long run, ethical conduct generally works out best for both individuals and societies. In the short run, however, complying with ethical duties typically requires the person with a duty to exercise at least a modest degree of self-restraint and sacrifice.

This is because ethical duties, including business duties, generally are intended to protect other people, like employers, customers, clients, contract counterparties, and the general public. Ethical duties require that we consider the welfare of others, not just our own welfare, in choosing how to act.

Having to respect the interests of others may not seem a very attractive prospect, especially if you're the only person doing so. Bear in mind, however, that business ethics set out general principles that apply to everyone in the business world. This means that, when businesspeople generally comply with ethical duties, you may have to sometimes consider the interests of others—but also that they have to sometimes consider your interests, as well.

What types of fiduciary duties exist?

In business ethics, the most common forms of ethical duty are called "fiduciary duties." There are a number of different types. We explore the definitions of fiduciary duties, and their meanings, more in Chapter 5. Because fiduciary duties are so common and central to many business relationships, it is important to understand them. Generally speaking, they fall into five basic categories. These are duties of *obedience*, duties of *care*, duties of *loyalty*, duties of *disclosure*, and duties of *confidentiality*.

Duties of obedience are relatively straightforward and apply most immediately to the employer–employee relationship and to our obligations as citizens. If you enter an employment or other business relationship in which you agree to follow someone else's instructions, the duty of obedience demands that you do your best to do so. The duty of obedience can also be seen in the general duty to obey the law. As a member of society, you have an obligation to follow its rules. Similarly, courts have held that corporate directors who manage corporations have a duty to take steps to ensure that their corporations obey the law.

Duties of care are more complicated. A duty of care generally requires that, in acting to protect the interests of others, you exercise a certain degree of prudence, caution, and attention. Duties of care apply in a wide range of contexts. The degree of care required to meet the duty of care, however, can vary considerably depending on the context. For example, tort law imposes a general duty on all people to avoid negligently injuring others, even total strangers. Corporate directors are only deemed to have violated their duty of care, however, if they have acted with "gross" negligence.

Duties of loyalty are among the most interesting and common form of duties in the business world. The duty of loyalty focuses on motivations, and especially on the need to ignore one's own material self-interest in favor of serving the interests of others. Like the duty of care, the degree of loyalty demanded depends on the nature of the business relationship. For example, corporate directors owe their corporations a very high degree of loyalty, and they should scrupulously avoid doing anything that would allow them to benefit at the corporation's expense. On the other hand, partners in normal contract relationships owe each other a more modest "duty of good faith," which typically precludes them from trying to harm their contract counterparty, but otherwise allows them to pursue the course of action that benefits themselves the most.

Duties of disclosure (sometimes called duties of candor) deal with the communication of information, and also are quite common in the business world. When a full duty of disclosure exists, the party subject to the duty must disclose all "material" (important) information relevant to the relationship or transaction. In other circumstances, the duty of disclosure is much weaker, and simply precludes a party from making statements that are false or deliberately misleading. When the duty of disclosure is very limited, silence is golden.

When a duty of confidentiality applies, the party subject to the duty must avoid disclosing to third parties the information that was entrusted to him or her in confidence. The duty of confidentiality is assumed to apply in certain business relationships, such as those between lawyers and clients or between doctors and patients. In other cases, the duty of confidentiality arises as the result of a formal contractual agreement, sometimes called a nondisclosure agreement.

To whom (or what) can businesspeople owe ethical duties?

If complying with business ethics were always easy and obvious, we would not need write to a book about it! One of the factors that can make ethical business decision-making difficult is the wide variety of parties to whom businesspeople owe ethical duties. A second factor is that some of the "parties" to whom businesspeople can owe duties are not human beings. Rather, they are intangible legal entities, like corporations. Although the idea of owing a duty to an intangible entity is difficult for many people to wrap their heads around, it is central to many ethical problems in business. In Chapters 5 and 6, we discuss in greater detail what it means to owe a duty to a legal entity.

Ethical duties frequently arise between different people who exercise governance roles within a single business organization. For example, partners in a partnership owe duties to each other. Similarly, directors and officers of corporations owe duties to the shareholders of the corporation and to the corporation itself as a legal entity. Shareholders even owe duties to other shareholders and, sometimes, to the corporate entity itself. Ethical duties within organizations are frequently labeled fiduciary duties.

Ethical duties also arise when businesspeople enter contractual relationships with each other. For example, employees owe duties to employers, and vice versa. Purchasers owe duties to suppliers, and suppliers to purchasers. Producers owe duties to customers who purchase their products.

Contractual relationships between certain kinds of professionals and their clients give rise to heightened ethical duties. Examples include the relationships between lawyers and clients, between doctors and patients, and between accountants and clients.

Finally, businesspeople, like other people, owe duties to the general public and to society as a whole. In Chapters 2 and 7, we discuss why people in the world of business should pay attention not only to how their conduct affects the people inside their organizations and those with whom they do business directly, but also to how their decisions affect society at large.

Why should I care about business ethics?

We must admit that, so far, the idea of paying attention to business ethics seems a bit unattractive. It sounds like hard work. And, in truth, ethical business decision-making can require thoughtfulness and self-restraint. Sometimes an ethical businessperson must make what seem to be, at least at the time, significant sacrifices.

Studying business ethics makes ethical decision-making a bit easier, however, for at least two reasons. First, studying business ethics can help you understand the rules that you should use in making moral business decisions, and alert you to some of the ethical dilemmas and pitfalls that you are likely to encounter during your career. Second, business ethics can also teach you some techniques and strategies that will help you summon the strength necessary to meet these challenges.

Some readers might still ask, why should I want to understand the rules, and develop the strength to follow them? In Chapter 2, we offer some answers to this question. As you'll see, organizations and societies with high ethical standards tend to flourish, while those with weak ethics often fail. The same is true for most individuals.

2

THE BENEFITS OF ACTING ETHICALLY

Being ethical sounds like hard work. What is the upside?

Having ethics means following certain moral rules without regard to your own self-interest. It should not be a surprise, then, that acting ethically sometimes requires both individuals and organizations to do things that they would prefer not to do, and to refrain from doing things that they would like to do. A commitment to ethics means accepting certain burdens, especially in the short run.

But there are many compensating benefits from choosing to act ethically—perhaps even especially—in the business world. First and foremost, embracing ethics in business benefits ethical individuals and business organizations themselves. But, as we will also see, when people and organizations behave ethically, the benefits of ethical behavior multiply. Just as unethical actions impose "external" costs on others, ethical behavior produces external benefits, for other people and for society as a whole. For example, when businesspeople act ethically, society needs to spend fewer resources enforcing rules; the transactions costs of doing business are lower; and we avoid costly disasters like the BP oil spill, the 2008 mortgage crisis, and the LIBOR price-fixing scandal. The benefits of business ethics can therefore be seen at the individual, organizational, and societal levels.

Many of the benefits that flow from ethical business behavior are "public goods," meaning that they are shared with others. When I choose to act ethically, I often benefit myself. But others benefit from my ethical action as well. Unfortunately, as economic theory predicts and experiments confirm, this means that ethical behavior tends to be "underprovided," unless some mechanism exists to reward ethical actions and punish unethical ones, at least occasionally. Without such rewards and punishments, many people eventually default to purely selfish and even unethical behavior. As discussed further in Chapter 4, this pattern has been seen in numerous experiments run by psychologists and economists.

This is one of the many reasons why it is important for both business organizations and societies to find ways to identify and reward those who act ethically, while ferreting out and discouraging unethical behavior. In fact, healthy societies and organizations typically *do* reward individuals who act ethically (and punish those who don't). This chapter explores the many external rewards that await both individuals and organizations that commit themselves to acting ethically in business. It also explores another important upside of ethical behavior for individuals: the substantial "internal" rewards that acting ethically offers in the form of better health, greater happiness, and more positive relationships with others.

Won't I be at a competitive disadvantage if I always act ethically?

It's easy to think of being ethical as disadvantageous. How can you compete against others successfully when you obey the rules of the game, and they don't? As this choice of words (compete, rules, games) suggests, being ethical can indeed be disadvantageous in "zero-sum games," in which one person can gain only if another person loses. If I can only win the game by making you lose, then winning any way that I can—including winning by cheating—seems the best strategy for the purely selfish player.

Luckily, zero-sum games are not that common in modern life, including modern business life. Most of the time, when people cooperate with each other and act ethically instead of selfishly and unethically, they generate substantial collective gains. To use the common economic analogy, people who co-operate receive more pie by making the pie larger, instead of simply fighting over the size of their particular slices. For example, when manufacturers tell the truth about their products, consumers are more willing to buy (and to buy more) because they have confidence that their purchases will meet their expectations. Both consumers and manufacturers are left better off. Similarly, when employers and employees trust each other, they focus their time and attention on getting the job done, instead of trying to detect employee misbehavior or looking for another job. Getting the job done better provides more in sales and profits for employers, and higher wages and greater job security for employees.

Of course, an unethical individual or organization can sometimes do better in the short run by cheating. The key idea here, however, is that this is generally true *only* in the short run. Eventually, the decision to behave ethically is usually advantageous, for both people and businesses. For example, in his book, *Give and Take: A Revolutionary Approach to Success*, business scholar Adam Grant demonstrates how workplace "givers" who work hard, share knowledge, and "take the high road" may do more poorly at the beginning than "takers" who focus only on advancing themselves, but givers typically outperform takers in their long-term careers.[1]

Ethical businesses and businesspeople tend to thrive for at least three reasons, which we explore in greater detail later, but introduce here.

First, being ethical helps individuals and organizations avoid or limit the serious, negative legal consequences that can flow from taking ethical shortcuts that seem advantageous in the short run, but prove disastrous. (These negative consequences are explored in greater detail in Chapter 8.) Consider the case of the accounting firm Arthur Andersen. Formerly one of the "Big Five" accounting firms, in 2002 Arthur Andersen was forced to surrender its license to practice accounting after being found guilty of criminal charges relating to the firm's auditing work for corporate giant Enron, which itself collapsed in 2001 in the wake of a massive accounting scandal.[2] In the short run, both Arthur Andersen and its partners who handled the Enron account seemed to benefit from cutting corners, including destroying documents.[3] In the long run, however, the 89-year-old firm's felony conviction led to its downfall.[4] (Now businesspeople talk about the "Big Four," or fewer, accounting firms.) Before you decide that unethical behavior is the best strategy for you, bear in mind that in the long run it frequently leads to fines, legal defense costs, the loss of a business license, or jail time. Conversely, choosing to behave ethically avoids these costs, leading to better odds of long-term business and personal success. In some cases—for example, making the difficult decision to "blow the whistle" on others' misconduct—may even bring you material rewards.

Second, developing a reputation for being ethical and trustworthy will bring you opportunities and advantages—such as support from superiors, loyalty from employees, the trust of customers and clients—that unethical competitors don't have. Conversely, indulging in unethical behavior can damage or even ruin your reputation, limiting your future opportunities by causing people and organizations to become unwilling to deal with you. (Even before Arthur Andersen surrendered its accounting license, it was hemorrhaging clients who did not want to be associated with its name. Although the Supreme Court eventually reversed Arthur Andersen's criminal conviction on technical grounds—the Court held that improperly vague jury instructions had been used at trial[5]—by then, Arthur Andersen's business reputation had become toxic, and the firm collapsed.)

Third and perhaps most important to most individuals, there are significant, intrinsic advantages to acting ethically. As discussed in more detail below, ethical people, it turns out, generally lead happier, healthier lives.

What are the material advantages of ethical action for individuals?

Let's start by considering the many reasons why an individual can expect to benefit materially from embracing ethics in business. One of the more obvious benefits is avoiding the legal sanctions—judgments, fines, loss of license, imprisonment—that we discuss in Chapter 8. But there are other material benefits for individuals as well.

One benefit from acting ethically is that meeting your ethical obligations to others makes you less likely to find yourself embroiled in conflict with them later. It's easy to underestimate this benefit, because unethical acts can bring immediate rewards, and the true costs of conflict often show up later. But, if you stop to think about it, you will realize that conflict with others is expensive. It drains away time, money, and attention better spent elsewhere. Of course, some conflict is inevitable in both business and in life. But, by reducing conflict, behaving ethically can save you valuable time and money (not to mention help you to avoid stress).

Another subtle but significant advantage of business ethics is that you don't have to put in effort and resources trying to cover up, explain away, or excuse your ethical lapses. As Mark Twain supposedly put it, if you always tell the truth, there is less that you have to remember.[6] Adhering to your principles not only makes your life easier, it allows you to focus your energy on getting the job done. This in turn makes you more likely to succeed.

A third key reward from embracing business ethics is that, over time, you will develop a strong and valuable reputation with others for having strong ethics. We live in a highly connected society in which information is readily available, and you bring your past with you when you deal with new people and organizations. Having a reputation for behaving ethically will bring you opportunities and advantages on which you would otherwise miss out. As an employee, you'll be sought-after for positions that require responsibility and conscientiousness. As an employer or supervisor, you'll attract loyal employees. As a professional or business owner, you'll be preferred by customers, clients, and suppliers. Not only will people and institutions be more willing to deal with you, they'll likely rely on less haggling and negotiation, and they will be more willing to forgo detailed (and expensive) formal contracts. Finally, they will be more inclined to "cut you slack" when things go wrong. (So will authorities. Judges, for example, routinely consider evidence of character and reputation when imposing criminal sentences.)

Given all these material benefits, why do some businesspeople still act unethically? Some may be psychopaths[7] without a conscience, as we discuss in Chapter 10. For many people, however, ethical lapses are the result of myopically focusing on immediate rewards, rather than long-term gains. After all, developing a good ethical reputation takes time, and you have to prove your ethics through your actions, not just your words. (You can't build a good reputation merely by making promises about what you're going to do.) This means building a reputation for ethics is a long-term investment; the gains, while substantial, come later. In contrast, the possible profits from acting unethically—trading on insider information, making sales by misleading customers—come quickly.

Before you succumb to temptation, though, remember that, while it takes a long time to build a good reputation, you can lose your entire investment almost instantly. As Benjamin Franklin said, "[i]t takes many good deeds to build a good reputation, and only one bad one to lose it."[8] And, once you've lost your reputation, you'll pay the consequences for years to come. If you're convicted of a felony, for example, you'll not only find it harder to get a job; you'll also face difficulties voting, renting an apartment, getting a loan, and visiting other countries.

Finally, a number of federal laws seek to promote business ethics by providing material rewards to individuals who "blow the whistle" on employers and firms that violate the law. The False Claims Act allows private citizens to sue employers that commit fraud against the government, and to receive a portion of any amount recovered.[9] The Act also allows employees to sue employers who retaliate against the whistleblower for damages.[10] The Securities and Exchange Commission (SEC) Whistleblower Program pays whistleblowers with awards of between 10% to 30% of monetary sanctions collected by the SEC in cases in which the whistleblower provided original information about federal securities laws violations.[11] The Internal Revenue Service (IRS) has a similar program for individuals who report people and businesses that fail to pay taxes.[12] The Whistleblower Protection Act in the Sarbanes–Oxley Act provides protection against retaliation for federal employees who report illegal government activity.[13]

In sum, there are many good reasons why an individual who practices good ethics in business can expect to be materially rewarded—in the long run, and sometimes in the short run as well. Knowing this can help you resist the temptation to seek short-term advantages by cutting ethical corners.

What are the physical and psychological advantages of acting ethically for individuals?

The likelihood of eventual material rewards is not the only reason to practice business ethics. The personal or "internal" rewards for individuals from acting ethically may be even more important. In *The Republic*, Plato famously wrote that "the just man is happy, and the unjust man is miserable."[14] Mahatma Gandhi held much the same view: "Happiness is when what you think, what you say, and what you do are in harmony."[15]

Plato and Gandhi were on to something. Extensive evidence confirms that embracing ethics and integrity in your life will make you a happier and healthier person. It may even help you live longer.

To give only a few examples, a 2003 study by Professor John Helliwell of individuals' self-reported happiness in the World Values Survey found that people who think it's never acceptable to cheat on taxes enjoy a higher level of happiness than people who think it's sometimes acceptable to cheat.[16] Another 2011 World Values Survey study by Professor Harvey James found that people who think it's sometimes justifiable to indulge in other types of unethical behavior (such as claiming benefits to which they are not entitled, not paying fares on public transportation, and accepting bribes) are less happy than people who believe these behaviors are unjustifiable.[17] Multiple studies confirm that people who volunteer, which is a pro-social behavior connected to ethics, are more satisfied with their lives than people who do not.[18]

Greater happiness, in turn, is associated with better health. In one experiment, subjects who reported higher happiness levels were less likely to become ill after being infected with a cold virus.[19] In another study, nuns who reported high levels of happiness in autobiographies written in their twenties were found to have significantly longer life expectancies six decades later.[20] Embracing ethics can make you not only healthier and happier, but also more popular;[21] another study found that people who score high on integrity are more well-liked.[22]

Why are people who embrace ethics and integrity happier, healthier, and more well-liked? There are several plausible explanations. One possibility is that people who embrace ethics are, by definition, willing to think about and value something other than themselves. This both makes them more attractive to others, and helps them avoid too much "self-focus," which is linked to anxiety and depression.[23] Another possibility is that ethical people simply have less to worry about—following the rules means that you can sleep better at night. Yet another interesting possibility is that ethical people are happier because they're happy with *themselves*.[24] One of the most basic human emotions is disgust; we are repelled by tainted foods and substances. We have the same emotional response (and use many of the same neural pathways in our brains) when we encounter behavior that evokes "moral disgust."[25] This is why you might say "John's behavior leaves a bad taste in my mouth," or "what Jane said doesn't sit right with me." So, imagine for a moment how you might feel if you did something unethical—and then had to experience self-disgust repeatedly whenever you looked in the mirror.

When we consider the enormous internal benefits that flow from choosing to behave ethically, it becomes easier to understand why, according to clinical psychologist Martha Stout, psychopathic individuals who lack a conscience and who are unburdened by ethics are also frequently bored, unhappy, and many times more likely than non-psychopaths to abuse drugs and alcohol.[26] Caring nothing for others, psychopaths self-medicate against the pain (in Professor Stout's words) of finding themselves "loveless, amoral, and chronically bored."[27] They are unable to follow the simple recipe for happiness that Eleanor Roosevelt laid out when she was 76: "a feeling that you have been honest with yourself and those around you; a feeling that you have done the best you could both in your personal life and in your work; and the ability to love others."[28]

What if being ethical means that I make less money—won't that make me unhappy?

Maybe—but probably not. The relationship between money and happiness has been the subject of extensive study. In brief, most researchers find that greater income and wealth are indeed correlated with greater happiness.[29] The relationship is only significant, however, at relatively low income levels. If you are very poor, and feel anxious and insecure in your ability to meet your household's basic needs (food, shelter), an increase in wealth or income that gives you security will make you significantly happier.[30] But the effect of an increase in income on happiness becomes much weaker once someone has achieved middle-class status. After that, even a very large increase in income or wealth does not have much effect. A famous study of lottery winners by sociologist Roy Kaplan, for example, found that only a few months after winning the lottery, they were not much happier than a control group of individuals who had not won the lottery.[31] In 1974, economist Richard Easterlin published a famous paper showing that, while real income per capita has increased substantially in Western countries during the past half-century, there has been no corresponding rise in reported happiness levels.[32] (Economists call this the "Easterlin Paradox," and it has been confirmed in subsequent studies.)[33]

When we combine the evidence that ethical people are happier with the evidence that money does not contribute much to happiness, it's hard to escape the conclusion that it's a mistake to trade your ethics for more money. Many people seem to recognize this intuitively. In his book, *What Price the Moral High Ground? How to Succeed Without Selling Your Soul*, economist Robert Frank showed how many people are willing to accept lower pay in order to work in careers in which they feel are making a social contribution.[34] Conversely, people demand higher pay to work in ethically questionable fields, like the tobacco industry, that are associated with social harms. This pattern suggests that most people recognize that they will be better off doing work that fits with their moral principles, even if they end up earning a bit less. (And, in the long run, they may not earn less, as we discuss above, and as Professor Frank also argued in his book.)[35]

At the same time, it's important to be aware of one situation in which earning less money may indeed make you unhappy: when you are earning less money than other people around you to whom you compare yourself. Although happiness is relatively insensitive to absolute levels of wealth and income (at least once people have achieved middle-class status), it may be more sensitive to *relative* income and wealth.[36] It seems part of human nature to want to "keep up with the Joneses." If you choose to live in a neighborhood in which most people are wealthier than you are, or a workplace in which most people earn more than you do, money may seem more important to you—and you might find it harder to hang onto your ethics.

What can I do to increase the chances that my ethical behavior will be rewarded?

Whether or not the business world rewards you for acting ethically, following your moral principles is something over which you have a good deal of control, and you can increase the likelihood of being rewarded for your ethics by choosing the right environment or workplace. In Chapter 4, we examine the psychology of ethics and the social factors that promote ethical behavior. These include support from authority ("tone at the top"), the belief that others behave ethically, and an understanding of why ethics leave everyone better off. You want to look for the same factors in your working environment. If you find them, you are likely to be in a place in which the value of ethics is recognized, and where ethical behavior is supported and rewarded. Conversely, you want to avoid a workplace in which your superiors and co-workers are ethically dubious, and where ethics are not widely recognized to be important. In such an environment, you're likely to be at a disadvantage, and your trustworthiness and responsibility may be neither recognized nor rewarded. You may even succumb to the temptation to act unethically yourself. (Remember the adage, "if you lie down with dogs, you'll get up with fleas.")

Another concern in thinking about being rewarded for ethical behavior is a business environment that relies too heavily on ex-ante incentive schemes to motivate people. As discussed in Chapter 9, it's harder for someone to remain honest when she or he can make enormous amounts of money, or avoid serious negative consequences, by acting unethically. And it's difficult—and perhaps impossible in most cases—to devise ex-ante incentive schemes that can't be "gamed" by acting unethi-cally. Not surprisingly, incentive plans have been implicated in a variety of recent scandals, including Enron's collapse in 2001; the widespread underwriting of fraudulent mortgages that led to the 2008 financial crisis; and the 2009 Atlanta teacher scandal (178 Atlanta public school teachers and administrators were found to have changed students' test scores on standardized tests to meet incentive targets). Rather than focusing on ex-ante incentives, it's ethically safer for a workplace to empha-size "after-the-fact" rewards such as raises, promotions, and discretionary bonuses.

A related concern in choosing a workplace that will reward ethical behavior is avoiding a highly unequal workplace that places too much emphasis on relative position. When people feel status is both important and threatened, they can become highly motivated to protect and improve their status, even, if necessary, by unethical means. Moreover, they can then per-ceive co-workers not as colleagues, but as competitors. The fight for status increases social distance between co-workers, encouraging more purely selfish behavior. Enron, for example, fell into this trap by adopting a "rank and yank" policy of grading employees annually and firing the bottom-ranked 10%. The firm's philosophy was "pressure makes diamonds."[37] Unfortunately, as the firm soon discovered, pressure also made felons. Similar behavior has been observed at Amazon and other companies.[38]

A second critical step that you can take to make it more likely that your ethics will be rewarded is always to be alert to, and protective of, your good reputation. This means thinking long-term and resisting short-term temptations to cut eth-ical corners. As already discussed, a good reputation takes a long time to build, but it can be lost very quickly. Building a reputation, however, requires more than merely acting ethi-cally—people need to *know* that you act ethically. This need to make a statement will be obvious in the unfortunate (and rare) case in which someone must make a great personal sacrifice to follow her or his principles. Consider Attorney General Elliot Richardson and Deputy Attorney General William Ruckelshaus, both of whom resigned their positions in the Nixon administration in 1973 rather than carry out President Nixon's illegal order to fire special prosecutor Archibald Cox, who was investigating the infamous Watergate break-ins. (Nixon then ordered Solicitor General Robert Bork to fire Cox. Bork did so—his posthumously published memoirs revealed that Nixon had promised Bork a seat on the Supreme Court[39]— but when Reagan nominated Bork to the Court in 1987, the Senate rejected his nomination.)

More commonly, you can help build your reputation for ethics by being willing to take the public position that ethics matter. This doesn't mean always standing on a soapbox and lecturing others, but it does mean that, when you spot significant ethical problems, you shouldn't hide in the crowd or "go along to get along." Tactfully, but definitively, raise the issue. Doing so may be stressful in the short term, but it will protect your reputation in the long term. (A 2006 study by psychologist Pat Barclay found that, in group games, subjects who acted as "altruistic punishers"—by taking it upon themselves to punish other players who were misbehaving—were deemed to be more trustworthy and more worthy of respect than subjects who themselves behaved, but did not also altruistically punish others.)[40]

How do organizations benefit when their employees and executives act ethically?

Because organizations are not people, they do not reap the physical and emotional rewards (health, happiness) individuals can from acting ethically. But, as much or even more than individuals, business firms and other organizations reap material benefits from embracing ethics. Most directly, more ethical firms are more attractive to—and face lower transactions costs when dealing with—important stakeholders like customers, employees, and investors. And, when ethical firms do make mistakes and face repercussions, they are more likely to survive and continue doing business.

Let's start with why ethical organizations do better with stakeholders. The benefits of an ethical reputation when dealing with customers are obvious: when customers believe that a firm will treat them honestly and fairly, they become more willing to purchase the firm's products and services. (This explains much of the success of franchises; customers perceive a franchise name like Dunkin' or Marriott as guaranteeing a certain level of quality and customer service.) In addition, as evidenced by the success of companies like the Body Shop and Etsy, some potential customers prefer—and are willing to pay a premium for—the products of companies that have a reputation not only for treating customers fairly, but also for behaving responsibly toward employees, local communities, and the environment.

Similarly, ethical firms also do better at attracting investors, both because those investors are less worried about being themselves defrauded, and because some investors prefer to invest in socially responsible companies. (The increasing role of socially responsible investing practices is discussed in Chapter 7). Last, but not least, ethical businesses find it easier to attract ethical employees, and may even have to pay them less. (As discussed above, employees demand higher wages when they feel that they are being asked to sacrifice their principles.) Ethical employees are likely to do a better job, with less in-fighting, more teamwork, and less need for management constantly to monitor for slacking, shirking, fraud, and theft.

Having a reputation as an ethical organization can be especially important when a firm runs into trouble. Both stakeholders and government regulators are more likely to "cut some slack" for an organization that has a good reputation, but that has recently encountered difficulties. In 1982, when Johnson & Johnson was one of the most successful and respected over-the-counter drug-makers in the United States, seven people died as a result of some then-unknown person, or persons, tainting Tylenol capsules in Chicago-area drugstores with cyanide. Johnson & Johnson immediately alerted consumers nationwide not to consume any type of Tylenol product; stopped producing and advertising the brand; and recalled all existing supplies in the U.S. on store shelves. It did not resume selling Tylenol until it had developed a new, triple-sealed safety package to prevent tampering. Due to the widespread perception that Johnson & Johnson handled the Tylenol crisis responsibly and ethically, the company soon completely recovered the market share that it had lost due to the crisis.[41]

Researchers who study the link between "organizational virtue" and firm performance have confirmed that, in the long run, business ethics pay off for organizations. Studies have found that "virtuous organizations" that score high on perceived compassion, integrity, and trust outperform less virtuous organizations on a number of performance measures, including profitability, productivity, customer retention, and employee loyalty.[42] For example, a study by researchers Jody Hoffer Gittell, Kim Cameron, Sandy Lim, and Victor Rivas of the U.S. airline industry after September 11, 2001, concluded that firms that tried hard not to lay off employees, and that were not highly leveraged, recovered their market share and stock price more quickly than those that were not.[43]

The lack of an ethical reputation also hurts organizations that may otherwise have experienced better results. For example, by 2015, the pharmaceutical company Valeant, whose CEO at the time was a former hedge-fund manager, had acquired a reputation for exploiting its customers and employees. When questions were raised about the company's accounting practices, its stock price plummeted by nearly 80%.[44] (So much for "maximizing shareholder value.")

How can organizations increase the chances that their ethical behavior will be rewarded?

As in the case of individuals, businesses that want to benefit from having a reputation for ethical behavior have to do their best to avoid ethical failures. In Chapters 10 and 13, we offer numerous suggestions for how organizations can minimize the risk of ethical lapses, such as establishing the right tone at the top, working to identify and remove unethical employees, adopting and communicating formal codes of conduct, establishing compliance and monitoring systems, and avoiding over-reliance on incentive compensation schemes. These are all essential tools for businesses that want to avoid the kinds of scandals that can so badly damage a firm's reputation.

But, to get the most from a good reputation, it's often useful for a company not only to "walk the walk" but also to "talk the talk," and deliberately communicate its commitment to ethics to its stakeholders. Possible methods include referencing ethics in its labeling, advertising, and recruiting; adopting a mission statement that incorporates the company's ethical concerns; and even launching a media campaign. Expressing a public commitment to ethics can be a valuable way for a company to attract important stakeholders, and to get them to do business on more favorable terms (for example, consumers may be willing to pay a higher price, or employees to accept a lower wage).

At the same time, there is risk in adopting a public commitment to ethics that is not backed up by action. Many companies have been criticized for "greenwashing" (making public claims about environmentally responsible behavior that are not supported by the facts). These accusations can be embarrassing: in 2002, "Greenwashing Academy Awards" were handed out to companies like BP and Exxon Mobil during the World Summit on Sustainable Development.[45] Nevertheless, greenwashing has become so common that the Federal Trade

Commission (FTC) has issued a Green Guide, cautioning businesses that seek to market products as "environmentally" friendly to avoid false or deceptive claims, and it has taken enforcement actions against businesses that fail to do so.[46]

Thanks to the prevalence of greenwashing, stakeholders today can be skeptical of corporate claims of social or environmental responsibility when these claims come directly from the corporation. One way to overcome such skepticism is to use "third-party certification." A number of independent organizations exist that can independently assess a business's products, manufacturing processes, or operating results, and certify that the company is meeting a specific performance standard. These third-party certifiers play a role similar to audit firms that certify businesses' financial results, except that auditors focus on non-financial factors like product safety, workplace conditions, or environmental sustainability. To give a few examples, the Leadership in Energy and Environmental Design (LEED) rating system is widely used to certify whether buildings meet certain environmental standards. The International Standards Organization (ISO) offers certification on a variety of different environmental and social performance measures, and voluntary guidelines on others.

More globally, several nonprofit organizations are now providing broader metrics for companies' environmental, social, and governance (ESG) performance. Examples include the Global Reporting Initiative (GRI), the International Integrated Reporting Council (IIRC), and the U.S.'s Sustainability Accounting Standards Board (SASB). These ESG reporting frameworks emphasize slightly different factors (for example, the GRI pays closer attention to stakeholder satisfaction and environmental impact, while the SASB focuses more on how non-financial factors impact investor returns).

Currently, for the most part, organizations are not required to provide ESG reports, but do so voluntarily, as a means of signaling their ethical commitments. This situation may change, however. There are signs that governments are moving toward mandatory ESG reporting. For example, European Parliament Directive 2013/34/EU requires EU member states to adopt laws requiring large, multinational corporations to disclose information relating to their environmental impact, treatment of employees, anti-corruption, and bribery efforts.[47]

How do societies benefit when individuals and organizations act ethically?

So far, we have focused on how acting ethically benefits individuals and organizations. But, when individuals and organizations behave ethically, the result can have enormous benefits for society as a whole.

As our world has become more interdependent and interconnected, the problem of "externalities"—harms that we impose on others or benefits we could (but don't) provide them—has grown. Without some means of limiting external costs and encouraging external benefits, our lives would indeed be (to quote political philosopher Thomas Hobbes) "nasty, brutish, and short."[48] As Hobbes himself argued, one important way we deal with the problem of externalities is through the law. Tort laws that require us to pay damages when we negligently injure someone, and antipollution rules that fine industries that damage the environment, are examples of laws that control external costs. Contract laws that make it easier for us to rely on each other when exchanging goods and services are examples of rules that encourage us to act in ways that benefit others.

But laws are expensive to create and enforce. They're also imperfect; many things that people do that violate the law may never be detected, or, if detected, may not be proven in court. And the law doesn't, and can't, cover every possible situation in which external costs and benefits come into play. This is why ethics are so important to a healthy society. When individuals and organizations commit themselves to behaving ethically, they are both less likely to harm others, and more likely to help them.

Consider, for example, how important ethics are in driving on the highway. Although we focus our attention on the occasional rude driver who cuts us off, or fails to use his or her turn signal, it's worth stopping to think for a moment what driving would be like if everyone behaved that way—and to think about how many more police officers we would have to hire merely to be able to travel down the road.

Similarly, business ethics make the business world flow more smoothly, and they allow us to spend fewer resources enforcing rules against behavior such as forming cartels, paying bribes, defrauding customers, sexually harassing employees, and polluting the environment. The result is a society with a stronger economy—more time, energy, and resources are invested in productive endeavors, and fewer are wasted on protecting against other people's bad behavior. Numerous empirical studies of the economic value of "social capital" have confirmed that countries in which more people believe that it is safe to trust others tend to enjoy higher rates of economic growth and investment.[49] Similarly, economic growth rates are stronger in nations where a greater proportion of people report in surveys that it is "never justifiable" to cheat on taxes or to fraudulently claim government benefits.[50] Even stock market returns are higher in countries where people report that they can trust others.[51]

Ethical societies are not only more prosperous—they also seem to be more pleasant places to live. As John Stuart Mill observed in his 1848 economics textbook, *Principles of Political Economy*, "[t]he advantage to mankind of being able to trust one another, penetrates into every crevice and cranny of human life: the economical is perhaps the smallest part of it."[52] Empirical studies find a positive relationship between the level of trust in others as well as the society's institutions, and the subjective well-being reported by the individuals in that society.[53] Similarly, a 2008 study by Professor Margit Tavits found a negative correlation between average levels of reported subjective well-being in a country and its level of corruption as measured by Transparency International.[54]

In sum, business ethics not only benefit individuals and organizations—they also benefit entire societies. When we all strive to be ethical, we all become better off.

3

MORAL PHILOSOPHICAL BASES FOR BUSINESS ETHICS

What are the major schools of philosophical ethical thought?

There are at least five major schools of ethical thought in philosophy that have built upon each other and responded to each other's strengths and weaknesses. Businesspeople making decisions need to be able to use tools from all of those major schools of ethical thought in order to challenge their established thinking from multiple perspectives.

Research has shown us that, if individuals do not rigorously examine their methods of thinking about choices, they tend to fall into the same traps and often start to justify increasingly worse behavior. It takes conscious will and effort to build ethical muscle. We benefit tremendously from the foundational work that philosophers have done before us to grapple with deciding what is the right way to act.

The five major schools of philosophical ethical thought are:

1. *Ethics of virtue, such as from Aristotle.* These ideas emphasize what personal virtues make someone a good human being. Forms of such character-based ethics trace from classical Greece, were popular in Judeo-Christian thought through the Middle Ages, and are often returned to by modern philosophers.

2. *Ethics of care, such as communitarianism.* These ideas emphasize a person's place in his or her community, and they prioritize the network of relationships that a person has with others over rewards for him or herself.

3. *Cost–benefit rationales, such as utilitarianism.* These ideas, such as Jeremy Bentham's utilitarianism, attempt to quantify moral questions in order to yield the largest benefit across numbers of people.

4. *Rights-and-duties rationales, such as Kant's categorical imperative.* Rights-and-duties rationales emphasize the development of moral rules to govern individuals in society. Immanuel Kant's categorical imperative, for example, appears similar to the traditional "Golden Rule," although with important distinctions.

5. *Distributive-justice rationales, such as Rawls's principles.* Distributive-justice rationales emphasize fairness and equality as fundamental to how society should be structured. John Rawls's principles would originate from behind a "veil of ignorance" and be applied after the lifting of that veil to create a more moral society.

What are the strengths and limits of virtue ethics, such as in Aristotle's writings?

The classical Greek philosopher Aristotle believed that people who developed personal virtues would make good human beings. He started a list of what he thought were the proper virtues that every person should develop. But his approach was not a hard-headed imposition of specific behavior in every situation. Rather, Aristotle argued that living up to the standards of being a virtuous person is a work in progress.

Key to implementing Aristotle's virtues is reasoning between extremes. The four commonly accepted, modern-day virtues from Aristotle's work are courage, temperance, justice, and prudence. Courage is facing fear with the proper balance between the extremes of cowardice (too much fear) and recklessness (too little fear). Temperance is controlling your desire for food between the extremes of gluttony (consuming too much food) and austerity (consuming too little food). Justice is the proper balance between the extremes of giving people too much—or not enough—of what they should receive. Prudence is knowing what is reasonable in situations, and it undergirds the implementation of the other virtues.

In the Middle Ages, the Catholic philosopher Thomas Aquinas added the virtues of religious faith, hope, and charity to Aristotle's list as a way for people to become closer to God. Additionally, Aquinas advocated for other changes, such as replacing Aristotle's virtue of pride with humility, which was viewed as more desirable for Aquinas's time.

Modern philosophers view virtue ethics' strength as providing specific, objective goals that anyone can follow to develop into a good human being. Virtue ethics provide structure and direction for individuals to follow in areas of action that can feel otherwise amorphous.

But philosophers have also argued that the additions of Aquinas and others to Aristotle's list involve too much social context for what traits might be desirable, and that the results of virtue-ethics analyses can become overly dependent on the norms of any particular time and place.

Two sets of questions then arise for virtue ethics today. The first set of questions involves which virtues to list. Modern philosophers have suggested that, in our world, important virtues are missing from the list, such as honesty, sincerity, persistence, dependability, and the ability not to engage in discrimination. At what point should these virtues be added or apply to our behavior? Similarly, should any of Aristotle's or Aquinas's virtues be phased out? When, where, and why?

The second set of questions for virtue ethics concern being overly reliant on current norms in finding the right balance between extremes to express virtues. How do you find this balance? How do you gauge where you are in this balance? Where are those extremes for you and how do you measure them? Is the middle always the right path? In modern business, for example, being caught in the middle of the road is sometimes exactly the wrong answer.

What are the strengths and limits of ethics-of-care rationales such as communitarianism?

The focus of virtue ethics on the individual is challenged by competing ethics-of-care approaches, such as communitarianism. Communitarianism asserts that the most important part of ethical choices is how we should relate to other people in a community. It teaches that we owe important obligations in our behavior to those in our community who have nurtured, cared for, and guided us, even over our shorter-lived relationships with other people. Therefore, a communitarian would argue for treating our family, close friends, and those with whom we share our background with preference over our own interests or the application of abstract principles.

Leaders of Asian cultures, in particular the modern founder of Singapore,[1] have criticized classical Western individualism for its lack of understanding of this issue. Although Western traditions might invoke the idea of bettering oneself first to work toward an over-arching common good, Asian traditions tend to prioritize a person's connections with his or her family, and other close personal relationships. The communitarian insight is that we are not isolated individuals, and that we should not act as though we are.

A strength of communitarian ethics is that they promote taking care of the people around us, including the elderly and those who might be neglected in Western, highly atomistic societies. Philosophers have looked to Korean "familism," for example, as a way to combat the brutal isolation of modern, work-driven, and splintered American life.[2] This aspect of communitarian ethics has also been attractive to Western feminist theorists thinking about the family and the role of women and mothers in society.[3]

Another strength of communitarian rationales is that individuals in society can be motivated to put their self-interests aside in favor of what can be defined as actions important to those around them. As Asian economies boomed in the 1980s and 1990s, for example, political leaders attributed to the region's communitarian ethics its ability to rapidly transform its economic structures.[4]

But the strengths of communitarian ethics can also be weaknesses in practice. Consider at least three major criticisms of communitarianism.

First, prioritizing the interests of family and friends so strongly can lead to corruption and favoritism. For example, if you work for a company, you might use a communitarian rationale to hire your relative into a certain position over a better-qualified candidate. Similarly, prioritizing your own network and relationships in making choices can be damaging for a company and culture because the results of your choices are limited to your own geographic and personal experience.

Second, communitarian rationales can lead to the burn-out of caregivers. Children are legally mandated, for example, to financially support their elderly parents in mainland China, India, Bangladesh, and Singapore.[5] There are questions of balance in how much financial support a person can give his or her elderly family members when the younger person may be trying to establish economic security for himself or herself, and possibly for his or her children. There are also questions about how a person should balance support for family members, even within a single generation, when there are multiple needs and not enough time, energy, or resources for everyone.

Third, communitarian rationales can lead to blindness in how others are treated outside of your own network. They have been blamed, for example, for political excesses and enabling violations of human rights. At least one South Korean philosopher has argued that his country's version of communitarianism has become a direct obstacle to the establishment of democratic rights.[6] These are debates that continue to be writ large on the international scene.

What are the strengths and limits of cost–benefit rationales such as utilitarianism?

Cost–benefit rationales seek to quantify ethical choices and arguably make them more objective. The eighteenth- and nineteenth-century philosopher Jeremy Bentham originated the most famous form of cost–benefit moral reasoning, called utilitarianism. Utilitarianism determines whether something is the right course of action by adding up the benefits to everyone affected, and then subtracting the costs of the action to those affected. Therefore, the classical version of utilitarianism asserts that there is only one correct moral course of action in any given situation: the action that most increases the net benefits to people in society.

Utilitarian and other cost–benefit calculations for moral actions can be helpful in that they can be intuitively easy to use in many situations. Businesspeople in particular may be attracted to a cost–benefit moral calculation because of its similarity to many types of modern economic analysis, and the relative ease of convincing others through what may appear to be the objective use of numbers.

But cost–benefit rationales have major weaknesses when applied as moral reasoning. A first set of problems has to do with measurement. A second set of problems concerns the lack of boundaries for distributing harms and benefits, and the failure of this technique to honor consistent moral rules for how people should treat each other in society. Both sets of problems leave cost–benefit rationales extremely vulnerable to abuse by individuals with a strong sense of self-justification and other biases.

First, because cost–benefit rationales depend heavily on the quantification of costs and benefits, problems with what and how you measure moral choices can profoundly influence outcomes. Initially, questions exist concerning whether the set of options you are measuring is the best set of options. Utilitarianism tends to herd a person's thinking into whether or not making a certain choice is correct—with the added burden that, if you determine that the net outcome for society is higher under one scenario than the other, then you are bound to make that moral choice. But what if there is another option you have not considered that would be a better choice? Even holding off on making the choice now might ultimately increase the utility for society.

Next, we cannot always know how other people value the utility of goods, such as their health, way of life, ability to commune with the natural world, and more. Economists often argue that we can simply ask people what they would pay for any type of good. But even asking them about tangible goods may not arrive at the best answers. Respondents may, for example, say that they prefer art to food (and be willing to pay more for art than for food), but people still need to eat, and society still needs to have food produced.

Similarly, we encounter measurement problems both when we fail to grasp all the implications of an action, and when we attempt to look into the future. We tend not to value future costs and benefits well. That choice to invest only in art, for example, may lead to a food shortage; and people in the future may then say that they would pay much more for food than for art. There are simply too many shifting circumstances and unintended consequences to actions for our valuations of costs and benefits to be accurate in many situations.

Second, because cost–benefit rationales may lack boundaries for the distribution of harms and benefits, they may fail to honor moral baselines for how people should treat each other in society. In merely adding up the benefits of actions and subtracting their costs without boundaries on the imposition of harms, cost–benefit calculations fail to consider what may be the unacceptable distribution of those benefits and costs.

Consider, for example, a cost–benefit analysis of slavery. A pure utilitarian may come to the conclusion—in fact he or she may be forced to come to the conclusion—that it would be the moral course of action to enslave a minority group because the accumulation of small benefits to the members of the majority would outweigh the extreme harm to the members of the minority. Modern society, however, rejects slavery as an unacceptable violation of any person's rights to bodily integrity and freedom.

Utilitarian calculations can run counter to many other modern social values as well. Although most other philosophical systems would agree, for example, that it would be an impermissible moral act to murder another person for personal gain, or to oppress another person because of the color of his or her skin, religion, sex, or other characteristic, classic utilitarian calculations can be manipulated to justify these socially unacceptable actions, as well as many others.

Ultimately, because utilitarianism is so dependent on case-by-case analyses, the philosophy fails to honor any set of moral rules for how people should treat each other. Some modern versions of utilitarianism have attempted to adopt the value of moral rules, but the endless bending of rules on a case-by-case basis, all depending on how they are formulated, means that these rules still fail to protect vulnerable members of society from the worst of others' self-interested behavior.

What are the strengths and limits of rights-and-duties rationales, such as Kant's categorical imperative?

The eighteenth-century philosopher Immanuel Kant moved in the opposite direction of Jeremy Bentham's utilitarianism to insist that the imposition of hard-and-fast moral rules would be the best way to create a moral society. Kant developed what he called a "categorical imperative" test for actions. The most common formulation of Kant's categorical imperative is that "I ought never to act except in such a way that I can also will that

my maxim should become a universal law."[7] Kant argued that
the test for our actions should be whether we would be willing
to have everyone else in society act the same way for the same
reasons. Actions under the categorical imperative must pass
the tests of being applied both universally—in other words,
the same way to everyone; and reversibly—in other words, to
you as well as to me, to them as well as to us.

Kant's categorical imperative may sound similar to the
Judeo-Christian "Golden Rule," which is often expressed as
"Do unto others as you would have them do unto you." But
Kant's formulation has at least three important differences.

First, Kant's formulation takes the test for our actions out
of the immediate person-to-person context of our relationship with specific people to ask a larger question about how
all people in society should be treated. This change has both
strengths and weaknesses in application.

A strength of Kant's emphasis on broad social application is
that his approach helps to discourage expectations of special
favors from friends. If you would expect your friends to lie
or cheat for you—and you would lie or cheat for them—then
using Kant's approach may help you realize that this behavior is not the rule that you would like to see across society as
a whole.

A weakness of Kant's emphasis on the larger society is
that his approach depersonalizes the context of a person's
actions enough that it may be difficult for a highly self-cen-
tered person, or someone utterly convinced of the need to justify an action, to empathize with the consequences. Reframing
choices as a social rule can distance our thinking too much
from the consequences of those choices. Cutting off the hand of
all thieves, for example, may sound to us like a good social rule
only if we personally will never have to steal food to stay alive.
Conversely, there may be people who believe so strongly in
cutting off the hands of all thieves that they would be willing to
have their own hands cut off if they were ever caught stealing.
But these people's conviction does not necessarily mean that

cutting off the hand of *anyone* who steals for *any* reason—even when driven by necessity or incurred by accident—is the best social policy, even if it were a consistent moral choice under Kant's rule.

Second, Kant insisted on the uniform application of rules to all people. Again, Kant's choice here has important strengths and weaknesses in application. On one side, the categorical imperative has an overwhelming benefit in requiring that all people—regardless of wealth, power, station, or other influence—be treated the same. This aspiration conveys a powerful message about the importance of equality in society. On the other side, a disadvantage of the forced uniform application of rules is that, under Kant's system, we may not be able to expand advantages for underrepresented groups or to compensate for certain wrongs in society without problematic formulations. This weakness of the categorical imperative becomes an issue in business, for example, if it impedes efforts to increase diversity. Even if special programs to attract diversity appear to violate the rule of equal treatment, they can serve important purposes for businesses as well as benefit society. Results of research show that diversification of gender and other representations enable teams to make better decisions, and that the significant presence of women in leadership, for example, makes a company consistently more profitable over the long term.[8]

Third, Kant's explanation of his categorical imperative puts particular emphasis on a person's motives for his or her actions, and it may not always be realistic about consequences. Therefore, there are certain situations in which a person may consider applying a rule that, in the abstract, sounds as if it would be the moral choice to make, but may lead to terrible consequences in the modern world.

Consider, for example, a rule that everyone should always tell the truth about everything. In the abstract, this may sound like the type of society in which you would want to live, and you may be motived by the best of intentions in formulating this rule for yourself. But, under a totalitarian political system, telling the truth when it requires revealing the identity of dissidents can put their lives in jeopardy, and threaten their ability to encourage social change, another important, yet conflicting, value in this scenario. Endlessly modifying and tailoring a universal rule to encompass all such caveats would be an impossible task.

Generally, the benefit of Kant's categorical imperative is the recognition and validation of some set of important rights that we believe we should protect for everyone. There tends to be universal agreement that most people would want their rights to food, shelter, and other basic physical needs to be protected. Where there tends to be more disagreement under Kant's categorical imperative is whether more nebulous rights—such as the freedoms of speech, association, religion, and the like—should be protected. And, even when people agree that these rights should also be protected, there is disagreement about the proper balance when such rights conflict.

Kant's theory reflects each person's own value system writ large on society, and it emphasizes respect for others. However, it is not always an easy system to use in practice, and there can be wide disagreements in its application and results.

What are the strengths and limits of distributive-justice rationales, such as Rawls's principles?

The modern philosopher John Rawls tried to improve on Kant's theory of the categorical imperative by encouraging the recognition of additional rights, and by focusing on fairness. Rawls argued that there should not be a conflict between freedom and equality when everyone focuses on fairness—fairness is justice. And when fairness is the basis of a society, that society becomes a moral one.

In order to form a fair society, Rawls would focus on granting equal liberty to all and reducing inequalities. His principle of equal liberty posits that there are basic liberties to which everyone has an equal right, and that these liberties should be as equal as possible for everyone. To reduce inequalities, we must provide fair and equal opportunity for all people to compete for a society's top positions. Rawls argued that this means we should help the least advantaged in society, and that we should give them access to the same educational opportunities, training, advantages, and other benefits as everyone else.

To encourage individuals to focus on fairness, Rawls advocated a technique that he called making choices behind a "veil of ignorance." We all know our gifts and attributes, and the position that we currently occupy in society. But imagine that we had to create rules for a society when we do not know who we may end up being in that society. From behind this veil of ignorance, if we knew that we could end up being the most disadvantaged person, or part of the most disadvantaged group, we are more likely to come up with rules that enable that person, or group of people, to better their lives and share in the benefits that the society can offer.

Rawls's principles and other distributive-justice rationales have strengths and weaknesses in practice. First, not all of us are in the heady position of being able to rewrite the rules for our society. We may have access only to limited resources and we may be constrained in how we can distribute those resources. We may not, for example, be able to compensate all disadvantaged people for all of the ways in which they have not had the same opportunities as others.

But other people argue that this weakness is actually a strength of Rawls's very practical theory. Within the constraints under which we work, we can make choices that help make our society more fair. A businessperson, for example, can use the opportunity presented in filling a position to hire a candidate who may not have had access to the same opportunities in his or her background as others. And often, these hires make excellent business sense and provide real advantages to the business in reaching out to new markets. There is nothing in Rawls's theory that prevents the business doing the hiring from benefiting as well. In fact, this type of win-win situation enables the growth of society to provide additional benefits to more people.

A second criticism of Rawls's approach is that it may not always help us come up with the most optimal or most moral set of rules, especially when rights conflict. To best protect freedom of speech, for example, we may have to protect speech that is especially damaging to the least advantaged members of our society. Utilitarians, in particular, may argue that we may need to tolerate more disruption and inequality in society to advance the greatest benefits for us all.

A third criticism of Rawls's approach is that his ideals are a particular product of their Western cultural roots, and are often limited in international application. Rawlsianism blends many different ideals about how to be a good person and how to operate in society, but businesspeople in particular may need to compromise more when dealing with other societies and cultures that may not accept his premises.

Later in his life, Rawls wrote on international relations and he conceded that sometimes people had to tolerate decent, if not politically liberal, societies. He was intolerant of human rights violations, but he argued that leaders had to work to open up societies so that improvements could be made for the next generation. Rawls himself was clear-eyed about his system being aspirational, and he sought room for reasonable pluralism.[9]

Where do the Golden Rule and other common maxims fit in?

Often businesspeople retort that all that they need to know about ethical rationales are maxims, such as the aforementioned "Golden Rule,"[10] or a public exposure test, such as how they would feel if their actions were on the front page of the *New York Times*. Many of these maxims utilize important psychological techniques to check actions and make sure that we consciously build and flex our moral muscles. Chapter 4 will explore more deeply the behavioral science research on human psychology and ethics. But almost all these maxims share with the work of moral philosophers in searching for a positive system outside of ourselves, and the demands of our immediate circumstances, to evaluate the larger implication of our actions.

In practical terms, we know that slowing down, thinking critically, and recognizing ethical decisions when they arise help change outcomes. Some practical techniques for ethical decision-making are as simple as:

- asking for more time, and slowing down the decision-making process;
- addressing our own basic physical needs, such as sleeping more, eating well, and feeling less anxious and scared;
- finding someone outside the pressure of the situation to ask for guidance;
- acting with empathy;
- taking time to reframe a choice in our own minds as an ethical issue instead of as a business rationale;
- broadly disclosing the problem instead of acting in secret;
- standing our ethical ground on small issues so that they do not cascade into larger problems;
- not engaging in euphemisms for our actions, but instead facing their impacts directly;
- not using other people's questionable ethical decisions to justify our own; and
- not falling prey to reward systems around us that incentivize us to engage in unethical behavior or blind us to it.[11]

All of these techniques engage us in taking extra, worthwhile time and effort to make moral decisions in the rush of the modern workplace. We encourage you to come up with your own way to grapple with the big questions of moral philosophy, and to recognize the benefits of engaging in these discussions to improve the quality of your own life and those around you.

4

WHAT DOES SCIENCE TELL US ABOUT ETHICAL BEHAVIOR?

Are people innately ethical?

We may be more innately ethical than classical economists have believed—and, most importantly—we *want* to believe that we are ethical.

A common economic view of ethics is that people are born as, and remain, rational maximizers. Rational maximizers, a species affectionately dubbed *Homo economicus*, are individuals who focus on their own self-interest.[1] This does not mean that individuals will always act selfishly, but rather that their actions are determined by what provides the most for their self-interest.[2] Consider this thought process in the context of the decision to rob a business:

> According to this perspective, people would consider three aspects as they pass a gas station: the expected amount of cash they stand to gain from robbing the place, the probability of being caught in the act, and the magnitude of punishment if caught. On the basis of these inputs, people reach a decision that maximizes their interests. Thus, according to this perspective, people are honest or dishonest only to the extent that the planned trade-off favors a particular action.[3]

But experimental evidence demonstrates that the classic *Homo economicus* understanding of human beings is of limited practical value in explaining much of human behavior. One of many experiments testing whether people do act in practice primarily as rational maximizers asked participants to play the "Prisoner's Dilemma" and "Dictator Game."[4] These games essentially assign a number of "endowments" (sums of money) to players and then create various scenarios in which players can bestow endowments on other participants, or keep the money for themselves. The results found that 7% of participants kept all of their endowments, qualifying for *Homo economicus* status. Only another 8.7% of participants distributed less than 15% of their endowments, qualifying them for status as merely "Quasi-*Homo Economicus*." The vast majority (84.3%), then, did not fall into either of these calculating categories.

Additionally, when individuals are asked about times that they might behave unethically, a clearer picture of the rational maximizer appears. There may be important governors on behavior, for example, when the action occurs within a reciprocal relationship and when the person believes that he or she will be caught. As psychology professor David DeSteno describes why humans do not outright trust everyone they meet, "90% of people—most of whom identify themselves as morally upstanding—will act dishonestly to benefit themselves *if they believe they won't get caught*."[5]

This may sound like versions of a rational maximizer cost–benefit analysis, but because other things impact behavior around ethics, our behavior as humans is not as grim as rational-maximizer explanations would predict. There seem to be important internal checks on us, and even quirks that push us to behave ethically in situations in which rational maximization expectations would predict exactly the opposite. For example, in experiments in which researchers dropped "lost" wallets with cash inside them, the more cash that was in the wallet, the more likely the wallet was to be returned with all of its cash inside.[6] The wallet was also more likely to be returned if it had cash in it than if it didn't have cash. Forty-six percent of wallets with no money, 61% of wallets with about U.S. $13, and 72% of wallets with nearly U.S. $100 were returned intact by complete strangers to their owners. The "big money" studies were done in the U.S., U.K., and Poland. The rest of the findings held across more than 17,000 "lost" wallets in 40 countries over more than two years.[7]

The researchers explain their wallet findings by pointing to two basic phenomena: altruism, but also how people want to see themselves. Again and again in follow-up interviews, people explained that they did not want to feel like thieves. As lead author Alain Cohn explains, "the *more* money the wallet contains, the *more* people say that it would feel like stealing if they do not return the wallet."[8] As economist Dan Ariely then describes, the results of this study and others show that "our decisions about dishonesty are not about a rational cost–benefit analysis, but about what we feel comfortable with from a social norm perspective and how much we can rationalize our decisions."[9]

We may all have experienced similar phenomena that do not comport with a purely "because I can get away with it" view of the world. One of the authors of this book, for example, returned from a lengthy business trip and handed a cab driver—whom she would never see again and would have no easy way of tracking down—a U.S. $50 bill for the fare instead of a U.S. $20.[10] The cab driver was the one who pointed out her mistake, and gave her back far more money than he might have needed to. Everywhere and every day, people are doing ethical things simply because they know that they should be doing them.

Accordingly, as discussed further in Chapters 8 and 9, social norms—and the personal internalization of these social norms—seem to govern the vast majority of people's behavior. Most of us not on the extreme ends of the ethical spectrum tend not to cheat, or at least not to cheat much.[11] On the ends of the ethical spectrum, as noted later, roughly 7% of people (and the same people) cheat in many formats, be these in on-line gambling communities or in their MBA applications.[12] By contrast, perhaps 2–3% of the population stand out as doing what they believe to be the right thing all the time regardless of social pressure.[13] If roughly 10% of the population (7% + 3%) are set in doing what they are going to do anyway, then the most interesting discussions are around what social norms and environments make the 90% of the population in the middle act ethically in any given situation or not. For this vast middle, ethical behavior is cultural and driven by expectations. Thus many of the remaining chapters of this book—especially Chapters 10 and 13—present what we know about how to create environments that will encourage people in that vast middle to engage in ethical behavior.

How do people develop the capacity to be ethical?

Researchers and experts agree that human beings are not born with fully developed ethical capacity, but that, as the discussion of social norms suggests, ethical behaviors are developed and learned through experiences.[14] As our parents, peers, and society teach us right from wrong, we begin to behave ethically. Everyone's particular experiences may be different, but for the vast majority of those who are taught how to behave ethically, a capacity to be ethical will develop.

Researchers have put this social development theory to the test, examining how people of various age groups behave across different games. By using different age groups, researchers could test whether "prosocial" behavior—behavior that benefits others—tends to vary by age.[15] The data demonstrate an increase in "prosocial" behavior as age increases. This increase also occurs regardless of the game that participants play. In results that will surprise few parents or college professors, one of the largest increases in prosocial behavior comes in individuals between their early twenties and their late twenties and early thirties.

The results of this experiment align with psychologist Lawrence Kohlberg's stages of moral development. Kohlberg described how, as humans grow older, they develop "moral reasoning," which serves as the foundation for ethical behavior.[16] The first of his six stages is what he referred to as "Punishment and Obedience Orientation." In this stage, young children learn what is good or bad based on the physical consequences of their actions. Children are focused on avoiding punishment rather than on making ethical choices, but their experiences teach them the foundations of moral reasoning.

Kohlberg's second stage is the "Instrumental Relativist Orientation." In this stage, children focus on satisfying their personal needs. Ethical behavior at this stage can almost be considered a marketplace, as children are willing to help others if there is something in it for them. According to Kohlberg, some semblance of ethical behavior is present, but children are predominately driven in negotiations to satisfy their own interests.

In the next two stages, children begin to mature and enter society. As they enter society, they adapt to the expectations of the society around them. In Kohlberg's third stage, the "Interpersonal Concordance," humans seek the approval of others and often receive that approval by being "nice." In the fourth stage, entitled the "Law and Order Orientation," humans feel pressure from authority. What is considered right depends on how authority defines it, and we respond in kind. To put this reaction another way, "[r]ight behavior consists in doing one's duty, showing respect for authority, and maintaining the given social order for its own sake."[17]

In Kohlberg's final fifth and sixth stages, individuals begin to define their own ethical values independent of society's beliefs. Kohlberg's fifth stage is the "Social-Contract Legalistic Orientation," and its foundations come from previously described stages three and four. At this stage, we look to society to determine what is right and conform to social expectations. As we continue to mature, however, we begin to determine what is right based on our own personal values. As the stage progresses, our own ideas become more important in our determining what is ethical. Kohlberg's final stage, the "Universal Ethical-Principle Orientation," is when humans finally define their ethics based on their own personal beliefs. At this point in our lives, we select our own ethical principles, and we use them to guide our decision-making processes. Although the guidelines may be as simple as the Golden Rule, the individual rather than society will determine and enforce his or her own principles.

What sorts of pressures drive otherwise-ethical people to do unethical things?

Otherwise ethical people may do unethical things under social pressure. In fact, such social pressures may reformulate an ethical person's principles, depending on how the person reacts to the unethical pressure.

The emotional response an individual exhibits to challenges under pressure may indicate how firmly internalized his or her ethical principles are, and it may help explain how otherwise ethically formed individuals may eventually commit unethical actions. Once an individual has formed his or her own ethical framework, how he or she defends that ethical framework emotionally matters. Some people are more susceptible to re-formation by social pressures than others. The combined process, like most other ways in which we mature, is both intellectual and emotional. A person's emotions may thus have an important role in both *formulating* and *re-formulating* personal ethical frameworks. If we use anger (either self-righteous or for others) to defend our ethical frameworks when they are under attack, we are far more likely to preserve them. If we react, on the other hand, with guilt (which contains elements of self-doubt and self-blame) we are much more susceptible to having our ethical frameworks modified.

Studies of otherwise-ethical employees implanted within unethical organizations confirm these flags.[18] For example, an ethical employee acting on a consistently ethical basis may be continuously disciplined for not taking unethical actions. Such disciplines (social pressure) may take the form of missed promotions, lost bonuses, or even outright firing. Sometimes the pressure form may be more subtle, such as not being a part of the "in" club and selected for the best assignments or opportunities. Generally, such unethical actions under pressure benefit the company to a larger extent than any of the employee's ethical actions. If an employee reacts to disciplinary signals with anger, he or she is most likely to refuse to act unethically and to continue in his or her ethical ways. However, if an employee primarily feels guilt for failing to conform with the organization, he or she is more likely to abandon his or her ethical compass and begin to act like the other employees in the organization.

Similarly, compliance firm Starling Trust divides employees along axes of social conformity that tend to manifest themselves within the first weeks and months of when an employee starts a job.[19] Signs of social conformity can be seen, for example, from anonymous filters of email to see how readily an employee mirrors the language and reactions of those around him or her. Employees who do not readily conform may be drummed socially out of organizations, but they may also—interestingly—be the ones least likely to cheat along with others, and most likely to blow the whistle on behavior that other employees may be more easily conditioned to accept.

Our emotional responses protect us and remain key to how we form, preserve, maintain, and arguably propagate—as we help form children and others around us—our ethical frameworks. As discussed in the context of the wallet example earlier, we want to feel good about ourselves and our behavior. As also discussed above, when we are put in situations in which we do not feel good about the ethical signals we are receiving, we may either shift our own ethical behavior to conform, or defend it to preserve our sense of positive ethical identity.

What sorts of social environments encourage ethical or unethical behavior?

Although environmental pressures may cause different reactions in different individuals, environmental pressures can have a significant influence over most individuals' decisions to act ethically. Some types of surveillance in the workplace may cause people to act in a more ethical manner. Researchers who examine this phenomenon believe that the pressure to maintain one's reputation, or abide by societal norms, encourages people to act in ethical ways.[20] When being watched, individuals believe that their unethical deeds may become public, so they avoid committing unethical acts while being watched. Note that too much surveillance, however, suppresses otherwise helpful employee engagement and ownership of an ethical environment.[21]

In general, overly competitive environments appear to breed unethical behavior, as shown by multiple examples of businesses facing legal trouble due to the actions of their employees.[22] Whether at Wells Fargo or Enron, when employees are placed in hyper-competitive environments, they may look to cut corners in an unethical manner in order to produce results.[23]

These findings are also supported by laboratory studies, which indicate that subjects will act in a more aggressive manner, at times without typical rational limitations, once competition is introduced into an experiment.[24] For example, in an experiment to test the impact of competition on negotiation, researchers created two scenarios: one in which a single seller had to sell an item to a buyer, and one in which multiple sellers competed to sell a good to a single buyer. Each time, the buyer was allowed to make one offer, which sellers could accept or reject. When the researchers ran the experiment with only one seller, buyers' most frequent offers were on a scale between 40 and 50, and any offers 10 and under were rejected 100% of the time. However, when competition was introduced via more sellers, the rejection rate for buyers' offers 10 and under fell about 20%. At 10 and under, the discount was so extreme that the sellers could not be breaking even, and were being distracted by their sheer desire to win in competition. Thus, when the sellers competed with each other, one was often willing to suffer economically as long as he or she could "win" inside the game. Many other restraints, including ethical boundaries, also succumb in situations to driving competitive impulses.[25]

Additional research indicates that, when a person enters an environment with low ethical expectations, they may lower their standards to conform. An informal survey of mangers at various businesses found that those who expected their employees to act in an unethical manner received just that, while those with better expectations received better performance.[26] This "Pygmalion Effect" created a cycle in which "the way people are seen influences the way they are treated, consequently prompting them to act accordingly, and thus confirm the original view of them. In this way people set up self-fulfilling prophecy, resulting in widely differing behavior within divisions of the same company."[27]

Finally, environments based on over-emphasizing the accomplishment of goals can lead to unethical behavior. History is filled with examples of pressure-filled environments causing people to turn to unethical behavior. For instance, Sears once asked its automobile repair mechanics at stores to produce at a rate of U.S. $147 an hour.[28] In a short time, its mechanics began to overcharge customers, or perform unneeded repairs, in order to meet Sears's leadership's goal. When the unethical behavior became public, Sears Chairman Edward Brennan acknowledged that it had been the company's "goal[-]setting process for service advisers [that] created an environment where mistakes did occur."[29] Sears is not the only company to run into this issue, indicating that high-pressure, goal-driven environments can cause employees to act unethically.[30]

Why does "tone at the top" matter so much?

At its best, an ethical tone by corporate leaders—so-called "tone at the top"— will inspire lower-level employees to behave in an ethical manner.[31] However, even at a minimum, it can encourage employees to report unethical behavior when they notice it. As research on ethical tone-from-the-top indicates, "[t]he ethical behavior of boards of directors can influence both the ethical behavior of corporate agents, and the ability to have unethical behavior disclosed and addressed."[32] People below the level of the board of directors are watching. If the directors are perceived as acting unethically, "the likelihood of a corporate scandal causing significant harm to the company only increases."[33]

Supervisors possess a great deal of influence over the type of work subordinates do, and how the subordinates perform that work. Experiments show that just one statement from a supervisor can cause an employee to prioritize completing a project over completing the project in an ethical manner.[34] When a supervisor holds such power, it is important to place an emphasis on ethical and legal behavior. Outside of a direct employee–supervisor relationship, this effect can be magnified when such a statement comes from the C-suite. When the statements and actions of leadership discourage ethical behavior, employees will respond in kind.[35]

As discussed above, incidents at Sears and other corporations demonstrate just how much influence the tone at the top can have over employees. Enron is another important example, as the constant unethical actions of company leadership caused employees to believe that ethics were not a priority at the company, and act in kind. When ethics are simply thrown out of the window and rational maximization is left to guide decisions, people "who would otherwise behave ethically . . . will opt for an unethical decision if put under pressure by . . . sheer economic calculi of company owners."[36] As discussed in greater depth in Chapter 10, leaders must realize the influence that their actions and statements have, as "tone at the top" is an important factor in creating an ethical environment.

How do ethical and unethical individuals influence others?

As the behavior of individuals is often influenced by the behavior of those around them, it seems logical that the behavior of ethical and unethical people can influence each other. Researchers have investigated this phenomenon, and specifically how unethical behavior impacts that of others. After examining the responses of 655 undergraduate business students, the researchers found a correlation between those who responded that they constantly observed unethical behavior and those who responded that they consistently behaved unethically.[37] The authors dubbed this the "Monkey See, Monkey Do Phenomenon," but found a few exceptions to this rule. The first exception is that those with strong moral identities will resist the urge to copy unethical behavior. Secondly, those who are introverted are less likely to be influenced by the unethical behavior of their colleagues. We discuss these issues more in Chapter 9.

How do incentive plans encourage ethical or unethical behavior?

As discussed above, the use of strict goals or benchmarks can create situations in which employees will behave unethically to achieve business goals. When reaching these goals provides an employee with additional rewards, the urge to act unethically can grow.

Instituting performance goals can lead workers to game, or falsify, metrics to reach those goals. For example, in a 2013 U.S. survey, 24% of managers admitted that they had witnessed other employees significantly altering financial information to meet goals.[38] In operations departments, 33% of employees admitted that they had witnessed other employees falsifying expense and time reports. When all of the respondents who had witnessed false reporting by other employees were asked why the employees might falsify their reports, 64% of them explained that the employees were reacting to "pressure to do whatever it takes to meet business goals."[39] Similarly, attorneys investigating the GM ignition switch scandal, in which 127 customers lost their lives when faulty ignition switches stalled, identified how incentives encouraged employees to focus on costs, causing them to look the other way when safety issues arose.[40] Although incentive plans can be a significant motivator for employees, they may also cause employees to act unethically in pursuit of those incentives.

What does where you work say about you?

Industry sectors, and the companies within those sectors, differ dramatically in the ethicality of their behavior.

As this book will discuss in greater detail in Chapters 9 and 10, our ethical behavior can be greatly influenced by our environment. One of the easiest things an employee can do to ensure that he or she is able to meet his or her own ethical standards is to find an industry, and a company within that industry, that comports with his or her own standards. Yes, this may mean switching companies, or even industries if there are not companies within the industry behaving the way that you want to see in your work life. (For those with an entrepreneurial streak, discovering that there is no such company within your industry may prompt you to found one, gathering other such like-minded people, and leading with your ethics as a selling point. Such ethically driven firms are now present in finance, among other sectors touched on below.) Although we will discuss more warning signs of problematic business environments in Chapters 9 and 10, there are some company patterns in high-pressure industries that are worth discussing here in considering where you want to work, and what that ends up saying about you.

The financial industry stands out in the data as a particularly troubling place for unethical behavior. One in 13 financial advisors, for example, have a record of misconduct.[41] But there are good companies in almost every sector. In surveys of business executives and academics for examples of companies with "exemplary ethics and business practices," they were able to identify 12 such companies within the finance industry alone.[42] In total, the participants were able to identify 86 companies as having such good business practices across nine industry sectors.

Other sectors, such as automotive manufacturers and the oil and gas industry, have also had particularly checkered recent histories. Some of the pressure on these industries, as well as on the ethical judgments of their employees, seems to come from the need to adapt to elevated standards, while being under intense pressure to make profits. In January 2017, for example, Volkswagen Auto Group ("VW") agreed to pay U.S. $4.3 billion to settle criminal and civil charges against the company stemming from violations of air pollution standards.[43] Two of VW's other suppliers/contractors were also implicated.[44] By 2018, almost no carmaker remained untouched by either suspicions or proven cases of large-scale emissions cheating.[45]

It is true that these were new U.S. air pollution standards that the companies were trying to meet (and cheated to reach them in an affordable way).[46] But, most significantly at Volkswagen, and other companies displaying these cheating patterns, there was a culture of fear inside the company that "discouraged open discussion of problems, creating a climate in which people may have been fearful of speaking up."[47]

Across Volkswagen (automotive manufacturing), BP (oil and gas), and Wells Fargo (banking), each of which have had scandals from widespread ethical wrongdoing, the pattern seems to have been that the companies set particularly lofty goals to increase profits, and then either perpetuated—or at least turned more than a blind eye to the use of—risky and unethical means to achieve these goals.[48] When employees questioned the risky practices, leadership in each of the three companies responded to such questions by suppressing dissenting opinions. Thus the leadership of the companies created the "strong social norm . . . that dissent was not appreciated."[49]

Without any ability to dissent and question the leadership's goals or tactics, employees received the message that unethical behavior was expected. The leadership's rigidity worked to "condone and even normalize [widespread unethical] behavior within the company."[50] There seem to be particular red flags for the ethical quality of a company if it uses intimidation tactics against employees. All three companies above (VW, BP, and Wells Fargo) used intimidation tactics against employees in their leadership's quest to obtain its goals and suppress dissent, including public shaming.

Such ethically problematic companies may also breed intensely internally competitive environments that encourage the behavior. Red flags to diagnose such an environment include when "small differences in performance can cause high differences in how employees are treated."[51] Such environments can be especially toxic for women—so it can be a danger sign that there are few women in the company, and especially at top levels of leadership. Survival in potentially unethically pressured environments "requires ambition, ruthless, and domination;" traits for which women "are more likely to be disliked and punished if they display."[52]

So be cautious about entering into a company with a "predatory culture," and also being changed by exposure to unethical pressures in these environments.[53] Think about where you work and what it says about you. At the end of Chapter 10, we offer some advice about speaking truth to power, and surviving in the workplace. In Chapter 12, we outline whistleblowing options. And, in Chapter 15, we discuss cooperating with law enforcement investigations to protect your own reputation, and potentially emerge from legal damage that the commission of widespread wrongdoing may do to a company.

But, if you have the choice, do not get yourself into those more troubling situations in the first place. If you are having ethical questions about what you are being asked to do at your company, and leadership is responding as tyrannically as at these other companies headed toward scandals, start thinking about other options, as well as what where you work says about you. The next few chapters describe the legal duties of businesspeople, what corporations and other legal "persons" are, and why such entities should act ethically in society.

5

LEGAL FOUNDATIONS OF BUSINESS ETHICS

What is the relationship between law and business ethics?

No matter what business you are in, you probably have to deal with a web of legal rules. Perhaps you contract with suppliers, manage employees, or take out business loans. Even these ordinary activities bring you into the legal world. It would be a mistake to think that you can "leave it to the lawyers" to always answer the question whether your conduct meets legal requirements. As we explain in Chapter 8, in many business contexts, you can be held legally responsible and required to pay damages, or even go to prison, for violating legal rules of which you may not even have been aware. Because of this, it is important to have a solid understanding of the law, both as it relates to basic legal standards for business transactions, and as a minimal baseline for business ethics.

Ethics and the law are not the same thing.[1] Ethical rules come from your own sense of right and wrong; your ethics are your moral code.[2] You may be able to violate this moral code without suffering punishment other than pangs of conscience. But someone who violates the law may be subject to external punishments such as fines, civil damages, and even jail time.[3]

Nevertheless, at times the law and ethics are closely related.[3]

First, most laws protect people from being cheated or harmed, ensure business is fair and competitive, and preserve the environment for the benefit of present and future generations. In other words, laws are often grounded in ethical concerns.[4] Therefore, being familiar with the legal rules that apply to your industry and workplace can help you understand the ethical implications of choosing one course of business conduct over another. It is important to know, however, that ethics go beyond the law: something can be lawful, but not ethical.[5]

Second, as a member of society, it is generally your ethical duty to obey the law. As discussed in Chapter 8, this is true even when breaking the law would be difficult to detect or punish. Ideally, obeying the law springs from your principles, and not simply from your fear of consequences. Someone who obeys the law only for fear of punishment—Kohlberg's "preconventional morality" discussed in Chapter 4—can be easily tempted to violate a rule "just this once."[6] That bending of rules can lead to the more dangerous ethical slide, as discussed in Chapter 9. Strong ethics are an important backstop to help you avoid succumbing to the ethical slide. Similarly, the threat of legal punishment can be a useful bulwark against the occasional temptation to do something that violates your own moral code.

While law and ethics typically reinforce each other, there may be situations in which they seem to be in tension.[7] You may face a situation in which two laws conflict. Or, perhaps you entered into a contract, but when you attempt to fulfill it, the contract turns out to be illegal.[8] Moreover, you may sometimes discover that the law is ambiguous. Ethics can help us decide what to do in such cases. Ethics will rarely demand that we knowingly violate the law to accomplish a moral purpose, but such situations can and do arise. Think of the man who steals a loaf of bread to keep his children from starving. His actions may be ethical, but they are not lawful.

The most helpful way to think about the law, as it relates to business ethics, is in terms of duties. A duty is an obligation to act (or to refrain from acting) in a certain way.[9] The law helps to clarify ethical situations by instituting rules: when you are in *this* situation, you are legally obligated to act *this* way.

The first two questions in this chapter explore the nature of legal duties and to whom you may owe them. The next four questions discuss the "cardinal duties" that arise in the business world: the duties of obedience, loyalty, good faith, and care. In the subsequent three questions, we explore additional duties related to information: duties of confidentiality, truthfulness, and disclosure. Finally, we circle back to the relationship between ethics and the law, and we address why a businessperson should act more ethically than the law requires.

What does it mean to owe a legal duty to a partner or other natural person?

Most of us sense intuitively what it means to owe a duty to someone or to something else. The easiest context in which to think about duties is in relationships among people. We think that parents *should* take care of their children.[10] We think that people *should* keep their promises to one another.[11] When we say that someone "should" act in a certain way toward another person, we are already in the land of duties.

But what makes a legal duty different? The answer is: not much. Owing a legal duty simply means that the law creates an obligation to act in a specific way toward another person or entity.[12] As discussed above, the law is often grounded in ethics. The law identifies an ethical duty, such as the duty to care for children or to avoid carelessly injuring others, and it makes that duty legally enforceable. A popular example is Ralph Nader's legal efforts to make the automobile industry liable for its dangerous products.[13] His efforts turned ethical concerns for the safety of others into new legal standards that sparked massive reforms in the industry.

Another way to think about these relationships is that a legal duty may give teeth to an ethical duty.[14] While an ethical duty may be enforced by a guilty conscience, a legal duty is enforced by the state. Once a legal duty exists to bind people or entities, it must be satisfied.[15] Moreover, once you have a legal duty toward another person or entity, that person or entity has a legal right to have your obligation fulfilled.[16] The obligation may be to follow through on a specific act, such as paying an amount owed under a contract.[17] Or, it may be an obligation to reveal certain information, such as telling a business partner about opportunities that you might discover in the course of the business.[18] Whatever your legal duty is, the law is a mechanism to ensure that you fulfill your obligations.[19]

Legal duties also take two different forms: a legal duty may exist as the "operation of law," or it may exist uniquely between two parties.[20] A legal duty through an "operation of law" means that the duty exists for anyone who fills a certain role. In a partnership, for example, a partner *always* owes certain duties to his or her fellow partners.[21] If a unique legal duty exists between two parties, it means that those parties formed an agreement with each other that the law recognizes as enforceable. Without such an agreement, however, they would not owe each other legal duties. Additionally, under some circumstances—think of the partnership described above—an agreement between two parties may overcome or limit a duty that otherwise arises through the operation of law.

The person to whom a duty is owed has a legal right to have his or her welfare considered.[22] When you enter into a legally binding contract, for example, your promise to fulfill the contract becomes a legal duty.[23] After that, you must make an effort to fulfill the legal obligations that the contract has created.[24]

Sometimes, you may owe a legal duty to another person without ever having entered into a formal agreement with them.[25] These legal duties arise based on the nature of your relationship.[26] Many relationships are so important that the law imposes duties to ensure that the parties behave according to certain standards in those relationships. Consider, for example, the special quality of some of the following relationships: a lawyer to a client, a trustee to the trust's beneficiaries, a corporate director to the corporation, a partner to the partnership, a doctor to a patient, and more.[27] These relationships underpin society, touching on the economy, finance, law, business, and medicine. The law wants to ensure that these relationships are ones of trust, and that those who enter these relationships treat them with more gravity than they would otherwise.[28]

If you are involved in one of these important relationships, the law may impose on you what are called "fiduciary duties."[29] A fiduciary is simply someone who exists in a relationship of trust with another person or entity.[30] A fiduciary duty is a "duty of utmost good faith, trust, confidence, and candor owed by a fiduciary (such as an agent or a trustee) to the beneficiary (such as the agent's principal or the beneficiaries of the trust)."[31] The person who owes the fiduciary duty must act honestly, loyally, and in the best interests of the party to whom the fiduciary duty is owed.[32]

As we just discussed, you do not need to volunteer or agree to have fiduciary duties; they may arise automatically based on your position and relationships. For example, anyone who enters into a partnership owes fiduciary duties to the partnership and to his or her fellow partners.[33] Without ever signing a contract, each partner is now obliged by law to act with fairness, loyalty, and honesty toward his or her other partners.[34]

The broadest duty—one that every person owes to every other person—is the general duty of care to avoid injuring others.[35] This duty requires exercising the care that a reasonable and prudent person would exercise to avoid harm to others.[36] Thus, even outside of contracts or special "fiduciary relationships," a person can be liable under the law if that person fails to exercise ordinary care toward others.[37] Of course, the law accounts for what it defines as "ordinary" in special situations. For example, the law typically requires the exercise of a higher duty of care from a professional within his or her expertise than from an ordinary person.[38] A doctor should treat patients with at least the care of a reasonable doctor; an accountant should handle a client's finances with at least the care of a reasonable accountant.[39] We discuss the duty of care further below.

If all of these legal duties seem imposing, keep in mind that the law does not require utter sacrifice for others.[40] Taking every possible precaution would render many businesses inoperable—not to mention unprofitable.[41] In tort law, you are allowed to analyze the risk in a given situation, and you should take precautions only when a burdensome injury is likely to occur without the precaution.[42] For example, a company should not employ careless workers or operate faulty machinery, but it is not obliged to spend all of its resources on screening and inspecting to eliminate every last possibility of injury; rather, it should identify problem areas and take reasonable precautions to avoid injuries where it knows of them.[43]

This method of weighing risk against probability was famously articulated by Judge Learned Hand in *United States v. Carrol Towing*.[44] In that case, a barge broke away from its moorings, and it struck a ship, causing serious damage. To decide whether the barge owners were liable for damage to other ships, Judge Hand reviewed three factors: "(1) The probability that [the barge] would break away; (2) the gravity of the resulting injury, if she does; [and] (3) the burden of adequate precautions."[45] By weighing the likelihood and gravity of the injury against the burden of preventing it, some of this analysis can be reduced to a basic equation: if the burden of preventing an injury is less than the probability of injury, times the gravity of the injury, then there is a duty to prevent the injury.

In addition to limits on what the law requires of behavior in everyday life, there are exceptions to almost every duty. What if the contract into which you enter turns out to be illegal?[46] The law provides exceptions to legal duties when circumstances require it.[47] You do not have a duty to fulfill an illegal contract, and you do not have to carry out a promise to commit an illegal act.[48] Similarly, you are not allowed to enforce an illegal contract. In an early case regarding illegal contracts,[49] two companies submitted bids for a public works project. Each secretly agreed with the other that, if one of them won, they would split the work. Sure enough, one company won the contract, but it refused to share the work. When the second company sued to enforce the contract, the court declined to enforce the parties' agreement because keeping the agreement secret from the public works project had been illegal.

And what if a client asks a lawyer to lie? Legally, no one has a duty to lie, even if a lie might benefit another party.[50] Additionally, some circumstances simply fall outside of a lawyer's (or other professional's) "line of duty." For example, lawyers must be zealous advocates for their clients' best interests, but they do not have to pay their clients' rent.[51]

When considering legal duties, it is important to keep an eye always on the ethical side of issues. The law does not always enforce ethical duties.[52] It is possible to act unethically and harm another person without breaching a legal duty.[53] For example, you may make a promise that is not in the form of a binding legal contract.[54] Breaking that promise may be unethical, but it is not illegal. The law steps only in when someone violates a legal duty.[55] The law, therefore, typically creates a threshold of minimally enforceable ethical behavior. Often, going above and beyond legal duties may be the right thing to do.

What does it mean to owe a legal duty to a corporation or other "legal person"?

In the business world, we also often have to think about legal duties in a broader context, rather than merely person-to-person. It may be simple enough to understand that you owe a duty to the living, breathing person who signs your contract. What may be more difficult to grasp is that you may also, or instead, owe a duty to the business that person represents. Understanding legal duties to business entities is important because, without this understanding, we can fall into both illegal and unethical behavior without even knowing that we owed a duty in the first place.

Let's start with the legal basics. It is not merely flesh and blood people who possess legal rights. The law grants legal rights to business entities like corporations, partnerships, and limited liability companies, and it treats them as "legal persons."[56] These entities are not on completely equal footing with flesh and blood people in all ways and in all circumstances; for example, these entities have some constitutional rights (like Due Process and Equal Protection) but not others (like Privileges and Immunities related to citizenship and other cross-border transactions).[57] In the business world, however, you should consider businesses as having essentially equal standing with human beings. When two business entities make a contract, that contract can be as legally binding as if it were made between two human beings.[58] With this in mind, you can see that the flow of legal duties is not merely to and from other humans, but can be to and from "legal persons"— business entities—as well.

Courts have recognized the legal rights of corporations for a long time.[59] (For simplicity's sake, we will refer in this text to "corporations" or "companies" rather than to "business entities," but these principles apply in varying degrees to all types of business entities.) Because of these legal rights, a corporation can own property like a human being.[60] A corporation can enter contracts like a human being. A corporation can sue, and it can be sued like a human being. You must respect the legal rights of corporations as if you were dealing with another human being.[61] Just as importantly, you must fulfill legal obligations to corporations the same way as if you owed those obligations to a human being.[62]

Another important concept to understand is that a corporation is separate from the people who own its shares.[63] A corporation is also legally distinct from the people who operate it and oversee it.[64] A corporation is *not* merely an amalgam of its shareholders, directors, and officers.[65] It has different rights, duties, and liabilities from all of these parties.[66] Similarly, it is a misperception to conceive of a legitimate corporation as the "alter ego" of the people who control it.[67] The law provides separate treatment to the corporation from those who control or operate it.[68]

Only if the entities behind a corporation use it to subvert justice will the courts look past the "corporate fiction" of separate personhood and hold those entities liable for harms caused by the corporation.[69] For example, in one case, Mr. Lincoln Polan, a businessman, created an empty shell of a corporation that he used to obtain funds, despite the fact that the corporation contained no assets or collateral.[70] Because Mr. Polan created the corporation strictly to protect his personal assets, and he did not take the time to observe basic corporate formalities, the court found Mr. Polan personally liable for debts owed by his corporation. Although it is rarely done, when the corporate form is abused, courts may "pierce the corporate veil" to hold shareholders or operators liable.[71]

We discussed above how legal duties may automatically arise as a result of certain relationships. By this same operation, certain people, by nature of their relationships with a corporation, owe the corporation duties.[72] The three groups of people who typically owe duties to a corporation include first, directors and corporate executives (the "officers" of the corporation); second, certain shareholders; and, third, employees.[73] Directors and officers (D&Os) owe fiduciary duties to the corporation, which were mentioned above and will be explored in greater detail in later questions.[74] D&Os must abide by standards of strict honesty and fair dealing when it comes to the corporation.[75] Similarly, a shareholder who, by his or her position, can control the actions of the corporation also owes these fiduciary duties.[76] Finally, employees are considered "agents" of a corporation, and therefore owe the corporation fiduciary duties as well.[77]

All of these relationships will be discussed in more detail below. What is important to remember for now is that, in the business world, you must consider both your promises to people, and your relationships to people, before you know what legal duties you owe. When thinking about legal duties, remember that you owe such duties not merely to the flesh-and-blood people you meet every day, but also to the corporations and other legal business entities with which you may interact.

When do I have a duty of obedience?

Now that we have explored what a legal duty is and to whom you may owe duties, in the next few questions we will discuss the four "cardinal duties" that the law imposes in the business world. These cardinal duties are the duties of obedience, loyalty, good faith, and care.[78] We begin with obedience.

When we think of obedience, we think of authority. Children (usually) obey their parents because their parents have authority over them. Employees (usually) obey their supervisors because their supervisors are in a position of authority over them. To understand the legal duty of obedience, you merely have to understand what the law places in authority over other things. For example, an employer really does have some legal authority over his, her, or its employees.[79] Therefore, the law imposes a duty of obedience on the employees.

Because we say that we live in a country that abides by the rule of law, the first and greatest authority to follow is the law itself. No matter who you are—a shareholder, a CEO, a director, a supplier, or the corporation itself—a duty to obey the law underpins every other duty.[80] Courts also generally view disobeying the law as a violation of other, more specific duties, such as the duty to act in good faith.[81] Furthermore, when directors or officers cause a corporation to disobey the law, it is not merely the corporation that has violated its duty of obedience to the law; those causing it to violate the law have themselves violated their duty toward the corporation.[82]

Most often, however, the duty of obedience requires obedience to a particular person or entity, rather than to the law in general. This means that the law recognizes one party or entity as having legal authority over the other. The most common example of this application is in an agency relationship. An agency relationship arises when a "principal" hires an "agent" to act on his, her, or its behalf.[83] In this situation, the agent has a legal duty to obey the principal's instructions and behave as the principal directs.[84] You can see agency relationships every day in the world of employment: every employee is an agent for the employer.[85]

Agency relationships also commonly arise in corporations. Because a corporation is a fiction created by law, it has no hands or mind to conduct its own business in the world. Rather, it acts through agents such as officers, directors and employees.[86] A corporation's "decisions" are ordinarily those made by its board of directors. The board of directors is responsible for hiring (and firing) executives, overseeing, and advising the corporation.[87] A board of directors must ensure that the company's executives and employees fulfill their duty of obedience to the corporation. Maintaining such oversight is part of the directors' fiduciary duty to act for the benefit of the corporation.[88]

Sometimes, the authority to be obeyed is not even a person or business entity, but a document. Every corporation must have a corporate charter and bylaws.[89] These are its governing documents, setting out the "law" of that corporation. In turn, a corporation's governing documents must follow the rules established by the state in which the corporation is incorporated.[90] Meanwhile, directors, officers, and employees of the corporation must conform with the corporation's governing documents. In the same way that justices on the Supreme Court owe a duty of obedience to the U.S. Constitution, directors and officers must obey a corporation's articles of incorporation (or charter) and bylaws.[91] Furthermore, because a charter typically specifies that the corporation may only conduct lawful activity, the failure to obey the laws of the state in which the corporation is incorporated automatically violates the duty to obey the corporation's internal rules.[92]

But what if obeying corporate authority conflicts with obeying the law? For example, what if an employer asks an employee to do something illegal? In these situations, the duty to obey the general law trumps the duty to obey the corporation's authority. Despite the stringent duties placed on an agent to be loyal to the principal, this loyalty will not excuse an agent's unlawful behavior.[93] Absent very specific circumstances, claiming that you were "only following orders" is not a legal defense.[94] Even when a principal specifically instructs an agent to violate the law or act against public policy, such an instruction will not excuse the agent's behavior.[95]

This message was clearly conveyed when the president of a Teamsters Union Local ordered the union's business agents to participate in embezzling union funds.[96] The business agents argued to the court that they owed a duty to follow instructions given by the union's president. The court unreservedly denied this defense: "Loyalty to a superior [here in the form of following orders] does not provide a license for crime."[97]

What does the duty of loyalty mean?

As with the duty of obedience, we know intuitively what it means to be loyal to someone. It means having an allegiance to someone, working for his or her benefit, watching out for his or her welfare, and not seeking personal gain when it could cause him or her harm.[98] The law takes these same principles, and it enforces them by imposing a duty of loyalty.[99] The duty of loyalty is one of the fiduciary duties discussed earlier. In its simplest form, it obliges those who owe the duty (such as directors or officers) to do what is best for the party to whom the duty is owed (which may be an "it," such as a corporation).[100]

Another way to say this is that the duty of loyalty requires selflessness. When you owe a duty of loyalty to someone or something, you must ignore self-interest, and you may not be controlled by the interest of any third party.[101] A good litmus test is to ask: who is receiving the benefits of my actions?[102]

The party to whom the duty is owed should be receiving the benefits of your actions.[103] If an action, such as entering into a contract, appears to benefit you while it harms your company, your duty of loyalty may be compromised.[104]

When it comes to corporations, many scholars and commentators believe that the duty of loyalty is the most important of the fiduciary duties owed by directors, executives, and controlling shareholders to the corporation.[105] But that does not mean that the duty of loyalty only applies in the corporate context. The law deems several other relationships important enough to impose a duty of loyalty on parties. For example, doctors owe a duty of loyalty to their patients.[106] Lawyers owe a duty of loyalty to their clients.[107]

Perhaps the best way to understand what the duty of loyalty entails is to discuss what breaches it. The most common way to breach the duty of loyalty is with a conflict of interest. A conflict of interest occurs when directors or officers, acting on behalf of a corporation, benefit themselves.[108] Acting for yourself while acting on behalf of the corporation is referred to as "self-dealing." Such behavior is dangerous territory because it can easily result in breaching your duty of loyalty.[109]

To determine if you are in this dangerous territory, ask yourself whether the actions you are helping to direct for the company will result in personal gain to you or to those close to you. In an example, a company assigned its right to redevelop a strip mall to a construction partnership.[110] Unfortunately, because one of the company's directors owned the partnership, he received personal gain from the transaction in the form of revenue to his partnership. Although the court ultimately approved the director's actions despite his conflict of interest, his self-dealing put him in the danger zone, and it required taking litigation all the way to the state appeals court.

Another way in which you may breach the duty of loyalty is to take opportunities that rightfully belong to the corporation.[111] Courts have developed three different approaches to determining whether someone is taking a corporate opportunity: the "interest or expectancy approach," the "line of business test," and the "multiple factors test."[112]

The first test, called the "interest or expectancy approach," finds a violation only when the corporation has an *existing interest*—such as an interest in real estate—and officers or directors usurp that interest and take it for themselves.[113]

The second test, called the "line of business" test, is much broader.[114] The "line of business" test holds that any opportunity in the corporation's general line of business, or any opportunity of which the corporation could reasonably be expected to take advantage, belongs to the corporation.[115] This test applies whether the corporation takes the opportunity or not.[116] As an illustration, the Loft company manufactured beverages and candy.[117] Loft's president bought Pepsi-Cola's secret beverage formula, formed a new company, then used Loft's factories, equipment, and employees to perfect a new drink, which he then sold to Loft. The courts held that the new drink opportunity was so closely tied to what the Loft company did that it was in their line of business. Therefore, when the president formed another company and made additional profits by its sales to Loft, he violated his duty of loyalty to Loft because he took an opportunity properly in Loft's line of business.

Finally, the third test, called the "multiple factors" test, creates a balancing scheme in which the court reviews eight factors to determine if a director or officer violated his or her duty of loyalty.[118] The eight factors are as follows:

- whether the opportunity was valuable to the corporation, and needed for the corporation's operation or expansion;
- whether the officer or director discovered the information because of his or her inside position with the corporation;
- whether the corporation actively sought the opportunity, or whether it had abandoned its efforts;
- whether the officer or director was specifically involved in obtaining the opportunity for the corporation;

- whether the officer or director utilized corporate resources to obtain the opportunity for him or herself;
- whether taking the opportunity set the officer or director in an adverse position to the corporation;
- whether the officer or director intended to turn around and "resell" the opportunity to the corporation; and
- whether it was feasible for the corporation to take advantage of the opportunity, or if it had been out of the corporation's grasp.[119]

Weighing all of these factors, courts will determine if an officer or director improperly took an opportunity that belonged to the corporation.

You may also breach the duty of loyalty when you use the corporation to channel private benefits to yourself.[120] Consider, for example, whether it is really acting in the best interest of the corporation to use the company jet to fly on personal vacations or to have the company extend you personal loans.[121] Anytime you receive personal benefits from your position at the company, beyond those for which you contracted in your employment agreement, you must fully disclose those benefits, and possibly reimburse the corporation for expenses it incurred when providing them to you.[122]

Taking corporate opportunities for personal benefit or self-dealing, however, only breaches the duty of loyalty if the company does not give its fully informed permission. You may obtain permission from a company to take corporate opportunities for yourself or engage in a self-dealing transaction.[123] Such permission is called a "corporate opportunity waiver," and it is an expanding trend, including in Delaware and in the Model Business Corporation Act.[124] If you wish to seek a waiver of the corporate opportunity, however, you *must* provide full disclosure to the company; arguing that your company had "constructive knowledge" of the situation or that it may have given its implicit approval to an interested transaction will not suffice.[125]

If you are in doubt about whether a course of action will breach your duty of loyalty or impermissibly take a corporate opportunity, you should always err on the side of caution and seek pre-approval from the company. It is especially important to seek such permission in advance because, while a corporation can exculpate and indemnify you for many business-related activities, it cannot do so if you have violated the duty of loyalty.[126] In addition, states are divided on whether they will allow a company to insure against damages caused by a breach of loyalty.[127] Although many states, including Delaware, now permit a corporation to insure against violations of the duty of loyalty, such a breach could lead to personal liability.

When do I have a duty of good faith?

Although the duties of obedience and loyalty are at least partly intuitive, the duty of good faith is a little more difficult to tease out. It is a pillar of fiduciary duties.[128] Technically, however, the duty of good faith is not a separate duty, but a "subsidiary element" of the duty of loyalty.[129] You may think of it as a related, or milder, version of the duty of loyalty. Acting in bad faith violates the duty of loyalty, and a subsidiary duty of acting in good faith as well.[130] (Merely to flag the issue, good faith in contracts is another body of law. The discussion in this chapter stays with corporate fiduciary duties.)

But what *is* the duty of good faith? It may be easiest to understand this concept through its opposite: acting in *bad* faith means acting with intentional disregard or conscious carelessness toward responsibilities. In practice, such actions typically include reckless behavior and the waste of corporate assets. Courts, however, do not readily find instances of bad faith. For example, in 1995, Disney hired Mr. Michael

Ovitz as its new president.[131] After merely 14 months on the job, Disney terminated Mr. Ovitz without cause, and the board, which had not even met or voted regarding the decision, allowed the company to pay a U.S. $130 million termination package. Despite this massive expenditure with a minimal review, the court held that the board's actions did not rise to the level of bad faith because paying off Mr. Ovitz had been "a rational business decision."[132]

The requirement to act in good faith precludes you from intentionally harming a company, gaining personal advantage from company dealings, or allowing the company to take such wasteful actions that your actions can only be seen as irrational.[133]

When asking whether you are acting in good faith, consider these questions:

- Are you pursuing a course of action that you know, or are at least fairly certain, will result in harm to your company?
- Are you trying to get something out of another person, or a business, in a way that is unfair? Do your negotiation tactics involve threats if your demands are not met?[134] This evaluation includes not merely outright threats like those of physical harm in *The Godfather* ("either your signature or your brains will be on the contract"),[135] but also more nuanced duress, such as implying that you will breach the contract if you do not get your way.[136]
- Are you fraudulently misleading another person or business?[137] Misleading the other party in a contract is acting in bad faith because it means that the other party did not fully understand to what they were agreeing.[138] Typically then, contracts entered into as a result of fraud will not be enforced.[139]

Finally, it is important to note that a duty of good faith is implied in every contract.[140] The parties do not need to specify that the duty applies to their dealings when they make agreements.

When do I have a duty of care?

The duty of care can be tough for a businessperson to pin down because it applies in such a wide variety of contexts. At its broadest, every person has a duty of care toward every other person.[141] But that duty can change based on who you are (doctors and lawyers have different duties of care from others), or your position (landlords have a different duty of care than tenants). We briefly explore these dimensions, then address the duty of care in the business world. Even inside the business world, the duty of care has many nuanced features, which we touch on below. Finally, we will discuss the possibility of insuring your business or people against breaches of the duty of care.

We'll start as broadly as possible, with the general duty of care that tort law imposes on everyone. No one escapes a legal obligation to act with the care necessary to avoid harming others.[142] The degree of care due is a flexible standard based on context. The duty of care obliges people or entities to exercise the caution that a "reasonable and prudent person" would exercise in the same or similar circumstances.[143] Everyone is obliged to avoid or minimize the risk of harm to others. The duty of care is focused almost entirely on avoiding harm to others: very few courts will impose a positive duty to rescue someone from a danger or to a prevent harm that you have not caused.[144]

At this point, the duty of care seems simple enough: after all, shouldn't everyone avoid harming others when they can? Things get difficult, however, when trying to decide whether, in fact, a person acted reasonably to avoid harming others. In limited circumstances, the person will be liable if there is an injury, regardless of the care that he or she exercised, and regardless of whether he or she intended harm.[145] The imposition of a duty not to harm others regardless of circumstances is called "strict liability" because parties are liable strictly when an event occurs, not because they were careless or acted with intent to harm. Strict liability is used to encourage utmost caution in a limited number of areas. For example, if your dangerous dog escapes the fence around your property and attacks someone on the street, you will probably be held strictly liable for that person's injuries, no matter how high a fence you put up around your yard.[146] This is because the law wishes to encourage the maximum level of care from people who own potentially dangerous dogs.[147]

Usually, however, the standard of care that courts apply is "negligence."[148] Although negligence is a nuanced concept defined by tort law, it generally signifies unreasonably risky behavior, or behavior that is risky enough that a person can be found at fault for engaging in it.[149] To prove negligence, you must show four things: (1) that a person had a duty toward another; (2) that the person breached this duty; (3) that breaching the duty resulted in an injury; and (4) that the injured person actually sustained harm.[150]

The level of care that you are responsible for exercising toward others may fluctuate with the responsibilities that you take on. Joining a profession or becoming an expert in a specialized skill may create heightened duties of care.[151] A doctor's care for a patient is measured against how a reasonable and prudent *doctor* would act, not against how a reasonable and prudent pedestrian would act if he or she walked into a hospital and put on scrubs.[152] This heightened duty of care for people with specialized expertise applies across many professions, including lawyers and psychiatrists.[153]

Even without joining a specialized profession, your duty of care can change based on the position that you hold. The best example of this is a landlord. Landlords owe different duties to people who enter their property than to people walking past the property on the street.[154] To make it more complicated, the duties owed to the person entering a property change based on whether that person is an "invitee," "licensee," or "trespasser."[155] A landlord may be liable for an injury to someone who is invited over to the property to attend a cocktail party or a business meeting, but not liable for the exact same injury if it happens to a trespasser.[156] Although the details of how the duty of care is applied in these various circumstances are too nuanced for our purposes here, it is important to remember that one's legal duty of care can change based on context and relationships.[157]

We turn now to the duty of care as it manifests in the business world. The duty of care, like the duty of loyalty, is one of the fiduciary duties owed to a corporation by its directors, officers, and controlling shareholders.[158] The duty of care is extraordinarily important in the business world because, when directors fulfill the duty of care (as well as the duty of loyalty discussed above), their actions are given deference under the "business judgment rule" (BJR).[159] Applying the BJR means that a court will not second-guess or try to make business judgments in hindsight for the directors, even if their judgments resulted in harm to the business. Because the BJR is a deferential standard that makes liability unlikely, directors of corporations want to have the BJR apply. If the directors do not abide by the duty of care as included in the BJR, however, courts will not defer to their business judgment.[160]

The most famous business case about breach of the duty of care is *Smith v. Van Gorkom*.[161] In that case, the president, chairperson, and CEO of TransUnion (Mr. Jerome Van Gorkom) met privately with a potential buyer and came to an agreement to sell TransUnion for U.S. $55 per share. Mr. Van Gorkom waited until the last minute to inform the board, and the board approved the deal in less than three days without so much as reviewing a financial analysis or asking how Mr. Van Gorkom had arrived at his price. The court found this type of lack of information and inquiry in business dealings unacceptable, and, denying the board deference under the BJR, found them liable for breach of their fiduciary duty of care.

In the end, the BJR is a tacit agreement between courts and the business world: if you agree to act carefully toward your company, we agree to stay out of your business.

Employers should keep a careful eye out for breaches of the duty of care because they can be liable when a subordinate breaches the duty. Liability for a lack of care can sometimes pass "up the chain" to the employer.[162] The doctrine in which liability is passed up the chain is called "respondeat superior," or Latin for "let the superior speak." Generally, the employer will only be liable for an employee's lack of care when the employee was acting on the employer's behalf and within his or her scope of employment.

Finally, we consider the silent mover in a lot of these cases: insurance. In the business world, it is quite common to purchase insurance to cover negligence in the form of "liability insurance."[163] Purchasing such a policy provides protection because the insurance company will pay for legal liabilities accrued as a result of careless acts.[164] As money is often the simplest way to pay for harms caused by carelessness, this area of law is largely propelled by the terms of liability insurance, which ultimately determines who gets paid and how much.[165] This insurance picture may change, however, when someone is liable for extremely careless acts or commits intentional harm.[166] Most liability insurance policies will not pay for injuries that are intentionally caused. In addition, when the carelessness is extreme—sometimes called "gross negligence"—courts may impose punitive damages, which are also typically excluded from coverage under insurance policies.[167]

What are duties of confidentiality?

Now that we have explored the "cardinal duties" of obedience, loyalty, good faith, and care, we turn to additional duties that relate to information. Ordinarily, we assume that it is permissible to share information with others. After all, businesses—not to mention the market as a whole—rely on a flow of information to operate. Normally, sharing information is necessary to keep a business running.

In three situations however, legal duties related to sharing information may arise. First, you may have a legal duty to keep information confidential. Second, you may have a legal duty not to lie about information. Third, you may have a legal duty to disclose information. In this subsection, and the answers to the next two questions in this chapter, we'll examine these three situations.

First, we explore duties of confidentiality.

Put simply, sometimes you are legally prohibited from sharing information. This duty goes beyond a moral obligation to refrain from sharing, as when you promise to keep a secret.[168] A duty of confidentiality chiefly arises from two sources: relationships and contracts. In other words, just as a relationship can establish fiduciary duties, your relationships can also oblige you to keep certain information confidential. Moreover, just as you can bind yourself to act in a certain way through a contract, you can also bind yourself through contract not to disclose something.

When information originates through a business or professional relationship, the parties are often obliged to keep it confidential.[169] If you have access to information because you are in a business relationship, you should typically seek the other party's permission before you disclose that information to another person or entity. Certain professional relationships spell out rules for confidentiality: for example, a lawyer has a duty to keep all information relating to a client's representation confidential unless the client gives permission to share.[170] And it is not solely lawyers who have this duty; many professions, such as being a doctor or journalist, come with some form of the duty of confidentiality.[171]

In the business world, duties of confidentiality are everywhere. Directors have a duty to keep confidential information about their corporation confidential.[172] A director's duty of confidentiality is part of the broader duty of loyalty: how loyal are you being to a company if you reveal its secrets?[173] Specific areas of the law, such as securities laws, focus on information sharing and regulate not merely whether a party can disclose information, but also what parties may do with the confidential information that they have. For example, if you have access to material, nonpublic information at a company that could affect the stock price, buying or selling stocks based on that information is illegal in most circumstances.[174]

While some people are bound, as a matter of law, to keep the confidential information that they acquire confidential, those who are not otherwise bound can still be bound to keep confidentiality in the form of nondisclosure agreements.[175] A nondisclosure agreement ("NDA") is simply a contract not to reveal confidential information. NDAs are common between businesses, or between a business and its employees, and courts will ordinarily enforce them.[176] Even if the parties do not sign a separate NDA, many business contracts contain a provision mandating confidentiality.[177]

There are two parts to policies motivating confidentiality: first, enforcing confidentiality protects privacy; second, it encourages people fully to disclose information that may be needed by the professional whom they have hired.[178] Lawyers and doctors are unlikely to help their clients and patients achieve the best results if they are not told all salient information.

Meanwhile, establishing rules around the handling of confidential information is important because confidential information must often be shared in the context of a business relationship.[179] For example, a company that is considering purchasing another company will need to see inside information before it can make an informed decision about whether to proceed with the acquisition.[180] Business ventures are unlikely to get off the ground if parties refuse to share information with one another. Duties of confidentiality—both stemming from the nature of relationships and from contracts—protect and restrain parties in ways that allow them to share important information with each other without fear of harm.

As with most rules in the legal world, the duty of confidentiality contains important exceptions. Under limited circumstances, confidential information between an attorney and a client may be disclosed if the opposing party cannot obtain the information in any other way.[181] Additionally, if lawyers know that their clients plan to commit crimes or fraud, lawyers may disclose otherwise confidential information to prevent such harms.[182] Moreover, if a client sues a lawyer, the lawyer can disclose otherwise confidential information if it is necessary for his or her legal defense.[183] Finally, you generally only have a duty to keep information confidential if it is actually a secret; there is no duty to keep otherwise public information in confidence.[184]

When do I have a duty not to lie?

A duty not to lie is one of the most widely recognized duties in ethics.[185] In its simplest form, lying is when you make a statement that you know to be false, and you want another person to believe that it is true.[186] Moral philosophers from Augustine to Kant have described lying as a "contemptible" practice, and have asserted that the act is "wrong in principle."[187] That lying is, in principle, unethical is almost universally accepted: most major religions, societies, and legal systems agree on this issue.[188]

When people lie for their own benefit, it is almost always unethical.[189] A more complex situation is a "white lie," in which you tell a falsehood to benefit—and usually protect—someone else.[190] Many religious and legal traditions excuse this form of lying when it is done to protect innocent victims or to prevent wartime enemies from discovering confidential information. Despite this acceptance, some schools of ethics, such as virtue ethics, consider telling even white lies unacceptable because a white lie still contradicts the virtue of honesty.[191] This tension can create a complex ethical situation in which a white lie may oppose one virtue (honesty) but embody another virtue (compassion).[192] To help navigate these ethically complex situations, virtue ethicists recommend imagining what an ideally virtuous person would do, and then committing to that course of action.[193]

When it comes to imposing liability for telling lies, the law imposes duties primarily when there is a special relationship between the parties in which candor would be expected. Such situations may include, for example, when a patient has to make an informed decision about his or her healthcare; when a client has to decide whether to accept a legal settlement; when someone holds a special position of financial trust; and when a person is dealing with the government or signing documents under oath. Lying in the marketplace is dealt with chiefly through fraud provisions, which we discuss in Chapter 11. The most important thing to remember in the legal sphere is that it is possible to commit fraud without expressly stating a falsehood.[194] Leaving information out or misrepresenting information may have the same legal consequence as telling an outright lie.[195]

What are disclosure duties?

As we discussed above, fraud includes situations in which you may mislead someone through an omission or partial truth. A partially truthful disclosure of information can paint a false picture, and legally speaking, this can be as bad as an outright lie.[196] Ordinarily, however, omitting a fact only becomes fraud when the fact you left out is material.[197] When considering disclosure duties, it is important to understand the concept of "materiality." Laws often require the disclosure of all "material" facts, and fraud is often a result of an omission of a material fact.[198] A fact is material if it would influence a person one way or another in making a decision.[199] (Note that securities-law cases have an even broader definition of materiality.) Materiality in contracts is usually determined from the viewpoint of the person disclosing the information.[200] In some special situations, however, such as when a doctor informs a patient about the possible effects of a treatment, materiality is determined by what a *patient* would deem material.[201]

Some parties, such as directors and officers of a corporation, are encouraged to go above and beyond what is normally required and *ensure* no one has been misled by the disclosures they make.[202] For example, when a director or officer has something personally at stake in a corporate transaction, he or she should not only disclose the facts of the transaction, but he or she should relate the implications of those facts to ensure that the other officers and directors fully understand the situation.[203]

The law identifies several situations in which disclosure is not optional, but affirmatively mandated. To name a few, if a lawyer knows that a client intends to commit a crime related to his or her representation, and the only way to prevent the harm is for the lawyer to disclose the client's plans, the lawyer must reveal that information.[204] Directors have disclosure obligations when they seek shareholder action or provide proxy statements.[205] Both state and federal law impose various disclosure requirements on companies when they advertise or furnish sales materials.[206]

In addition to these general disclosure requirements, there are at least four categories of disclosure requirements that appear frequently in the business world:

- *Hidden defects*: If a product or a property contains a hidden defect, you are not allowed to let it slip past a buyer; instead, you must proactively disclose the defect. Many states imply a warranty in a company's sale of items that the items being sold are free of hidden defects.[207] Failure to disclose such a defect may lead to legal rescission of the sale. For example, a landowner sold his property, but he failed to mention in his property disclosures that the property had drainage problems, which the buyer could not discover until the rainy season. The court allowed the buyer to rescind the purchase because the seller had not disclosed this hidden defect.[208]

- *Insurance applications*: When you apply for insurance, either personally or for your business, both the law and your insurance contract typically require full and accurate disclosure of all risks.[209]
- *Public companies and securities*: Disclosure requirements tend to be particularly stringent when it comes to public corporations.[210] Companies that wish to sell securities to the public must, for example, provide extensive and accurate information about the company.[211] The law further requires public corporations to disclose extensive financial information to shareholders on a regular basis.[212] Federal statutes, like the Sarbanes–Oxley Act[213] and the Dodd–Frank Act,[214] require additional myriad disclosures from corporate directors, officers, and outside auditors about corporations.[215]
- *Drug companies and side effects*: Some products, such as pharmaceuticals, pose sufficient health risks if misused that the Federal Drug Administration maintains special disclosure requirements for labeling and side effects.[216] Such disclosures help consumers make informed decisions regarding their health.[217]

Why should businesspeople act more ethically than the law requires? Isn't the law enough?

It can be tempting to let legal requirements dictate your ethical choices. After all, legal requirements are the minimal standards that can be legally enforced. The law, however, is not enough. Although the law can prevent some ethical wrongs, it is a higher level of social ethics and duties that create a positive and ethical business culture.[218] Moreover, at times, legal requirements are not ethically correct. Sometimes ethically correct decisions are not legally required. Or even, when government control is being misdirected, such as in Nazi Germany or dictatorships, complying with the law can be explicitly unethical.[219] This means that the businessperson must venture beyond minimally complying with the law and do his or her own thinking about what is ethically required in situations.[220] Only by thoughtfully considering his or her larger duties to act ethically in the business world can a businessperson properly satisfy true social responsibility.[221]

Additionally, the law cannot perfectly enforce all of the duties that it mandates. Our legal system lacks the resources required to ensure compliance and to effectively deter all wrongdoing.[222] And, even if absolute enforcement of rules were possible, the government itself cannot always make correct decisions about how to rectify ethical harm or enforce ethical principles.[223] Therefore, it is up to you, as a businessperson, to ensure your own ethical behavior and to build a culture of ethical behavior around you.

Another misconception is that conforming with the law must mean that what you are doing is a good thing. This assumption is often incorrect. When a course of action is profitable and legal, it may still be harmful.[224] The lawful pursuit of profits can still bring about great social harm, such as the destruction of the environment or massive layoffs to increase profits. Movements to encourage corporations to think more broadly about the social costs and benefits of their actions beyond a simple floor of profit and legality are actively trying to counter this thinking from both legal and cultural perspectives.

Finally, legal duties and ethical duties can conflict, and in these situations, it is important to have your own working ethical compass as a guide.[225] As we talked about in Chapters 1–3, you must examine the law critically, and take ethical considerations into account when determining what actions to take in business decisions.[226]

6

UNDERSTANDING CORPORATIONS, LLCS, AND OTHER "LEGAL PERSONS"

What is a corporation, LLC, or other "legal person"?

In order to act ethically in business, we have to understand what businesses are, and how we, as people relate to them. The law has changed a lot in this area. Businesspeople must be updated on the legal environment in which they now find themselves.

Many people think of a corporation as an amalgam of people, or possibly as the "alter ego" of a physical person like a shareholder or chief executive officer (CEO). These common misunderstandings are erroneous and dangerous. Rather, corporations are their own "legal persons," that is, they are legally treated as their own individuals.[1] Although it is a legal fiction for a corporation to be considered a person, this treatment allows the corporation to have rights, duties, and obligations separate from the human beings who run it.[2]

Just as there are many types of natural people, there are many types of legal business entities, including corporations and limited liability companies. We will discuss some of these different types below. A corporation, like other business organizations, is a separate entity from its owners, shareholders, and executives. Corporations may typically be organized for "any lawful activity," from traditional for-profit business enterprises to organizations with more social, charitable, religious, or quasi-governmental activity.[3] There are a series of advantages to the corporate form, as opposed to other choices of business form.

There are at least five important attributes of the corporate form.

First, corporate shareholders typically enjoy limited liability.[4] Limited liability is a protection extended to shareholders that shields them from most personal liability for corporate actions. Generally, when you buy stock in a corporation, your liability for the actions of the corporation is then limited to the amount that you paid for its shares, which may become worthless. Thus, should the corporation engage in some form of unlawful conduct and be sued—for example, for hitting a person with one of its delivery trucks—the injured party would not typically have a cause of action for his or her losses directly against you. This makes a corporation a much safer entity in which to invest than one in which you may be liable for actions that you cannot control.

Second, corporations typically enjoy perpetual existence.[5] Perpetual existence is the assumption that a corporation will continue to exist as its own entity in perpetuity, and without regard for the mortal lifetimes of its directors, officers, employees, or shareholders. Thus, the Walt Disney corporation, for example, is still going strong and "making" things long past the death of its founder, Mr. Walt Disney, and presumably past the deaths of many of its directors, officers, shareholders, and employees who will have contributed to its success.

The power of having such a perpetual life is that a company can own property, commission work, borrow money, and otherwise enter into contracts without regard for the health or mortality of the people currently financing or running it. This quality, in theory, should make corporations important vehicles for the successful completion of intergenerational or large-scale projects that go beyond the ability of groups of people to otherwise fund or organize.[6]

Third, a corporation has centralized management in the form of its board of directors (BoD).[7] Corporations can organize large numbers of people by having chains of command that come to a head and are supposed to be overseen by their boards of directors. It is a corporation's BoD that hires and fires its CEO and other top officers. A corporation's BoD is supposed to set out and be guided by the corporation's purpose. The BoD is assumed to be monitoring and guiding (see the famous *Caremark* case)[8] the corporation at all times to be heading in the right direction, in the right way, and conducted lawfully along its path.

Accordingly, we watch the BoD carefully, and the members of that board have special duties to the corporation, which it is presumed will outlive them. Directors are caretakers and guides for the time that they serve on the board. As was described more fully in Chapter 5, the duties owed to the corporation by the people who serve it are supposed to preserve the corporation to continue its work beyond the interests of any one person or group of caretakers.

Fourth, corporate shareholders can generally freely transfer their interests in the corporation.[9] Free transferability means that shareholders can, typically, sell their shares to other people without obtaining the permission of the corporation. There are distinctions in the transferability and forms of investment among public, private, and closely held corporations, which we will discuss more toward the end of the chapter.

A public corporation cannot screen its investors.[10] On the public market, anyone can buy into a corporation, and they can exit when they are unhappy. Hence, the theory is that the market will discipline corporate actions by lowering the valuation of its shares. If a public corporation were behaving badly, its shareholders would sell their shares and leave, causing the stock price to decline. (This may not be possible for shareholders of closely held or private corporations.) If a corporation were behaving well, its shareholders should be rewarded through the increase in value of their shares, and the corporation may also be able to raise money by selling additional shares at a higher price each.

Fifth, as a legal person, a corporation has many legal rights similar to a natural person.[11] A corporation may, for example, sue someone, be sued, hold property, and sign contracts.[12] These abilities mean that corporations exist as members of our society, interacting with human beings and other business entities to transact deals, employ people, and get things done.

Unfortunately, although corporations and other business entities may walk among us, do not be fooled into thinking that they necessarily operate on the same scale or with the same limitations as the rest of us. As has been well documented by other academics, the last half-century has seen a greater concentration of power and resources into the hands of public corporations.[13] Together, the top 200 corporations collect more in revenue than the combined economies of all the countries in the world except for the largest ten.[14] In 2016, the single corporation, Apple, had more cash on hand than the combined gross domestic products (GDPs) of two-thirds of the world's countries.[15] Walmart takes in more annual revenue than either Spain or Australia.[16] One-hundred-and-fifty-seven of the world's 200 richest entities, are, in fact, corporations, not governments.[17] Merely because you can contract with a corporation the way you might with another natural person, do not imagine that the corporation will behave over the course of the contract the way a natural person might.

This point leads us to a few limitations on the corporate form. Corporations are special entities regulated in their internal governance primarily by the state in which they are incorporated.[18] Incorporators, the people who form corporations, must follow the rules of the state in which they seek to form their corporate entity. Essentially, when a state agrees to issue the equivalent of a birth certificate (often called a "corporate charter" or "certificate of incorporation") to a corporation, it wants to ensure that corporation will follow certain procedural rules for its decisions. Moreover, even if a corporation commits an act outside the state of its incorporation, it may often be sued in the state in which it is incorporated. When a corporation seeks to do business in another state, the other state may additionally have rules to authorize or "qualify" the corporation to do business there.

As far as many state and local governments, as well as the federal government, are concerned, corporations are typically responsible for paying their own taxes. For the investors and other people who then receive income from the corporation, the stream of revenue is then taxed twice—once when the corporation generates it, and then again when the corporation pays it out to individuals or other entities who are also responsible for their own taxes.[19] This is different than the tax treatment of other business entities like partnerships and sole proprietorships that are taxed only once when proceeds are distributed to individuals. The subject of business taxation is extremely complex and is discussed in more detail below. Fundamentally, as we have witnessed how corporations can move money, operations, and their headquarters around the world, changes in tax policy and tax treatment can affect a lot of corporate behavior.[20]

For anyone deciding to create a corporation, a key decision is where to incorporate it. Within the United States, corporations, as noted above, are largely creatures of state law, and the law of that state will be binding on it.[21] When a state issues a charter (birth certificate) to a corporation, the charter typically requires the name of the corporation, the corporation's purpose, service of process information, incorporator identification, and the types of stock that the corporation will offer.[22] Historically, corporations were required to give a specific purpose for their existence. Today, many states have moved toward greater flexibility in corporate purpose.[23]

For example, under Delaware corporate law, a corporation can be formed for "any lawful business purposes."[24] Then, an incorporator needs to file the charter (and a fee), usually with the state's Secretary of State.[25] After properly executing the charter, the corporation exists.[26] The corporation, however, still needs to organize itself. At an organizational meeting prior to its first annual shareholder meeting, the corporation will elect directors, appoint officers, adopt bylaws, and issue the corporate stock.[27]

Within the world of corporations, there are public versus private corporations, for-profit versus non-profit (and related not-for-profit corporations), as well as so-called "C" Corporations ("C-Corps") and "S" Corporations ("S-Corps"). We take apart some of these distinctions now. The major differences between a public versus nonpublic (also known as private) corporation is whether it has shares for public sale. The public may invest in a public corporation that is listed on the public markets and regulated by securities laws. When a corporation is private, it is owned by specific people (often organized behind other business entities), and it is not required to disclose the same types of information as required of public companies. Historically, in order to become a large corporation and raise enough money to engage in large-scale projects, corporations had to "go public" and list on public markets. Increasingly today, however, privately provided money ("private equity") is available at levels and on terms that were not conceivable before. The private equity market is estimated at U.S. $7 trillion and growing.[28] This allows more corporations than ever to conduct large-scale operations without becoming legally "public," and therefore being regulated under the rules for public companies in the marketplace.

Somewhere between public and private companies are closely held companies (or "close" corporations). These are corporations that issue shares, but those shares are held by only a small number of people and not readily available at a market price on an exchange.[29] Close corporations can often be held by families and have significant overlap between shareholders and management.[30] Not all such close corporations are small-scale enterprises, however.[31] Hallmark Cards, Inc., a U.S. $4 billion enterprise by revenue, is as of this writing, still a close corporation.[32] The Mars candy and food company is a close corporation with some U.S. $37 billion in revenue.[33]

Another important decision is whether a corporation is registered as for-profit or as a non-profit. A for-profit corporation's purpose, while generally unspecified, tends to emphasize making financial profits.[34] A non-profit corporation's focus is on a charitable or publicly beneficial purpose.[35] Although most corporate governance rules apply to both types of corporations, a non-profit corporation can receive special tax benefits, including tax-exempt status.[36] Additionally, while corporations have traditionally fallen into the for-profit or non-profit categories, there are a growing number of corporate forms that blend the two categories. A not-for-profit corporation generates profits, but it allocates its profits to charitable causes.[37] Also, in many states, a for-profit corporation can elect to become a benefit corporation.[38] In a benefit corporation, a corporation asserts that it has a public benefit purpose that supersedes any expectation that it will first maximize profits.[39]

There are also tax implications to consider in choosing a corporate form. Unless otherwise specified, corporations are considered "C" corporations for tax purposes under the Internal Revenue Code.[40] As mentioned above, revenue through a C-Corp is subject to double taxation unless paid out to tax-exempt entities. Certain corporations can avoid such double taxation by electing to be an "S" corporation.[41] An S corporation is not a taxable entity; instead its profits are taxed when they become its investors' income.[42] In order to be eligible for S-corporation status, a corporation must have fewer than 100 shareholders, who all must be residents of the United States, and solely one class of stock.[43]

Finally, to round out briefly our discussion of common business entities, there are sole proprietorships, partnerships, and forms that blend aspects of corporations with partnerships. A sole proprietorship is a person doing business as him or herself. Typically, sole proprietors may use their own names (such as "John Smith, Dentist"), and are responsible for the revenue and expenses of their businesses as extensions of themselves.[44] According to the Small Business Association, 72% of U.S. business entities are sole proprietorships.[45] A partnership is typically a common venture between two or more people. Although it is an entity, a partnership is still largely tied to the finances and credit of the individuals behind it. Although a general partnership may sign a contract, its individual partners are still typically responsible for the debts of the business, and for each other's professional actions.[46]

In order to provide a degree of protection for themselves in their business, sole proprietors and partners may opt for business forms that legally protect them from the business's liabilities more similarly to the protection shareholders receive via the corporate form. A limited partnership (LP), for example, limits the liability of partners not generally engaged in running the business.[47] Moving farther along the spectrum of business forms from partnerships to corporations, a limited liability company (LLC) is a non-corporate entity that melds aspects of partnerships and corporations.[48] All states have an LLC form, but there are many differences between states' LLC laws.[49] Similar to partnerships, LLCs typically enjoy single taxation and are not required to have centralized management. Although LLC members have an interest in the LLC, their interest is not in stock form. However, like a corporation, all of an LLC's members receive limited liability. Given their hybrid nature, LLCs are a particularly attractive option for small businesses that are interested in limited liability but that do not want to completely adopt a corporate structure.

What is the purpose of a corporation?

A corporation's purpose describes its goals and the nature of its business.[50] As such, its purpose delineates the bounds of how the corporation's directors and officers should act.[51] Historically, states required corporations to have a specific, well-defined purpose. Today, a corporation's purpose can be increasingly general and varied. With modern corporation statutes taking an enabling approach, corporations can often easily meet their purpose requirement.[52] For example, in Delaware, a corporation's purpose can be to "conduct or promote any lawful business purposes."[53]

Even though general corporate purpose clauses are broad, they do articulate limitations. Most importantly, as the Delaware general-purpose provision indicates, a corporation cannot engage in an unlawful business purpose.[54] Thus, a corporation cannot be created in order to, for example, fraudulently conceal earnings or murder people.

Additionally, under the "ultra vires" doctrine, a corporation can only act within the scope of its purpose and powers.[55] With the increasing expansiveness of corporate purpose clauses under states' laws, the ultra vires doctrine does not have the limiting power that it used to. The idea behind the ultra vires doctrine was that, because corporations used to be chartered for more specific purposes—to engage in a specific trade or to conduct activities within a specific territory, for example—the existence of the corporation would be void if it exceeded its foundational mandate.[56]

But the law is still uncomfortable with granting the privileges of a corporate entity to engage in potentially fraudulent or abusive behavior. Another doctrine that may come into play in this area is "piercing the corporate veil." When the people behind a corporation, for example, begin to use the corporation as an extension of themselves (an "alter ego" theory), fail to respect the formalities of the corporate structure, or undercapitalize corporate assets, courts may "pierce the corporate veil" to find a shareholders or shareholders legally responsible for the corporation's actions.[57] Courts pierce the corporate veil to remove the limited liability shield we discussed above.

There are certainly other ways in which a corporation's purpose may be hijacked to the detriment of the corporation, its investors, its employees, and its other shareholders. Much discussion in business school concerns how to preserve a corporation's purpose from those who would corrupt it or otherwise abuse the corporation for their own ends. For example, Professor Colin Mayer, of Oxford University's Saïd Business School, has written extensively on the power of commitment to positive corporate purpose, and the trust this engenders in others.[58]

When corporations are hijacked for unethical outcomes, those situations can violate both corporate purpose and other laws. Sometimes corruption of a corporation's purpose can happen slowly with unrealistic pressure to meet targets over time: consider how the Volkswagen emissions scandal unfolded in response to management pressure to meet air pollution targets with diesel technology, or Wells Fargo's fraudulent accounts scandal evolved in response to demands to hit cross-selling targets—examples discussed more extensively in Chapters 8 and 10.

But there are other examples in which corporations appear to have been explicitly designed for the primary purpose of perpetuating a fraud.[59] Enron's financial house of cards is an example from this second category. Enron was founded to take advantage of deregulation in the energy industry, and its methods exploited poor accounting standards.[60] The company used "mark-to-market" accounting, which enabled it to report the value of its assets based on what Enron projected the assets might be worth, as opposed to what the assets were currently worth. For example, when Enron built a power plant, it marked down all the profit that it expected from the plant on its books before the plant even opened. When the assets ended up being worth less than Enron had projected, such as when a plant failed to meet targets, the company would not adjust its books to account for its losses.[61] Instead, it pushed its losses into special-purpose vehicles (SPVs), and special-purpose entities (SPEs), businesses whose sole purpose appears to have been to hold Enron's stock and absorb its losses.

At its height in late 2000, Enron shares traded at over U.S. $90, and the company was worth over U.S. $60 billion.[62] It was number seven on the *Fortune* 500 list.[63] However, by the time its accounting games caught up with the company, and it declared bankruptcy in December 2001, its shares traded at 26 cents.[64] Because Enron owed nearly U.S. $67 billion to over 20,000 creditors, its employees received little severance or healthcare benefits,[65] and they lost millions of dollars in savings through their company's 401(k) retirement accounts, which had often been heavily invested in the company's stock.[66] Public retirement plans around the country and other investors in the company also suffered severe losses. For example, Florida's teachers and public employees lost U.S. $328 million as a result of the Enron scandal.[67] In total, nationwide, pension funds for union members, teachers, and public employees lost as much as U.S. $1.5 billion from Enron's fall.[68]

When Enron's assets were distributed by the bankruptcy court, 4,000 of the company's lower-level employees each received U.S. $13,500. However, this payout did not include compensation for the company's decimated 401(k) program, which left many employees without their retirement savings.[69] By contrast, top corporate executives received payouts from Enron in the year before its bankruptcy of U.S. $681 million.[70] Some were later convicted of insider trading and securities fraud, and they served time in prison.[71]

The important underpinning of this discussion about corporate purpose is also about who relies on a corporation to play a role in society, and what people expect of that role. When Enron collapsed, it became clear that the company had been run for the benefit of its top management, and not necessarily for its investors, employees, or other stakeholders. A corporation's purpose, as we will discuss more extensively during our introduction of corporate social responsibility (CSR) in Chapter 7, should be at a minimum lawful behavior, but ideally also to provide a benefit for the world. To whom a corporation owes its benefits is a larger, and actively debated, question. When corporations were historically granted charters by a sovereign, benefits were to accrue to the sovereign, or the corporation would no longer be entitled to exist. The corporation's investors were entitled to benefits as well; its employees received jobs, their families might have received support, and industries and trade could be spurred by economic development.

In the 1970s, a group of economists and others based primarily in Chicago (the so-called "Chicago School" of thought) began to argue for a more restrictive understanding of corporate purpose as primarily to generate profit for shareholders. The economist Milton Friedman is largely credited with this push,[72] as well as professors Michael Jensen and William Meckling,[73] and others. By 1991, a generation of finance professors had been steeped in the teachings of the Chicago School, and the U.S. Business Roundtable's statement of corporate purpose focused on maximizing profit to shareholders.[74]

These deeply held assumptions about shareholder primacy so permeated our business culture and assumptions about corporate purpose that, by the mid-1990s, it was common to misquote the former president of General Motors as saying "What is good for General Motors is good for the country."[75] What he had actually said back in 1953 was "What is good for our country is good for General Motors, and vice versa."[76] In other words, his assumption had been that, should the community around GM prosper, the company would too. It was not that he believed that looking out for the interests of shareholders over the interests of employees and communities would somehow give the country a trickle-down-effect benefit from GM's primarily self-interested orientation.

Much scholarship in the past 20 years or so has focused on establishing more of a balance of interests within corporations and allowing a more expansive expression of corporate interests. By 2001, Professor Jensen, for example, wrote that, "[i]n order to maximize value, corporate managers must not only satisfy, but enlist the support of, all corporate stakeholders- customers, employees, managers, suppliers, [and] local communities."[77] Indeed, running corporations for the public good, or more specifically, to honor the interests of a wide variety of stakeholders, is now explicitly protected in many states' laws. Delaware, for example, broadly protects the ability of corporations to make business decisions that consider, even in the most narrow context of deciding whether to block a hostile takeover, social and broad economic factors such as the "nature and timing of the offer, questions of illegality, the impact on 'constituencies' other than shareholders (i.e., creditors, customers, employees, and perhaps even the community generally), the risk of non-consummation, and the securities being offered in exchange."[78]

Many states have now enacted constituency statutes that explicitly allow, and even encourage, corporate directors to consider the interests of many parties in making corporate decisions.[79] For example, Pennsylvania's statute allows the board to consider the interests of any group affected by the action, including shareholders, employees, customers, and the community.[80] Moreover, no one group has a more important interest than others. Additionally, many states have created new corporate forms that explicitly and formally place the interests of broader stakeholders over maximizing profits.[81] Benefit corporation statutes grant boards even more insulation to place socially responsible priorities over profit-maximizing conduct.[82] Kickstarter, for example, became a public benefit corporation in 2015 under New York law.[83] The company's new charter explicitly protects a number of corporate values, including helping to generate creative projects, limiting the company's environmental impact, and donating a percentage of its profits to support arts education.[84]

By 2019, the U.S. Business Roundtable finally dropped shareholder primacy—the idea that had been pushed by the Chicago School that the primary purpose of a corporation is to maximize shareholder value.[85] Instead the Roundtable's definition of corporate purpose describes a more textured set of responsibilities to consult with, and to provide for, customers, employees, suppliers, communities, and shareholders. In

recognition of expectations in modern corporate law and social values, the Roundtable's statement places corporations
as legal individuals in society with complicated social
responsibilities.

What is the role of the board of directors?

Since a corporation is an artificial person, it requires actual
people to act on its behalf. The board of directors (BoD) exercises
the corporation's powers and manages the corporation's business affairs.[86] Its role tends to focus on big-picture, corporation-
wide management, with officers handling the day-to-day
affairs.[87] In general, boards set the corporation's goals, select
the CEO and other officers, determine executive compensation, and provide advice to officers.[88] At the end of the day,
however, a corporation's board is ultimately responsible for
the management of the corporation.[89] Because directors exercise a great amount of power, state corporate statutes and the
courts have created legal safeguards to prevent directors from
misusing the corporation.

We have already discussed some of the duties that directors
and other top officers have toward the corporation in Chapter 5.
Before delving into the board's powers, it is important to understand a board's composition. A board is composed of directors.
There are multiple types of directors. An inside director is
someone who acts as both a director and as an officer for the
corporation.[90] An outside director is not an officer or otherwise
employed by the corporation.[91] Outside directors are often independent, that is, individuals who should have no conflict
that would interfere with their independent judgment in considering questions that come before the board.[92] Directors are
typically elected at the annual shareholders' meeting, and
serve one-year terms.[93] It is becoming common, however, for
directors to serve multiple-year terms that are staggered in duration. This staggering helps preserve expertise and prevent
hostile takeovers.[94]

A corporation's BoD, as the primary authority of the corporation, possesses broad powers.[95] The board has managerial power, which includes the ability to make investments, devise strategies, and pay stock dividends.[96] The board also makes decisions concerning the nature of the corporation, such as mergers and takeovers. In exercising these powers, the board must act as a unit, that is, a single director cannot act on behalf of the corporation without appropriate authority from the rest of the board.[97] Even though state statutes grant directors broad powers, directors must act within the scope of their authority.[98] And many of their actions, especially in the realm of mergers, takeovers, and charter amendments, must be ratified by shareholders as well.

As introduced previously in Chapter 5, directors act for the benefit of the corporation, and thus owe fiduciary duties to the corporation and its shareholders.[99] Specifically, directors owe duties of loyalty and care. Under the duty of loyalty, directors must act in the best interest of the corporation and respect the ability of its shareholders to vote.[100] A director cannot use his or her position to further his or her own interests over those of the corporation. The duty of loyalty generally comes into play with self-interested transactions and taking corporate opportunities. A self-interested transaction occurs when a director may have interests on both sides of a transaction and may gain a personal benefit from the transaction.[101] In this situation, the director is presumed to be interested and should not participate in the transaction.[102] For example, executive compensation is an area with potential for self-dealing transactions, especially when an inside director occupies a place on the executive team of the corporation as well as on its board.[103] There is also a potential violation of loyalty when a director takes advantage of a corporate opportunity that would have been useful to the corporation. We further described such examples in Chapter 5.

Another fiduciary duty that directors owe corporations is the duty of care, which requires directors to act as a reasonable person would act in similar circumstances.[104] To quickly re-view our longer discussion of this subject in Chapter 5, the duty of care also requires directors to be well-informed before making business decisions.[105] As often articulated by courts, the duty of care is more concerned with the process that was followed by directors to make substantive decisions than, at times, the merits of those decisions. Accordingly, courts will presume that, when a director acts in good faith, and is well-informed, that the director acted with due care. This pre-sumption is called the "business judgment rule" (BJR), and it often protects directors from liability for their actions.[106] See Chapter 5, and our previous answer to a question about the BJR in this chapter, for additional information.

In addition to the duties of care and loyalty, there are also duties of good faith, oversight, and disclosure. The duty of good faith is violated when there is intentional misconduct or a conscious disregard of one's responsibilities.[107] The duty of oversight, which can be connected to both the duties of care and loyalty, requires that directors implement a compliance system within the corporation, and that they ensure that the system adequately provides them reliable and timely infor-mation about possible legal or ethical violations. (For more on ethics and compliance systems, see Chapters 13 and 14.) Directors' duty of disclosure requires directors to provide in-formation to shareholders when requesting that shareholders take an action. It mandates that corporate directors be honest and candid with shareholders in communications.

In addition to fiduciary duties, there are other requirements that limit director power, specifically, prohibitions against il-legal actions and corporate waste. As the ultra vires doctrine highlights, directors cannot act illegally even if doing so would profit the corporation.[108] Corporate waste occurs when corpo-rate assets are essentially given away as a gift. The waste doc-trine assumes that giving away corporate assets in exchange for nothing of value (not even goodwill) cannot have been in the proper conduct of business.

What are the roles of corporate officers and other employees?

Within a corporation, officers and employees are the people who actually perform day-to-day operations. Officers usually have managerial duties, possess authority over employees, are in positions of trust, and may require advanced knowledge for their positions.[109] Corporations tend to be hierarchal in structure with the board of directors (BoD) at the top. The board chooses the corporation's officers, who then select the employees below them, with the corporate structure having as many levels as it requires.[110] As this hierarchal structure suggests, the BoD has the power to fire officers because it selects them. Depending on contract and default rules, officers and the employees below them may be fired either with or without cause. In the United States, the default tends to be that people serve in positions at-will, which means that they typically can be fired without cause, although they may be entitled to severance depending upon their contract with the corporation. They serve at the pleasure of, and on the terms set or negotiated by, the corporation.

There are a variety of officer positions that corporations are increasingly modifying to fit corporate needs. The same position in different corporations may have different names. Some state corporate statutes require certain officer positions like president, secretary, and treasurer. Others, like Delaware, allow the BoD and a corporation's bylaws to determine what officers to appoint, although Delaware does statutorily require a corporate secretary.[111] Top officers are generally included in what is called the "C-suite," which may include the chief executive officer (CEO), chief operating officer (COO), chief financial officer (CFO), chief information officer (CIO), chief administrative officer (CAO), and chief legal officer (CLO).[112]

Since a corporation is an artificial person, it requires corporate officers, employees, and others to act on its behalf. In the older law of master-and-servant (now agency law), the corporation is the principal (master) and the officers and employees are the agents (its servants).[113] As agents, officers and employees must act according to the authority given to them by the corporation. This authority may stem from a variety of sources, but, most commonly, comes from a job description approved by a corporate officer or BoD, a board resolution, or the corporation's bylaws.[114]

This type of authority given to corporate agents tends to fall into one of four categories: expressed actual authority, implied actual authority, apparent authority, and inherent authority.

Actual authority is present when an agent acts with overt corporate permission.[115] Actual authority may be expressed or implied. Expressed actual authority is present when the general corporate statute, charter, bylaws, some other written document, or direct order gives the agent authority to act.[116] Implied actual authority is when there is no written description or direct order for the agent's authority, but the agent reasonably infers what the corporation wants the agent to do based on corporate manifestations and the powers that the agent needs to carry out his or her job.[117]

Agents also may have apparent authority.[118] Apparent authority may be inferred based on corporation manifestations through the agent's relationship with third parties on the corporation's behalf. Apparent authority is the authority that a third party would reasonably believe that the agent possesses based on what the corporation has done.[119]

Finally, especially the CEO and executives of a corporation have inherent authority to act on the corporation's behalf in many matters. By virtue of their positions, they have the authority to act within the general goals of the corporation's business and, importantly, to bind the corporation to perform certain actions.[120] A CEO has the greatest degree of this authority.

Although these forms of authority may appear fairly straightforward, much litigation concerns when and whether a particular corporate office had authority to bind the corporation.[121]

What is the relationship between the corporation and its shareholders?

In order to raise money (capital), corporations may sell stock.[122] Shareholders are the people who purchase that stock.[123] In exchange for financing the corporation, shareholders receive an interest in the corporation and its residual corporate profits via dividends or theoretical distribution rights upon the liquidation of the corporation.[124] Because shareholders own stock, and not an outright interest in the corporation itself, their liability, as described above, is typically limited to the amount that they have invested in stock.[125] This is an important distinction. Although the language around shareholders' relationship with the corporation can be loose, they are not the "owners" of the corporation. What they own is *stock* in the corporation. Owning stock in the corporation allows for certain rights to sell stock, vote on corporate actions, and to sue for corporate harms. It does *not* allow shareholders to run the corporation as though they owned it: a common shareholder may not, for example, take items off the shelves of the corporation's warehouses without paying for them, or insist on minutiae such as that the corporation must produce a certain flavor drink.

Remember that a corporation is its own legal person. First, it would be against that framework for anyone to literally "own" another person. Second, corporations are run by their boards of directors and, through delegations of authority, by their management teams. Third, as was discussed above in the context of piercing the corporate veil, should any person start to exercise personal ownership of a corporation as an extension of his or herself, he or she may be subjected to legal liability for violating the protections of the corporate form (e.g., through courts piercing the corporate veil). Part of the bargain that shareholders make for their limited liability protection is that they will not become too intimate with the corporation, such as the way that the owner of a business is.

Shareholders are investors who have limited their liability for their investments to the amount that they have bought in stock. They have certain rights as owners of equity (typically stock) that distinguish them from owners of the corporation's debt (known as creditors). A longer description of the different rights of owners of corporate equity (the "residue" of corporate assets after all fixed claims are paid), versus owners of corporate debt (some of those fixed claims on corporate assets), is beyond the scope of this chapter, but owning stock comes with basic rights to sell, vote, and sue.[126] We will talk more about these three rights now before moving on to other topics.

First, courts will typically protect shareholders' right to sell their stock—to get out of their investment in the corporation at a fair market price.[127] If shareholders do not like what is happening at a corporation, they should have the right to leave. Indeed, someone else in the marketplace may feel differently about the corporation's actions, and he or she may value the corporation's stock for a higher amount. However, selling may not fix the problem for a given shareholder if other marketplace participants also disagree with what is happening at the corporation, and they discount the price they are willing to pay the shareholder for his or her shares accordingly.

Generally, when shareholders of public companies sell their stock, they sell over the public exchanges, and they are able to leave the company almost instantly.[128] It is this "liquidity" (ease of sale and transfer) of stock over the public markets, as well as limited liability—the limit of shareholders' liability is the stock that they own—that contributes to making investments in the corporate form attractive.[129]

Second, should a stockholder not want to leave—or at least not want the corporation's behavior to continue such that he or she sells at as much of a loss—shareholders may make proposals about the corporation's direction, and vote on proposed candidates for its BoD candidates.

Under many states' organizational laws, shareholders elect and remove directors, approve certain fundamental changes (such as sales of all or substantially all of a corporation's assets), and weigh in on the corporation's bylaws.[130] Taking Delaware's general corporation law as an example (and 82% of U.S. public companies are incorporated in Delaware),[131] shareholders have the right to an annual meeting, and they have the right to vote on certain shareholder issues.[132] Under Delaware law, in addition to electing directors, key actions that would trigger a shareholder vote include amending the corporate charter, approving a merger, the sale of all (or substantially all) of the corporation's assets, and the dissolution of the corporation. Shareholders may also present proposals to the BoD. If approved by a majority of votes at a shareholder meeting, the proposals become binding on the corporation.[133]

The shape and enforcement mechanisms for these rights vary by jurisdiction, but savvy lawyers can make money advising shareholders on how to influence corporate boards, and advising corporate boards on how to influence or shape deals so as not to trigger shareholder votes.

Because it can be uncommon for the thousands of shareholders who may hold a public company's stock to show up in person at shareholder meetings, typically shareholders fill out "proxy" forms. Such proxy forms give someone else the power to vote on a shareholder's behalf, either binding the proxy's vote for the shareholder's established position, or allowing the proxy to decide the direction of the shareholder's vote (or votes).

Ahead of a shareholder meeting, shareholders review written (or now electronic) materials sent out by the corporation in advance to describe the votes to be held at the meeting. U.S. corporations' materials must include shareholders' proposals, if the proposals pass review under the U.S. Securities & Exchange Commission's (SEC) proxy rules.[134] These rules govern issues such as shareholder eligibility, the length and number of proposals, and their subject matter. Shareholder proposals will be rejected if they concern a personal grievance, violate state law, relate to less than 5% of the corporation's assets, or attempt to control the corporation's ordinary business operations. Generally, shareholder proposals are written in a less-binding, suggestive form to pass review.

Third, should a shareholder feel that there is an injury to the corporation—and the shareholder does not want to sell his or her stock, or change the direction of the BoD through voting—he or she may be able to sue the corporation to correct or be compensated for the corporation's alleged wrongs. When the shareholder is bringing suit for alleged damage to him or herself, the suit is called a "direct" suit.[135] When the shareholder is suing the BoD for alleged harm to the corporation itself, the suit is "derivative" of the corporation's own claims: a "derivative suit."[136] Theoretically, in a derivative suit, the shareholder is bringing suit on behalf of the corporation itself because its BoD is functioning so poorly that the corporation is unable to pursue the suit or correct the issues itself. Typically, the plaintiffs must allege that the BoD is unable to correct the issues inside the corporation itself because its members have conflicts of interest (such as violations of the duty of loyalty described both above and in Chapter 5, or other problems).

Along with the different purposes of direct versus derivative suits, there is a major difference between who gets paid in the end.[137] In a direct suit, the shareholder is suing on his or her own behalf and recovers the remedy him or herself. In a derivative suit, the shareholder sues on behalf of the corporation, and the corporation recovers the remedy.

Derivative suits are the primary way to hold officers, directors, and majority shareholders accountable for fraud, mismanagement, and negligence that causes shareholders' investments to lose value.[138] Despite the importance of holding corporate directors and officers accountable to the corporation, derivative suits involve myriad procedural requirements that make bringing a successful suit difficult. One such requirement is the demand on directors. Before filing a derivative suit, shareholders typically must demand that the corporation's directors first rectify the cause of the suit, or show why asking its directors to do so would be futile.[139]

In addition to these three main rights (to sell, vote, and sue), shareholders have a number of ancillary rights, including the right to information.[140] This right helps shareholders keep an eye on the corporation to see how its business is being conducted. Through this right, shareholders can inspect the books and records of the corporation. Shareholders may typically only request such information when it is for a legitimate purpose connected to their interest as an investor in the corporation.

Although shareholders may wield a fair amount of power through these rights, the corporation has ways to limit shareholder power. Two common limitations are staggered boards and non-voting shares.

When a board's terms are staggered, only a certain number of board positions are open for re-election each year. For example, if only one-third of the positions are open at the annual shareholders' meeting, each director actually may serve a three-year term.[141] Shareholders may generally replace by vote without cause directors whose term has finished, but they typically may only remove for cause those directors whose term has not finished.

To protect itself against shareholder action, a corporation may also issue different classes of shares.[142] For example, it may have non-voting common stock and voting stock. The corporation sells common stock to the public while it sells voting stock to only a few individuals—usually managers within the corporation. A variation on this technique is to create classes of shares that have far more votes than other forms of stock, or certain triggers that make them more valuable should a takeover or other specified event occur. The purpose of such different classes of stock and provisions is to protect the positions of managers, founders, and others who do not want to lose their positions or their control over the company's decisions.[143] These structures are permitted when a company initially sells its shares to the public, but subsequent charter amendments to achieve a "dual class" system—so-called "midstream recapitalizations"—are effectively barred.

Another limit on shareholder power may come from a controlling shareholder or group of shareholders. We describe these issues more in the question below.

What can a controlling shareholder do?

The first thing to know about a corporation for the purpose of evaluating what a controlling shareholder can do is whether the corporation is public or private. As described earlier in this chapter, a public corporation typically lists its stock on a public exchange, and its shares are freely available for trade.[144] Because public companies usually have hundreds, if not thousands, of shareholders, there are usually enough of their shares for sale, and people eligible to buy such shares, that economists consider the market "thick" enough to fairly price their stock.

But when a company is closely held by a small number of shareholders, or privately held by shareholders who are not trading the company's stock on the public markets, problems may arise in how shareholders treat each other and the company. Shareholders in such situations may not have the practical ability to sell their shares at a fair price in order to leave, or have a meaningful vote at shareholder meetings. They may thus only be able to sue.

Of special concern to courts in such situations is when the power to control the corporation has been concentrated in the hands of a single controlling shareholder, or group of shareholders who act together to create the same effect. A controlling shareholder may not need to actually own a majority of the corporation's stock if he or she (or it) effectively exercises control anyway.[145] Minority (non-controlling) shareholders may find themselves consistently locked out of decisions, or their interests disregarded, as the controlling shareholder elects the directors of the corporation, and can cause the corporation to sell or buy assets on unfair terms. The controlling shareholder may also sell his or her stock, and hence control of the corporation, at a premium or extreme discount to someone else opposed to the minority shareholders' interests.[146]

Essentially, the concern is that minority shareholders may be locked into corporations that they cannot control; and they may be exploited by their fellow (controlling) investors. To help protect minority shareholders in these situations, courts may impose a duty on controlling shareholders that would not exist among shareholders who might otherwise have access to a fair market solution. Typically, courts describe this duty as a duty of good faith, similar to, but slightly weaker than, the good faith expected of directors toward the corporation. Depending on the state, courts may enforce this duty of good faith by, for example, not allowing a controlling shareholder to remove a minority shareholder from the company's board, or to fire him or her from the company's employment.[147] In certain cases involving closely held corporations, courts enforce a stronger duty to act with the utmost good faith and loyalty. In those cases, controlling shareholders should not, for example, withhold dividends, reduce salaries, or deprive key stakeholders of employment.[148]

Courts impose echoes of other duties that we may recognize as typically imposed on BoDs in the context of controlling shareholders as well. They simply appear far weaker and much more difficult to trigger in the controlling shareholder context. In an echo of the duty of loyalty, controlling shareholders may not usurp a corporate opportunity if it harms minority shareholders.[149] Courts have used an intrinsic fairness test to determine whether a controlling shareholder is receiving such a benefit to the detriment of minority shareholders.[150]

Finally, if a controlling shareholder exercises too much direct control over a company, the shareholder risks exposing him or herself to personal liability. As we mentioned above, courts will pierce the corporate veil (reach through the protection otherwise afforded to shareholders behind the corporate form) to hold shareholders or directors personally liable for corporate actions when they have abused their power and become so entwined that they have essentially "merged" with the corporation.[151] Controlling shareholders who too overtly pull a corporation's strings may be accused of using the corporation as their "alter ego," and invalidate the protection of the corporate form by rendering the entity a "dummy corporation."[152] Important indicators for courts that controlling shareholders have merged with their corporations include undercapitalization, the failure to observe corporate formalities, fraud, abuse, lack of good faith, and the commingling of funds.[153]

What is the business judgment rule and why does it matter?

From our previous discussion of the three main powers of shareholders—to sell, to vote, and to sue—we can see how directors (and sometimes controlling shareholders) may be keenly aware of their liability to shareholders should the shareholders decide to sue. Directors are often sued for alleged violations of their fiduciary duties and need to think about how to defend themselves from these suits. In addition, courts, not wanting to entertain what could be massive numbers of suits from shareholders complaining about directors' every action, have developed defenses for directors' behavior.

The primary defense in Delaware law to protect directors from shareholder suits is the business judgment rule (BJR). For the presumptive protection of BJR to apply and insulate a director's actions from liability, the shareholders must prove that the director has not (1) acted in good faith, (2) in a way that is not self-interested, (3) been reasonably informed, and (4) rationally believe that his or her decision was in the best interest of the corporation.[154]

Taking apart the elements of the BJR, we recognize the standard of good faith from earlier descriptions of directors' duties. We recognize the requirement to act in a way that is not

self-interested from the duty of loyalty. We recognize the requirement that directors be reasonably informed from the duty
of care. And we recognize the requirement to act in the best
interest of the corporation as a variation of the duty of loyalty
to have the corporation's best interests at heart. So, directors
should be fulfilling these basic requirements anyway—the
issue for the courts is not to have to go through a mini-trial on
the fulfillment of each duty.

When shareholders attempt to bring suit against directors
for alleged violations of their fiduciary duties, the first thing
the Delaware courts—and the many other courts that follow
their example—will do is to allow directors to raise the BJR
as an initial defense. If shareholders can establish violations
of the BJR, then the court may hear the rest of the case. If they
cannot, the court will dismiss the case.

Permitting the BJR to serve as such a strong bar to further
litigation has positives and negatives. First, it focuses an enormous amount of attention on the BJR itself as something of
an abbreviated understanding of directors' more comprehensive duties. Second, it provides relief for directors to know that
courts will largely defer to their judgments if their behaviors
satisfy the BJR's minimal standard. This effect both makes it
easier to find directors willing to serve the corporation, and
it reassures directors that they may largely run the corporation as they see fit, including taking substantial business
risks.[155] Third, the BJR allows courts not to be involved in the
intricacies of most corporate decisions, and it vastly reduces
their caseloads.[156]

In practice, the BJR contains both procedural and substantive concerns.[157] Procedurally, directors need to be attentive
and reasonably informed when making business decisions
and, substantively, these decisions need to be reasonable.

Most directors can live within these basic limitations. Note
that the BJR does still insulate them from liability for mistakes
that may seem stupid on the merits. There is always a problem
in business cases that directors' bad decisions will look

worse in hindsight than they did at the time that they were made, with the information and understanding then available. Directors are seldom sued by happy shareholders when decisions have turned out well. They are typically sued when things go badly, and shareholders want to be compensated and have them removed. Courts and judges do not want to be drawn into such fights to second-guess what directors should have done, and to estimate hypothetical damages. They would prefer to grant directors more discretion and have to engage in less intimate review, even if this means that some bad behavior goes unchecked.

When courts have gotten involved in business cases, it is usually because there have been procedural irregularities and the BoD failed to gather the information it would have needed to make a properly informed decision. Cases such as *Caremark* now require boards of directors to institute reporting and monitoring programs within their corporations that will provide them ways of collecting timely and accurate information about what is happening inside their organizations.[158]

Additionally, in practice, corporations have found other ways to insulate their directors from liability. Among the most common approaches are exculpation, indemnification, and insurance. When a corporation exculpates its directors from liability, it typically includes a provision in its articles of incorporation that eliminates (or severely limits) its directors' personal financial liability for breaches of fiduciary duties.[159] Under Delaware law, however, certain violations of the duty of loyalty (e.g., acts not committed in good faith, or transactions in which the director received an improper benefit) cannot be so eliminated and, for everything else, injunctive relief remains available.[160]

Should a director breach a fiduciary duty that is still owed to the corporation, the corporation can indemnify (indeed must indemnify) its director in specific situations. Indemnification occurs when the corporation pays the director's expenses. Typically, the director (or other corporate agent) must have acted in good faith and reasonably believed that his or her actions were in the best interests of the corporation (hints of the BJR).[161]

Finally, almost all public companies in the United States and Canada, as well as in other countries around the world, purchase so-called "Directors and Officers" (D&O) insurance. "Side A" D&O insurance covers the company's indemnification responsibilities. "Side B" insurance often covers their directors, officers, and other key employees or agents for amounts not covered by indemnification. Unlike indemnification, Side B insurance coverage is not usually limited in its terms to actions taken in good faith and in the best interests of the corporation,[162] but many states' laws may not permit insurance companies to cover criminal and other illegal acts.[163]

Cases concerning violations of fiduciary duties and the BJR typically center on the actions of a corporation's directors and officers. The BJR is available for them to raise as a defense to claims, although there is some question whether officers are held to the same standards of duties to the corporation as its directors.[164] In addition, it is even less clear whether controlling shareholders—whose behaviors may trigger fiduciary duties, but only at lower rates and with much lower standards than directors—may be entitled to protections under the BJR. Because there has been so little demand in the case law for a rule in the controlling shareholder context, the answer may effectively be that they, and the courts, do not need the BJR.

What kinds of conflicts of interests are common in corporations and how can they be addressed?

The most common conflicts of interest inside a corporation involve decisions for the corporation being made by someone who has a potential personal benefit connected to the outcome. These conflicts may involve the director whose husband is the real estate agent for the property the corporation could buy; the vice president whose daughter the corporation could hire;

or the accountant who wants to run trades for the corporation through the firm that his friend owns to receive a cut of
the transactions. At each point, the actual decision to proceed
may or may not also be in the corporation's best interest, but
a benefit from the transaction accrues to the individual, the
individual's family, or close friend helping to make the decision on the corporation's behalf.

For directors, officers, and controlling shareholders of the
corporation, proceeding with such transactions can constitute
a violation of the duty of loyalty. Remember that directors and
officers owe duties of loyalty to the corporation to act in its
best interest, and controlling shareholders may be bound by
their special accumulation of power not to abuse their influence over the corporation and its minority shareholders.

But there are examples of interested transactions—
transactions in which a decision maker is on both sides of
the transaction—that take place in corporate life all the time.
Consider, for example, negotiations over salary (especially
when the chief executive sits on a corporate board), directors
buying corporate assets, and a director selling assets or stock
to the corporation.[165] Even receiving frequent-flyer miles in
your personal account for travel taken on behalf of the corporation can trigger concerns about loyalty. We will talk later
about how to disclose and have such transactions approved.

Meanwhile, even though interested transactions may be
among the easiest potential violations of the duty of loyalty to
spot, another significant category of loyalty violations involves
taking a corporate opportunity away from the corporation. As
we discussed, corporations only act through the people who
work for them (their "agents"). A corporation cannot do anything on its own except through the people who perform
tasks on its behalf. In the course of doing their jobs for the
corporation, those people may come across information and
opportunities of which the corporation may want to take advantage. Think about all the real estate deals that a real estate
company's directors or officer, for example, may hear about in

a week. It would be a serious problem for the corporation if its agents shifted those deals to their own personal accounts or to other business entities in which they have an interest instead of presenting those opportunities to the corporation that employs them.

Part of what the corporation is paying for by engaging individuals as its agents is their promise to let the corporation know about the opportunities that they discover. In considering what generally constitutes the "taking" of a corporate opportunity, courts' analysis typically inquires whether (1) the opportunity in question was within the corporation's "line of business," in other words the type of industry, subject, or deal in which the corporation might want to engage; (2) the corporation has a tangible interest in the opportunity, in other words, property, money, or other reasons why it might be involved; and (3) the taking was fair on the part of the director, officer, or other person involved—a much more nebulous test that tries to weigh the equities of the situation.[166]

In Delaware, the courts narrow these questions a little more to ask:[167]

- Could the corporation financially take advantage of the opportunity? (If the corporation has no cash to buy the property and could not borrow the money, for example, it is hard to claim that the corporation would be able to take advantage of the deal.)
- Similar to above, is the opportunity within the corporation's line of business? (In other words, would the corporation have had interest in the deal anyway?)
- More immediately, does the corporation already have an interest in the opportunity?
- And—especially for directors, but for officers and employees as well—does the opportunity place the agent at odds with the corporation, in violation of his or her duties to the corporation? (In other words, if the director buys the land that

the corporation needs, does that mean that the director and the corporation will be on opposite sides of the table soon?)

Rather than trying to thread arguments for a transaction through these tests, however, a better strategy is often to simply *disclose what you are doing and get permission from the corporation*. This method—as long as there was full and fair disclosure—waives the conflict and alleviates worry over any later objections. Early, full disclosure and waiver is the easiest, safest strategy, and the one taken by most directors, officers, and others with potential conflicts. As a practice tip, it is best to both make the disclosure and get the permission in writing (even if you are memorializing over email an oral conversation with someone after it happens). Because being excused by fully disclosing and getting permission is so easy, actions taken without permission close to the line also tend to look suspicious by comparison.

Moreover, the consequences for not disclosing and getting permission for actions that violate the duty of loyalty can be severe. First, remember that violations of the duty of loyalty are among the very few actions that cannot be exculpated (excused in the articles of incorporation), indemnified (reimbursed for litigation and liability costs by the corporation), or often insured (covered by outside D&O insurance of other policies under the terms of various state laws).

Second, even if you do not end up in litigation personally, you may not end up with the benefit of the deal either. The corporation can move to void the transaction— meaning undo the deal that you made. The transaction does not *have* to be voided (that means that voidability is at the corporation's discretion). The corporation can instead choose to waive the conflict and allow the transaction to occur if properly disclosed afterwards.[168] But this option is risky, and it would be easier to have asked for permission beforehand.

If you do find yourself in the very awkward position of trying to get a corporation's permission for a transaction after it has happened, Delaware law does provide a painful way to ensure the deal will not be voided. If you really need to, you can go back to the board of directors and shareholders for them to approve the deal, and effectively waive the loyalty violation after it has closed. A deal is no longer voidable if (1) it is disclosed to the board and a majority of disinterested directors (directors who do not have a personal stake in the deal) approve it; and (2) it is disclosed to the corporation's shareholders and a majority of them approve it; or (3) the taking was fair (not the most well-defined safe harbor that may involve litigation to determine).[169] Thus, as uncomfortable as an earlier conversation for permission might be, it is simply a better idea to fully disclose and receive permission in advance from the entity to whom you owe a duty.

What special rules apply to corporations?

At the start of this chapter, we discussed how corporations are increasingly full legal persons. Then we talked about how those legal persons can function in the world through the actions of agents, who are bound by fiduciary duties toward the legal entity that they serve.

Now in the final questions for this chapter, and into Chapter 7, we discuss what the place of these legal persons is in society. We mentioned that they are often bound in contract like natural persons—though notice some unusual qualities like the ability to void contracts not properly approved through the corporation's operations as described in the question above—and that many laws apply to corporations to restrict their behavior as though they were natural persons (e.g., the corporate delivery truck has to stop at the red light like everyone else). But there are some laws that are primarily aimed at corporations, and people who work for corporations should be aware of them.

The main subjects of these laws and rules at the federal level are securities regulation, anti-fraud, antitrust, anti-corruption, and intellectual property (IP) and technology transfer. We will very briefly survey those special requirements for corporations before closing this chapter with a focus in the next question on how corporations can be legally disciplined for breaking laws.

First, a note of caution, what follows is a survey of major *federal* requirements for corporate entities. As already mentioned, much regulation of corporations, similar to regulation of natural people, takes place at the state and local levels. Traffic rules, licensing, permitting permissions and use allocations, many taxation decisions, and other regulations govern corporate behavior at those levels.

At the federal level, the U.S. SEC is primarily in charge of enforcing the two main securities regulation laws and amendments to them.[170] The two main securities laws are the Securities Act of 1933[171] and the Securities Exchange Act of 1934.[172] The 1933 Act largely governs the issuance of securities. The 1934 Act then largely focuses on how those securities are traded and the regulation of public companies. Significant changes to these 1933 and 1934 Acts have been made over time, but most prominently by two laws discussed often in the corporate setting: the Sarbanes–Oxley Act of 2002 (SOX)[173] and the Dodd–Frank Wall Street Reform Act of 2010 (Dodd–Frank).[174] Among other things, SOX elevated accounting standards in the wake of the Enron and WorldCom scandals.[175] Dodd–Frank created additional reporting and other requirements in the wake of the 2007–08 financial crisis.[176]

Public corporations that issue stock (a form of security) are heavily regulated by the SEC. Closely held and private corporations may be regulated as well when they offer financial instruments such as stock or other securities to their investors. Even non-corporate forms of business entities may be regulated when they start raising money from investors and issue financial promises.

Public corporations spend significant time and energy filing regular forms and disclosures with the SEC. Typically, these forms are filed with the SEC, and then available to the public either at the same time, or after a short embargo period. This means that, should you have questions about a public corporation, such forms are important sources of information about its financial health and plans.

Whenever a corporation offers securities (e.g., issues stock), it must file a registration statement with the SEC that includes information on the security being offered, the corporation's business, as well as its management, finances, and anticipated risks.[177] Public companies must file corporate 10-K forms annually.[178] 10-K forms contain much of the same information as the company's annual report released to shareholders before annual meetings, but in significantly greater detail. Public companies file 10-Q forms quarterly to provide up-to-date developments on the corporation.[179] They also file 8-K forms to provide investors with information about major developments that did not occur in time for the other filings.[180]

Another major area in which corporations file forms with the SEC concerns shareholder voting. We discussed above shareholders' rights to sell, vote, and sue. Shareholders vote during (at least) annual meetings, often through the proxy system described above.

Proxy statements must be filed with the SEC before they are sent to shareholders, generally at least ten days beforehand.[181] The SEC is concerned, among other things, that proxies clearly state who is soliciting proxy votes, and that the information upon which the proxy is granted is fairly presented.[182] Corporations cannot make false or misleading statements in proxy contests.[183] Violating this "anti-fraud" rule would subject corporations to SEC enforcement.[184]

Major public company corporate shareholders and insiders must file forms about their control of the corporation with the SEC as well. Forms 3, 4, and 5 are designed to discourage insider trading—when someone who has material nonpublic information about the corporation trades or helps someone else trade on that information.[185] Form 3 discloses to investors which insiders own corporate securities. Form 4 discloses material changes to the holdings of corporate insiders—in other words, whether there is unusual activity in their patterns of buying and selling. Form 5 discloses additional transactions not reported on Form 4, and it needs to be filed with the SEC within 45 days after the corporation's fiscal year or within six months of when the insider leaves the corporation.

Still at the federal level, other government agencies enforce the antitrust rules. Antitrust is an area of law that attempts to prevent the overconcentration of market power by a single corporation or a group of businesses working together to shut out competition. The U.S. Federal Trade Commission (FTC) polices unfair methods of competition in interstate commerce.[186] The U.S. Department of Justice (the "DOJ," the federal government's main litigator) may bring suit for violations of the Sherman Antitrust[187] and Clayton Acts.[188] Under the Sherman Act, which forbids unreasonable restraints of trade, the DOJ focuses on price-fixing, bid-rigging, and customer-allocation behavior.[189] Under the Clayton Act, which is concerned with mergers and acquisitions that may inhibit market competition, the DOJ and FTC require advance disclosures and filings.[190]

Federal anti-corruption rules are enforced through a series of agencies. One of the most visible of these rules in current times is the Foreign Corrupt Practices Act (FCPA), which requires filings with the SEC and can also be enforced by the DOJ.[191] The FCPA's goal is to reduce or eliminate payments directly to, or made in order to influence the behavior of, foreign officials, candidates, or parties.

The law is broad in scope, applies both inside and outside the U.S. (to people and entities with a U.S. connection), and contains no monetary minimum. For a while under the U.S. Obama administration, corporate fines under the FCPA reached very high levels, but observers are waiting to see how much emphasis FCPA enforcement will currently be given.

Finally, technology transfer restrictions are gaining a higher profile for corporations under the U.S. 2018 Export Control Reform Act (ECRA), which was passed as part of the defense budget that year.[192] The ECRA joins other laws controlling the transfer of intellectual property (especially advanced devices and technical expertise) bought, sold, or otherwise exchanged to certain places. The 2018 legislation created a now-permanent authority for export regulations within the Commerce Department, and it focuses on trying to keep certain information out of the hands of other governments. It tightened export controls on emerging and foundational technologies, created a higher level of scrutiny for export licenses, and expanded the definition of U.S. persons (especially corporations) providing aid to foreign defense intelligence services.[193] The ECRA joins the government's recent wave of activity toward more aggressive limits on the terms of international trade through export controls, sanctions, tariffs, and other methods of which corporations need to be particularly aware.

How can laws be enforced against a "legal person"?

If corporations and other entities are bound by laws like other people, a reasonable question with which to end this chapter is whether business entities—as "legal persons"—can be disciplined the way that natural persons can. In some ways they can be, and in some ways they cannot. Corporations and other legal persons can be fined, can be prevented by courts from engaging in certain behavior (enjoined), and can lose privileges for misbehavior (loss of licensing, ability to bid for contracts, and other penalties). They can even be convicted of crimes that are marked on their records. But they cannot be jailed. They have, as the Lord Chancellor of England complained in the late eighteenth century, "no soul to be damned, and no body to be kicked."[194] We will leave to the next chapter (Chapter 7, "The

Corporation as an Ethical 'Person' in Modern Society"), to comment on the third part of the Lord Chancellor's complaint that he did not "ever expect a corporation to have a conscience."[195]

There is a unique way in which a corporation can be disciplined, however, that does not exist for a natural person. Theoretically, because states grant corporations their charters (recognition of a corporation's coming into being as a legal entity that will be recognized by the state), states can revoke those charters as well. This penalty is highly unusual and serious, but states will take this step where there has been corporate fraud and mismanagement.[196] When a state revokes a corporation's charter, the corporation can no longer conduct lawful business in the state and must dissolve.[197]

A less drastic step is to suspend a corporation's license to conduct business (or even its charter) temporarily, meaning that the corporation cannot legally operate for a set period of time.[198] States may, for example, suspend a corporation's license for failure to pay taxes or to file appropriate reports.

Returning to more typical forms of actions against corporations, civil suits against corporations may be brought by individuals, other business entities, the government, or joined in combination against the corporation. The corporation may be sued as a legal entity, and sometimes its directors, officers, and other employees may be sued in their official capacities (in their roles for the corporation) or in their individual capacities (as responsible for their own actions). Corporate directors and officers may also be sued by shareholders, either in the shareholders' individual capacity (if suing for a direct harm that they incurred as a result of corporate action), or as part of a derivative suit (a method discussed above to recover damage done to the corporation itself).

Finally, we described above some of the laws particularly focused on corporate behavior. The government encourages reports of corporate wrongdoing and may either pursue a case against the corporation itself, or it may allow a private individual to take the lead for a percentage of the profits (a procedure described as *"qui tam"* litigation). In some cases, the individuals who have helped the government establish its case may be paid a bounty but only if the government's recovery is high enough (see more on whistleblowing laws and options in Chapter 12, and Chapter 16, the appendix of resources to this book). For more on official government policies about, and procedures for, suing corporations, you can visit the DOJ's manual on federal prosecution of business organizations.[199]

As a final note to this chapter, the DOJ's approach toward prosecuting individuals as well as corporations for corporate wrongdoing continues to evolve. At times, such as during the Savings & Loans failures in the 1980s, the DOJ prosecuted hundreds of financial executives for their misconduct. Conversely, after the 2007–08 financial crisis, which resulted in the disappearance of up to 40% of the world's wealth,[200] not a single top executive went to jail.[201]

The DOJ has issued internal policy guidelines to encourage greater prosecution of individuals in addition to corporations, but such prosecutions reached a 40-year low in April 2018 under the Trump administration.[202]

Nonetheless, one of the most active areas of individual prosecutions may remain violations of securities laws. Between 2000 and 2014, the SEC named individuals in 88% of its enforcement actions.[203] In most of those cases, the SEC named individuals and a corporation, but in 25% of cases the SEC named individuals alone. Individuals were also more likely to suffer severe penalties from these securities suits than corporations. Individuals suffered severe penalties in 62% of the SEC's cases, whereas corporations suffered severe penalties in merely 18% of cases. In only 4% of cases did the SEC impose severe penalties on corporations without imposing them on individuals. We discuss additional repercussions for individuals from participating in corporate wrongdoing later, in Chapters 8, 9, and 15.

7

THE CORPORATION AS AN ETHICAL "PERSON" IN MODERN SOCIETY

What role should corporations play in modern society?

In thinking about the role that corporations should play in modern society, we should consider why we have corporations in the first place. Governments have generally enabled corporations to exist as legal entities because they make worthwhile economic and other contributions to society.[1] Corporations, as we discussed at greater length in Chapter 6, allow for reduced individual liability, thus enhancing the accumulation and retention of investment, and enabling new transactions, often at large scale.[2] Ideally, the government's agreement to limit individuals' liability in different forms for a corporation's shareholders, managers, and employees empowers groups of like-minded individuals to "experiment on socially-beneficial undertakings."[3]

As former President of Columbia University and Nobel laureate Nicholas Murray Butler has expressed, corporations can do wonderful things and be engines of development. In his opinion, "the limited liability corporation is the single greatest discovery of modern times, whether you judge it by its social, its ethical, by its industrial or, in the long run . . . by its political effects."[4]

But, as philosopher and business ethicist Thomas Donaldson has noted, we need to articulate the basis of this bargain that the corporation has made with society. A corporation has been granted unique protection to take risks and alleviate transactional costs. What does the corporation owe society for those protections? In his book, *Corporations and Morality*, Professor Donaldson describes how the existence of the "social contract" between corporations and society helps to justify corporations' protections.[5] Under Social Contract Theory, corporations owe society certain duties in exchange for those protections.[6] Professor Donaldson would conceptualize corporate duties through: (1) imagining a society without corporations; (2) determining what societal problems would exist in a world without corporations, and which such problems could be remedied through corporate action; and (3) facilitating a contract between corporations and society by laying out the rights and responsibilities of the parties.[7] For example, without corporations in society, there may be a lack of entities to produce certain goods. Therefore, to remedy this problem, a social contract might exist between society and corporations to produce the goods. The basis of this bargain is that corporations are then given the right to use society's natural resources to help produce the goods, but their right to use those resources comes with a social responsibility on the part of the corporations to minimize pollution.

This idea of the corporation as embedded in society, and responsible to society, segues into one of the most important developments in defining the role of corporations: stakeholder theory. The 1932 *Harvard Law Review* debate between corporate-law scholars Adolf A. Berle, Jr. and Merrick Dodd laid out some of this framework for the corporation's role in society.[8]

Professor Berle had argued on behalf of "shareholder theory," now called shareholder primacy, under which a corporation's primary purpose is to make money for its shareholders. Shareholder primacy had been adopted by the Michigan Supreme Court in the 1919 case of *Dodge v. Ford*.[9] In that case, the Dodge brothers, shareholders in the Ford Motor Company, sued the company, claiming that it had erroneously withheld shareholder dividend payments and invested those funds back into the company. The company countered that, since it had already returned to shareholders dividends in the amount of their initial investment, its additional cash flow could be used to hire more people, thus helping the surrounding community. The 1919 court believed that:

> [a] business corporation is organized and carried on pri-
> marily for the profit of the stockholders .... The discretion
> of directors is to be exercised in the choice of means to at-
> tain that end and does not extend to a change in the end
> itself, to the reduction of profits, or to the nondistribution
> of profits among stockholders in order to devote them to
> other purposes.[10]

By contrast, Professor Dodd believed that the corporation should serve a social function in addition to profit-making.[11] More commonly known today as "stakeholder theory," his belief was that corporations should take broader account of those affected by their actions.[12] Such stakeholders so impacted may include employees, customers, investors, non-governmental organizations (NGOs), interest groups, governments, surrounding communities, and others.

The dominant view of corporate purpose in the U.S. during the latter half of the twentieth century was to maximize shareholder wealth. In the twenty-first century, in part due to reputation of the argument that shareholders could be meaningful residual owners of corporations (see Chapter 6), many legal scholars recognize that this view is incorrect.[13] Shareholders are not the "owners" of companies.[14] They are merely a type of investor in the company. And there are other types of investors who have invested in the company in other ways. Shareholders hold special rights that other stakeholders do not, such as the ability to elect officers and directors, not because of a unique claim on directors, but rather because they were thought to be in the best position to represent the coalition of people and groups that have all made investments in, and contribute to, the company.[15]

Our understanding of the role of corporations has thus moved away from shareholder primacy to a broader purpose comprised of both profitability for, as well as social responsibilities to, stakeholders. A corporation is merely an organizational form, which can be employed by different persons for different purposes, and such purposes should not be limited to making profits for shareholders.[16] Historically, corporations have been formed for myriad purposes such as serving customers, rallying suppliers, coordinating employees, and providing infrastructure. Returning to these roots, the purpose of a corporation is not merely to maximize wealth and attain profitability, but may, and should, include other goals, including taking into account the effects of corporate decision-making on all its stakeholders.[17]

Are corporate managers required to maximize shareholder value?

No, corporate managers do not have a legal duty to maximize profits for shareholders.[18] As Justice Alito wrote for the majority of the U.S. Supreme Court in *Burwell v. Hobby Lobby*, "[w]hile it is certainly true that a central objective of for-profit corporations is to make money, modern corporate law does not require for-profit corporations to pursue profit at the expense of everything else, and many do not do so."[19] In support of the Court's holding, Justice Alito relied on a standard tenet in U.S. business law that corporations may be formed for *"any lawful purpose* or business."[20] The "lawful purpose" language had been previously broadly interpreted in *A.P. Smith Manufacturing Co. v. Barlow*.[21] In that case, the New Jersey Supreme Court had upheld a corporation's charitable donations to Princeton University. In defending its ability to allocate resources to charity rather than to shareholders, the company explained that donating to the school would, in turn, benefit the corporation by providing it educated workers.

By contrast, shareholder primacy—the idea that corporate managers were required to maximize shareholder value to the exclusion of other priorities—misunderstands corporate purpose. It is true that, when a corporation is first created, it may be indistinguishable from its shareholders, as its founders tend to be its primary shareholders. However, as corporations mature and take on additional investors in the form of shareholders, these shareholders should not take an active part in running the company; to do so would be to weaken the corporate form and invite piercing of the corporate veil (described previously in Chapter 5). Shareholders as a group should not then control the ordinary business operations of the corporation.[22] Thus, shareholders are not the "owners" of the corporation in terms of control.[23]

Shareholders are not the "owners" of the corporation for several other important reasons as well. First, although some have argued that shareholders are entitled to any residual profits after the corporation's contractual obligations to other parties have been fulfilled, this typically has no practical value in reality after bankruptcy. Indeed, whether shareholders have the legal right to any residual at all—in other words, whether they might claim (or "own") any property or interests that may be left behind by the dissolution or restructuring of the corporation after other claims have been satisfied—is also increasingly contested.[24]

Second, corporations are their own legal "persons" (see discussion previously in Chapter 6). Under U.S. law—and the laws of most modern countries after the abolition of slavery—a person cannot own another legal person.[25] This point was made in the *Statement on Company Law*,[26] which was signed by 51 corporate-law experts. As the *Statement* emphasized, corporations, as "legal persons," exist separately and independently of their directors, officers, *shareholders*, and other human persons with whom the corporation as a legal entity interacts.[27]

Moreover, no U.S. statute has ever specifically required corporate managers to maximize shareholder value.[28] The majority of U.S. states have even adopted "corporate constituency statutes," which explicitly protect managers who consider constituencies other than shareholders for decision-making purposes. In addition to these statutes, the American Law Institute (ALI), which generally interprets law across the country, states that a corporation, in its conduct of business, "[m]ay take into account ethical considerations that are reasonably regarded as appropriate to the responsible conduct of business; and [m]ay devote a reasonable amount of resources to public welfare, humanitarian, education, and philanthropic purposes."[29] The ALI notes that, although corporate managers must meet a certain standard of care in the decision-making process, "that standard can be satisfied even when . . . a prospective profit cannot be particularized."[30]

In sum, corporate managers have no duty to maximize shareholder value at the expense of everything else.[31] The law permits managers to act under ethical and social considerations in addition to considering shareholder value for decision-making purposes.

Finally, as previously discussed in Chapter 6, the business judgment rule (BJR) protects such managerial discretion. The BJR generally notes that a corporate manager will not be legally liable for decisions made (1) in good faith, (2) in a manner he or she reasonably believes to be in the best interest of the corporation, and (3) with the care that an ordinarily prudent person would reasonably be expected to exercise in a like position under similar circumstances.[32] In exercising this discretion, a manager must (1) not have a personal interest in the decision, (2) he or she must be reasonably informed about the decision, and (3) rationally believe that the decision is in the best interests of the corporation. The BJR thus protects managers who make decisions that they reasonably believe are in the best interests of the corporation, even when such decisions will not directly maximize shareholder profits.[33]

What is corporate social responsibility (CSR)?

Although there is no single definition of corporate social responsibility (CSR), the United Nations Industrial Development Organization defines CSR as "a management concept whereby companies integrate social and environmental concerns in their business operations and interactions with their stakeholders."[34] CSR expands beyond traditional stakeholder theory.[35] Rather than simply focusing on ways to protect stakeholders (i.e., people who are affected by corporate actions such as shareholders, employees, and the communities in which a corporation operates), CSR posits that companies should take an active role in fixing problems in society as a whole.

Although Google's first corporate code of conduct famously began with "don't be evil,"[36] CSR demands more of companies than not being evil: it requires actions to help bring social good to the world. Under CSR, a corporation has an affirmative duty to use its power and resources to alleviate social and economic problems. CSR theory is related to Adam Smith's view on markets. Because trade should make parties better off, pursuing one's own advantage should naturally lead to actions that are advantageous to society as a whole.[37] According to the Conference Board's Committee on Economic Development (CED), another way to express this exchange is that, because the "corporation is dependent upon the goodwill of society, which can sustain or impair its existence through public pressures on government," CSR is not only a moral engagement, but also contributes to the success of the corporation in the long term.[38]

One tangible form of supporting social good is to engage in Socially Responsible Investing (SRI). Modern SRI began in 1928 when the first ethical investment fund was created.[39] This fund avoided purchasing interest in "sin stocks," referring to investments in companies that produced liquor, tobacco, or had a financial interest in gambling. Another method of SRI is portfolio screening, sometimes known as an "investor boycott," which refuses to invest in enterprises that are in opposition to broader moral beliefs. This practice was popular during the South-Africa-divestment movement, in which companies pulled out of economic activities connected to South Africa in protest of Apartheid.[40] SRI is becoming an increasingly popular investment option for both corporations and individuals.

There are more than 200 companies in the U.S. that explicitly invest their resources in SRI.[41] Most large investment advisors currently offer these types of investment plans.[42] By 2018, SRI funds managed U.S. $30.7 trillion worldwide.[43]

CSR can be more comprehensive than SRI. In its foundational 1971 report, *Social Responsibilities of Business Corporations*, the CED outlined the trajectory of CSR, stating that "[t]he basic purpose of business . . . is 'to serve constructively the needs of society—to the satisfaction of society.'"[44] Although traditional "profit maximization" can result in positive outcomes, such as additional jobs and a higher standard of living for workers, the CED statement highlights that society expects more than mere profit maximization from corporations. Some of these expectations include addressing poverty, the unequal distributions of opportunities, educational deficits, needs for employment, and livable communities.

In terms of recognized international standards, in 2003–04, the United Nations Global Compact announced ten principles to which companies should aspire.[45] These were grouped into the categories of human rights, labor conditions, the environment, and anti-corruption. Under human rights, (1) "[b]usinesses should support and respect the protection of internationally proclaimed human rights;" and (2) they should "make sure that they are not complicit in human rights abuses." Under labor conditions, (3) "[b]usinesses should uphold the freedom of association and effective recognition of the right to collective bargaining;" (4) "the elimination of all forms of forced and compulsory labo[r];" (5) "the effective abolition of child labo[r];" and (6) "the elimination of discrimination in respect of employment and occupation." Under the environment, (7) "[b]usinesses should support a precautionary approach to environmental challenges;" (8) "undertake initiatives to promote a greater environmental responsibility;" and (9) "encourage the development and diffusion of environmentally friendly technologies." Under anti-corruption, (10) "[b]usinesses should work against all forms of corruption, including extortion and bribery." The organization also adopted 17 specific sustainable development goals to help management orient itself toward those changes.[46]

In 2020, the U.N. Global Compact proposed benchmarks for these goals, which include metrics for companies to gauge their progress.[47] Under human rights and labor, for example, "100% of employees across the organization [should] earn a living wage," and there should be a "gender balance across all levels of management." Under the environment, five such metrics are (a) "[z]ero discharge of pollutants and hazardous chemicals;" (b) "[n]et-positive water impact in water-stressed basins;" (c) "[z]ero waste to landfill and incineration;" (d) "100% re-source recovery, with all materials and products recovered and recycled or reused at the end of life;" and (e) "[g]reenhouse gas emissions reduction in line with a 1.5 °C pathway" to slowing global warming. Finally, under anti-corruption, there should be "[z]ero incidents of bribery."

Who are the stakeholders in a corporation?

Stakeholders have traditionally been defined as any person who has a "stake" in corporate actions.[48] Professor R. Edward Freeman, one of the most prominent authorities on stakeholder theory, defines stakeholders as "any group or individual that can affect or be affected by a company's purpose."[49] Other scholars have preferred a more narrow definition of stakeholders as those who "bear some form of risk [in corporate activity] as a result of having invested some form of capital, human or financial, of value, in a firm."[50] Professor Freeman, as well as accepting others,[51] has defended his broader definition of stakeholders because it can more flexibly be used to identify who might be integral to the value creation process.[52] In identifying stakeholders, it may be helpful to ask who is affected, or who can affect, a corporation in a significant way? And who bears either the benefits, or risks, of a corporate action?[53]

"Primary" stakeholders are traditionally customers, suppliers, employees, communities, and financers.[54] These groups often hold considerable power to affect the value-creation strategy of a business, and are "indispensable to the function of the corporation."[55] For example, if employees do not feel appreciated at a company, they may not work as hard, and the company will lose potential profits.

"Secondary" stakeholders are more removed from the business, but can still affect its value-creation processes.[56] These groups include governments, the media, interest groups, critics, and other non-governmental organizations (NGOs). Although these groups may not be directly represented inside a company, they can sway opinions, change conditions, and put pressure on a company. A government, for example, may place restrictions on companies for environmental reasons. The media and NGOs may scrutinize and pressure a company that has a reputation for heavily polluting the environment more so than a company that has independently reduced its pollution.

Importantly, stakeholders are real people. They should be treated as human beings with names, faces, needs, emotions, and families—rather than described as assets, liabilities, accounts, or products. Stakeholders should not be "means to an end" to create profitability for the corporation.[57] Rather, benefiting such stakeholders should be the end goal of corporate actions.[58] Corporations do not simply provide customers with a product: that product comes with a promise, and the promise is different depending on the stakeholder. For example, when providing a product to a customer, the transaction may come with the promise that the product will not cause harm. For a financier, a potential product may come with the promise that company sales will turn a profit for investors.

Why should corporations act in economic, socially, and environmentally sustainable ways?

In our modern, interconnected world, it is advantageous for a corporation to take into account the desires and needs of all of its stakeholders. As Professor Freeman notes, a "survival-of-the-fittest" narrative in capitalistic practices will be harmful in the long-run because it debases how human beings work together to produce value.[59] The idea that profitability and ethical responsibilities may be inherently in conflict is fundamentally false, and it is the duty of managers to look for places where these interests intersect. It may seem, for example, that profitability and ethical responsibility are in opposition in many examples, when thinking harder about options allows them to intersect. For example, when a local company employs a dirty process to make its goods, and the local community demands a clean environment, it may seem at first as if these interests are in opposition. But, if a thoughtful manager were to reexamine the production process, he or she may find that cleaning up the current process could be less expensive and better overall for the company. It takes this thoughtfulness and concern for reconciling different interests to make beneficial changes for stakeholders happen.

Recognizing and accommodating the needs of stakeholders is key to both shareholder value and long-term profitability. The modern corporate environment is much more complex than simply making money for shareholders.[60] In fact, basing corporate decisions primarily on whether they will create profits for shareholders has led to massive corporate scandals, including those at Enron, WorldCom, Tyco, Arthur Anderson, and Volkswagen. These scandals have forced some proponents of shareholder theory to refocus on *long-term* shareholder value, rather than on providing immediate benefits to shareholders.[61] The 2009 case of *In re Citigroup, Inc. Shareholder Derivative Litigation*,[62] for example, permitted corporate managers to "maximize shareholder value in the long-term."[63] The way to "maximize shareholder value in the long-term" is to focus on profitability in the long term.[64] In order to focus on long-term profitability, corporations must assess and respect the values that are important to their stakeholders, including sustainability, economic objectives, and social demands.[65]

Corporate actions that respect stakeholder concerns result in long-term profitability by increasing corporate efficiency, reducing its risks, enhancing its reputation, and ultimately lowering its cost of capital.[66] Engaging in corporate social responsibility—and particularly respecting its stakeholders—can be profitable for a corporation in many ways.

First, respecting its stakeholders can increase corporate efficiency. One such example is in solving corporate "commitment" problems among its corporate managers, employees, and outside entities.[67] As an illustration, when companies pay a "piece rate" to employees, employees are paid per unit for what they produce. Although management may believe that paying a piece rate incentivizes employees to produce units as quickly as possible, employees may be concerned that, if they work too efficiently, management will reduce the piece rate per unit. A way out of this dilemma is for managers to establish trust with their employees. When employees trust that management will act ethically, and take their interests into account, they are more likely to continue to produce quality units at a fair rate.[68] This result actually both better compensates employees, and it increases the long-term profitability of the firm by maintaining an efficient employee base.

Second, respecting stakeholder concerns can reduce corporate risks in many ways. For example, many studies have shown that consumers are willing to pay increased prices to support socially responsible corporations.[69] Similarly, consumers are willing to pay more when corporations can ensure the quality of the service or product that they deliver.[70] Reducing such risks means respecting the values of stakeholders, and communicating this respect through the company's actions.[71] When StarKist Tuna decided to source only "dolphin-safe" products, many feared that the company's sales would drop because of the increase in unit price that would be necessary.[72] Sales increased, however, because the brand's consumers were willing to pay extra for a cause about which they cared.[73]

Moreover, StarKist did a good job of communicating both what it was doing and why.[74]

Third, enhancing corporate reputation through investing in stakeholders and their concerns can be profitable in many ways. As we discuss more extensively in Chapters 4 and 8, most employees want to work for ethical companies. People are often willing to take a lower salary to work in a job that gives them moral satisfaction. For example, in a 2017 study, 89% of respondents would take a 21% pay cut to work for a more ethical company than they currently do.[75] Notably, millennials were willing to take the largest pay cut—on average 34%—to work for a company that is socially conscious and has values that align with theirs.[76] Thus, an ethically responsible firm may be able to recruit employees for less than its competitors, in effect offsetting increased costs from its more ethical behavior.[77] Additional savings come from the fact that acting ethically reduces companies' average employee turnover rate. Ethical firms save on replacement costs an average of between 90% and 200% of an employee's salary for each employee that they retain.[78]

Finally, and arguably most importantly, corporations should engage in ethical behavior, and respect their stakeholders, because those are the right things to do. As discussed previously in Chapter 3, the moral philosophical bases for business ethics compel us to think about who we want to be as human beings, and how our behavior impacts others. Corporations are merely organizational forms that band individuals together to accomplish more than they could by working alone or in small groups.[79] But each person should still retain his or her moral compass and sense of ethical purpose. Similarly, the individuals working together to animate the corporate form— and to create a new legal person—should ensure that the corporate person also considers who it wants to be, and how its behavior impacts those around it: its stakeholders, including its employees and the community into which it is embedded.

How should a corporation account for external costs?

Corporations make decisions every day that can either positively or negatively affect third parties. When a company, for example, decides to maintain green space on its property, that action may reduce storm-water runoff to adjacent properties. This consequence can be described as a *positive externality*, or a benefit incurred by third parties from the corporation's behavior.[80] For our purposes, however, we are going to be focusing on *negative externalities*, or "costs imposed on third parties."

The classic example of a negative externality is pollution. When a corporation pollutes, the corporation may gain the economic benefit of inexpensively disposing of undesirable products, such as old electronics, smoke, or chemicals, while third parties also bear the cost of a polluted environment.[81] Negative externalities, though, may be much more nuanced than pollution. For example, in the years leading up to the 2008 mortgage crisis, banks profited by issuing people mortgages that they could not pay back. When the subprime mortgage bubble burst, families lost their homes and financial security; neighborhoods were decimated as abandoned homes brought down surrounding property values; and municipalities lost much-needed property-tax revenues.[82]

As previously discussed in this chapter, corporations have reputational and financial incentives to engage in corporate social responsibility, which, in part, includes accounting for external costs, commonly known as *internalizing externalities*. There are several traditional methods for corporations to internalize externalities. These include following an internal code of conduct, voluntary self-imposition of civil regulations, and responding to changes in the law. Additionally, there are suggestions that the U.S. Securities and Exchange Commission (SEC) should implement new rules requiring companies to submit "social disclosures," detailing their actions taken under CSR in conjunction with their standard financial disclosure forms.[83]

The most widely practiced method for corporations to internalize externalities is to work with private regulators to meet community standards.[84] Private regulators are often NGOs and other professional associations that create standards of practice for certain types of businesses and organizations.[85] These standards differ from traditional legal regimes in that they rely on decentralized enforcement mechanisms, referred to as "soft laws" or "civil regulations." Traditional laws utilize formal sanctions to moderate behavior, whereas "soft laws" rely on voluntary reporting and compliance under the threat of reputational damage.

Violating standards of conduct promulgated by an NGO, such as environmental practices, will not come with formal fines, but such a violation may substantially affect the company's reputation in the eyes of the public. Companies incur further consequences in loss of goodwill with customers, suppliers, and other stakeholders, who may penalize them in the marketplace, and who may lobby formal regulators for greater enforcement. Many companies understand the consequences of such violations, and they incorporate "soft law" standards into their internal codes of conduct.[86] Additionally, almost all global industry sectors have private standards setting out responsible business conduct. Such codes often integrate measures for environmental and social responsibility.[87]

Companies may be concerned about which consequences of internal procedures should be counted toward internalizing externalities, and which may be disregarded in that calculation. Industry-wide guidance and best practices are often the best standards to follow with these concerns. In addition, the more procedurally regular the accounting process for external costs is, the better. The reason is that, under the above-described business judgment rule (see Chapters 5 and 6), courts seem reluctant to second-guess the substance of corporate decisions, but they may address the procedural quality of decisions.[88] Reliably following internal procedures and codes of conduct help indicate higher procedural quality in the corporation's decision-making process, thereby helping to insulate corporate decision-making from legal scrutiny after the fact.[89]

Why should a corporation want its actions to be transparent?

Corporations are increasingly adopting principles and procedures that make their business and activities more transparent.[90] There are several important strategic reasons why such transparency benefits the company, and it can be a competitive advantage in the marketplace. Transparency benefits companies with consumers, with investors, in courts, and with regulators.

First, when a company is transparent around its business and activities, consumers are more willing to help it survive shocks and scandals.[91] For example, the fact that Nike had been hiding the use of child labor in making its products infuriated the public, and that revelation in 1998 made its earnings fall dramatically.[92] Soon thereafter, Congress added a provision to the Treasury Department's appropriations prohibiting products made with "forced or indentured child labor" from being imported into the United States.[93]

By contrast, consumers were far more willing to forgive Johnson & Johnson, the maker of the drug Tylenol, when seven people died in 1982 from ingesting its product.[94] Johnson & Johnson recalled all of its Tylenol bottles, and the company promptly responded to authorities.[95] Although no one knew it at the time, law enforcement ultimately determined that the Tylenol had been laced with cyanide by someone tampering with the product once it was already on store shelves.[96] By recalling its product, Johnson & Johnson's share of the over-the-counter pain medicine market initially dropped from over 35% to 8%.[97] But Johnson & Johnson also launched a public media campaign explaining its actions, and warning the public not to use the product until it was safe to do so. The company worked with federal regulators to invent and manufacture new tamper-proof packaging, which has become standard for the industry today.

Even though the deaths had nothing to do with Johnson & Johnson's initial production lines, the company's transparency, and its pledges to investigate and fix the situation, were incredibly well received. As a result of its transparency and its efforts to protect consumers, Johnson & Johnson's Tylenol earned deep trust and loyalty from its customer base. Within a single year, Johnson & Johnson's share price had completely recovered from the time of the murders.[98]

Second, transparency benefits corporations in their relationships with investors and access to capital. Capital may often be less expensive for transparent companies with good reputations for quality corporate governance and disclosures.[99] We know that, in regard to sustainability, "an increase by one unit in a country's overall sustainability metric [leads] to an average decrease of 69 basis points in the cost of corporate debt. In other words, a loan or bond that would otherwise be priced at 3% [would] now [be] priced at 2.31%."[100] Moreover, investors often consider both economic and noneconomic factors when deciding to invest, and the relative transparency of a company can be more than the tipping point in such decisions.[101] Socially responsible investors may require information about a corporation's CSR initiatives to qualify the corporation for their funds. Conversely, lack of transparency may be equated with potentially poor corporate governance, and increased risk of legal noncompliance, which both increase company costs through fines and other penalties, and reduce potential profits for investors.

In the absence of transparency, shareholders can also bombard corporations with books-and-records inspection requests, which can be time-consuming and costly to respond to.[102] Moreover, to set expectations, corporations do not have the same right to privacy under U.S. constitutional law as do human beings.[103] Absent a statutory reason, such as the protection of intellectual property, corporations cannot refuse government requests for disclosures under such arguments about privacy.[104] The default is that corporations should then be transparent, and look good for being proactive about their disclosures, because they may have to share the information eventually.

Third, transparency benefits corporations when their actions are examined by courts and regulators. As mentioned above in this chapter and in Chapter 6, the primary legal rule protecting the management of corporations—the BJR—insulates from initial challenge disinterested, procedurally fair decision-making. Corporate transparency in the decision-making process helps, in particular, to allay concerns that company management is trying to hide its behavior because its decisions are not disinterested, and may violate its duty of loyalty (see Chapter 6 for a longer discussion of the duty of loyalty and the BJR).[105] Similarly, corporate transparency may help to establish a perception that the company's decisions are procedurally fair. It is a natural instinct in litigation to question corporate decisions that are made without transparency, and it is easier for plaintiffs and courts to assume the worst when transparency is lacking.

Regulators often have many of the same instincts as courts. There can be additional and more stringent penalties on companies who fail to be transparent or cooperate with regulators during the oversight process. Compare, for example, the previous description of Johnson & Johnson's cooperation with regulators, and the goodwill that the company reaped for years afterwards, with Volkswagen's deceptive behavior toward regulators during its emissions-cheating scandal.

As revealed in 2015 and since, Volkswagen (VW) had engaged in a cat-and-mouse game with regulators for years, which resulted in both much larger, and much swifter, penalties for the company than it ever expected.[106] Regulators provided plenty of warning to the company, for example, before the U.S. Environmental Protection Agency (EPA) refused to certify the company's 2016 diesel models "until the company c[ould] explain the discrepancies" between the amount of emissions it had informed regulators that the cars emitted, and the actual amount that the cars emitted on the road, which was up to 40 times their emissions levels under testing conditions.[107] By September 2015, it was too late to repair Volkswagen's relationships with U.S. regulators when the company, under pressure from its U.S. dealers who could no longer sell upcoming model-year cars, had to confess that it had cheated on emissions standards to regulators. The EPA issued an unprecedented "Notice of Violation" that made news headlines worldwide, and then ordered the recall of 500,000 cars.[108] It was far too late to repair the company's relationship with regulators, consumers, and worldwide public opinion by the time Volkswagen's U.S. president and its German CEO both apologized—the latter profusely, twice.[109] The resignation of the company's German CEO and other top executives did not fix the situation either.[110]

Discovery of multiple more types of cheating[111] has only solidified the company's reputation as untrustworthy and hypocritical in the public's eye. VW's stock dropped 40% after revelations of its cheating, and it faced fines in the U.S. alone of up to U.S. $37,500 per vehicle, or $18 billion.[112] The company had to warn of massive job cuts, and it had to put its entire set of U.S. $73 billion investment plans on hold.[113] In sum, VW's lack of transparency created "a crisis that threaten[ed] the existence of the company" that was unprecedented in its 78-year history.[114]

When we consider such impacts on corporations' relationships with customers, investors, outcomes in courts, and results with regulators, corporate transparency starts to look not only like the most strategically smart option for a company, but a comparatively inexpensive one as well.

How do sustainability, accountability, and transparency work together in CSR?

Sustainability, accountability, and transparency work together in CSR to provide for the long-term profitability of a company and improve the world around it. Focusing on sustainability, accountability, and transparency helps companies reorient their decisions to favor long-term value creation over potentially more destructive, short-term behavior. These are the mechanisms through which companies keep their eyes on what they should be doing in the world, and how they should be doing it. Taking each of the three elements in turn, we can see how they individually, and collectively, interact to keep a corporation's culture focused on its longer-term contributions to itself, to society, and to the world.

"Sustainability," for example, does not, in this context, refer only to traditional environmentalism, but to thinking about what practices are sustainable for both human beings and the planet long term. Thus, although sustainability is linked to improving the health of the environment—and the lives of all human beings who depend on it for their very existence—it asks managers to consider the long-term costs, and consequences, of the choices we make in managing both "human and natural capital."[115]

"Accountability" requires us to impose metrics by which we measure results to ensure both that we are asking the right questions about contributions to long-term value, and that we are holding ourselves to the appropriate standards for doing so. Accountability metrics can take many forms, but they are often stated as goals against which the company, and its managers, can measure themselves to assess its transformation. If, for example, a company were to adopt the U.N. Compact's 2020 goal of gender equality in management, the company would need to (a) measure where its gender equality in management is now; (b) identify pathways to move from where the company is now to where it wants to be; and (c) regularly assess its progress by measuring the company's completion of interim results along the way.

Accountability involves an iterative process, however. If the company is not on-target to meet its goals, managers need to know this, and be prepared to adjust what they are doing. Moreover, if the company is serious about meeting its stated goals, its measurement and adjustment to meet goals must happen at all levels of the company. The CEO and board of directors have to be asking how close the company is to gender equity on a regular basis, and meaningfully maintain their focus on the issue over time, for the message to filter down to all levels of management. Accountability also means that there must be consequences for not meeting goals and not taking issues seriously. Managers should be rewarded for meeting targets, and they should be coached or removed if they are not making progress toward the company's CSR goals.

In order to achieve accountability, a company must have transparency as well. We provided many reasons above in this chapter why companies profit from external transparency, but to that list we here also add the mechanisms of internal governance to enforce CSR. External transparency permits companies to be accountable to the public, regulators, and their other stakeholders. Internal transparency allows corporations to best manage their own affairs to achieve for themselves. Returning to our gender-equity example, if the company does not have internal transparency to see how many women are in its management, and why they are not being promoted when they should be within the company, then it may be far more difficult—or even impossible—for the company to make the changes that it needs over the long term to reach its goal. The corporation further fails to benefit fully from the talents of more than half the Earth's population, and may fail to cultivate many of the best corporate leaders of the future.

Finally, when sustainability, accountability, and transparency work together to implement CSR within the corporation—as well as to allow other stakeholders to see what the corporation is doing from the outside—the culture of the organization changes. Culture is the internalization of norms within an organization that permit behavior to be self-reinforcing. Best practices for sustainability, accountability, and transparency eventually build norms within organizations such that less and less formal feedback is necessary to keep the organization on track. Culture itself, of course, needs to be monitored so that it stays healthy and embraces the company's stated goals as they evolve, but "culture eats strategy or procedures for breakfast" when fully internalized and core to an organization's identity.[116]

Without such a culture focused on strong, long-term goals at the company, "more than half of executives and directors . . . say their company would delay a new project to hit quarterly targets[,] even if it sacrificed value."[117] Companies seeking to achieve long-term value to make the impact that they want to have in the world, must ensure that all parts of sustainability, accountability, and transparency support CSR, and are ultimately embedded in their cultures.

What authorities have adopted CSR principles, and how are corporations accountable for CSR?

Many international, national, non-governmental, and business entities have announced CSR initiatives. Corporations are accountable through law for many of these standards as adopted by national governments, particularly in the areas of environmental, social, and corporate governance (ESG), which have increasingly growing power in the financial sector.

At the international level, this chapter has already described the U.N. Global Compact.[118] Also through the United Nations, many countries have signed on to enforce and implement the Universal Declaration of Human Rights (UDHR). The UDHR recognizes the inherent dignity, equality, and inalienable rights of human beings around the world.[119] Under the UDHR, there should not be discrimination on the basis of race, color, sex, language, religion, political or other opinion, national or social origin, property rights, conditions of birth, or other status.[120] The United Nations also helped develop the Covenant on Economic, Social, and Cultural Rights, which requires countries to submit annual reports to the U.N. Secretary General on their progress in addressing issues from living wages, equal pay and workplace advancement, maternity leave, educational access, and protection for intellectual property.[121] There are also key international conventions on the Elimination of Discrimination Against Women,[122] the Rights of the Child,[123] and Against Corruption.[124]

Large, non-governmental organizations have partnered with business leaders and others to promulgate standards that often have their own enforcement mechanisms. For example, businesses that join the Fair Labor Association must adopt internal codes that meet or exceed certain standards, they submit to external monitoring of their employment processes, and they must work to remediate grievances in a timely manner.[125] Similarly, businesses that join the Coalition for Environmentally Responsible Economies (CERES) report annually on their environmental performance.[126] They pledge to protect the biosphere, use natural resources sustainably, conserve energy, reduce and recycle waste, minimalize environmental risks to their employees and the communities in which they operate, strive to use safe products, and restore the environment. In order to implement such principles, CERES businesses pledge to inform the public when there is a danger to health, safety, or the environment; to keep their own CEOs and boards of directors briefed on environmental issues, and informed on environmental policy; and to support generally accepted environmental audit procedures. CERES has also launched the Global Reporting Initiative (GRI), which attempts to push environmental and corporate sustainability reporting to higher standards worldwide.[127]

More traditionally conservative business groups have moved toward CSR as well. The Caux Round Table (CRT) is an international network of business leaders promoting principled capitalism. The CRT principles include moving from "beyond shareholders toward stakeholders" (Principle 1), to "beyond the letter of law toward a spirit of trust" (Principle 3), to "avoidance of illicit operations" (Principle 7).[128]

Similarly, within the United States, the Business Roundtable (as discussed previously in Chapter 6) announced in 2019 that "Americans deserve an economy that allows each person to succeed through hard work and creativity and to lead a life of meaning and dignity."[129] In businesses' "fundamental commitment to all our stakeholders," they should put first "delivering value to our customers," then "investing in our employees," "dealing fairly and ethically with our suppliers," "supporting the communities in which we work," and finally "generating long-term value for shareholders."[130] It was a sign of the times, and the widespread acceptance of CSR's emphasis on stakeholders, that the preamble explicitly commits to stakeholders more generally, and that the last priority on the list is shareholders—and then, shareholders' explicitly long-term value, not their short-term profits. The statement was signed by 196 chief executive officers of America's largest companies, including Walmart, Target, Amazon, PepsiCo, Johnson & Johnson, J.P. Morgan Chase, Goldman Sachs, and Citigroup.[131]

The financial world has experienced some of the most dramatic recent changes in expectations and enforcement. In 2005, the U.N. Secretary General invited select CEOs of major financial institutions to focus on the need for ESG initiatives. Under the auspices of the U.N. Global Compact, the International Finance Corporation, and the Swiss government, the resulting report argued that embedding ESG factors into capital markets not only made good individual business sense, but would collectively help markets and society.[132] Soon thereafter, the Freshfield Report demonstrated how important ESG issues are for financial value.[133]

In 2006, the Principles for Responsible Investing (PRI) initiative launched in an announcement from the floor of the New York Stock Exchange.[134] The PRI's mission explicitly ties the promotion of ESG initiatives to enhancing long-term value creation. As the PRI states, "[w]e believe that an economically efficient, sustainable global financial system is necessary for long-term value creation. Such a system will reward long-term responsible investment[,] and benefit the environment and society as a whole."[135] The six principles of the PRI are that:

1. "we will incorporate ESG issues into investment analysis and decision-making processes;"
2. "we will be active owners and incorporate ESG issues into our ownership policies and practices;"
3. "we will seek appropriate disclosure on ESG issues by the entities in which we invest;"
4. "we will promote acceptance and implementation of the Principles within the investment industry;"
5. "we will work together to enhance our effectiveness in implementing the Principles;" and
6. "we will each report on our activities and progress towards implementing the Principles."[136]

By 2020, the PRI had over 3,000 signatories.[137] As of 2017, its signatories accounted for approximately U.S. $70 trillion in assets under management.[138]

Worldwide, governments are increasingly mandating ESG disclosures. By 2015, a report by Harvard Kennedy School's Initiative for Responsible Investment found that, since 2000, 23 countries had enacted legislation to require public companies to report environmental and/or social information.[139] In 2018, Professors Cynthia Williams, Jill Fisch, and other cosignatories petitioned the U.S Securities and Exchange Commission to join this group in requiring U.S. companies to disclose ESG factors related to their operations.[140] Many stock exchanges already require such ESG disclosures for companies to list with them.[141]

Companies have also announced their own CSR initiatives that have garnered them attention and acclaim. XEROX, for example, was ranked in 2018 among the "100 Best Corporate Citizens"[142] for the twelfth consecutive year for its large range of CSR initiatives, including participating in the Green

World Alliance, the Electronic Industry Citizen Coalition, and launching its own XEROX Community Involvement Program. Since 1974, the Program has sponsored over 18,000 projects involving over 400,000 employee participants.[143] TOMS Shoes has traditionally matched every pair of shoes sold with the gift of a new pair to a child in need.[144] As of 2019, TOMS Eyewear's initiative has helped restore the sight of over 780,000 people; and TOMS has provided over 722,000 weeks of safe water to people in six countries.[145] In 2011, the Levi Strauss company launched its Worker Well-Being initiative to help "transform the apparel industry by setting a new standard for valuing and investing in apparel workers' lives."[146] The company's initiative collects information from workers on what their needs are, and it partners with various NGOs and non-profit organizations to address the needs its workers identify. The company has since seen tangible changes in the well-being of its workforce in Bangladesh, Egypt, Haiti, India, and elsewhere.[147]

Finally, when corporations make business decisions, they can sometimes enact social changes much more quickly and efficiently than governments. For example, three weeks after the deadly 2018 Parkland, Florida, high school shooting, Dick's Sporting Goods announced that it would no longer sell assault-style weapons, and that it would cease selling guns or ammunition to anyone under the age of 21.[148] Walmart, at the time the world's largest retailer, followed suit later the same day.[149] By contrast, it took the Florida state legislature nearly a month after the shooting to address the issue of gun control.[150]

NGOs, public pressure, and consumer boycotts can also move companies toward CSR.[151] As seen from some of these examples, however, the most deep and impactful CSR changes come from when CSR becomes part of a company's expectations for itself. Companies can garner the most benefit from CSR when they are seen as, and understand themselves to be, leaders helping to shape positive expectations for their industries and transforming society.

8

THE COSTS OF ACTING
UNETHICALLY

What are the legal consequences to individuals for unethical business behavior?

The term "unethical business behavior" covers a wide range of behavior, some legally punishable, and some not. Individuals who engage in unethical business behavior may face legal consequences across a wide spectrum. In the most extreme cases, a legal consequence for unethical behavior can be prosecution for murder. More common financial crimes may be punished with prison terms, fines, restitution, and community service. Furthermore, especially in regulated industries such as finance and government contracting, individuals may be banned from working in the industry for finite terms up to bans for life.

Acting for the benefit of an organization is not a justification for an individual's choice to engage in unethical business behaviors. There are personal consequences for engaging on behalf of an organization in unethical business behavior ranging from financial manipulation (such as accounting misconduct or price-fixing behavior), to endangering people's lives (such as circumventing safety procedures or shipping out tainted products). Depending on the magnitude of the harm, individuals may face prison terms for these crimes. In 2012, for example, two executives of the Taiwanese electronics firm AU

Optronics Corp. convicted of fixing the prices of liquid crystal display screens were each required to pay a U.S. $200,000 fine and sentenced to three years in prison.[1] In 2015, Peanut Corporation of America CEO Stewart Parnell was convicted of intentionally shipping contaminated product that poisoned over 700 people with salmonella and killed nine of them.[2] He was sentenced to prison for 28 years.[3]

Many classical so-called "white collar" crimes involve engaging in financial misconduct for personal gain. The most common white collar crime is fraud, which is taking someone's money under false pretenses. Examples of fraud through different mediums include computer fraud, wire fraud, Internet fraud, and credit card fraud. Other forms of fraud refer to the scheme or the potential victim involved, such as healthcare fraud, bankruptcy fraud, securities fraud, insurance fraud, elder fraud, and defrauding the government.

Some forms of financial white collar crimes involve routing money or valuables into the hands of people who should not have it. Bribery, kickbacks, and money laundering all route money ostensibly earmarked for one purpose to fund another. Embezzlement is taking money from an organization to which a person is not entitled. Tax evasion is not paying the government money that it is owed.

Other forms of white collar crime involve the mishandling of information. Insider trading is trading or tipping off someone else to trade on nonpublic information. Theft of trade secrets is stealing an organization's specialized process, formula, design, or instrument as defined under state and federal trade-secret laws. Theft of intellectual property may also include the unauthorized use of inventions protected under patent, original expressions of an idea protected under copyright, and distortions of the source of products as protected under trademark.

In many industries, unethical business behavior may include the failure to properly file forms or reports under state and federal laws. Such a failure may sound like a minor technical offense, but it may be punishable by fines, prohibitions from future contracts, or worse. Although it may seem counterintuitive that failing to file a form would rise to the level of an ethical violation, this perception can rest on faulty assumptions about the purpose of filing the forms. Often the forms are designed to protect human health, the environment, the fairness of the trading markets, and other social goods that moral philosophers define as requiring ethical attention. Consider, for example, the loss of lives and the penalties paid by Toyota (described more below) resulting from not reporting problems with sticky accelerator pedals on a government form.

Finally, under the "responsible corporate officer doctrine," executives in many cases may be individually liable for the behavior of others within the organization even if they did not personally participate but should have known about the behavior. The U.S. government is increasingly using this prosecution technique in regulated industries such as healthcare and food production.

What are the reputational penalties to individuals for unethical behavior?

Individuals who engage in unethical behavior incur reputational penalties both inside and outside of their workplaces. Most people react to behavior labeled as unethical the way that they react to epidemic disease—they distance themselves from the individuals as fast as possible. We know, for example, that when people in positions of authority engage in unethical behavior, they drive talent out of organizations. We also know that unethical people tend to surround themselves with other people who engage in unethical behavior, which adds to their problems and compounds the reputational damage.

First, in the workplace, individuals who engage in unethical behavior suffer because they lose the best people from their teams. Studies show that employee engagement explains 96%

of the attitudes that drive voluntary turnover rates for work units,[4] and that employee engagement specifically suffers when people are given orders to commit unethical behavior. In fact, subjects who receive an unethical request even from an experimenter in a laboratory perform worse on cognitive tasks.[5] In the wake of being given an unethical order, employees suffer increased anxiety at work and a subsequent decrease in intrinsic job motivation. The number-one reason why people quit their jobs is to get away from their bosses.[6] But having an unethical coworker can drive employees out as well. The third-most common reason given by employees for leaving a job is the perception that their coworkers are not committed to quality.

Second, a major reputational problem for individuals who engage in unethical behavior is that their unethical choices start to contaminate all of their relationships. Unethical people tend to surround themselves with other unethical people. This tendency can be demonstrated in studies of cheaters in online gaming communities, where it is particularly easy for researchers to quantify social behaviors.[7] Among the 12-million-strong Steam online gaming community, for example, computer probing reveals that approximately 7% of individuals are cheaters, and that cheaters tend to stick together. In the online gaming world, while "nearly 70% of non-cheaters have no friends that are cheaters, 70% of cheaters have at least 10% cheaters as their friends. About 15% of cheaters have [as] over half of their friends other cheaters."[8] Cheaters were thus playing the games primarily with other cheaters. And, since there was no advantage in the games from associating with other cheaters, the cheaters were choosing this company of other cheaters based solely on their own preferences.

Third, being publicly identified as a cheater has significant social consequences. Cheaters seem to be particularly interested in the socially competitive nature of games, rather than in their content. For cheaters so invested in their social standing, it may be particularly painful to be publicly identified as a cheater. When the online gaming community tagged cheaters, the "newly banned cheaters were over twice as likely to change their profile to a more restrictive privacy state than non-cheaters."[9] And the community as a whole does punish cheaters who are identified cheaters. Cheaters tend to lose friends immediately after the cheating label is publicly applied. The authors of the gaming study also return to the parallels between cheating labeled as cheating and the avoidance of epidemic disease.[10]

What are the other consequences to individuals for unethical behavior?

Engaging in unethical behavior not only harms people's effectiveness in the workplace and in their social life, it harms their physical and mental health. Lying, for example, increases stress levels and saps mental energy. Over time, lying has been linked to lower-back pain, tension headaches, a rapid heartbeat, menstrual problems, and even infertility.[11]

In a 2012 study, when subjects told three fewer lies per week, over the course of ten weeks they had fewer physical complaints and fewer mental-health issues.[12] Tension and melancholy subsided; sore throats and headaches cleared. The same improvements in mental and physical health held for reductions of both minor and major lies.

Interestingly, among subjects who completed the study in a supportive environment encouraging them not to lie for the ten-week period, the mental and physical health benefits of not lying were two to three times as strong. Subjects' close personal relationships improved, and their social interactions went far more smoothly.

The takeaway lesson seems to be that an individual's entire life suffers when he or she engages in unethical behavior. We are social creatures, we need positive personal relationships, and we need to feel good about ourselves. Engaging in unethical behavior damages us and, by extension, the people around us whom we care about.

What are the legal consequences to organizations for unethical behavior?

Just like individuals, organizations can be civilly liable for their actions, criminally liable for their actions, or both. The legal consequences to organizations from unethical behavior range from being barred from future work, approvals, and contracts, to massive fines and penalties that can threaten the existence of the organization.

The organization itself cannot be thrown into jail, but, traditionally, criminal penalties are more severe than civil penalties. Criminal penalties require a higher burden of proof and tend to be brought in the wake of more harmful actions than civil penalties, and having an organization's behavior labeled as criminal carries a higher reputational penalty in the marketplace as well. In fact, surveys show that being convicted of a criminal act is the number-one most-significant form of damage to an organization's ability to recruit talent.[13] Additional damage to an organization's reputation from unethical behavior will be discussed in the next section.

Unethical behavior on the part of an organization that can lead to being barred from future work, approvals, and contracts includes a wide variety of crimes. Any fraud or felony against the U.S. Department of Defense, for example, may trigger a ban for at least five years;[14] against a federal or state healthcare program, a ban for five years or more for an individual, and a minimum of ten years or more for an entity;[15] and against any part of the drug approval process, the same.[16] Bans from other dealings with the U.S. federal government may result from "any other offense indicating a lack of business integrity or business honesty that seriously and directly affects the present responsibility" of the organization.[17]

Organizations may incur massive fines and penalties for actions ranging from negligent homicide to not filing forms. For example, in 2012, Toyota was fined U.S. $17.4 million for failing to report on a form to the U.S. government that the accelerator pedal of certain automobile models might stick to the floor.[18] The defect caused significant numbers of preventable deaths and injuries. Toyota ultimately had to pay U.S. $5 billion in penalties for the way that it handled the sticky accelerator problem.[19] Worse, the courts found that Toyota's failure to file the proper report when the organization learned of the defects had constituted fraud. As the judge approving the final criminal settlement of Toyota's case warned, the consequences of fraud may not always be minor. Fraud "can kill."

A final point is that regulators are human, and that an organization's pattern of unethical behavior can be a significant factor in the ultimate determination of its legal fines and consequences. In 2011, for example, Bridgestone admitted to fixing the prices of marine hoses and other equipment. The company agreed to cooperate with antitrust investigators and, in return, it received a reduced penalty.[20] In 2014, because regulators discovered that Bridgestone had also been fixing the prices of rubber car parts and had failed to report its behavior, the organization's next fine jumped to U.S. $425 million.[21] Similarly, between 2009 and October 2014, large banks were forced to pay out U.S. $204 billion in fines in the United States, largely in response to public outrage over repeat misbehavior.[22]

The 2015–16 Volkswagen scandal also demonstrates the elevated legal consequences of an organization's repeat unethical behavior.

Back in 2005, Volkswagen had been warned by U.S. regulators about not properly reporting a defective emissions part, and the company paid a modest U.S. $1.1 million fine.[23] At the time, regulators did not require VW to admit wrongdoing, and the company signed a consent decree promising to enhance its "defect tracking, investigating and reporting system."[24]

By contrast, in 2015–16, after cheating again and lying about its emissions-defeat devices, Volkswagen received very different treatment from regulators. The company then faced fines in the United States of up to U.S. $45 billion at the federal level and another U.S. $45 billion at the state level.[25] Additional costs came from recalls, compensation for VW car owners, and other remedies stemming from the more than 500 piggy-back class-action suits filed against the company. U.S. regulators were still evaluating criminal charges against Volkswagen, as were prosecutors in Germany, France Italy, Sweden, and South Korea.

In the 2015–16 scandal, Volkswagen admitted to three new forms of emissions-control cheating. With those revelations, the company, which used to have U.S. $227 billion dollars in annual revenue, lost 50% of its stock value.[26] In October 2015, Volkswagen warned of massive job cuts, and it put its entire set of U.S. $73 billion investment plans on hold.[27] By November 2015, Volkswagen's monthly sales had slid 24.7% from the year before at a time in which the rest of the car industry as a whole was on track for new sales records.[28] The chairman of the VW supervisory board admitted that the new cheating created "a crisis that threatens the existence of the company," unprecedented in its 78-year history.[29]

Furthermore, documents from inside Volkswagen show that the company repeatedly underestimated the cost of its unethical behavior to its relationship with regulators. At first, when the wrongdoing revealed in 2015–16 began in 2006— only a year after signing the company's 2005 consent decree—Volkswagen technicians believed that the company had only a slim chance of being caught.[30] Then, by the time that it was easier for regulators to catch the cheating, managers at Volkswagen had convinced themselves that the repercussions of the company's actions if caught would not be so bad. Even as late as 2015, after Volkswagen had been on notice for a year that U.S. regulators were investigating the company's emissions, the company repeatedly lied to regulators and denied wrongdoing until it was finally forced to admit cheating. By this point, U.S. regulators were very angry with the company.

Yet VW executives were still caught flat-footed. They were apparently "shocked" at the regulators' response. In November 2015, the U.S. government gave the Volkswagen government-relations manager a mere 30 minutes of warning before releasing the bombshell public announcement that Volkswagen had admitted to the cheating.

Still in denial, Volkswagen thought that it might have "months" to control release of the news. Instead, Volkswagen was blindsided by release of the cheating news, and the resulting public relations disaster has further compounded the damage to Volkswagen's reputation. If the company had maintained a better relationship with regulators, and if it had left some reservoir of goodwill, it might have been able to control release of the news.

But, even more fundamentally, if Volkswagen had maintained better ethical standards and kept its agreements with regulators under the 2005 consent decree, the company would not have found itself in the middle of its 2015–16 scandal in the first place. The next section specifically addresses the reputational penalties that organizations incur from unethical behavior.

What are the reputational penalties to organizations for unethical behavior?

Organizations incur significant reputational penalties from unethical behavior. These reputational consequences are felt in the marketplace with customers, in the organization's ability to recruit and keep talent, and in the organization's opportunity costs from the loss of partnerships and goodwill, including its relationships with sources of funding and, as noted above, with regulators.

First, customers inflict a penalty on organizations with reputations for unethical behavior by demanding a steep discount for goods. In a study of the prices that coffee could command in the market, for example, consumers exposed to negative information about a company's ethics demanded a steep discount for its beans. Consumers with high ethical ex-' pectations set the discount at 40%, while others set it as low as 15%, but the average consumer would demand a full 30% discount for beans produced by unethical methods.[31]

Organizations should be particularly aware of this financial penalty because the consumers most likely to inflict it are becoming a larger segment of the marketplace. Millennials, commonly defined as the generation born after 1982, tend to have higher expectations for ethical behavior from organizations than previous generations, and they tend to penalize an organization's unethical behavior more harshly. Conversely, firms that lose millennial customers also lose out on the higher premium that millennials are willing to pay for ethically produced products. Because millennials are becoming a larger and larger part of the consumer market, their preferences are reshaping the entire marketplace. In 2013, for example, 50% of all consumers would pay extra for ethically produced products.[32] By only two years later in 2015, the number was 66%.

As a generation, 75% of millennials pay more for ethically produced products.[33] Among millennials making over U.S. $100,000 a year, 79% pay more for ethically produced products. Ninety-two percent of all millennials prefer ethical organizations in their purchases.

In addition, millennials tend to be well-informed customers who do their homework on organizations. As the Nielsen firm summarizes its findings on the new global marketplace, these customers check "labels before buying," they look "at web sites for information on business and manufacturing practices," and they pay "attention to public opinion on specific brands in the news or on social media."[34] An organization that damages its reputation for ethical conduct with the millennial generation in particular does so at risk of great financial cost.

Furthermore, among millennial customers, those in Latin America, Asia, the Middle East, and Africa are even more willing to pay a premium for sustainable offerings than those in the developed world. Twenty-three to 29% additional millennial customers in these regions are willing to pay a premium for sustainable offerings.[35] These customers consider global warming, environmental degradation, the abuse of workers, and other ethical wrongdoing to be even more immediate threats to their well-being than customers in the developed world. These findings should be particularly important to organizations because the developing world is where the vast majority of new customers and purchasing power will also be located.

Second, organizations that engage in unethical behavior have a hard time finding and keeping good talent. Employees actively penalize organizations that engage in unethical behavior. Even when considering job offers, employees strongly prefer not to work for organizations with reputations for poor ethical behavior, and they take a harder line toward salary negotiations when considering offers from them. According to a 2015 survey, for example, 77% of respondents, even if unemployed, are unlikely to accept a job offer from an organization with a bad reputation.[36] This number has remained unchanged since 2012 even through difficult economic times. If respondents do join an organization with a damaged ethical reputation, they require an average 57% increase in pay.

In fact, the link between employee behavior and an organization's ethical standards is strong enough that consultants can use employee turnover to flag whether an organization may be harboring ethical problems.[37] Additionally, any organization that fails to cultivate its ethical reputation vis-à-vis its competitors becomes especially vulnerable to losing its best talent. In the 2015 survey, 92% of respondents said they would consider leaving their present jobs to join a company with an excellent reputation for ethics.[38]

The costs of employee turnover add up. The rule-of-thumb estimate is that replacing an employee costs an organization 1.5 to 5 times that employee's annual salary.[39] When turnover is too high, the workplace can become unstable. In addition, when the competition for top talent within an industry or across industries is fierce, the hiring of talent can help determine the future of an organization. These numbers on employee turnover are worth paying attention to.

Third, organizations suffer reputational penalties for poor ethical behavior in the form of opportunity costs from the loss of partnerships and goodwill, including in their relationships with funders and regulators. The section above described Bridgestone and Volkswagen's elevated penalties from their losses of goodwill with regulators.

Developments in the palm oil industry help illustrate how an organization's poor ethical reputation can lead to loss of access to funding. Palm oil is used to produce a wide variety of consumer products from toothpaste to chocolate, and there are environmental concerns about the way that tropical forests have been destroyed to make way for palm oil plantations. In March 2016, an industry group suspended the certificate of environmental sustainability for Malaysia's IOI Group, a large producer of palm oil. By the end of that same month, major palm oil customers such as Unilever, Nestlé, Kellogg, and Mars had stopped trading with IOI. By that May, Moody's rating service was reviewing IOI's credit rating for a possible downgrade that would substantially affect IOI's ability to borrow from credit markets. Analysts describe the IOI case as "a tipping point."[40] From now on, at least within the palm oil industry, "if a company loses its certification the international banks will not be able to support it."[41]

What if I think that I won't be caught?

Rather like Volkswagen discussed above, many individuals and organizations harbor the secret belief that either they won't get caught, or that the consequences for being caught will not end up being serious. The next chapter describes major ethical traps in modern business and talks about the role of whistleblowers and others in reporting unethical behavior.

But a note here should highlight that many types of ethical misconduct are also discovered through computer monitoring, which is becoming increasingly more sophisticated. Computer-screening techniques to flag market irregularities first caught both the 2008 LIBOR and 2013 foreign-exchange rate manipulations.[42] Even garden-variety fraud such as paying someone to write your MBA application essays can be caught with anti-plagiarism computer software. Interestingly, as an aside, the rate of business-school admissions application fraud hovers year after year at around 8%[43]—almost exactly the same as the 7% figure discussed above revealed by software probes of the online gaming community.

In addition, regulatory agencies are increasingly sharing information, which has led to a big increase in international antitrust and other prosecutions. Joint investigations between the United States and Japan initiated in 2010, for example, have resulted in guilty pleas from 26 firms for the manipulation of the prices for 30 auto parts.[44] In 2014, experts estimated that the prices of another 70 to 120 parts might have been manipulated, which will significantly increase the ultimate number of firms that may be prosecuted. As of that year, 24 individuals had been charged in the cases, and U.S. $2 billion in fines had been paid.

If the toll on your health, your relationships, the quality of your work, and your reputation were not enough, it is now increasingly possible that you will be caught cheating in a way that you never saw coming. Let's turn in the next chapter to describing the major ethical traps in modern business.

9

MAJOR ETHICAL TRAPS IN MODERN BUSINESS

What are some of the most common unethical business behaviors?

Many businesspeople wonder what the most common unethical business behaviors are in the workplace. According to a 2011 survey, the most common form of misconduct is the misuse of company time (33%).[1]

Other common unethical behaviors involve negative character traits such as engaging in abusive behavior (21%), lying to employees (20%), abusing company resources (20%), and violating the organization's Internet use policies (16%—and somewhat related to the abuse of other company resources above).

The next most common cluster of unethical business behaviors includes interpersonal choices such as discrimination (15%), conflicts of interest (15%), and inappropriate social networking (14%).

Outright bright-line violations round out the list of the top unethical behaviors: health and safety violations (13%), lying to outside stakeholders (12%), stealing (12%), falsifying time reports or hours worked (12%), employee benefit violations (12%), and sexual harassment (11%).

These numbers add up to more than 100% because disciplinary reports on a particular employee may include several of these behaviors.

What patterns do common unethical business behaviors take?

As can be seen from the survey numbers above, and as confirmed by research, individuals with negative personality traits often manifest those traits as unethical behavior both at home and at work.[2] The key difference for organizations is that, in the workplace, these individuals have access to an organization's information and resources—including its people—to inflict damage on a much larger scale than is possible in their private lives.

We know that patterns of unethical business behavior in the workplace tend not to be isolated events. As discussed in Chapter 8, not only do cheaters tend to surround themselves with other cheaters, but individuals who engage in unethical behavior tend to repeat unethical behaviors, and the severity of their unethical behavior increases over time.

At the end of the line, one in 20 workers in U.S. firms is fired for toxic behavior.[3] Behaviors for which employees were fired include sexual harassment, workplace violence, falsifying documents, fraud, and general workplace misconduct. All of these behaviors were defined as egregious violations of the organizations' policies. More than a quarter (26%) of misconduct is part of an ongoing pattern of behavior, and 41% of the behavior is being repeated at least a second time.[4]

Three personality traits play a large role in these findings. Researchers concluded in a 2015 study that "workers who are overconfident, self-regarding, and profess to follow the rules are much more likely to be terminated for toxic behavior" than are other employees.[5] Overconfident workers exaggerate their skills before they are hired and may interview better than other candidates, but they may also be more willing to lie and manipulate once on the job. Within the first year of employment at an organization, overconfident employees are 15% more likely than the average worker to be fired for toxic behavior. Self-regarding workers, who are less oriented toward others—meaning less pro-social—may be less sensitive to injuring others. These employees are 22% more likely than the average worker to be fired for toxic behavior. Like the overconfident employees, workers who profess to follow the rules all the time may be telling employers what they want to hear rather than actually internalizing and maintaining personal moral standards. Employees who profess that they will follow the rules all the time are 25% more likely than the average worker to be fired for breaking those rules.

While 70% to 88% of the firings for toxic behaviors may stem from an employee's personality traits, the rest of the misconduct can be linked to the culture of the organization. An organization's culture becomes more significant the longer the employee is at the company. Exposure, especially to a cheating culture, has a particularly strong effect on the behavior of self-regarding employees and employees who profess that rules should always be followed. If either of these types of employee ends up in situation in which he or she is surrounded by unethical managers or co-workers, he or she is 20% more likely than the average worker to commit unethical behavior for which he or she will be terminated. For overconfident employees, the statistic is 11%.

How are most unethical behaviors caught?

Many businesspeople wonder how unethical business behaviors are caught. As mentioned at the end of the previous chapter, computer programs routinely comb the marketplace and other sources of information such as reports and applications for unusual activity. International regulators are increasingly pooling such data and cooperating on investigations.

Additionally, reports to law enforcement can come from customers, vendors, and other outside parties. Any person up or down an organization's supply chain can report unethical business behavior. This, for example, is how the Japanese auto parts investigation described in the previous chapter was broken open. In fraud investigations, roughly 40% of tips come from sources outside the company.[6]

Most reporting of unethical business behavior, however, comes from inside organizations. Continuing with the example of fraud investigations, more than half of all reports of fraud come from an organization's employees.[7] Organizations receive another 14% of fraud reports anonymously, which may include additional reports from employees who do not wish to be identified. As mentioned in the previous chapter, unethical conduct in the workplace is a major source of job dissatisfaction, and how supervisors address misconduct is a major indicator of whether a firm will be able to retain its best talent.

There are increasing incentives for whistleblowers to bring the details of large-scale frauds to regulators. Under the 2010 Dodd–Frank Wall Street Reform and Consumer Protection Act ("Dodd–Frank"),[8] whistleblowers may be entitled to 30% of the U.S. government's recovery for cases worth over U.S. $1 million. We are still collecting data on who whistleblowers are, but they seem to come in two forms. Some whistleblowers are able to identify misbehavior from outside of an organization, such as consultants or other third parties. More commonly, however, whistleblowers come from inside the organization, and, by definition, they have either been a party to the behavior or have come across the behavior in the course of their work.

Of course, many businesspeople have conflicting feelings about internal whistleblowers. Defense counsel may argue that there is no difference between the terms "whistleblower" and "snitch." But prosecutors have the same problem in business cases as in street-level drug and gang crimes. Informants are often a prosecutor's best witnesses: who else but someone on the inside knows as much about what is happening? The justice system makes its peace with the witnesses' previous involvement in wrongdoing through reduced penalties as a reward for their cooperation.

Finally, given the information that we do have about the patterns of cheating and cheaters clustering together (see more on this in Chapter 8), having one person inform on unethical business behavior can often ripple widely through an organization. Once potential targets discover that it is in their best interest to cooperate, prosecutors can work their way up a chain of command. Chapter 15 discusses prosecutorial tactics in more detail. But the point here is that anyone who thinks he or she will not be caught for unethical business behavior should not trust his or her co-workers, and the people around him or her, to keep his or her secret even if they are complicit themselves.

What is the ethical slide?

Among all types of individuals, unethical business behaviors tend to start out small and grow in seriousness. We call this phenomenon "the ethical slide," but it has also been described as "the slippery slope" or the ethics "snowball."[9]

Sometimes unethical behavior is simply the result of making poor decisions in small matters. Consider the very human case of Jonathan Burrows, the former managing director at Blackrock Assets group. Mr. Burrows's two mansions outside of London were worth over U.S. $6 million, but he ducked paying a little over U.S. $22 in train fare each way to the city for five years.[10] Perhaps Mr. Burrows had calculated that being fined would be less troublesome than the inconvenience of complying with the train fare rules. Unluckily, the size of his U.S. $67,200 total repayment caught the eye of Britain's Financial Conduct Authority, which banned Mr. Burrows from the country's financial industry for life.[11] That is how we know about his story.

But how do small bad ethical choices snowball into large-scale frauds? How do we go from dishonesty about a U.S. $22 train ticket to a U.S. $22 trillion loss in the financial crisis?[12] We know that, once they cross their thresholds for misconduct, individuals find it easier and easier to justify misconduct that adds up, and that their acts of misconduct often become more serious.[13]

The taxonomy of the ethical slide seems to be that individuals delude themselves into believing that small ethical violations do not qualify as ethical violations. The environment around these individuals fails to check their actions early and consistently enough to force them to confront the violations as ethical violations. The violations pile up over time, and typically become more egregious. Because the individual has become desensitized to the violations, the ultimate scale of his or her ethical misconduct can be overwhelming.

These conditions can be duplicated in a laboratory. For example, in research subjects, exposure to the permissive conditions for an ethical slide doubles the incidents of unethical behavior.

As Bernard Madoff, the financial advisor who stole over U.S. $17 billion from investors over nearly 30 years, has explained, "Well, you know what happens is, it starts out with you taking a little bit, maybe a few hundred, a few thousand. You get comfortable with that, and before you know it, it snowballs into something big."[14] Mr. Madoff's fraud was a simple Ponzi scheme: he collected money from new clients to pay off earlier clients and never placed the trades that he said he was making in the market. When the market tanked in 2008, and investors wanted their capital back, Mr. Madoff's fund collapsed. By then, the financial losses to investors were massive.

The Enron energy company scandal bears many of the same hallmarks of the ethical slide. By the time Enron self-destructed in 2001, the company's bankruptcy cost U.S. $60 billion in market value, U.S. $2.1 billion in employee pension plans, and over 5,600 jobs.[15] According to detailed accounts of the fraud, "[a]lthough questionable, the accounting tricks that Enron pulled in [its] early years were not illegal."[16] The repetition of accounting tricks, however, "did push people's morals into the gray zone."[17] Over time, "a steady accumulation of habits and values and actions that began years before . . . finally spiraled out of control" into the largest bankruptcy in U.S. history.[18]

Our refusal to acknowledge and label our own unethical behavior initially for small acts explains, for example, why the rate of cheating in research experiments is higher for subjects compensated merely U.S. $0.10 or $0.50 for every math problem solved, versus those compensated U.S. $2.50 or $5.[19] It is easier for us to justify cheating for a dime or two quarters than for more generous amounts of money.[20] We can tell ourselves that a dime or two quarters doesn't "matter"—that lying to obtain those small amounts of money cannot rise to the level of an ethical violation. Researchers suggest that individuals with otherwise-high self-standards can ultimately engage in unethical behavior for larger amounts of money because the experiment is replicated without consequences over time.[21] These findings are not dissimilar from the appalling results of the incremental increases in voltage during the famous Milgram electric shock experiments.[22]

The ethical slide also involves denial of how damages accumulate. Many people feel guilty when they commit damaging unethical acts and seek to "balance out the scale" by engaging in compensatory, good moral conduct. This "balancing out the scale" helps them to continue to think about themselves as moral people.

Hence, like Kenneth Lay, the founder and CEO of Enron, even deeply religious people fall victim to the ethical slide in spectacular ways.

Another example of a deeply religious person who committed large-scale unethical behavior is the infamous lobbyist Jack Abramoff. Mr. Abramoff studied scripture every night, he gave 80% of his income away in charity, and he was a pillar of his community.[23] His family took in children who had no other homes. Yet he also corrupted public officials, engaged in tax evasion and fraud, and ended up serving three-and-a-half-years in prison. As Mr. Abramoff explains, "I was so far into it that I couldn't figure out where right and wrong was. I believed that I was among the top moral people in the business. I was totally blinded by what was going on."[24] At the same time he admits, "I thought it was—it was wrong of me to do it."[25]

Because the ethical slide is a known phenomenon, research also indicates the best ways to curb it. We can help an individual to own his or her ethical violations and to internalize damages by imposing consequences for small actions early on and by publicly labeling his or her behavior as an ethical violation.[26] Criminologists and sociologists, for example, propose a "pyramid" technique of intervention for preventing white collar crime, from early reeducation to eventually more serious consequences ending in prison.[27] Similarly, more common prison sentences of shorter duration would be more effective to deter white collar crime than the few headline-grabbing sentences that we tend to impose now.

Even simple, nonpunitive psychological interventions may help to prevent the ethical slide. A change suggested by one attorney frustrated with the prevalence of white collar crime is to heighten social awareness by calling the behavior outright "stealing."[28] In a math cheating experiment, reminding individuals of their own high standards for honesty by making them sign an honor code at the outset reduced the cheating rate.[29]

Nonetheless, even after being reminded of the honor code, many people still cheated in small versus large ways. In the math experiment, "among the 791 participants who could cheat, we encountered only 5 (.6%) who cheated by the maximal amount . . . whereas most [participants] cheated only slightly."[30]

And the cost to society of most participants cheating slightly ends up being far greater than the cost of the few participants who cheat as much as they can. Total costs increase even more dramatically when the ethical slide is added to the equation and the severity of the cheating increases over time. If everyone starts to cheat, and to cheat with increasing severity, we are talking about real harm to us all everywhere.

When are you crossing the line into your own ethical slide?

No system for checking the ethical slide is perfect, and much depends on the environment in which we choose to place ourselves. Positive environments will provide early responsive checks for violations and rewards for ethical behavior. Toxic environments will push individuals toward cheating. And ultimately, individuals may have to change the quality of their environments in order to feel better about themselves and their choices. We discuss the process of speaking up in a later subsection and the challenges of ethical leadership in the next chapter.

But, short of quitting your job and walking away, consider this four-point framework developed by the ethicist Kirk Hanson for helping individuals check their own ethical slide.[31] This book's authors annotate Professor Hanson's points.

1. *"**Listen to your instincts**. Don't disregard that disquieting feeling when something doesn't feel right or you're being asked to do something that makes you uncomfortable."*

There is a reason why internal alarm bells are a part of our psyche. The key to halting the ethical slide is to listen to those alarms early and to take the time to examine our own behavior. People who are under pressure, feeling stressed, tired, or hungry, for example, are more likely to make poor ethical decisions.[32] And we may deny that it is in our economic interest or competitive nature to examine our behavior carefully. However, given what we know about the ethical slide, we have a much greater chance of preserving our careers and mitigating the damage that we may do through unethical behavior if we check ourselves early in the process.

2. *"**Look for backup**. Approach someone within the organization who you believe has a good 'moral compass,' and whose values will stand strong in the face of bad behavior."*

These points of reference can be either inside or outside of the organization. Individuals can look to their spouse, family, close friends, religious leaders, or others for their moral compass or reality check. But whether your reality check comes from inside or outside of your organization, people who will tell you uncomfortable truths and challenge the pressures that you feel for conformity or competitive advantage help you to slow down and solidify decisions as ethical issues in your own mind. Talking to someone whose moral compass you trust also allows you to process the confusion and anxiety you may feel in having to make difficult ethical judgments.

These moral compass conversations do not have to be confrontational. Professor Hanson suggests sounding out sources of moral authority with language as mild as the comment that "it seems kind of odd to me" to be given an order to engage in unethical conduct by a manager, or to follow a certain procedure in the office. But make sure that you accurately describe the behavior that gives rise to your ethical concerns, and that you do not whitewash the subject. You want the person who is your moral compass to be able to evaluate the true dimensions of the problem.

3. *"Collect information. "You don't want to come out and say I think these people are a bunch of unethical so-and-sos, but just say 'hey, I'd like a little bit more information' . . . . You may make your own judgment that, even though it is acceptable behavior in your organization, you're not going to do it."*

We would put Professor Hanson's point about collecting your own information and making your own decision about ethical issues more forcefully. It is *you* who have your neck on the line, not the person from human resources or the legal department. The fact that your boss may be involved as well will not save you. You will have to serve the prison time, pay the fine, incur the reputational damage, and have to explain the situation to your family and loved ones. You will take the fall for engaging in unethical behavior. And other people may take you down with them. But no one else is going to bail you out of the bad situation that you are creating for yourself.

Attempting to shut your eyes to the situation by not asking questions makes it worse. Ignorance is not a defense in the law. Willing blindness only makes you look incompetent, ignorant, or unable to control the situation. Life is a series of choices—choosing not to act or not to ask questions is as much of a choice as collecting the information that you need to be in control of your behavior and its consequences.

4. *"It's never too late to pull back. Even if you've engaged in behavior that may be unethical[,] . . . you can stop the behavior and start being honest. While you may still have to own up to bad decisions, 'the point is that once you either get moral[] clarity or you realize the risk you're taking, then you can change your behavior.'"*

Pulling back is a particularly important step to protect yourself and your reputation from legal consequences. And we have to state this point more forcefully than perhaps Professor Hanson would. Especially when we are discussing unethical behavior with legal consequences, you must go farther than merely refusing to engage any longer in the unethical behavior if you want to mitigate the damage that you have done. To receive co-operation credit from prosecutors once you are caught, you will have to help them build cases against other people. If you do not want to be prosecuted in the first place, you may have to prevent the crime and report what you know before you are caught.

To avoid liability for the full extent of a coordinated crime, the law protects you only if you renounce the conspiracy, which can mean reporting it to authorities and preventing the crime from succeeding. In the words of the U.S. Model Penal Code, "[i]t is an affirmative defense that the actor, after conspiring to commit a crime, thwarted the success of the conspiracy, under circumstances manifesting a complete and voluntary renunciation of his criminal purpose."[33] If you start down the path into criminal behavior, this is the standard up to which you will have to live as a defendant in a legal case.

In Chapter 15 we discuss how to cooperate with authorities during an investigation of your organization. Merely reporting the behavior to representatives within your organization may not be enough to spare you the consequences for unethical behavior.

Refusing to engage in the behavior is a good first step, but once you know—or should have known—about bad behavior, that knowledge cannot be undone. You may, as we discuss in Chapter 5, also have a duty to report the behavior and correct it. Participating in the bad behavior requires more to mitigate. The longer that you know about the behavior, and certainly the longer that you participate in the behavior, the worse your own culpability becomes.

Of course, once you are in a hole, the smart move is to stop digging. Stop participating in unethical behavior on your own before you get caught by authorities or pulled in deeper by your co-conspirators.

But we have to be honest that you're still in a hole. The next steps are to figure out how to climb out of the hole, and that may involve going to see an outside attorney who works for you—not for your organization—and eventually reporting to law enforcement.

How can I handle peer pressure and negative reaction to halting my ethical slide?

Once you have abandoned unethical behavior, you can expect peer pressure to return to it. The pressure may come in the form of friends or co-workers who feel rejected by your unwillingness to continue along the ethical slide. Pressure may come from bosses who notice a difference in hitting performance targets and other indicia for rewards. Pressure may come from the organization itself for questioning procedures and take the form of resentment for substituting your interpretation of rules for its own.

Because you are making an informed decision about your own behavior, however, you are in the driver's seat. Here is some advice for how to handle the peer pressure and negative reaction you may experience when halting your ethical slide.

First, as Professor Hanson suggests, if you are in a subordinate position in the workplace, your withdrawal from the behavior for your bosses and co-workers does not have to be noisy. Professor Hanson recommends "tell[ing] them that you're personally uncomfortable with the behavior, but don't make it a judgment on them." You may be able to "[c]arve out your own moral[] space." But we would recommend also that you privately document any conversations that you have with co-workers or bosses in which they attempt to exert undue pressure on you, and bring this evidence to your own attorney.

Second, in case you needed additional evidence that your workplace may be toxic, look for signs that the organization is exerting pressure on employees to engage in unethical behavior, and that it does not respect employees' concerns about unethical behavior. Both of these reactions are bright red flags that the organization itself is headed into real trouble.

The sociologist James O'Toole describes being called in to consult with Cowles Media Corporation, for example, after the notoriously controlling John Cowles, Jr., had assumed leadership. During a focus group in which senior executives refused to answer even basic questions about the company's culture, Professor O'Toole was passed an unsigned note that read: "Dummy, can't you see that we can't speak our minds? Ask for our input anonymously, in writing."[34] In three years, the organization's net income tumbled from U.S. $12.2 to $0.7 million, and soon Mr. Cowles was fired by his family from the company.

As Professor O'Toole aptly sums up more than four decades of research into troubled organizations, "[t]he failure to openly examine . . . behavior-driving assumptions leads to what commonly is called 'group think,' a state of collective denial or self-deception which often has disastrous business and ethical consequences."[35] Once "group think" conformity sets in, you have to ask yourself whether you want to go down with the ship. Jumping ship from an organization with a toxic culture before it is underwater may be by far the best option.

Third, there is a skill in speaking truth to power. Integrity by itself is not always the most important quality. It must be combined with virtue. As Professor O'Toole notes, Hitler had plenty of integrity in the sense that he said what he was going to do, and then he did it. The virtuous decision to speak truth to power is instead a blend of sociologist O'Toole's analysis and law professor Stephen Carter's examination of moral philosophy and rules.[36] In sum, the speaking of truth to power should be:

1. truthful;
2. not harmful to innocent parties;
3. not motivated by self-interest (in other words, the benefits must go to others or to the organization);
4. the product of moral reflection;
5. a message for which the messenger must be willing to pay the price; and
6. not a product of spite or anger.

Make sure that you are speaking up in the right way for the right reasons, and then be confident in your approach. The next section provides practical advice for how to deliver your ethical message with confidence, and also with the highest chance of successfully convincing others to rethink their positions.

How do I speak up when I need to challenge unethical behavior?

Once you have decided to speak up about unethical behavior, how you prepare to address the issue is of special importance. Professor Mary Gentile has trained students and employees of many organizations how to speak their minds when they feel that they are witnessing or being asked to engage in unethical behavior. Her excellent Giving Voice to Values (GVV) movement distributes free materials, videos, and in-depth explanations of techniques and how they work.[37] GVV is based in scientific research on how to be persuasive, and it is culturally relevant for contexts around the world.

We survey Professor Gentile's technique below and add our own comments. Professor Gentile recommends drafting an actual speech or presentation that can be delivered in a conversation with your boss, co-worker, potential allies, or to whomever you need to talk. Writing out—or at least creating the bullet points for the conversation—and then practicing your presentation of the points are important elements of the technique. To be your most persuasive, you need to anticipate counterarguments, think of the best way to present your solution, and be confident in your proposal and delivery. It is helpful to rehearse the points out loud to other people whom you trust to give you emotional support and constructive feedback. But even practicing the conversation several times in front of a mirror is a good start.

This is Professor Gentile's "to-do" list for drafting your presentation, with annotations by this book's authors:[38]

1. *"Values. Know and appeal to a short list of widely shared values: e.g., honesty, respect, responsibility, fairness and compassion. In other words, don't assume too little—or too much—commonality with the viewpoints of others."*[39]

One of the great myths of ethics is the assumption that we all have different values. Actually, research shows that we have a fairly short list of common values across cultures, and that we are far more similar than we believe. In order to pitch your presentation to hit common values and themes, think about how those values may be expressed in your organization and how to tap into the language that your organization uses to express its mission.

2. *"Choice. Believe you have a choice about voicing values by examining your own track record. Know what has enabled and disabled you in the past, so you can work with and around these factors. And recognize, respect and appeal to the capacity for choice in others."*

Especially after having discussed the ethical slide in the earlier section of this chapter, we know that important parts of the solution are empowering yourself and others to be conscious of making ethical choices and exercising ethical muscle. Professor Gentile herself couches the discussion in terms of the exercise of free will, but the authors of this book would use the terms self-empowerment and self-awareness. To be successful in business, you have to believe that you control your own destiny though hard work and good judgment. Taking control of your ethical decisions is part of that empowerment.

3. *"Normality. Expect values conflicts so that you approach them calmly and competently. Over-reaction can limit your choices unnecessarily."*

Professor Gentile makes an excellent point here in three parts, which we interpret, generalize, and elaborate. First, disagreement over ethical matters is simply a part of business and, more generally, a part of life. By analogy, it is not reasonable to go into business and expect that you will not, for example, ever have to negotiate your salary, the terms of your employment, or have any other uncomfortable conversation with your boss. Conflicts are a part of life. And ethical conflicts are a very regular part of life. Ethical conflicts are so common, in fact, that we often resist recognizing and labeling them as ethical conflicts—leading to the ethical slide.

Second, just as you would go into any other type of negotiation prepared to ask for what you want, having considered your range of acceptable solutions, and what your alternatives might be to any agreement, you should be making the same conscious evaluations in your ethical negotiations. Not every issue, for example, is a make-or-break point. Sometimes there is a continuing conversation and an ongoing evolution of positions. That is worth recognizing. You do not need to overreact. You will have many ethical conversations over your successful career. Get used to them, do not shy away from them, and evaluate them the same way you would other types of negotiations with important consequences.

In addition, before you consider only a single method of confrontation, we would emphasize that there are many ways to win long-term negotiations. Some classic methods that Professor Gentile mentions include "looking for a win-win solution; changing the boss's mind through persuasion and logic; going over the boss's head within the organization; building coalitions of like-minded employees; and so on."[40]

Third, there are times in which it is worth going to the mat for an issue. You have to know when those times are and prepare yourself for them. Donna Dubinsky at Apple Computer always kept a reserve of "go-to-hell money" if she had to walk away from a situation to preserve her own reputation.[41] Other successful executives describe themselves as feeling either young enough or senior enough (completely a matter of your own perspective) to take a stand for their careers. To be successful, you have to be willing to take a certain amount of risk—and sometimes that risk is leaving an organization that you feel is conducting itself in the wrong way.

4. We would combine Professor Gentile's next two points. She lists her points as:

- *"**Purpose**. Define your personal and professional purpose explicitly and broadly before conflicts arise. What is the impact you most want to have? Similarly, appeal to a sense of purpose in others"; and*
- *"**Self-Knowledge, Self-Image[,] and Alignment**. Generate a 'self-story' about voicing and acting on your values that is consistent with who you are and that builds on your strengths. There are many ways to align your unique strengths and style with your values. If you view yourself as a 'pragmatist,' for example, find a way to view voicing your values as pragmatic."*

When you have a sense of purpose and know what type of professional you want to be, it is much easier to act in your own interest. You know who you are, what you want, and how you want to be remembered. Then you need to do things in your own authentic style. Not only will you be more at peace with your decisions, but you will be more convincing to other people if you come across as genuine in your concerns and as consistent in your reasoning.

5. *"**Voice**. Practice voicing your values in front of respected peers, using the style of expression with which you are most skillful, and which is most appropriate to the situation, and inviting coaching and feedback. You are more likely to say those words that you have pre-scripted for yourself and already heard yourself express."*

Literally practicing your script and what you want to say makes your delivery more powerful, no matter what method you choose for its delivery. If you practice in front of a friendly group, or at least enough times in front of the mirror that your delivery is easy, polished, and balanced, you are much less likely to be thrown off track by objections and counterarguments that you have overlooked.

6. *"**Reasons and Rationalizations**. Anticipate the typical rationalizations given for ethically questionable behavior and identify counter-arguments. These rationalizations are predictable and vulnerable to reasoned response."*

There are four very common rationalizations that individuals and organizations offer in the workplace for unethical behavior. You should be crafting your delivery with these predictable responses in mind when you know the actors involved. Professor Gentile documents that objections to being called out on ethical behavior tend to fall into one or more of the following categories:

- *"Expected or Standard Practice*: 'Everyone does this, so it's really standard practice. It's even expected.'
- *Materiality*: 'The impact of this action is not material. It doesn't really hurt anyone.'
- *Locus of Responsibility*: 'This is not my responsibility; I'm just following orders here.'
- *Locus of Loyalty*: 'I know this isn't quite fair to the customer[,] but I don't want to hurt my reports/team/boss/company.' "[42]

When combatting arguments about standard practice, remember that there may be more ambiguity in what constitutes that practice than the person to whom you are talking realizes. Consider that the person may never have learned that what he or she is doing is wrong, and he or she may need education about the ethical problem and some suggestions for alternative methods.

If the person to whom you are talking already understands the problem and what the potential alternatives may be, then his or her standard-practice objection may be rooted in his or her resentment toward taking time and attention to rethink the issue. But remember that you can make a compelling case for doing things in a better way with long-term advantages for both the person with whom you are talking and the organization.

When combatting arguments about materiality, the person needs to understand that the issue is not merely something that he or she can gloss over. The ethical issue may need to be specifically flagged as an ethical violation, and you may need to describe the reality of the ethical slide previously discussed. Additionally, especially with many reporting requirements and legal standards, there is no such thing as "just being a little wrong." Either the organization's reports and accounting comply, or they do not. And if they do not, that definitely becomes everyone's problem.

When combatting arguments about responsibility, you may be hearing that the person you are talking to is scared to get involved in the issue. He or she may already recognize that the unethical behavior makes him or her uncomfortable, and he or she may need help to act on a solution. These signs are good openings for you. You can help offer him or her a solution, and enlist him or her as an ally in talking to other people to build a consensus for changing the situation.

When combatting arguments about loyalty, remind the person that there are many ways to exhibit loyalty, including working together to solve problems that could impact everyone in the organization. A more expansive definition of loyalty would be to speak up, to help out, and to solve the problem together. It is of real value and benefit to the team/boss/company to get the issue right and to protect the organization's reputation and profitability over the long term.

Use your voice, add value, and do well!

10

SPECIAL ISSUES OF ETHICS IN LEADERSHIP

Do managers behave less ethically than other employees?

We know from research findings that managers are some of the worst violators of business ethics. According to a 2013 survey, managers perpetrate 60% of workplace misconduct.[1] Within these numbers, the more senior the manager, the more likely the manager is to be perpetrating workplace misconduct. Low-level managers are responsible for 17% of misconduct, middle managers for 19%, and senior managers for 24%.

It is particularly disturbing that these leaders, who are expected to set the tone for the other employees in an organization, are failing spectacularly in their stated missions.

Additionally, when individuals higher up the chain of command at an organization commit fraud, the losses to the organization tend to be greater. A 2016 report documents that the median damage to organizations from fraud on the part of owners or executives was ten times worse than when committed by a lower-level employee.[2]

Why should managers, who are otherwise supposed to be role models in the workplace, have such disturbingly high rates of unethical behavior? There are at least three main explanations.

What is the dark triad?

One explanation that psychologists have offered for disturbingly high rates of unethical behavior among management is that managers are drawn disproportionately from specific personality profiles. These profiles include the personality traits of Machiavellianism, narcissism, and psychopathy. Psychologists label these traits the "dark triad" because "all three entail a socially malevolent character with behavior tendencies toward self-promotion, emotional coldness, duplicity, and aggressiveness."[3] Machiavellianism is a cold and manipulative personality. Narcissism is marked by "grandiosity, entitlement, dominance, and superiority." Psychopathy is "high impulsivity and thrill-seeking along with low empathy and anxiety." There tends to be significant overlap among these personality traits in individuals.

All three personality traits have been linked in research to "fast life" strategies that have short-term success but ultimately lead to poor long-term outcomes. Because such individuals may lack self-control, they often "exhibit short-term mating, selfishness, and other antisocial manifestations."[4] A large body of research has shown that individuals with these personality traits typically derail, leading to characterizations of "toxic leadership," "snakes in suits," and "bad bosses."[5] Because individuals with these personality traits are inherently unstable in both their personal and professional lives, over the long term, they tend to derail whether they are in positions of leadership or not.[6]

High levels of dark triad traits, in combination with other factors such as intelligence and physical attractiveness, can help an individual advance in the workplace hierarchy.[7] Except for psychopaths, these toxic workers tend to be highly productive.[8] Curiously, however, tests show that the actual quality of the work that they produce is lower.

Individuals with dark triad traits may be more interested in how they are perceived than in engaging in high-quality work, and they may trade faster "check-off-the-box" accomplishments for slower, more hard-won gains in quality. These findings are echoed by the studies described in Chapter 7 of cheating in on-line gaming communities.

When compared to the overall population, cheaters are generally less interested in quality and content, and more interested in their social positions.[9] The substantive quality of a person's work tends to be linked to whether he will engage in unethical behavior. The lower the quality of an employee's work, the more delusional he or she may be about his or her intellectual and social skills,[10] and the higher his or her likelihood of being fired for unethical behavior.[11]

What is the effect of pressure to produce results as a manager?

An explanation that behavioral ethicists have offered for high rates of unethical behavior among managers is that people who otherwise describe themselves as ethical are more likely to commit unethical behavior when under pressure to produce results, especially when there are no meaningful checks on the methods that they use to produce those results. We discussed the conditions of the ethical slide in Chapter 8. But the more extreme the pressures to produce, the more excuses individuals may make for their behavior.

As Professors Max Bazerman and Ann Tenbrunsel famously discuss in their book *Blind Spots*,[12] and as has been documented through decades of behavioral research, people rely on defense mechanisms to preserve their own sense of ethical selves when committing unethical acts. Almost everyone believes that he or she is more ethical than in reality, and also more than other people judge him or her to be.

There are three stages in which these mechanisms work. First, we make consistent prediction errors in our own favor when we anticipate how we would act in ethical situations. We routinely overestimate, for example, the outrage that we would express when faced with an unethical situation, and we underestimate how much we would respond to pressure from our co-workers or boss.[13] We absolutely respond to our environment, and we may significantly change our behavior depending on where we find ourselves and who is around us. (See additional discussion in Chapter 4.) Research demonstrates that even employees' campaign contributions—a reflection of how we identify ourselves and our core values—change dramatically when we get a new boss.[14] The study found that "employees direct approximately three times more of their campaign contributions to political candidates supported by their firm's [CEO]"[15] This result is not because the CEO and his employees already shared the same values. Instead, the change in the employees' donations is a direct result of the chief executive's influence over his subordinates. The employees in organizations watch the CEO and redirect their own contributions to follow his lead.[16]

Second, we justify to ourselves what we want or need at the time that we make ethical decisions. We may think of ourselves as thoughtful and rational, but in the moment that we make decisions, research shows that we act much more impulsively and emotionally than we acknowledge.[17] If we are hungry, tired, overwhelmed, or desperate to look good in front of our superiors or shareholders, we allow the ethical dimensions of our choices to fade away.

"Ethical fading" is the re-labeling of ethical decisions as situations controlled by other types of reasoning to reach the outcomes that we desire in the moment.[18] Too often, for example, instead of tackling ethical questions as ethical questions, we re-label them as business requirements, job necessities, or cost–benefit analyses. A classic case of ethical fading took place in the 1970s when Ford decided to manufacture the Pinto for U.S. $11 less per car even though the company knew that, by doing so, its gas tank could explode on impact. As Professors Bazerman and Tenbrunsel describe, "[i]n the case of the Pinto fuel tank decision, the pressures of competition likely produced feelings akin to the survival instinct."[19] Lee Iacocca, the Ford executive who was closely involved in the Pinto launch, refused even to hear concerns about the car's safety.[20]

Similarly, news reports in 2016 reveal that General Motors and eventually 16 other car manufacturers installed cheap ammonium-nitrate-based airbags from Takata, despite explicit safety warnings that the airbag inflators would rupture under the pressure of explosion and propel shrapnel into vehicles.[21] In fact, as early as the 1990s, Takata's Swedish-American rival Autoliv refused point-blank to manufacture ammonium-nitrite-based airbags because of these safety concerns. As the *New York Times* summarizes, the automakers were not, as they now claim, "the victim of Takata's missteps," but rather "pressed their suppliers to put cost before all else."[22] Like Ford with the Pinto fuel tanks years before, GM—and then eventually the other automakers, too—chose the cheaper auto parts without directly acknowledging the safety implications of their decisions.

But, as is also true of Ford's decision about the Pinto, even when suppressed, ethical problems refuse to fade away. By 2006, Takata's airbag factory had been shut down by ammonium-nitrate explosions that "blew out the windows of nearby homes and forced hundreds of workers and local residents to evacuate."[23] In 2016, a truck carrying ammonium-nitrate inflators exploded so forcefully that the remains of a woman killed inside her house from the blast could not be found for two days, and pieces of the vehicle's engine were discovered two miles away.[24] More than 100 million ammonium-nitrate-based inflators worldwide have been declared defective, and the explosions of ammonium-nitrate airbags in vehicles are directly responsible for at least 14 deaths and 100 injuries.[25] Takata is fighting for its very survival; the car companies are facing huge costs. Ammonium-nitrate airbags are the subject of the largest recall in history, affecting one out of five cars on the American road.[26]

The third stage at which people utilize defense mechanisms to self-justify committing unethical acts is after they commit them. We edit our own memories of events to make ourselves look better in our own eyes, and we are expert in deflecting the blame for our choices. Typical justifications here include "I just did my job," "everyone was doing the same thing," and—especially for managers—blaming employees.[27]

The next section will describe in more detail the mechanics of how we deceive ourselves under pressure.

How do we deceive ourselves under pressure?

In their path-breaking paper describing the ethical fading process, Professors Tenbrunsel and David Messick focused on what they called the "four enablers of self-deception," which allow people to behave self-interestedly while falsely believing that they are upholding their moral principles. The authors highlight our use of language euphemisms, the slippery slope of decision-making, errors in perceptual causation, and constraints induced by representations of the self.[28]

Examples of the euphemisms that allow us to hide from the impact of our ethical decisions are descriptions of "aggressive" accounting practices, instead of illegal ones; "externalities" associated with a business strategy, instead of outright harm to people or the environment; and "collateral damage" in military campaigns, instead of civilian deaths. Business schools teach about "transaction costs, profit maximization, and rationalization" instead of directly taking on the human and potential ethical dimensions of decisions.[29]

The slippery slope of decision-making is what we described in Chapter 8 as the "ethical slide." In brief, the phenomenon has two parts. The first is a "numbing" of ethical outrage from repeat exposure and lack of repercussions. The second is growth in the magnitude of unethical behavior over time.[30] Sloppy accounting practices at an organization, for example, often become more and more questionable before they cross the line into outright fraud.

Errors in our perceptual causation of ethical events often boil down to faulting individual people for what are actually systemic issues, or not recognizing that our omission of an important fact may have as much impact as a direct misrepresentation.[31] We discuss in Chapter 11 issues such as when it is ethical to lie or stay silent during negotiations.

Constraints induced by self-representations acknowledge the fact that we are always the narrators of our own stories. Of course we are going to see events through the lenses of our own position, experience, and desires. As discussed in Chapter 2, part of the important work that moral philosophy forces us to engage in is the search for positive systems outside of ourselves and our immediate circumstances to evaluate the larger implications of our actions when we make decisions.

How do ill-conceived goals, motivated blindness, and indirect blindness affect managers under pressure?

In addition to ethical fading, three other issues are tightly linked to the particular challenges of being a manager under pressure: ill-conceived goals, motivated blindness, and indirect blindness. Ill-conceived goals encourage unethical behavior. Motivated blindness allows managers motivated by their self-interest not to recognize the unethical behavior. And, if the unethical behavior can be delegated, indirect blindness permits managers to add an additional layer of denial. These three issues feed each other and compound the scale of unethical behavior in the workplace.

A classic example of ill-conceived goals is the flat quotas that organizations may give employees to keep their jobs. As mentioned in Chapter 4, in the early 1990s, the Sears, Roebuck chain told its auto mechanics that they had to meet a sales goal of U.S. $147 per hour.[32] Instead of working faster and more productively under the sales quota, the chain's employees began routinely overcharging for their services and "repairing" parts of customers' vehicles that were not broken. Undercover investigators found the behavior so pervasive that it occurred in 34 of 38 transactions.[33] Examples of similar widespread quota-driven unethical behavior appeared in 1993–97 at Bausch & Lomb from "channel stuffing," and in 2013–15 with the gaming of Veterans Affairs hospital wait lists.

Thus, it was anything but a shock in 2016 that Wells Fargo had to pay a U.S. $185 million fine and refund another U.S. $2.6 million in inappropriate fees for setting up a system of incentives that pushed employees to open roughly 1.5 million bank accounts and apply for 565,000 credit cards that were not authorized by the bank's customers.[34] Even more significantly, Wells Fargo's market value dropped by U.S. $20 billion after the settlement was disclosed.[35]

Wells Fargo had been famous for pushing employees to "cross-sell" its products to achieve sales quotas. Meeting each branch's sales goals became an obsession inside the company. Some employees reported that branch managers met with employees hourly about their sales goals, and branch managers reported their sales numbers to higher-ranking managers seven times a day.[36] Employees were encouraged to hunt for sales prospects at bus stops and retirement homes. Managers pushed employees who had fallen short of sales targets to open accounts for their mothers, siblings, or friends. If employees missed targets, they had to work extra hours when the bank was closed. Product sales goals were wildly unrealistic, and, when a branch failed to meet its goals for the day, the shortfall was added to the next day's goals.

The Wells Fargo case illustrates motivational blindness on the part of management as well. As novelist Upton Sinclair famously wrote about human psychology, it "is difficult to get a man to understand something, when his salary depends upon his not understanding it."[37] Wells Fargo executives saw themselves in an aggressive race to overtake China's Industrial &

Commercial Bank to become the most valuable bank in the world.[38] In 2015, the company posted revenue of U.S. $86 billion, and had 268,000 employees.[39] Wells Fargo Chairman and CEO John Stumpf personally made over U.S. $100 million between 2011 and 2015 on the back of the aggressive cross-selling tactics.[40] Even when pressed by the evidence of employee misconduct to give them up, Stumpf clung to them because "[t]hat's how we've grown so much."[41]

Managers also hide from their own ethical accountability though indirect blindness. We are particularly lenient in our judgment of bad ethical behavior when the most questionable part of the behavior has been pushed off onto someone else. Managers thus "routinely delegate unethical behaviors to others, and not always consciously."[42] Apple, for example, tried to hide in 2010–12 behind the fact that human rights violations in producing its iPhone were conducted in the name of a Chinese subcontractor. But we cannot absolve ourselves of ethical responsibility by merely telling someone else to "do what it takes" and refusing to ask the questions that we should about how those actions are carried out. Apple still incurred heavy reputational penalties when information surfaced about worker suicides, filthy cockroach-infested dormitories, numbingly repetitive work, and the pressure to put in maximum overtime hours that all fueled the company's bottom line.[43]

Similarly, managers at Wells Fargo put tremendous pressure on employees to "get the job done," regardless of *how* the job was done. For example, according to employees, if an employee asked, "This doesn't make sense. Where are you getting these sales goals?," managers would answer, " 'No, you can do it' or 'You're negative' or 'Oh, you're not a team player.' "[44] When employees objected that customers did not need another credit card, "The answer was: 'Yes, they do.' "

Even more insidiously, and in apparent direct violation of the law, Wells Fargo began to retaliate against employees who questioned the ethics of its sales tactics. A former human resources official reports that the bank established a method to get rid of anyone who objected.[45] In "retaliation for shining light" on unethical sales practices, managers would monitor the employee to find a way to fire him or her. Eight days after a Pennsylvania employee called an ethics hotline and sent an email to human resources objecting to being ordered to engage in unethical sales tactics, he was terminated for alleged tardiness. Another employee "endured harsh bullying[,] . . . defamation of character, and eventually being pinned for something" she did not do.[46] In fact, one employee was fired this way after sending an email questioning ethical issues directly to Chairman and CEO Stumpf.[47]

What are the psychological effects of being in a management position itself?

A third explanation that former managers and management consultants offer for disturbingly high rates of unethical behavior among management is that the higher up in a chain of command an individual rises, the more his or her moral bearings start to become subjective. As Harvard Business School's Bill George describes, "Leaders who lose their way are not necessarily bad people; rather, they lose their moral bearings, often yielding to seductions in their paths. Very few people go into leadership roles to cheat or do evil, yet we all have the capacity for actions we deeply regret unless we stay grounded."[48]

Some executives describe the phenomenon of drifting out of touch with their moral compass while in power as losing perspective after having been "kissed up to for too long." There are, in fact, measurable psychological changes that occur when people are in positions of power over time. They, for example, lose their ability to gauge whether a laugh is real or not; they tend to lose contrarian voices and input around them; and, when their ego is always fed and they are told that they are making the right decisions, it becomes easier to justify even unethical decisions to themselves and to others.

As the unusually candid CEO of Novartis, Daniel Vasella, explains, "for many of us the idea of being a successful manager—leading the company from peak to peak, delivering the goods quarter by quarter—is an intoxicating one. . . . It is a pattern of celebration leading to belief, leading to distortion."[49] Eventually, "you begin to believe that the figure at the center of all that champagne-toasting is yourself. . . . You are idealized by the outside world, and there is a natural tendency to believe that what is written is true." The problem at this stage is that it can become "difficult if not impossible to change the course you and your company are on. Your mind whispers, 'You must make the targets—must keep delivering record results at whatever cost to continue the celebration.'" But this response is particularly unhealthy when dealing with ethical problems: "in reality things don't go in only one direction; they go up and down."

A brief anecdote from the 2016 Wells Fargo scandal illustrates how out of touch with reality CEO Stumpf became during his champagne party. In the organization's 2010 annual report, Stumpf responded to questions why Wells Fargo's cross-selling product goal for each of the bank's customers was eight.[50] At the end of years of fraud in 2015, the average for Wells Fargo customers was 6.3. Stumpf's answer was that eight "rhymed with 'great.' Perhaps our new cheer should be: 'Let's go again, for ten!'"

As Mr. George describes the rest of the intoxication with power phenomenon, leaders trapped in this cycle of their own need to succeed start to push away honest critics who speak truth to their power. They surround themselves instead with sycophants who echo what they want to hear. As time passes, leaders may become "unable to engage in honest dialogue" and their subordinates "learn not to confront them with reality."[51] The ultimate effect is a "loss of authenticity" that prevents people in power from making grounded ethical decisions. As Mr. Vasella sums up, "if you want to cheat, you will always find a way. You might get caught, but many [executives] don't. And every time they don't, the tyranny of self-deception gets stronger."[52]

The management consultancy McKinsey & Co. also warns executives against the self-deceptive changes that come with being in power. Consultants can measure how dominating executives become, and the findings often come as a surprise—and annoyance—to the people trapped inside this phenomenon. During a 20-minute brainstorming exercise between a senior vice president and five of his subordinates, for example, the "senior vice president contributed about 65 percent of the comments, interrupted others at least 20 times, and was never interrupted."[53] When the executive left the room, his subordinates were accurately able to report those results. By contrast, when asked what he did during the session, the senior vice president "recalled making about 25 percent of the comments, interrupting others perhaps 3 times, and being interrupted 3 or 4 times." When confronted with the actual results and the fact that his subordinates had been far more accurate in perceiving the power dynamics of the situation, "he was flabbergasted and annoyed."

What are the consequences of retaining unethical managers in an organization?

Organizations need to understand the consequences of retaining unethical managers. Mr. Jack Welch, the Chairman and CEO of General Electric for 20 years who guided the company to a 4,000% increase in value, describes unethical managers as "Type VI" workers. In General Electric's 2000 annual report, he famously defined Type VI as "the manager who doesn't share the values, but delivers the numbers."[54] In Mr. Welch's colorful language, he described this individual as "the 'go-to' manager, the hammer, who delivers the bacon but does it on the backs of people, often 'kissing up and kicking down' during the process." Mr. Welch admitted that these type of managers are the "toughest to part with because organizations always want to deliver—it's in the blood—and to let someone go who gets the job done is yet another unnatural act. But we have to remove these Type IVs because they have the power, by themselves, to destroy the open, informal, trust-based culture we need to win today and tomorrow."

As leaders, these individuals have significant weaknesses. As noted previously, dark triad traits may help individuals to "get ahead" in the workplace but not necessarily to "get along with" other people.[55] These workers may not be ultimately interested in quality, they drive out high-quality talent, and they may destructively prioritize short-term over long-term gains. Research shows that avoiding the hiring and certainly the promotion of these toxic workers—even putting aside the moral problems in having such workers in an organization—is bottom-line "better for the firm in terms of net profitability" given their impact on the rest of the organization, despite the loss of that one potentially productive worker.[56]

In an organization, another major problem with keeping individuals with dark triad traits is that their inability to get along with other people means that they eventually fall from grace, and sometimes in spectacular ways.[57] In negotiations, for example, "psychopaths favor threats, Machiavellians favor manipulation of others, and narcissists try to use their appearance and charm to influence others."[58] Separate studies have found that leaders with dark triad traits are characterized either by "insensitive, manipulative, demanding, authoritarian, self-isolating, aloof, or critical" behavior, or "arrogance, melodrama, volatility, excessive caution, habitual distrust, aloofness, mischievousness, eccentricity, passive resistance, perfectionism, and eagerness to please."[59]

As these individuals tend to be unsuccessful over the long term, so do the business ventures that they run. For example, "organizations with narcissistic CEOs tend to perform in an extreme and fluctuating way; their year-to-year performance is less stable than organizations led by less narcissistic CEOs."[60] Abusive leadership, unethical decision-making, a willingness to lie, and other associated negative behaviors have magnified, organization-wide consequences.

Moreover, the behaviors of people in power echo throughout their organizations. How top executives behave interpersonally is often modeled directly by their subordinates as appropriate leadership. As McKinsey & Co. reports, "[w]hether or not they know it, their followers monitor, magnify, and often mimic their moves."[61] In one large company, for example, the "CEO did almost all of the talking in meetings, interrupted everyone, and silenced dissenting underlings." Although the CEO's executive vice presidents "complained about him behind his back, . . . when he left the room, the most powerful EVP started acting the very same way. When that EVP left, the next-highest-ranking boss began imitating him in turn."

How can the difference in power between managers and subordinates affect the decisions that businesspeople make?

In thinking about organizational culture, managers must always consider the imbalance of power between themselves and their subordinates. A strong theme that continues to resurface in business ethics scandals is how blind managers can be to the power that they wield consciously or unconsciously over the people underneath them.

First, as McKinsey & Co documents, "[w]hen CEOs have far more pay and power than their direct reports do[,] . . . performance can suffer if their subordinates feel they can't stop them from making and implementing lousy decisions."[62] CEO of FiveStars, Mr. Victor Ho, advises that "the strongest lesson I learned at McKinsey that I now share with every single new hire is what they call the 'obligation to dissent.' It means that the youngest, most junior person in any given meeting is the most capable to disagree with the most senior person in the room."[63]

In fact, "[a]n absence of psychological safety, in concert with fear of the boss, can be dangerous or downright deadly" in the workplace.[64] Nurses who fear their supervisors hesitate to report errors in drug treatment and put patients' lives at risk. Commercial airline pilots who fear their superiors or who are overly bound in hierarchical relationships fail to take control during crashes, even when they know that there is something seriously wrong.

Second, in business ethics scandals, the public is particularly sensitive to issues of inequality and hubris. The perception that low-level employees at Wells Fargo bore the brunt of punishments while top executives uncaringly got rich was inflammatory enough in 2016 to unite the politically divided United States Senate Banking Committee for the first time in ten years.[65] Wells Fargo executives appeared spectacularly out of touch in refusing to acknowledge that massive wrongdoing could have anything to do with the bank's flawed incentive structure or its overly aggressive emphasis on sales.[66] CFO John Shrewsberry blamed the crisis on low-level employees alone. Speaking at a financial-services conference in New York, he dismissed the 5,300 employees involved as not "high performers." They were merely "people trying to meet minimum goals to hang onto their job."

The backlash was immediate. CEO John Stumpf was raked over the coals by the U.S. Senate Banking Committee. A U.S. senator, calling for Mr. Stumpf's resignation, labeled his attempt to push accountability onto low-level employees "gutless leadership."[67] The country was reminded that, for Wells Fargo's branch employees who were making roughly U.S. $12-an-hour with base salaries at U.S. $30,000 a year, their bonuses and incentives made a big difference in their ability to provide for their families and to make ends meet.[68] Headlines stressed that people making so little money and working under tremendous organizational pressures "Needed a Paycheck."[69] Acid humor about the divide in compensation and power between managers and low-level employees was highlighted by a cartoon in which a banker intoned, "If teller and bankers make those sales numbers each day, at the end of the month everybody in the branch will get a $5 gift card to McDonald's. The district manager will get a $10,000 cash bonus."[70]

Moreover, the lack of accountability for top executives made the country furious. Not a single top executive responsible for the incentive system pushing the thousands of low-level employees was fired.[71] In fact, Mr. Stumpf made U.S. $19.3 million in 2015 compensation,[72] and the executive in charge of sales made U.S. $27 million over her last three years and retired under the cloud of the scandal with an almost U.S. $125 million exit package.[73] Under tremendous public pressure, the board eventually clawed back some of their compensation—just in time for Mr. Stumpf to endure a second grilling before a U.S. House Committee.[74] The entire spectacle highlighted how out of touch Wells Fargo's executives had become in power, and how blind they had become to their impact on the people who struggled to survive under them at the bank.

How does business culture affect what ethical decisions businesspeople make?

An organization's culture has an enormous impact on the ethical decisions that businesspeople make. As McKinsey & Co. describes, and research supports, "[g]ood bosses spark imagination and encourage learning by creating a safety zone where people can talk about half-baked ideas, test them, and even make big mistakes without fear of ridicule, punishment, or ostracism."[75] In addition, research on ethical collapses such as at Enron emphasizes that moral leadership must be "a conscious task in which the leader needs to consider the emerging situations and decide on a response that best caters toward overall moral development."[76]

There should not be an overt tension between the ethics of an organization's leaders and the image that the organization seeks to project. "To be a great boss, you must constantly ask and try to answer many questions. Perhaps the most crucial is, 'What does it feel like to work for me?'"[77] Managers are living in a fool's paradise and ripe for a fall if they overly rely on external messages and do not understand the impact of their words and deeds on employees.

Wells Fargo is also a spectacular example of what happens when the internal and external descriptions of an organization's culture do not match. The bank, for example, had issued a public 37-page "Vision and Values" brochure that explained, at length, how it would put the interests of its customers first.[78] The brochure uses the word "trust" 24 times. In an astonishing setup for its own demise, Wells Fargo's promotional material announced "If you want to find out how strong a company's ethics are, don't listen to what its people say. Watch what they do." Indeed, employees, regulators, and eventually the rest of the world will discover the difference between an organization that merely "talks the talk" on ethics versus one that ultimately "walks the walk."

Employees were far more attuned to the bank's internal culture, which emphasized cross-selling, product quotas, and pushed out anyone who failed to comply with intense sales pressure. In online forums, former Wells Fargo employees shared their stories of the dissonance between their formal training and the "on-the-job reality" of being hounded by managers to meet wildly unrealistic sales goals.[79] Many of the fake accounts in fact were opened with simple forged signatures and "wellsfargo.com" emails.[80] As an executive in the same industry objected: "The phrase 'cross-selling' is all about profitability, not about meeting client needs. When employees hear it over and over in meetings[,] . . . they know what it really means."[81]

Organizations do need goals, but research demonstrates that rewarding employees for achieving narrow goals, such as sales quotas and exact production quantities, increases both risky and unethical behavior.[82] Well-run organizations know this. Truly ethical and effective organizations properly establish their ethical values and remain consistent in their internal messages to employees. They make a point of rewarding ethical and punishing unethical behavior. Southwest Airline's former CEO Herb Kelleher, for example, explained in 2013 that he pushed his employees hard to come up with solutions to save the company when it was on the edge of bankruptcy, but that "having a simple set of values" for his company was "very efficient and expedient."[83] At Southwest, "if somebody makes a proposal and it infringes on those values, you don't study it for two years. You just say, 'No, we don't do that. And you go on quickly.'"

As savvy executives who last in the long term understand, high-quality leadership is not simply about pushing harder, but about being clear both internally and externally what you stand for.

What can employees do to promote ethical environments without leadership support?

In order for employees to promote ethical environments even without leadership support, we discuss the "Giving Voice to Values" method extensively in Chapter 8. One of the great challenges for anyone within an organization is how to speak truth to power, and to do so in an effective way. In addition, we discuss in Chapter 12 the procedures and protections available for whistleblowers. Chapter 14 describes how to respond to investigations, and to protect your reputation.

11

NEGOTIATIONS

Why are there special ethical issues in negotiations?

Business negotiations present special ethical issues for individuals and companies. There is a natural tension in any negotiations, such as in business, during which both parties, to paraphrase Professor James White, seek to passively mislead the other about their real bottom lines.[1]

This chapter explores the large grey area between the basic, legal floor of acceptable negotiations and the effect of tactics on opponents during the process. But we must start with the fact that the way that a negotiation itself is framed makes a large difference in how parties behave. If the parties see themselves as working together toward mutually beneficial goals, they tend to be more cooperative, forthcoming, and creative in their solutions. They also tend to embrace long-term time horizons. If the parties perceive themselves to be in opposition to each other, however, they tend to operate more with short-term goals, and they are more likely to resort to questionable tactics. Questionable tactics can trigger negative emotional responses such as anger. Anger may fuel competitiveness, but it also creates blind spots and reduces the parties' creativity.[2] Thus, framing a bargain for oppositional gain alone may impede the quality and value of the negotiation result.

The parties' time horizons affect other behaviors as well. When the parties assume that the relationship has no future, they may engage in tactics with poor reputational consequences such as misrepresenting themselves, and then surprising the opposing party with different terms when the agreement is reduced to writing. With the right language, the contract may or may not be binding, but no one in an industry will want to do business with that party again.

Savvy negotiators, therefore, must play beyond the short term also for the long term if they want to add value long-term. Equally important is presenting the negotiation for the opposite party as an opportunity for adding potential value long-term.

In addition, deciding ahead of time how you will approach ethical issues in negotiation significantly alters the quality of your interactions and outcomes. The best negotiators decide early where they stand on ethical issues, and they maintain consistency in their reputations and dealings with other people.

As Professor G. Richard Shell reminds us from his extensive experience running Wharton Business School's Executive Negotiation Workshop, a reputation for high personal integrity ranks as one of the four most effective tools that you can wield as a skilled negotiator.[3] Professor Shell defines personal integrity in negotiations as being counted on to "negotiate consistently, using a thoughtful set of personal values that [the person] could, if necessary, explain and defend to others."[4] The authors of this book also refer the reader to Chapter 3's discussion of moral philosophical bases for ethics, and the similar need to think consciously about the impact of our decisions.

With this set of conscious decisions in mind, sections of the following chapter discuss major ethical issues triggered in negotiations, such as "What is fraud?," "When it is permissible to lie?," "When is it permissible to stay silent?," and "What special responsibilities flow from power imbalances?" The chapter then describes ethical issues that emerge in specific business situations such as negotiating for a job, negotiating for a business or someone else, and negotiating solely for price. Finally, we devote a section to relationships as of utmost importance in negotiation.

What is fraud in negotiations?

Traditionally, any person who "fraudulently makes a misrepresentation of fact, opinion, intention or law for the purpose of inducing another to act or to refrain from action in reliance upon it, is subject to liability to the other in deceit for pecuniary loss caused to him by his justifiable reliance upon the misrepresentation."[5]

What does this definition mean? There are a couple of key pieces to the interpretation of fraud. First, there must be a misrepresentation. Second, that misrepresentation must be fraudulent. Third, the other party must have justifiably relied upon the misrepresentation. Fourth, there must have been some resulting damages.

First, what is a misrepresentation? According to the classical definition, a "misrepresentation is an assertion that is not in accord with the facts."[6] Not disclosing a fact is the same as asserting that the fact does not exist when (1) the negotiator knows that disclosing the fact would correct a mistake of the other party as to a basic assumption; (2) when not disclosing would lead to fraud or material misunderstanding; or (3) when there is a special relationship of trust between the parties such that it is reasonable for the other party to expect disclosure.[7] Misrepresentations can be so severe that courts find that the contract was never formed[8]—and therefore cannot bind the parties—or that the contract is voidable,[9] and that the injured party may leave.

Second, when are misrepresentations fraudulent? For misrepresentations in a contract to be fraudulent, they must not only be "consciously false," but they must "also be intended to mislead another."[10] Parties can still be awarded separate damages, however, if the person making the statement insulates him or herself from the facts and does not necessarily know that "the matter is not as represented."[11] Failure to investigate and assertions of plausible deniability may not be a defense.

Third, when may the other party have justifiably relied upon the misrepresentation? Cases hold that even otherwise-protected expressions of opinion can create liability when the person asserting the opinion is in a special position of authority over the other, such that he possesses "special skill, judgment, or objectivity with respect to the subject matter" upon which the other party may reasonably rely.[12] If the head of your engineering department, for example, pronounces on the reliability of the widgets that are the subject of the negotiation, it is reasonable for the other party to believe what he or she says about the topic. In fact, that may be the reason why the party asked to speak to the head of engineering, or why you may have offered for the head of engineering to become involved. Definitely do not allow that person to lie!

Fourth, there must have been some resulting damages. Pecuniary damages describe monetary losses,[13] but additional statements of the law extend liabilities to cover physical harm,[14] and still others may provide compensation for opportunity costs.[15]

Finally, contracts may be unenforceable for other reasons as well. Parties must have the capacity to bind themselves to the agreement; they must mutually agree on the terms, and not have large gaps in their understandings of them; and there must have been no material misrepresentations, duress, or undue influence in the negotiating process.[16] These issues overlap with the concerns about power differences between parties expressed in other chapters of the book and again in a special section below.

When is it permissible to lie?

There are really three answers to when it is permissible to lie depending on the context. This subject comes up constantly in negotiations.

The first answer is the easiest one: It is never permissible to lie in any legal or investigatory proceeding, when testifying under oath (whether in person or on paper), or in signing any document that is submitted to a regulator. Such actions can trigger a prosecution for false statements or perjury, and, if the lie concerns a material issue, the case may be pursued without regard for the reason why the person lied.

The second answer is that it is a really bad idea to lie when you know that someone may change his or her behavior based on your answer. This broader category of lies—including the omission of information that you know could change a person's mind—can easily become the basis of contract, tort, and securities regulation lawsuits. Even if you win a suit, these suits are headaches that savvy businesspeople do not want to invite for the welfare of their organizations, and for the future of their own careers.

The third answer is that there are certain lies that, although permitted for commercial purposes in negotiations and other contexts, you have to evaluate whether telling them is worth the potential damage to your reputation. Interestingly, for example, there is a specific carve-out in the legal ethics of negotiations for the price and value of deals. Puffing up the value of an item, embellishment, and some misdirection with respect to your true settlement objectives are legally permitted, but they may still come with reputational consequences.[17]

In brief, the line between "puffery"—exaggerated statements that may mark a sales transaction—and fraud is how reasonable it is for the opposing party to rely on the statements in context. Thus, for example, most buyers would know to be skeptical of claims that "this is the best widget in the world!" Most buyers, however, would reasonably expect to rely on technical specifications that the widget is adequate for peeling 20 potatoes an hour, that it cuts through five sheets of paper at a time, or that it meets environmental protection standards.

When is it permissible to stay silent?

Another major question in negotiation is when it is permissible to stay silent. There are at least two ways to address this issue. The first, most basic, socially acceptable way, is not to volunteer information that you do not have to; but, if you do volunteer information, make sure that it is not overtly misleading or an actual lie.[18] If you do, for example, offer the opposing party technical production numbers and other figures, you must ensure that they are accurate.

The second, savvy way to preserve your reputation and operate as a successful repeat player is to ensure that the opposing party is not laboring under a misunderstanding that affects the basis of the deal. Yahoo!'s negotiators, for example, should have informed Verizon of the full extent of the three-billion-account breach of their system if they knew it before the companies' merger, even if Verizon had not asked.[19] This is a harder standard to which to hold yourself and your firm, but it does prevent expensive litigation and painful choices later down the road.

The law is very limited here. Unless there is a special quality to the relationship—as described more below—parties do not generally have a legal duty to disclose relevant facts when negotiating.[20] But there are exceptions that do compel speech, such as when the failure to speak assists criminal conduct or fraud.[21] Nondisclosure alone may constitute fraud when there is a duty to speak, and the party knows that his or her nondisclosure is going to cause a certain action.[22] Moreover, if a lawyer's work "has unwittingly been used to further an ongoing fraud, the lawyer has a duty to correct the misapprehension."[23]

What special responsibilities flow from power imbalances in negotiations?

Legal fraud in negotiations takes a variety of forms, but it is almost always exacerbated by power imbalances. As mentioned above, courts often take a very different view of the facts depending on the quality of the relationship between the parties. Partners, fiduciaries, and others who owe each other elevated duties cannot behave toward each other the way that two large corporations might that operate at arm's length. (See Chapter 5 for a longer discussion of duties.) Traditional awards of liability calculate the damages that powerful parties' misstatements inflict on parties with fewer resources or options, such as a landlord's fraudulent ultimatum for a tenant to pay a large increase in rent or move out because the landlord claims that a fictitious third party is bidding for the space.[24]

As Wells Fargo discovered in unpleasant hearings before the U.S. Congress, the fact that there may be a large gap in both resources and the availability of other options can raise assumptions about coercion and, when something goes wrong, will reflect particularly badly on the more powerful party. We do not negotiate in a vacuum. The fact that you are someone's manager, or that you control the lease on the property where he or she lives, will always be a factor when the ethics of a negotiation are evaluated. Because you have more power, you also have more responsibility to disclose information and to be sure that the other party is making at least a reasonably informed decision. In the best outcome, both parties are ultimately happy with their experience and the result of the negotiation. In the worst outcome, at least you have protected yourself and your organization's interests by understanding and not abusing your position of power.

Power differences in negotiation have both legal and complex ethical implications. In simple terms, a contract that is negotiated against the background of too much of a power imbalance will not be legally enforceable. In more complex ethical terms, the party that feels strong-armed may not actually comply with the terms of the deal, and the party seen as abusing its power will be unable to find partners willing to do business with it.

Reputation has an immediately translatable economic value. Individuals and companies find that they can "punch above their weight" when they cultivate reputations for adding value and being trustworthy business partners. Conversely, not only do individuals and companies that abuse their power in negotiations invite lawsuits and intervention by regulators, they also find that potential partners and opportunities melt away as their negative reputation proceeds them.

What are some special ethical issues in negotiating for someone else, such as a business?

Negotiation practitioners note that some of the most difficult ethical issues in negotiations may occur when a conflict arises between your employer's expectations or interests, and how you feel you must treat the other party with whom you are negotiating.[25] "[M]isleading and duplicitous tactics" toward the other party may be expected of you, and employers or clients such as businesses may pressure you to use them.[26]

There still remain some bright-line rules for negotiating on behalf of others that allow you to push back against these expectations. First, under Rule 4.1 of the Model Rules of Professional Conduct, attorneys and other negotiators bound by the Rules may not lie.[27] Second, under the same Rule, attorneys and other negotiators may not fail to disclose a fact when hiding the fact would enable the business or person for whom they work to engage in a criminal or fraudulent act.

One of the fathers of modern negotiation literature, Professor Rodger Fisher, has developed a model memorandum to those for whom you negotiate on "How I Propose to Negotiate" as well as a "Code of Negotiating Practices for Lawyers."[28] We summarize some of his key suggestions here, although we do not present this list in Professor Fisher's order or necessarily in his language:

- Establish your authority to negotiate as clearly as possible, along with your ability to "discuss questions, develop recommendations, make procedural [and final] commitments on behalf" of the business or person who will be the client you represent.
- Clarify the client's interests as he or she would express and prioritize them.
- Generate the broadest array of options possible, so that the client has a sense of where the negotiation outcome may land, and how he or she may be creative in meeting his or her own needs as well as what the other party would like from the negotiations.
- Ensure that the client understands the alternatives presented, including what it means to walk away from the table.
- Resist having the client become attached to any one alternative before the negotiation is concluded, but do honor points of agreement as they are made and closed so that the negotiation process can move forward.[29]

What are some special ethical issues in negotiating for a job?

In negotiating for a job, there are some particularly thorny issues that stem from the structural imbalances between a potential employer and employee, as well as the fact that the terms of the bargain will influence potential performance and feelings on the job.

The employee does not want to bargain so hard that he or she is not welcome when showing up for work, but he or she doesn't want to leave money on the table when the starting salary may become the basis of raises and other evaluations. The employer does not want to push the employee out the door before he or she has started, but the market may be competitive, and price may be a sticking point in the employer's choice of whom to hire.

The fact that both the employee and the employer are hoping for a good long-term relationship, but have a power imbalance, may introduce further twists in the negotiation. As Drs. Deborah Kolb and Judith Williams describe, when there is a special connection between certain parties, either "differences never get fully aired or appreciated" or "collaborative overtures can be misconstrued as signs of weakness."[30]

Moreover, as Professor Carrie Menkel-Meadow enumerates the elements needed to make negotiations ethical and satisfying for both parties, many of these basic requirements are not present in the new job situation.[31] The authors adapt and abridge Professor Menkel-Mendow's list below, and add comments for the situation of negotiating a job.

- "Is the structure of a particular negotiation fair?" By definition, there is a power imbalance between a potential employer and employee. Although there are star employees who may name their own price and receive it, other employees must be careful not to offend a potential employer in the negotiating process, especially while the employer is courting multiple people for the position. For this reason, most experts recommend leaving salary negotiations to the end of the process, once many other boxes have been checked, and the employer has narrowed down the candidates to those in whom the employer is most interested. A longer interview process additionally provides opportunities for the employer and employee to develop common interests and expectations.
- "Are the rules of process and proceeding clear to all?" The interview process should address the ground rules for the negotiation. Engaging in initial process discussions builds understanding between the parties, setting the groundwork for more content-laden discussions ahead.

- "Do the parties understand their respective purposes and goals?" This is perhaps the most important phase of the job negotiation, when each side's expectations of the relationship can be fleshed out and explored. An employer who feels strongly about an issue—for example, the specific hours that the employee must be available for tasks—should make that expectation clear. The employee who needs to know the hours that he or she will be working, and the duties that he or she will perform, should ask those questions of the employer if the information is not forthcoming.
- "Do the parties have a fair shot at achieving a mutually satisfactory solution, or is one . . . 'unfairly' positioned to take advantage of the other side?" "Unfair" positioning in the employment negotiation can take many forms. On the employer's side, an employer who has no interest in investing in the employee, and misleadingly induces the employee to take an offer that has no future, has harmed the employee, and will find the employee soon disenchanted. Similarly, the employee who misrepresents his or her intention of staying with the employer, and leaves right after training and investment, has harmed his or her relationship with the employer. Failing to explore or reach understanding on these issues reduces each party's investment in the other, and it leaves the joint enterprise worse off.

Finally, there are behavioral effects that can create problems in new job negotiations. See Chapter 4 for more detailed explanations of these phenomena. Throwing out an arbitrary salary number, or unfairly inferring the value of an employee from a previous salary, for example, can "anchor" salary negotiations in ranges that inhibit satisfactory agreement.[32] For this reason, some jurisdictions, such as the U.S. states of Massachusetts, California, Delaware, Oregon, and the territory of Puerto Rico, as well as cities such as New York and Philadelphia, forbid employers from asking applicants about their previous salary history.[33] "Planning fallacy" can lead to unrealistic expectations of what an employee can do in a specific amount of time, and both parties should resist including unrealistic expectations in job targets and goals.[34] "Confirmation bias" may reinforce harmful pre-existing judgments and lead to discriminatory results in hiring.[35] Utilizing blind-screening and objective metrics for accomplishments, skills, and credentials before meeting candidates helps to reduce these effects.

What are some special ethical issues in negotiating solely for price?

Negotiations solely for price can be among the most ethically fraught negotiations. Research shows that people typically feel more constrained in their dealings with others when they anticipate repeat interactions and a long-term relationship. When negotiators perceive that the only object in a transaction is price, they are more likely to lie, to push boundaries, and to engage in behavior that they would otherwise regret.

Professor Shell has developed a list of common factors that people lie about in negotiations, and alternatives to telling those lies.[36] These are the areas in which parties often utilize negative tactics to apply pressure. Shell lists:

- issues of truthfulness surrounding each party's bottom line;
- negotiators' degree of authority to bind their side to the terms of the deal;
- whether there are alternatives available, and whether the parties have other options;
- the degree to which parties are really committed to their positions;
- the injection of "phony" or give-away issues to concede in exchange for additional value;
- the use of threats and emotional escalation;
- the misrepresentation of ultimate or short-term intentions; and, finally,

- the distortion or outright misrepresentation of facts material to the parties' decision to buy, sell, or settle on the terms of the deal.

Regardless of what tactics the other party uses, there are ways of yourself avoiding lies or material misrepresentations. Deflecting the question, answering it with another question, or being clear that you are expressing your own opinion—rather than a statement of fact—all save you from lying or abusing the opposing party in a negotiation. Pause. Probe. Ask for time. You don't have to lie.

Professor Shell further includes a chart of alternatives to lying in his book *Bargaining for Advantage,* which we reproduce with permission here.

Alternatives to Lying	
Instead of Lying About	*Try This*
1. Bottom line	Blocking maneuvers: • Ask about their bottom line. • Say, "It's not your business." • Say, "I'm not free to disclose that." • Tell the truth about your goals.
2. Lack of authority	Obtain only limited authority in the first place. Require ratification by your group.
3. Availability of alternatives	Initiate efforts to improve alternatives. Stress opportunities and uncertainties. Be satisfied with the status quo.
4. Commitment to positions	Commit to general goals. Commit to standards. Commit to addressing the other side's interests.
5. Phony issues	Inject new issues with real value or make a true wish list.
6. Threats	Use cooling-off periods. Suggest third-party help. Discuss use of a formula.

Alternatives to Lying	
Instead of Lying About	*Try This*
7. Intentions	Make only promises you can and will keep.
8. Facts	Focus on uncertainty regarding the facts. Use language carefully. Express your opinion.

How important are personal relationships in negotiations?

Harvard Business School Professor Michael Wheeler writes about the importance of personal relationships in negotiations, and he notes the double-edged nature of using—versus abusing—your relationship with someone for economic advantage.[37] The data, however, show that building trust in a relationship, even with minor acts such as engaging in small talk or offering someone a cup of coffee, makes it more likely that the parties will reach an agreement.[38]

Conversely, losing sight of relationships as part of the negotiation hamstrings negotiators from accomplishing their best outcomes. Lawyers, in particular, often perform poorly in negotiation when they treat it like litigation. They tend overly to focus on "playing to win (or to not lose)," by "sharing as little information as possible," and "continuously demonstrating the strength of their positions."[39] Some of this behavior stems from lawyers' focus on the minimum conduct required by legal rules, and some of it stems from a lack of emphasis in their legal training on cultivating long-term relationships and goals.

Professors Art Hinshaw and Jess Alberts recommend that lawyers—but we would expand this advice to anyone in a negotiation—should independently verify information, and "maintain a healthy skepticism of statements that cannot be independently confirmed."[40] Of course, "document and confirm in writing any material representations and incorporate them into any agreement."[41] But, most of all, do not risk your own reputation, career, and capital by abusing relationships, nor attempt to justify unethical actions with arguments that unethical behavior is the currency of the land. Relationships are the currency of the land. Parties achieve better outcomes for themselves, and for those for whom they negotiate, when they keep that fact top-of-mind.

In conclusion, utilizing the techniques suggested in this chapter, and considering what type of negotiator you want to be, will help you to achieve great success. We hope that you end up with the best negotiated outcome *as well as* good relationships into the future.

12

SPECIFIC LIABILITY
QUESTIONS AND
WHISTLEBLOWING OPTIONS

How should businesses report ethical violations?

A business acts through its employees and agents. (See Chapters 5 and 6 for how businesses are legally structured.) As such, a business is often held to answer for the illegal behavior of the people it directs (we will use the shorthand of "employees" here), even if the major part of the business itself did not behave in an unlawful manner. If a business discovers that it broke the law—or that some of its employees broke the law—leaving the company open to government fines, civil penalties, and even criminal liability, the business should take decisive action to remedy the situation. Although the knee-jerk reaction for a business might be to conceal wrongdoing and to hope that authorities do not find out, this decision leaves the company open to larger penalties if the unlawful activity is discovered later through other means.

Instead, the business should engage in what federal law describes as "mitigating" activity. When a business or other organization is charged with legal violations, there is a range of fines and punishments that a court may impose on the business depending on the nature of the illegal activity.[1] A court may reduce the penalties that it would otherwise assign based on the business's mitigating activities. One of the major mitigating factors that a court will consider is whether the company had in place an effective compliance program to try to prevent the misconduct. (See Chapter 13 for extensive discussion of such compliance and ethics programs, expectations, and requirements.) An effective compliance program is one "reasonably designed, implemented, and enforced so that it generally will" prevent and detect criminal conduct.[2] The company should actively establish compliance standards, appoint individuals to oversee those standards, and conduct due diligence on employees, especially those whom the company puts in situations with a higher likelihood of unlawful activity. The company should actively monitor for violations, and it should encourage its employees to come forward to compliance personnel without fear of retribution.

Once illegal activity occurs, it is too late to initiate these procedures for compliance-system credit. The company can still engage, however, in mitigating conduct by conducting its own investigation into the misconduct and involving legal counsel. The investigation's findings should be recorded, including its conclusions. Once the company determines that unlawful conduct occurred, it must take action to discipline those involved, regardless of their positions in the company. The federal sentencing guidelines suggest that individuals who should have detected the violation, but who failed to do so, should also be disciplined. Internal disciplinary action may range from reporting the employee(s) to law enforcement, to discharging the employee(s) who were involved in the unlawful activity, to instituting broader reforms within the company.

If there is no immediate threat to health, safety, or other pressing harm, the company, after completing a sufficient internal investigation, and taking appropriate action against those responsible for misconduct, should report the activity to the authorities. Regulators and prosecutors will want proof that the company took appropriate steps to have a strong compliance program and internal controls, that it engaged in a legitimate internal investigation after it became aware of the wrongdoing, and that it followed through with reporting and changes.[3]

If the company has handled the violation well internally, and put steps in place to prevent the violation from occurring again, regulators and prosecutors may decide not to initiate legal action against it. At a minimum, businesses' coming clean about occurrences and handling legal violations well may greatly reduce the fines and penalties that a court or regulatory agency imposes.

For example, in 2013 the U.S. Securities and Exchange Commission (SEC) entered into a non-prosecution agreement with Ralph Lauren Corporation after the company reported that employees had bribed officials of a foreign government in violation of the Foreign Corrupt Practices Act.[4] A non-prosecution agreement (NPA) is when the government agrees not to prosecute a company, usually only after full disclosure of all the facts, and usually after the company promises to continue making changes. (See Chapter 15 for more details on business prosecutions.) In the case of Ralph Lauren, the SEC decided not to pursue substantial fines, and a further investigation into the company's affairs, because the company had promptly reported the results of its internal investigation to the SEC, produced relevant documents, and implemented substantial changes to address the legal violations, including the elimination of one of its foreign subsidiaries. Ultimately, the SEC imposed a U.S. $1.5 million dollar fine, which was a relatively small amount compared to the companies against which the SEC pursued legal action. Other companies that engaged in similar unlawful activity paid fines ranging from U.S. $15.8 million to U.S. $398 million.[5]

In addition to fines, the company and its employees may face criminal charges, and the company may be required to engage in mandatory monitoring.[6] Monitoring usually involves expending additional resources to pay for court-approved third parties to observe the company's activities and the implementation of control policies, typically for a period of three to five years after entering the agreement with government regulators. The agreement may further impose requirements on company executives to certify that the company is following all of its terms. If the company continues to engage in unlawful activity, or it fails to follow other terms imposed by its agreement, its executives may incur additional criminal penalties for making false statements.

Although it may seem counterintuitive for any business to *want* to report its illegal activities to government regulators or law enforcement, penalties for failing to report such conduct are clearly higher.[7] The government takes corporate responsibility and cooperation seriously. Government regulators, in the words of one commentator, expect corporate compliance departments to serve as "quasi-government agents" to prevent illegal conduct. If the government believes that a company is making a sincere attempt to comply with the law—rather than breaking the law, or attempting to walk the line of illegal behavior—it will impose far less in penalties, if it imposes any penalties at all.

How should employees report ethical violations?

What is an ethical violation? What activity is unlawful? If there is a violation, how serious is it? We address these questions more fully in Chapters 1, 2, 3, and 5. This chapter answers these questions in terms of what major rules are in place that employees should know about for reporting, and who enforces them. In order to report ethical violations properly, employees should be clear about *what* rules have been broken, *who* enforces those rules, and, if the employee can find out, who else may be involved in the wrongdoing. We survey the landscape of rules and entities typically enforcing them, and then we address strategy and what it means for the employee that other people may be involved.

What are some sources of rules, and who are the enforcement entities?

Unlawful conduct can be more or less severe depending on what type of law, rule, or regulation is broken. Generally speaking, there are many sources of laws. This chapter will focus on U.S. federal law, but there are also international laws, state laws, and local laws such as within cities and counties. At the federal level, laws are passed by Congress and then administered through agencies with specialized jurisdictions. Agencies engage in rulemaking to implement regulations and attempt to apply federal laws as they were passed. Courts can be called on to dispute an agency's interpretations, as well as whether the federal law itself is constitutional, but they generally defer greatly to agencies and their subject-matter expertise.

Violations of laws and regulations can carry either criminal penalties, civil penalties, or both, depending on the severity of punishment permitted or deemed appropriate. For example, securities-law violations can carry either civil or criminal penalties, depending on how the violations are categorized by the SEC. The U.S. Department of Justice (DOJ) typically prosecutes criminal cases for other agencies of the U.S. government (although not always, for example, with the SEC). The DOJ also typically defends the U.S. government from civil cases brought against it, and it can prosecute civil cases for some agencies. But many agencies also have their own administrative processes and procedures for pursuing civil violations of federal laws and regulations. Some cases are tried entirely within agencies until potentially appealed to the U.S. courts at the end of the process. In fact, one of the largest administrative judicial systems in the world is inside the U.S. Social Security Administration, which issues more than half a million decisions on cases and appeals each year.[8]

These structures dictate that businesspeople must not only understand which key statutes (laws) govern their industry, but also how those statutes are interpreted by the administrative agencies that help enforce them. If you run a technology company, for example, your business may intersect with laws and agencies covering everything from use of the broadcast spectrum (the Federal Communications Commission, or FCC);[9] to truth in advertising (Federal Trade Commission, or FTC);[10] to the regulation of financial product transactions (the SEC;[11] the Commodity Futures Trading Commission, or CFTC;[12] the Department of the Treasury, including subdivisions such as the Financial Crimes Enforcement Network (FinCEN),[13] and the Office of the Comptroller of the Currency (OCC)[14]); to employee categorization issues (the Department of Labor, including the Wage and Hour Division (WHD),[15] or, if dealing with a union, the National Labor Relations Board (NLRB)[16]); as well as import and export controls, including the violation of trade sanctions (the Office of Foreign Assets Control (OFAC)[17] within the Treasury, the Examination and Criminal Investigation Divisions within the Internal Revenue Service (IRS),[18] the Department of Homeland Security,[19] the Department of State,[20] and others). If the technology company has a healthcare orientation, there are many agencies that touch on health products and services such as the Food and Drug Administration (FDA)[21] in approving medical devices; the Department of Health and Human Services (HHS)[22] in overseeing healthcare programs such as through the Center for Medicare and Medicaid Innovation (CMMI);[23] and the Department of Veterans Affairs, which runs the largest integrated healthcare system in the country and serves nine million veterans a year.[24] If the technology company is submitting an application for a self-driving vehicle, it may have to be approved by the Department of Transportation's National Highway Traffic Safety Administration (NHTSA),[25] as well as conform to standards for interconnectivity as set by the National Institute of Standards and Technology (NIST),[26] and others.

In politically charged times, businesspeople also have to watch developments closely inside the White House Office of Management and Budget (OMB),[27] especially its Office of Information and Regulatory Affairs (OIRA), which creates guidelines for other federal agencies in drafting, issuing, and enforcing regulations.[28] OIRA reviews proposed presidential executive orders. Additionally, it has the power to evaluate any "significant" proposed agency regulation across the federal government. These broad powers can impact industries as varied as coal mining to space exploration.

In addition to following the statutes and regulations that govern their industries, businesses may participate in specific programs with their own rules. In sales to the federal government, for example, the Government Services Administration (GSA) generally oversees the processes through which the government procures goods and services.[29] In bidding for a U.S. Department of Defense (DOD) contract, participants must follow the DOD's rules.[30] In grants and funding for research, the National Science Foundation (NSF) imposes restrictions on how entities may apply for the funds it awards, and on how funds may be spent.[31]

Violations of laws, regulations, and program rules may bring criminal penalties (such as prison time, fines, and court-ordered restitution); civil penalties (such as fines, restitution, and injunctions against behavior going forward); and regulatory penalties such as ineligibility to participate in programs and contracts going forward.

The violation of any criminal or civil statute or regulation is per se *illegal*, even if it does not result in criminal or civil sanctions. The violation of the terms of participation for many government programs—such as the Medicare or Medicaid health insurance programs—may also be illegal, and constitute stealing from the government or fraud. Businesspeople would be smart to report these issues right away to protect their own reputations, as well as to achieve the most credit possible for cooperation from agencies and prosecutors.

Another category of important regulatory rules and entities for businesspeople to watch is self-regulatory bodies such as industry groups, professional licensing associations, and third-party certification services. Industry groups may promulgate rules and standards for their member businesses to follow, such as the Marine Stewardship Council's limits on fishing to maintain global fish stocks.[32] An industry may also segment its rules to address concerns about specific parts of a market, the way that the Advertising Self-Regulatory Council (ASRC) has created subdivisions to address advertising to children (the Children's Advertising Review Unit, or CARU)[33] and electronic retailing (the Electronic Retailing Self-Regulation Program, or ERSP).[34] Members of an industry group may be in charge of disciplining violators within their own ranks, or the group may also refer the violation to a government agency with which it works. For example, the North American Electric Reliability Corporation (NERC) group's rules operate with the backstop of enforcement measures through the Federal Energy Regulatory Commission.[35] The Financial Industry Regulatory Authority, Inc. (FINRA) partners with the SEC.[36]

As a member of an industry group, the business is usually responsible for self-reporting to that group. Businesspeople should obviously be on the lookout for violations of industry-group standards wherever violations occur, and they should report them to the industry group and outside regulators as appropriate. Typically, violations that occur within a company, and are reported within a company, may be dealt with within the company before being self-reported to the company's industry group.

Here we need to add a few additional warnings, however, about entrusting a company to self-report, whether to an industry group or to regulators. First, some industry-group rules directly concern health and safety (consider airbag standards for the automobile association). Should people die or be injured, a criminal case is far more likely, and there are often safe harbors for individuals who skip internal reporting and report instead directly to back-stopping government authorities.

Second, if a large-enough monetary issue is involved (such as cartel activity violating antitrust provisions, or False Claim Act suits for recovering fraud against the government), reporting first to authorities may not only be protected by whistleblower provisions (see the discussion later in this chapter), but reporting and pursuing these cases externally could garner monetary compensation for individual reporters in the form of a whistleblower bounty, or in the recovery of a portion of the ill-gotten gains.

Third, in some industry-group reporting provisions, the groups have appointed a specific person, or group of people with certain job functions, within the company to report violations. Should you be such a person so designated to report, failing to report to the industry group or outside regulators, even if your company orders you not to, could lead to violations of contractual and other legal obligations that you probably do not want to invite. You may also have particular reporting duties as a professional to the government and other entities by virtue of your professional licensing while serving within the company.

Professional licensing associations tend to be organized by job function. Thus, lawyers are typically regulated through state bar associations, which have the power to remove (disbar) attorneys from practice, as well as to impose penalties short of disbarment.[37] Doctors are supervised both by state licensure boards, which regulate who can practice medicine in the state, as well as by medical specialty boards, which govern the use of occupational titles and sometimes the scope of a doctor's medical practice.[38] The National Association of State Boards of Accountancy (NASB) regulates the licensing of accountants, and it provides for standards of professional conduct.[39] Most such professional licensing associations, in addition to the state governments with which they work, promulgate professional codes of ethics that can, and do, bind businesspeople with these and other professional affiliations within, and as they represent, their businesses.

Because violating a businessperson's professional code of conduct could lead to that individual no longer being able legally to work in his or her chosen profession within any business, issuing, following, or not reporting orders that violate professional licensing standards is particularly dangerous and consequential. Professionals should consider the ethical codes of their professions to be above directives from their companies. Indeed, often reporting ethical issues to professional bodies grants a degree of immunity (or at least deference) within licensing processes to the person who reports and refuses a company order. Your fellow professionals may not be able to save your job at that company. (There is more information on whistleblowing protections later in this chapter, and, in Chapter 4, more on whether you want in the long-term to work at an unethical company.) But at least you will typically be able to keep your professional license and reputation, and to be able to continue your career at another firm. Given the years of training that you have invested in your professional certification process, and the future earning potential linked to it, doing what you need to protect your professional certifications and reputation is always a smart move.

Another potential source of rules and enforcement, third-party certification services, are organizations or businesses that a company typically pays to receive their stamp of approval based on the information that the company provides to the services and/or based on the services' inspections of the company's operations. There can be tremendous economic pressure on the company during difficult times to cheat in its certification processes by cutting corners, or otherwise fail to comply with certification requirements, when those requirements cost money to maintain. Although some third-party certification services are particularly diligent in their certification processes, others may be more willing to look the other way because they are being compensated by the company, and fees from companies are their primary stream of revenue.

It can be difficult to know, as a businessperson concerned about compliance, which of these situations defines the relationship between your company and its third-party certification service. A savvy businessperson may begin to feel this out with a representative of the third-party certification service when that person comes to visit the company in the process of inspecting operations or regulating information. Here, because it is the job of the third-party certification services to be looking for deficits in the company's processes, a mere word to the wise from a concerned employee about where to look, or what numbers might not add up, could be all that it takes. But, if the third-party certification service representative does not seem interested or willing to follow through with his or her own investigation, you can be disappointed, but maybe not surprised.

When reporting violations to third-party certification services, the same caveats about how serious the violation is in terms of health, safety, economic impact, and other factors as discussed above apply. You will usually need to report directly to the government in those circumstances. Nonetheless, if your attempts to report less dangerous concerns internally or to these enforcement bodies do not work, you may need to start quietly either advocating within the company for a change in its ethical culture (see "Giving Voice to Values" suggestions and outlines in Chapter 9), or starting to look for another job that better comports with your ethics and the values toward which you are contributing such a significant part of your life.

If you are experiencing a failure of your company's compliance and ethics system, see Chapters 13 and 14 for how companies should encourage internal reporting, and how important healthy internal reporting rates are to companies' well-being.

What are some strategies for employee reporting?

As mentioned above, the first thing that employees should figure out is *what* they are reporting, and then who is involved.

Once you know more about those things, you can be more savvy about to whom to report and how.

Before an employee reports, he or she should be as clear as possible about what standard or violation has been broken, and how it was broken. If you are unsure whether the conduct that you observed violates a law, professional, or ethical standard, it may be worthwhile to conduct some research, consult a lawyer, or ask someone who will be able to maintain a measure of confidentiality, such as a close friend. It may not be wise to discuss possible violations initially with corporate counsel or compliance until you are more certain that the conduct is, in fact, either unlawful or otherwise impermissible, and why.

The employee should then attempt to understand who else in the company (or outside) may be involved in the misconduct. If solely one employee, or a small group of employees, is engaging in the wrongdoing, it is more likely that managers higher in the company will take action to discipline the employee(s) and ensure that the conduct stops. On the other hand, if the individual, or individuals, committing the misconduct happen(s) to be the CEO, a managing partner, regional supervisor, or other person in a position of significant power, reporting internally may not be successful unless your report can be made to someone at least a level above the individual(s) engaged in the misconduct.

Try to determine the broader ethical culture of your company, and who knows what. It can be an awkward situation to document the wrongdoing of a group of employees, and march into their supervisor's office to report the wrongdoing, only to discover that the supervisor is, or his or her superiors are, the one(s) directing the unlawful activity. Another way to say this is that it's important to know not *only* who might be "shredding the documents," but who might have told them to shred the documents in the first place.

Figuring out who may be involved in the ethical misconduct helps to determine the best way to report violations.

Sometimes an employee can simply report the issue to his or her manager. Sometimes the employee will have to report higher up the company's structure. In some cases, the employee may have to go directly to regulators. Ideally, of course, the report can be made internally first to give the company a chance to self-regulate. But, given the scope and nature of some forms of misconduct, that option is not always a realistic possibility.

In trying to decide whether to report internally or externally, the employee should consider whether the company's Code of Conduct requires specific actions regarding where and how to report.[40] Companies usually publish their Codes of Conduct on their websites or in their employment handbooks. Some more minor situations may not be legally appropriate for external reporting, and should be dealt with internally.[41] The jurisdiction where an employee is located may also require internal reporting before making certain external reports.[42] Employees may have a range of internal reporting options, such as submitting an anonymous report via the Internet, reporting to an ombudsperson or compliance officer, or calling a hotline.

Although employees should try to follow a company's Code of Conduct or other procedures put forth in an employment handbook, such policies and handbooks are not always binding and enforceable against employees. If a policy or handbook, for example, seeks to prevent the reporting of violations, it is unlikely that a court will enforce it.[43] It is also possible that a company may not list the option to report misconduct externally in its materials. It is strange that U.S. federal law does not currently require companies to include the option to report externally in their corporate policies and handbooks. But even if an option to report externally is not listed, the employee may usually still do it (especially in severe cases). Public companies cannot prohibit an employee from reporting externally. Consult your own attorney, however, to understand what ramifications may follow.

As we have touched on earlier, some circumstances create immediate harm to others that require emergency reporting to authorities.[44] If, for example, an employee needs to call 9-1-1 as an emergency in the U.S. because someone is hurt in an industrial accident, there is little time to wade through a formal reporting structure. Similarly, if an employee observes the company dumping toxic waste into a river, there may not be time formally to report the issue to compliance before lives are on the line. Although it is usually better to report internally if the situation permits, if preventing the harmful conduct from continuing requires emergency intervention, the employee may have to go straight to authorities, or at least report to authorities and management simultaneously.

If the timing permits, however, you should do what you can to document the issue and who is involved with the issue before reporting it. It is typically better to know everything that you can, and have your own evidence to support what you are saying, before pulling the trigger on a report. Back up documents, when possible, to your own devices, or maintain separate paper copies, to prove your claims. It can be a very bad situation when evidence of the violation is destroyed, and it becomes an employee's word against the company's word. You will want to have your own evidence to prove your claim, especially if the company's compliance officers or upper-level management do not end up siding with you, or even attempt to blame you for the violation.

Holding certain positions in the company, such as serving as an attorney or auditor, may require that these employees report internally before they report externally.[45] As described above, these positions may also have their own codes of professional conduct, which can encourage them to follow up internal reports with reports to external authorities should no internal company action, or should a negative internal reaction, occur.

Regardless of your position, should the company's internal process fail you, you may want to report externally.

Filing externally is more likely to protect you from retaliation within the company. Companies can, and do, fire employees for reporting misconduct internally. In fact, under some laws, employees are protected from retaliation only if they report to external authorities within a certain period of time of when events happen. For example, the U.S. Supreme Court has held that employees are not protected from company retaliation under the 2010 Dodd–Frank Wall Street Reform and Consumer Protection Act unless they make an external report to authorities within 120 days of being terminated.[46] The Dodd–Frank Act applies to violations of federal securities laws, and it is only one example of a whistleblower protection law.

There are many other laws at both the U.S. federal and state level that may offer protection to someone who reports wrongdoing within a company. A key takeaway, though, is that protection from retaliation after reporting wrongdoing is far from guaranteed under current laws. An individual must make sure that he or she satisfies the requirements for protection under those laws.

Most of all, if you decide to report misconduct either internally or externally, one of the most important pieces of advice is to have your own lawyer and not rely on the lawyers within your company. Remember that those lawyers work for the company, and not for *you*. They are bound to preserve the interests of the company, which they may or may not understand as protecting you as well. The company may contest your claims, and try to discredit you. The company may also attempt to destroy evidence once it realizes that you have reported the violation. (Yes, this is often illegal, but it still happens, and it is something that whistleblowers confront.)

If you have documented materials on your own devices, or otherwise kept copies that the company cannot destroy, it will help to have that proof so that the case does not come down to your word against the company's, and so that you have something to show outside regulators. You may succeed in the case, win disciplinary actions against the company for its behavior, and be awarded compensation for reporting, but to achieve those results you will need to get through the process first.

What are my options if reporting within my organization does not work?

Once an employee reports internally, the question becomes how much time the employee should wait for a satisfactory response. How long is reasonable to wait before concluding that the company is either taking no action, or inadequate action, to stop the misconduct, and that the employee should report externally? The employee should give the company some time to correct the wrongdoing, and to conduct its own internal investigation. But, if no correction happens, and the unethical or unlawful conduct continues, it is a good rule of thumb to report externally no later than 120 days after reporting internally.[47]

Depending on the industry and relevant law, however, some reports must be made to external authorities as soon as possible.[48] For example, the Occupational Safety and Health Administration (OSHA), within the U.S. Department of Labor, may pursue companies for violating regulations only if the violation is either currently occurring, or the violation existed within six months of the date that an individual complains to OSHA.[49]

An employee may still be permitted to report misconduct externally after 120 days, but under many state and federal laws whistleblower protection may sometimes not attach after that window. The reporting period may also be shorter than 120 days. These varying parameters are another reason to consult your own attorney who should be familiar with your industry, or who handles whistleblower matters on a regular basis.

Whistleblower protection may not apply to an employee who misses the 120 days (or other window) to file because the law does not want individuals to learn of misconduct, and then sit on that information. Authorities want to know about unlawful activity as soon as possible. Another reason for time-limiting such protection is to discourage employees from using knowledge of a company's wrongdoing to prevent the company from firing them.[50] This rationale may be especially strong if the employee knows about the wrongdoing because he or she was extensively involved in its commission, or becomes complicit in it over time.

For these reasons and others, it is a good idea not to threaten your employer with reporting legal violations before reporting them, as the company may use your threat against it to argue that you acted with the ulterior motives of either attempting to preserve your job or extorting the company. If the company can convince a court that you tried to use your knowledge of the legal violations to ensure that it could not fire you, you may lose your claim of retaliatory discharge should the company fire you for reporting.

Another consideration of timing and strategy involves the relevant statutes of limitations. Statutes of limitations are federal, state, or local laws that put time limits on when civil or criminal lawsuits may be filed. Once those time limits expire, it can be nearly impossible to hold companies (or individuals within those companies) responsible for their unlawful conduct because a court will dismiss such a suit out-of-hand as untimely filed.

For example, the federal False Claims Act permits an individual who knows that a company or person is defrauding the federal government to bring suit as a private individual against that company or person to recover money due to the government in exchange for a portion of that payment.[51] The suit may move forward, however, only if it is brought within six years of the date that the fraud occurred, or within three years of when the government learns of the violation. Under some circumstances, the time period for suit may extend beyond six years, but ten years is the point beyond which almost no such claim may be brought. Similarly, the statute of limitations on bank fraud is ten years.[52] Again, although there are some exceptions, once ten years has elapsed from the date of the crime, the person who committed bank fraud may not be prosecuted for the fraud.

Statutes of limitations vary by offense. Some statutes of limitations are as short as a single year. One example of a single-year statute of limitations is on securities fraud.[53]

Although there are exceptions to statutes of limitations, employees should presume that a clock is running on their time to file with authorities unless their attorney informs them otherwise. This means that, if you are going to blow the whistle, do not overly delay your external reporting. Additionally, as time passes, the misconduct at issue can cause further injury to victims, and evidence may be lost or destroyed.[54]

When reporting externally, as discussed above in this chapter, the employee may have a choice of agencies to whom he or she may report, depending on the type of industry and violation involved. Some of the most common federal agencies to which whistleblowers report include OSHA, which handles workplace safety and health hazards, as well as matters related to 22 other federal statutes.[55] The SEC collects information about violations of federal securities laws that regulate the stock markets and most related investment activity.[56] The FTC handles issues of consumer protection, ranging from generic scams, to breaches of data privacy, to reports of companies that attempt to fix prices and create monopolies.[57] The Environmental Protection Agency (EPA) oversees issues impacting the environment from the inappropriate disposal of hazardous waste, to the regulation of carbon emissions, and other forms of pollution.[58] The Commodity Futures Trading Commission (CFTC) oversees the trading of commodities.[59] Commodities are items to which people commonly assign value and use, such as silver, gold, wheat, and even coffee beans.[60] The IRS collects taxes for the federal government.[61] The U.S. Department of Energy supervises the use of nuclear power, and other energy sources across the country.[62] The Federal Election Commission (FEC) is responsible for ensuring the integrity of federal elections, and it handles issues such as the misuse of campaign contributions.[63] The FDA regulates the safety of the nation's medicines and pharmaceuticals.[64] The powerful U.S. Department of Agriculture (USDA) monitors the nation's food supply.[65]

In addition to reporting to regulatory agencies, employees can report criminal activity to law-enforcement personnel, including prosecutors. Perhaps the best-known federal law-enforcement organization is the Federal Bureau of Investigation (FBI). The FBI investigates a wide range of criminal conduct, from financial crimes such as tax evasion, to matters of national security such as terrorism and espionage on behalf of foreign governments.[66] Although the U.S. Secret Service is best known for protecting the President and other high-ranking government officials, it is also responsible for investigating crimes that undermine the integrity of the country's currency, such as counterfeiting and certain cybercrimes.[67] The U.S. Marshals Service not only protects federal buildings, it tracks down wanted persons.[68] The Bureau of Alcohol, Tobacco, Firearms, and Explosives (ATF),[69] the Drug Enforcement Agency (DEA),[70] and the Transportation Security Administration (TSA)[71] are yet more examples of specialized federal law-enforcement agencies.

If an employee is reporting criminal activity, but he or she is unsure to which agency to report, the best catch-all agency to contact is the U.S. Department of Justice (DOJ).[72] The DOJ is the legal arm of the federal government most commonly charged with prosecuting criminals in court. Federal prosecutors handle a wide range of criminal matters, and the DOJ oversees a system of such prosecutors in U.S. Attorneys' Offices across the country.

All of the agencies mentioned above are federal, but, in addition to these, many states will have their own versions of such offices to enforce the state's criminal and civil statutes. For example, the most typical state equivalent of the FBI is the State Police. States may have an office of State Attorney

General that plays a role similar to the DOJ. Depending on the size of the state, and the unique challenges that the state faces, it may have important subdivisions of its state agencies. Many states, for example, have county, and even more local law enforcement agencies and prosecutors' offices such as District Attorneys (or State's Attorneys) for criminal cases, and County or City Attorneys for civil cases.

In sum, if one agency does not respond to the employee's report of unlawful activity, there may be plenty of other options to which to consider reporting when he or she thinks about all the levels of federal and state government organizations.

Another option for the employee, if federal and state government entities do not respond in a timely or adequate way, is to approach the news media. The First Amendment protects the news media as well as employees in some situations from retaliation for stories about public employee whistleblowers.[73] For limits on these protections, see your own attorney. Additionally, even if you are not explicitly protected from retaliation for communicating with the news media, news coverage of your case may help draw positive attention to your cause, and reporters can vigorously protect the anonymity of their sources.

Finally, it may be worth taking matters into your own hands in court by suing your employer as a private citizen. As briefly noted above, some federal statutes (and corollary state statutes) allow individuals to sue companies and/or groups of people on behalf of the government or classes of people affected by the wrongdoing. The federal False Claims Act (FCA) enables individuals who sue on behalf of the government to keep a percentage of the money the government would otherwise have lost as a reward.[74] In other situations, an individual may sue on behalf of a larger group of people who have been similarly harmed as part of a "class action." The benefit of a class action suit is that many people who might not have been otherwise able to afford to sue can combine forces to share attorneys' fees (or have an attorney work for them on contingency), and recover damages that they may not have been able to collect on their own.

What are my options when I report to authorities?

You need not always make your identity known when you report to authorities. Many government regulators allow individuals to submit reports confidentially, and to keep their identities anonymous.[75] The SEC, for example, allows individuals to submit tips anonymously online, or through calling the agency's whistleblower hotline. From May 2011, when the hotline was established, to 2019, the SEC had returned 15,413 calls, and it returned 3,124 calls in 2016 alone.[76] The SEC's website and hotline are available for use by whistleblowers of all types, attorneys, and members of the general public.[77]

Additional agencies have similar procedures, and governments rely heavily on such tips. In 2016, globally, 39.1% of fraud cases were initially detected through tips.[78] Employees submitted 51.5% of these tips to regulators. Anonymous tips accounted for 14% of the tips that revealed fraud. Beware of rules about hotlines internationally, however. In France and Sweden, calling such tip lines may violate local data privacy and employment laws.[79]

Also, in order later to claim a bounty for the information that you submit, the tip must be in writing,[80] and the government may have to be able to contact you. You may typically use your lawyer's information for such contact, but that does mean that you will need your own lawyer.

Like when reporting internally, once you report to authorities, be particularly careful when the company's lawyers question you. First of all, it is important to understand again that your company's lawyers represent the *company*, and not you. They operate in the company's best interest, which may not be the same as yours. You may not have the right to refuse to disclose information unless to do so would violate your own right to avoid criminal self-incrimination. In such a case, you should not answer questions, and you should invoke the Fifth Amendment. It is also a very good idea to have your *own* lawyer present during such questioning.

But the company may have the right to fire you for refusing to answer questions and failing to cooperate with the company's lawyers. In addition, whatever you tell the company's lawyers may be disclosed to other parties at a later date. Attorney–client privilege relates to the relationship between the company's lawyers and the *company*, and it may be waived by the company regarding the information that you disclose.[81]

If it is permissible, you may want to make your own recording of such conversations. If the organization attempts to cover-up the extent of the misconduct, it is possible that the company may attempt to frame you for it. In addition, the company may simply bury your evidence, and conclude that "no wrongdoing took place."

Should your employer retaliate against you for reporting, you may consider several options.

First, possibly while also pursuing other strategies, you may want to file additional claims with external regulatory authorities about the company's actions. Should the employer realize that a regulatory agency is investigating, and is actively being updated on claims, the company may start acting on its best behavior—at least as long as the active scrutiny keeps up. But that time may be long enough to encourage personnel changes higher up in the company, and that could make a difference in your ability to continue working there.

Second, you might bring a wrongful retaliation suit against your employer. The power of reporting to outside authorities is that it helps become more clear-cut when and how anti-retaliation protections apply. Consult your own attorney on these issues.

If you win a wrongful retaliation suit against your employer, a court may order your employer to pay you monetary damages, backpay for the time that you should have been working, and even order your employer to give you your job back.

Compensation may also be available generally for "adverse employment actions." These can be broader than the company firing you, and include other forms of retaliation, such as taking you off a key project, docking your pay, no longer giving you substantive assignments, or even moving your shifts to times that the employer knows are inconvenient for you. Consult your own lawyer about whether your company's actions might amount to retaliation, and whether a court would rule for you.

Whatever you decide to do, remember that the statutes of limitations may start to run from the time that you learn that you *will* be retaliated against, not from when the retaliation eventually occurs. So you must be actively vigilant to protect your claims. To be protected under the Sarbanes–Oxley Act of 2002 (SOX), an employee has 90 days to file his or her complaint with an agency (such as OSHA) from when he or she unambiguously learns that the company will retaliate against him or her in some way.[82] Environmental statutes of limitations are even more restrictive, and require that many retaliation claims be filed within 30 days.[83]

If you think that the company may retaliate against you in some tangible way that could constitute an "adverse action," talk to your own lawyer right away. Watch to see whether your company fires you, takes you off a key project, docks your pay, stops giving you work, or does anything that makes you think that it is retaliating against you for reporting to regulators. If this happens, you may not be able to wait too long to do something about it. If you wait, it may be too late to bring an anti-retaliation claim. The company may not change its mind. Cooler heads may not prevail. And you may have lost your best leverage to save your job and your position within the company.

To what benefits am I entitled as a whistleblower?

In addition to receiving protection under whistleblower-protection laws from retaliation, whistleblowers who report to authorities and meet certain criteria may be entitled to monetary awards from the government. One of the best-known whistleblower bounty systems is through the SEC. The SEC may pay bounties to whistleblowers whose information leads to a successful enforcement action against any company or individuals.[84] These bounties range from between 10% and 30% of what the government recovers.[85] By 2019, of the ten-largest whistleblower awards paid by the SEC, three had been awarded in 2017, and the highest amount that year was for U.S. $20 million.[86] The headline sums also seem to be getting larger. In October 2020, the SEC paid a whistleblower an award of U.S. $114 million.[87]

When paying out these awards, the SEC does not disclose information that may directly or indirectly reveal a whistleblower's identity.[88] The difference in bounty awards between 10% to 30% of the money collected by the SEC depends on how valuable the information was provided by the whistleblower.[89]

The prospect of obtaining a whistleblower bounty, however, should *not* be the main factor in whether an employee decides to report unlawful activity. It usually is not. The vast majority of whistleblowers are motivated by concerns about fairness and justice.[90] These findings have been repeatedly confirmed by studies. Even in healthcare fraud cases, in which 90% of cases are separate "qui tam" actions, during which whistleblowers sue on behalf of the government for a percentage of the recovery, the majority of whistleblowers were not initially motivated by money.[91] Nearly all of the insiders first tried to fix the company's legal and ethical problems internally by "talking to their supervisors, filing an internal complaint, or both."[92] Ultimately, most of the employees' reasons for suing when their attempts to report internally failed "coalesced around four non-mutually exclusive themes: integrity, altruism or public safety, justice, and self-preservation."[93] Every single participant confirmed that "the financial bounty offered under the federal statute had not motivated their participation in the qui tam lawsuit."[94]

Even when employees acted to preserve their own jobs, it was often because of the potential reputational consequences.

As one participant explained, "[i]f these guys go down[,] I'm not going to be the one that gets blamed for all this."[95] As another person described, "in the end[,] they were pushing me hard to break some more laws. I had just said, 'I'm putting my foot down. I'm being excluded from meetings. They're making decisions that I'm going to do things that are illegal.' So I felt like [my company was] just trying to set me up."[96]

The advice that successful whistleblowers give is worth repeating here. Hiring an experienced personal attorney is important. You will need mentally to prepare for a process "more protracted, stressful . . . conflict-ridden, and less financially rewarding" than many people expect.[97] But, as can be summed up, "I would say don't expect any money. It's going to be a long time. It's going to be frustrating. But if you're doing it for the right reasons? Then go for it. But if you're doing it because you think you're going to make millions? Don't do it."[98]

In fact, one whistleblower who used to work for Deutsche Bank explained in 2016 why he ultimately turned down his half of a U.S. $16.5 million award from the SEC.[99] He had been a risk officer at the bank, and he saw "the bank's shareholders and its rank-and-file employees who are now losing their jobs in droves" as the primary victims of top executives' wrongdoing.[100]

The whistleblower who turned down this money, like so many others, had called his company's internal hotline first. Deutsche Bank's lawyer had attempted to keep him from reporting externally, and the whistleblower had been fired. He did admit that, "[w]hen I first helped the SEC investigation, the whistleblower award was a powerful incentive."[101] However, once he was eligible for the award, "[a]lthough I need the money now more than ever, I will not join the looting of the very people I was hired to protect."[102] He objected that, in the Deutsche Bank case, unlike other SEC cases, no individuals at the bank were charged. He may not have known that the company's insurance company likely paid a large portion of the award (if not all of it), and that monies collected by the

SEC from such settlements, whether from a company or individuals, typically go into a fund to compensate victims.

The process of obtaining an award from the government is difficult. A complicated investigation can take several years, and there may be competing claims for the award.[103] Of the close to 4,500 tips that the SEC collected in 2017, only 12 individuals received financial awards from the agency. The odds of receiving an SEC award as a whistleblower that year were then about a quarter of 1% (0.267%).[104]

When a tip is submitted, the SEC analyzes the information, and it decides whether to initiate an investigation. After its investigation, the SEC may charge the company, individuals, or both. The agency's cases may settle before going to court, or they may (in more rare cases) go to trial. In the end, most charges brought are likely to result in penalties and sanctions. Fines, as noted above, typically go into the SEC's Investor Protection Fund.[105] Nonetheless, only certain SEC actions are eligible to become the basis of governmental awards to whistleblowers. (For more details, see the SEC's list on its Office of the Whistleblower website under "Notices of Covered Actions" (NOCA)).[106]

Once such a covered action reaches its conclusion, the whistleblower may file to claim his or her award.[107] Only after the SEC's award has been determined, and all appeals of its case have been resolved, may the government then pay a whistleblower bounty out of the Investor Protection Fund.

In order to qualify for a government bounty at that stage, the whistleblower's filing is evaluated for whether the whistleblower's tip to the agency was "voluntary," contained "original" information that "led to" the successful enforcement action, and whether the whistleblower otherwise had a formal duty to report. For the SEC, a whistleblower's information is "voluntary" when the whistleblower comes forward with the information "before a request, inquiry, or demand that relates to the subject matter of your submission is directed to you or anyone representing you."[108] In other words, file your tip early, before the SEC may ask you for the information or question you.

The information that you provide if you want a government award should be "original," meaning "derived from your independent knowledge or independent analysis," rather than someone else's work or knowledge.[109] You are not required ever to have been an employee at the company to claim this award. The SEC has granted whistleblower awards to people who were never company employees, but who were able to figure out that there was something wrong at a company by going through public information or by obtaining records from inside the company that they then use to help the SEC to put together its case.

For the SEC, information "leads to" a successful enforcement action (of which the whistleblower may claim a portion), if it triggers an investigation, contributes significantly to the success of an action, or is reported internally and used by the company/other entity in the company's internal investigation and report to the SEC.[110] The company, and/or individuals at the company, may pay money to the SEC as part of a settlement with the government to resolve its potential liability once it discovers the extent of its wrongdoing internally. Thus, if you do report internally, it is worth watching SEC settlements to see if your company may have used your report as part of how it resolved its case with the government. But, given that your company probably already had access to the information you provided, this can be difficult to prove. In addition, the basis of the company's settlement may be confidential, so it may be difficult for you have enough information about how it was settled to file your whistleblower bounty claim. These factors additionally argue for filing directly with the government, so that you maintain an easier record of what, when, and how you provided the information that became the basis of the case.

As a reminder, internal audit and compliance officers are not eligible for portions of a company's payment to the SEC from internal investigations because they have a pre-existing duty to report such information within the company (and possibly directly to regulators) in the first place.[111] There is an exception here for compliance personnel, like the Deutsche Bank whistleblower, who try to report internally (as they are supposed to), and then also report (outside the company's process, or when the company tells them not to) to the SEC. By setting up incentives this way, the SEC is trying to prevent an internal compliance officer from "rack[ing] up the damages" by allowing harms to fester within the company before ultimately reporting, in an attempt to collect his or her percentage of a larger award. It should be within such personnel's professional interest to stay on top of potential ethical violations and illegal activities (to which ethical violations may lead) before they escalate. By nipping problems in their earliest stages, these personnel further justify their jobs to save the company money and keep it out of trouble.

For similar reasons, officers, directors, trustees, or partners of the business may not be eligible for governmental awards if they learned of the misconduct through the company's established processes for addressing violations of the law, or from another employee communicating the information to them.[112] Such people should already have the correct financial incentives to stop the wrongdoing when they hear of it. If they do not, they may be liable for their failures to act, and these failures may become the basis of new external reports and charges against the company or individuals.

What protections will I have as a whistleblower?

Whistleblowers are protected from employer retaliation under various federal, state, and sometimes even local laws.[113] We will walk through some of the major considerations under federal law for being able to claim retaliation once a company has done something negative to you after reporting. (See also this chapter's previous discussion about what may constitute an "adverse" employment action for purposes of suit.)

The reason why we spent so much time earlier in this chapter on protecting yourself against retaliation (for example, save your documents!), and in this section on the protections you may have as a whistleblower against retaliation, is because retaliation against employees happens *a lot*. Companies are full of human beings who do not like to hear bad news. That's why there is an art to being able to speak truth to power and not being fired (see the discussion of "Giving Voice to Values" techniques in Chapter 9). Especially in the United States, in which the vast majority of employment relationships are "at will"—meaning only for the time that pleases both the employer and employee—people may be fired for bad news all the time. In fact, even when employees have contractual protections and are fired "for cause," the existence of misconduct on your watch that you did not prevent may leave you vulnerable to being blamed by the company for that behavior. It is really only whistleblowers—those who have reported the misconduct—who may have meaningful legal protection for their jobs.

Merely to prepare your expectations, despite the fact that, in one study, 91% of corporate codes promise "no retaliation" against employees, or explicitly prohibit retaliation,[114] another study found that 74% of whistleblowers had been terminated.[115] Although those numbers are grim, it must be said that we do not have the numbers on who else may have been terminated at those companies when the misconduct came to light, but at least we know about the whistleblowers. They were able to bring cases, and we know about them *because* they were the whistleblowers who reported.

As noted above, simply because you report (even to external authorities—although that helps significantly), there is no guarantee that you will be compensated either through a governmental bounty, or through the court system.

The general advice for employees, then, is to have savings if you can. As Silicon-Valley legend Donna Dubinsky, who co-invented the Palm digital organizing device, and who has worked at many companies with her "Midas touch," put it: "Get enough financial resources to pay for your costs of living."[116]

These funds will help you "when you don't like the way things are going in the company." They can be "your 'go to hell' money and . . . [help you] walk away.'" That ability to leave also enables you to conduct yourself with "'grace and integrity.' If you disagree with someone, speak up. If you're at fault, pick yourself up and move on." Your integrity is "N[umber] 1."[117]

This conversation additionally has to be placed in the context of larger labor-market dynamics, especially in the United States. Long-term, as Dubinsky describes in the tech space, but as employees need to think about across the labor market, "[b]ig companies don't always win." And "[d]on't depend on big companies" to necessarily protect or help you. Although Dubinsky was speaking about the entrepreneurial space, her warning about the limits of employee relationships with companies applies for employees across the workforce generally. "You really have to get into their shoes and understand and remember that you are really small to them."[118] You may think that your strong relationships with the people with whom you work may save you, but also realize that they may not, and it is important for you to have a plan for when something goes wrong.

Ideally, you can plan ahead for these situations. But, sometimes, and especially in potential whistleblowing situations, you cannot. In fact, depending on the industry, applicable law, and potential harm at stake (as described in this chapter above regarding the timeliness of whistleblowing reports), you may have to report right away to receive protections.

At least, in these situations, there may be protections for whistleblowers. If you are successful in a retaliation lawsuit against an employer, a court or government agency may order the company to restore your job, pay your back wages, reinstate your employee benefits, and provide other forms of relief.

When OSHA finds that retaliation has occurred, for example, it may explicitly order reinstatement of the employee, payment of back wages, the restoration of benefits, and additional special damages.[119] In another example, the U.S. Department of Labor ordered the reinstatement of a whistleblower, and payment of more than U.S. $1 million in back wages and other relief to him for violations of the Sarbanes–Oxley Act.[120]

If you are fired for reporting, typically you must demonstrate four things in order to succeed in a retaliatory discharge claim.[121] First, you must have been engaged in protected activity. Protected activities include, but may not be limited to, assisting an investigation, whether internal or external, testifying in proceedings related to an alleged violation, or reporting unlawful activity.[122] Many laws that protect whistleblowers from retaliation in initial reports additionally protect employees who file cases, testify, or otherwise cooperate with investigations as they proceed later against the company.[123]

Second, you must show that the company knew about, or at least suspected, that you were engaged in the protected activity.[124] This knowledge may be proven by circumstantial evidence, such as the timing of events. If an employee, for example, reports unlawful conduct to high-level managers, and the employee's direct supervisor disciplines the employee, an agency or court could conclude that the supervisor disciplined the employee because the supervisor learned of the employee's report to the higher-level managers.[125] The employee's reporting to higher-level managers would be a protected activity. The supervisor's disciplining of the employee after his or her report could be considered unlawful retaliation based on circumstantial evidence that the supervisor may have known about the employee's report, and the supervisor acted adversely toward the employee because of the protected report.

Third, you must show that the company engaged in an "adverse action" against you.[126] We described previously in this chapter how broad the concept of an adverse action can be. Depending on the statute, and the agency, it could be almost anything designed to punish, or to exact revenge against, an employee for whistleblowing. Examples of adverse actions, according to OSHA alone, include everything from "[a]pplying or issuing a policy which provides for an unfavorable personnel action" affecting the whistleblower; to "blacklisting," "demoting," "denying overtime or promotions," "denying benefits," "failing to hire or rehire," or "firing or laying off" the whistleblower; to "intimidation," "threats," reduction of "pay or hours," reassignment to a "less desirable position," or "suspension."[127] Under the Occupational Safety and Health Act, for example, OSHA also broadly considers it unlawful retaliation for a whistleblower to have been "punished in any other way because you used any right given to you under the . . . Act."[128]

Fourth, once you have been the victim of retaliation, you must show that your protected activity (whistleblowing) motivated or contributed to the company's decision to take the adverse employment action.[129] This element will almost always require the use of circumstantial evidence because a company is not likely to tell an employee that he or she was fired, demoted, or otherwise disciplined for whistleblowing.[130] In fact, it may be easy for the company to make up excuses for its adverse action(s). Therefore, an important piece of circumstantial evidence to prove the company's motivation here can be the timing of the adverse action. If the adverse action occurred relatively soon after the employee blew the whistle, then courts and agencies will sometimes presume that the employee's whistleblowing motivated the company's retaliation. Data tend to support this presumption: of whistleblowers who were the victims of retaliatory adverse actions, 79% reported that they were retaliated against within the first three weeks, and 90% reported that the retaliation occurred within six months.[131]

Indeed, some state courts, such as in Texas and South Carolina, have announced that they have a default rule that adverse actions against employees will be considered the result of retaliation if they occur within specific timeframes, such as either 90 days or one year after the employee blows a whistle. In these situations, companies then have the burden of showing that their actions against the employee were not taken for a retaliatory purpose.[132]

In addition, an employee in these circumstances does not have to show that his or her whistleblowing was the only, majority, or even a significant factor in the company's decision to take the adverse action.[133] Showing merely that the whistleblowing was a "contributing factor" in the employer's retaliatory behavior is often enough.[134] Another way to articulate this very low standard to prove retaliation is that "any factor, which alone or in connection with other factors, tends to affect in any way the outcome of the [company's] decision" to engage in the adverse action after the employee's whistleblowing, should be enough.[135]

In sum, although much of the law is not tilted in favor of whistleblowers, at least the standards for establishing retaliation are generous toward employees.

Procedurally, to establish that a company's adverse action against an employee was retaliation, the whistleblower may sometimes have to file an additional claim that includes a description of the retaliation within a certain period of time after the retaliation occurs. Under many of the 22 laws that OSHA enforces, for examples, the employee must report retaliation sometime within 30 to 180 days of when the employee discovers it.[136]

Finally, there are some defenses that companies may assert against being held responsible for a retaliation claim. For example, the company may argue that it would have taken the same action against the employee even if the employee had not reported.[137] By way of illustration, if a teacher has a long history of unprofessional activities, and is fired after complaining to a radio station about the school's uniform policy, the school may argue that the teacher was about to be fired anyway, and that the complaint to the radio station had no impact on his or her firing.[138] Similarly, a company may claim that an employee's conduct on the job (outside of the protected whistleblowing report) was too consistently disruptive or disloyal when the employee had a duty to follow proscribed methods of communication.[139] Once the employee has demonstrated, however, that his or her whistleblowing was a "contributing factor" in motivating the company to engage in an adverse action against the employee, a company can only overcome the presumption that it will be liable for unlawful retaliation by "clear and convincing evidence" that the employee's whistleblowing was not actually a contributing factor to its decision.[140]

In a related argument, if an employee were to use the whistleblower-protection laws for an improper purpose, the company would be able to use the employee's improper motive as a defense.[141] For example, whistleblowing protections should not apply when an employee blows a whistle only to delay disciplinary action, when there is no issue to report, or when the employee is otherwise improperly seeking to use the protection of anti-retaliatory discharge laws. Similarly, in some industries such as the nuclear, pipeline, environmental, and airline sectors, a company may defend against an employee's charge of retaliatory discharge based on the employee's deliberate misconduct.

Another important set of protections that whistleblowers should know about include the laws' ability to render void confidentiality or nondisclosure agreements (NDAs) that may prevent an employee from reporting unlawful activity.[142] The U.S. Supreme Court is clear that employees cannot be bound by such agreements in their employment contracts.[143]

SEC regulations additionally expressly prohibit anyone from using nondisclosure (NDA) or other agreements to limit or control the report of a securities-law violation.[144] Not only are the SEC's regulations in this area very broad, but they make it illegal for anyone to enforce—or even to threaten to enforce—an agreement seeking to control communication with the SEC about potential securities-law violations.[145] Employers cannot, for example, require employees—or former employees—to forgo whistleblower bounties; deny, or even threaten to deny, a severance payment to an employee until the employee says that he or she has not reported to the SEC; or attempt to make any agreement during arbitration with an employee that the employee not report wrongdoing to the SEC before, during, or after proceedings. Under the Dodd–Frank and Sarbanes–Oxley Acts, mandatory arbitration agreements may be illegal if they can be used to limit the rights of whistleblowers.[146] Even language in an agreement that could potentially discourage reports to the SEC may not be allowed—regardless of whether there is evidence that fewer people either reported or may report because of it.[147]

It is typically illegal for a company or anyone else to buy off—or to attempt to buy off—a whistleblower. In fact, settling any case with a whistleblower under the Sarbanes–Oxley Act requires the approval of the Department of Labor to protect the whistleblower.[148]

What else should I know about being a whistleblower?

The most pressing concern that many whistleblowers have about blowing the whistle is how it will affect their future careers. It is true that whistleblowing may make it more difficult to stay in your chosen industry going forward.[149] But, if you are a businessperson or professional, also remember that *not* blowing the whistle on observed misconduct, especially if your superior or company attempts to implicate *you* in the misconduct, could be career-ending. It is very hard, if not impossible, for example, to continue in a position of trust in the financial sector with an insider-trading conviction on your record. Similarly, if your company or division makes headlines for terrible behavior, you are in much better shape explaining that you were the ethical person who blew the whistle, than be tarred with the same brush as those who engaged in wrongdoing.

Be careful of other companies that are afraid of hiring whistleblowers. You have to wonder what might be going on inside that company, and whether you might be jumping from the frying pan into the fire. There could be serious wrongdoing happening inside of those companies too.

Look for firms that hold ethics among their core values. They may be seeking people like you who will take a stand against misbehavior.[150] There will be companies out there looking for principled employees who will do what is right, and that prefer to hire them over others. Check the company's website for mentions of ethics. Speak to people who work at the company, and gauge whether ethics are important to them. See whether ethics at the company is truly a lived creed, or mere lip-service.

If there are no ethical companies in your industry, seriously consider whether you want to stay in the industry. And then consider starting a company—there is most likely a business opportunity there to be had. (See more in Chapter 4 about what the conditions of a workplace say about you.) By starting your own company, you can make the choices about who you want as your partners, whom you decide to hire, and how you want them to act. Those are among the most powerful tools to shape an environment that you can have.

In the interim, managing the stress of being a whistleblower can be a serious challenge.[151] Find ways to be productive with your stress, and see a therapist if your stress manifests in unhealthy ways. How you deal with this stress can affect the outcome of your process, and your ability to pivot in your career going forward. Finding trusted friends, family, and advisors in whom you can confide will make things easier. Protect your relationships with your loved ones and family. If you are still at the job, trying to remain anonymous, and concerned about retaliation, be careful not to choose a confidant who may expose your role to your employer.

In terms of resources, the National Whistleblower Center is a good place to consult for blog discussions, attorney referrals, frequently asked questions on whistleblower topics, and other needs.[152] For the sake of your own security, consider accessing the National Whistleblower Center's site and other websites only from devices that are not part of your employer's network. Employees of all kinds, for their own legitimate reasons, keep separate laptops and other devices at home. If your mobile phone, for example, either has software from your employer on it or links to your employer's Wi-Fi, do not use it. If cost is an issue, consider going to a library to use a computer there, and bringing your own thumb drive or other way to save files.

In thinking about hiring a lawyer, the National Whistleblower Center is again a good place to start, and it runs a confidential attorney referral service.[153] Consider whether there may be specialized industry knowledge involved, how much experience and success a firm has had representing whistleblowers, whether the firm may help convince a state or local government to pursue the case (saving you significant money and effort), as well as the fee arrangement.[154] If a firm has more resources, it may be able to front more of the cost of your case at the beginning, and work for a contingency fee only taken from any earnings at the end.

Remember that lawyers typically bill by the hour, and be judicious with your lawyer's time. Be prepared in your initial meeting to explain the case. The lawyer will want to know who you are, where you work, what potential misconduct you observed, and what you did about it. Having detailed records (for example, a contemporaneous diary) can help make or break a case. Above all, do not lie to or mislead your lawyer. The lawyer whom you hire is your advocate, and he or she needs an accurate understanding of the case—flaws and all— to give you the best advice.

Finally, for the sake of your case, and your future, beware of compromising yourself. Companies may, for example, engage in tactics designed to keep you from reporting or to discredit your integrity. If you take "hush money," you may be implicated in the wrongdoing.[155] Remember that compliance officers and corporate counsel working for the company may not have your best interests at heart (as discussed in the chapter above), and do not take legal advice from them. Similarly, be cautious of company reporting hotlines, as they have been known to be used to tip off the wrongdoers being reported, and help the company engage in retaliation.[156] Follow the money, and document everything you can—and keep your documents away from the office, where the company will not be able to destroy them.[157]

We have not covered international whistleblowing, military service, and several other specialized whistleblowing circumstances, but for those issues, as well as others, we would recommend retaining your own lawyer who knows those areas of law. You will feel more confident with a capable advocate by your side. You are (hopefully) fighting for what is right, and for the right reasons. It is worth investing in yourself to get through this process. In addition, as mentioned above, many lawyers may not charge as the case progresses, but only recoup a percentage of the recovery in the end as their contingency fee. Find a good lawyer, and allow him or her to guide you through this process for the best results.

Know that you are doing something very important, and that we thank you for it.

13

HOW TO INSTITUTE BEST PRACTICES

Why do business leaders need to create and promote ethical environments?

The creation and promotion of ethics and compliance programs to shape business environments may arise out of necessity through legal enforcement actions, or through the threat of legal enforcement actions. (See later in this chapter on what an institutionalized compliance and ethics program looks like; Chapters 5 and 6 on the legal duties of businesspeople; Chapter 7 on corporate social responsibility; Chapter 8 on the costs to corporations and businesspeople of acting unethically; as well as Chapter 2 on the benefits of acting ethically.) But, as we have argued throughout this book, the best results for both businesses and for society are when business leaders affirmatively create and promote ethical environments, as well as advance the good of their employees and stakeholders, because they understand it to be for their own well-being.

We can make both the short-term financial case for that decision, as well as the long-term case for the company's (and businessperson's) future. We have explained the data and described the difference between ethical companies and unethical ones in the chapters above. Ultimately, your employees know whether you walk the walk, as well as talk the talk.

In thinking about ethics, 94% of U.S. workers describe it as "critical" or "important" that they work for an ethical company.[1] A typical business can lose 5% of its revenue annually to fraud.[2] Meanwhile, creating a positive, strong ethical culture can reduce ethical violations by as much as 40%.[3]

What does an appropriate compliance and ethics program look like?

There are several ways to answer this question. We start in this chapter with baseline legal expectations and methods of evaluation, and then build from there.

In terms of baseline legal expectations, prosecutors in the U.S. Department of Justice (DOJ) offer cooperation credit in sentencing to businesses that have an "effective compliance and ethics program."[4] The U.S. Sentencing Commission promulgates the Organizational Sentencing Guidelines, which are intended to influence judges, but prosecutors look to the Guidelines as well to persuade a court to accept the plea agreements they make with organizational defendants. To have an effective compliance and ethics program under the Guidelines, organizations must "(1) exercise due diligence to prevent and detect criminal conduct; and (2) otherwise promote an organizational culture that encourages ethical conduct and a commitment to compliance with the law."[5] Any such program should be "reasonably designed, implemented, and enforced so that the program is generally effective in preventing and detecting criminal conduct."[6]

Related to the need for *institutionalizing* ethical culture, which we address later in this chapter, to qualify as an effective compliance and ethics program for cooperation credit under the Guidelines, an organization must both "establish standards and procedures to prevent and detect criminal conduct," and "otherwise promote an organizational culture that encourages ethical conduct and a commitment to compliance with the law."[7] High-level organizational personnel should ensure that the company has an effective program, and "[s]pecific individual[s] within high-level personnel shall be assigned overall responsibility for the compliance and ethics program."[8]

Those individuals are to be "delegated day-to-day operational responsibility for the compliance ethics program," and "shall report periodically to high-level personnel and, as appropriate, to the [company's] governing authority" on the effectiveness of the program.[9] To carry out this operational responsibility, "such individual[s] shall be given adequate resources, appropriate authority, and direct access to the [company's] governing authority or an appropriate subgroup of the governing authority."[10] Typically, that "governing authority or appropriate subgroup of the governing authority" is the organization's board of directors.[11] (See discussion of boards of directors and oversight duty in Chapter 6.)

Moreover, it is not enough merely to *have* a compliance and ethics program in place: a company must communicate the program to its employees, and train them how to use it. As described in the Guidelines, the company "shall take reasonable steps to communicate periodically and in a practical manner its standards and procedures, and other aspects of the compliance and ethics program."[12] This effort should ensure that "the organization's compliance and ethics program is followed, including monitoring and auditing to detect criminal conduct."[13] It needs to be "evaluate[d] periodically" to determine "the effectiveness" of the program.[14] The program may also have a hotline, or other method by which an organization's employees and agents more generally can enjoy "anonymity or confidentiality" in reporting "potential or actual criminal conduct without fear of retaliation."[15]

Promotion and enforcement of a company's compliance and ethics program should be consistent throughout the organization. Prosecutors will be looking for whether (a) the organization has supported its program with "appropriate incentives to perform in accordance with the compliance and ethics program;" and (b) it has imposed "appropriate disciplinary measures for engaging in criminal conduct and [for] failing to take reasonable steps to prevent or deter criminal conduct."[16]

If there are problems with the company's compliance and ethics program, the company should be taking active measures to fix it. As the Guidelines continue: "The organization shall take reasonable steps to respond appropriately to the criminal conduct and to prevent future similar criminal conduct, including making any necessary modifications to the organization's compliance and ethics program."[17] To this end, "the organization shall periodically assess the risk of criminal conduct and shall take appropriate steps to design, implement, or modify" its program elements.[18]

The Guidelines are particularly concerned about the re-occurrence of similar misconduct despite a compliance and ethics program being in place. In fact, should such "similar misconduct" re-occur, it would "create[] doubt regarding whether the organization took reasonable steps to meet the requirement of this guideline."[19]

Under new "Factors to Consider in Meeting Requirements of the Guideline," the Guidelines elaborate that they will consider "(i) applicable industry practice or the standards called for by any applicable government regulation; (ii) the size of the organization; and (iii) similar misconduct." We briefly mentioned above what it means to have engaged in similar misconduct. Under "applicable industry practice," an "organization's failure to incorporate and follow applicable industry practice[,] or the standards called for by any applicable government regulation[,] weighs against the finding of an effective compliance and ethics program."[20]

The size of the organization matters under the Guidelines because large organizations are evaluated differently than small ones, based on their resources and sophistication. Thus, "[a] large organization shall devote more formal operations and greater resources in meeting the requirements of this guideline than shall a small organization."[21] Large organizations, however, should also "encourage small organizations (especially those that have, or seek to have, a business relationship with the large organization) to implement effective compliance and ethics programs."[22] Large organizations, for example, need to think about the effectiveness of the different compliance and ethics programs up and down their supply chain.

Small organizations have to "demonstrate the same degree of commitment to ethical conduct and compliance with the law as large organizations."[23] Given their smaller size, and potentially smaller access to resources, a "small organization may meet the requirements of this guideline with less formality and fewer resources than would be expected of large organizations."[24]

The Guidelines even contain specific suggestions for how a small organization could flexibly meet its requirement under this standard. Its board of directors (or other governing authority) could "directly manage the organization's compliance and ethics efforts."[25] The organization could "train[] employees through information staff meetings," and monitor its compliance through "regular 'walk-arounds' or continuous observation while managing the organization."[26] It could use "available personnel, rather than employing separate staff, to carry out the compliance and ethics program."[27] And it could "model[] its . . . compliance and ethics program on existing, well regarded compliance and ethics programs and best practices of similar organizations."[28]

What guidance has the DOJ given regarding its interpretation of the Organizational Sentencing Guidelines?

In June 2020, the DOJ's Criminal Division released updated guidance for its prosecutors to interpret the Organizational Sentencing Guidelines.[29] That guidance superseded previous guidance released in April 2019, and it built on the DOJ's Fraud Section's guidance from February 2017, as well as other policy statements.[30]

The DOJ's guidance, however, remains focused on three fundamental questions that continue to structure its analysis. This chapter discusses these questions in order:

First of all, "[i]s the corporation's compliance program well designed?"[31]

Second, is "the program being applied earnestly and in good faith?"[32]

Third, "[d]oes the corporation's compliance program work" in practice?[33]

Fundamental question one: Is the corporation's compliance program well designed?

To evaluate whether "the corporation's compliance program is well designed," prosecutors ask about (a) risk assessment, (b) policies and procedures, (c) training and communications, (d) the confidential reporting structure and investigation process, (e) third-party management of any such program, and (f) what happens to the program during mergers and acquisitions.[34]

In terms of (a) risk assessment, the guidance wants to know how much specific thinking the company has done, and whether it conducts periodic, data-driven reviews. Initially, "[w]hat methodology has the company used to identify, analyze, and address the particular risks that it faces?"[35] Next, "[d]oes the company devote a disproportionate amount of time to policing low-risk areas" instead of high-risk areas in which wrongdoing is more likely to occur?[36] Additionally, is its "risk assessment current and subject to periodic review?"[37] Is that "periodic review limited to a 'snapshot' in time or based on continuous access to operational data and information across functions?"[38] Indeed, has the company's review "led to updates in policies, procedures, and controls?"[39] Do the updates "account for risks discovered through misconduct or other problems with the compliance program?"[40] "Does the company really incorporate its lessons learned?"[41]

In terms of (b) policies and procedures, prosecutors are thinking about (i) design, (ii) comprehensiveness, (iii) accessibility, (iv) responsibility for operational integration, and (v) gatekeepers.[42] Evaluating the design and comprehensiveness of compliance and ethics programs makes intuitive sense, as does ensuring that employees and other have access to them. Under responsibility for operational integrity, prosecutors evaluate how "compliance policies and procedures [are] reinforced through the company's internal control systems."[43] In thinking about "gatekeepers," prosecutors consider "[w]hat, if any guidance and training has been provided to . . . those with approval authority or certification responsibilities."[44] Are they clear on "what misconduct to look for?" And, "[d]o they know when and how to escalate concerns?"

In terms of (c) training and communications, the DOJ describes "appropriately tailored training and communications" as "[a]nother hallmark of a well-designed compliance program."[45] Has the company "relayed information in a manner tailored to the audience's size, sophistication, or subject matter expertise?" Is the company's training and communications around its program "truly effective?"[46]

Factors to assess whether the company's training and communications are "truly effective" include reviewing for risk-based training (has "the company provided tailored training for high-risk and control employees?"); considering the form/content/effectiveness of the training; how the company communicates about misconduct; and the availability of guidance to employees and others.[47]

In terms of a compliance and ethics program's (d) confidential reporting structure and investigation process, prosecutors look for "an efficient and trusted mechanism by which employees can anonymously or confidentially report allegations of a breach of the company's code of conduct, company policies, or suspected or actual misconduct."[48] Does the company's "complaint-handling process include proactive measures to create a workplace atmosphere without fear of retaliation, appropriate processes for the submission of complaints, and processes to protect whistleblowers?"[49] How good are the company's processes for "handling the investigation of such complaints, including the routing of complaints to proper personnel?"[50] Is the company engaging in "timely completion of thorough investigations?"[51] And does the company conduct "appropriate follow-up and discipline" on the complaints and reports made to it?[52]

A fairly new question in the June 2020 version of the DOJ guidance is whether a company takes "measures to test whether employees are aware of the [reporting] hotline," as well as presumably other anonymous/confidential reporting mechanisms, "and feel comfortable using" them.[53] Is the company "periodically test[ing]" their "effectiveness . . . for example by tracking a report from start to finish?"[54]

In evaluating a company's confidential reporting structure and investigation process, prosecutors ask about (i) the effectiveness of the reporting mechanism; (ii) whether investigations are properly flagged ("scoped") by qualified personnel; (iii) the investigation response itself; and (iv) whether the company has invested sufficient resources in investigations, as well as tracked their results.[55]

In terms of (e) third-party relationships, prosecutors will "assess whether the company knows the business rationale for needing the third-party in the transaction, and the risks posed by third-party partners, including the third-party partners' reputations and relationships, if any, with foreign officials."[56] Prosecutors here think about (i) risk-based and integrated processes; and (ii) appropriate controls (for example, "what mechanisms exist to ensure that the contract terms specifically describe the services to be performed, that the payment terms are appropriate, that the described contractual work is performed, and that compensation is commensurate with the services rendered?").[57] The list of what prosecutors consider in this area further includes (iii) the management of relationships (such as, "How has the company [designed] the compensation and incentive structures for third parties against compliance risks?");[58] and (iv) the real actions and consequences of having the third party involved in the company's business.[59]

In terms of (f) mergers and acquisitions (M&A) of companies, prosecutors will want to know that the companies have engaged in "complete pre-acquisition due diligence," that the "compliance function [has] been integrated in the M&A process," and what the companies' processes will be "for implementing compliance policies and procedures, and conducting post-acquisition audits, at newly acquired entities."[60]

Fundamental question two: Is the program being applied earnestly and in good faith?

The DOJ's next big umbrella question is whether "the corporation's compliance program [is] adequately resourced and empowered to function effectively."[61] Here its questions revolve around the compliance and ethics program's degree of (a) "commitment by senior and middle management," (b) "autonomy and resources," and (c) "incentives and disciplinary measures."[62]

Essentially, the DOJ's concern is that "[e]ven a well-designed compliance program may be unsuccessful in practice if implementation is lax, under-resourced, or otherwise ineffective."[63] Prosecutors will probe whether a company's compliance and ethics program is merely a "paper program," or one with more teeth to support and create meaningful results.[64]

In reviewing whether there is sufficient (a) "commitment by senior and middle management" to the company's compliance and ethics program, prosecutors seek to determine whether, "[b]eyond compliance structures, policies, and procedures," the company "create[s] and foster[s] a culture of ethics and compliance with the law at all levels of the company."[65] In order to be effective, a company's compliance and ethics program requires "a high-level commitment by the company leadership to implement a culture of compliance from the middle and the top."[66]

A company's "top leaders"—typically its board of directors and executives—"set the tone for the rest of the company."[67] Have the company's senior managers, for example, "clearly articulated the company's ethical standards, conveyed and disseminated them in clear and unambiguous terms, and demonstrated rigorous adherence by example?"[68]

The DOJ is focusing more attention on the role of middle managers as well. Prosecutors look to how "middle management, in turn, have reinforced those standards and encouraged employees to abide by them."[69] Thus, prosecutors are not only interested in "conduct at the top," but they also look for "shared commitment" within the ranks of the company, and "oversight" to ensure that the correct actions are taken to enforce compliance and ethics throughout the company. For example, not only "what actions have . . . senior leaders"—but also "middle management stakeholders" such as "business and operational managers, finance, procurement, legal, [and] human resources"—"taken to demonstrate their commitment to compliance?"[70] "Have they persisted in that commitment in the face of competing interests or business objectives?"[71]

In considering the (b) autonomy and resources of a company's compliance and ethics program, prosecutors evaluate whether "those charged with a compliance program's day-to-day oversight" can "act with adequate authority and stature."[72] For example, do those within the compliance program have (1) "sufficient seniority within the organization; (2) sufficient resources, namely staff to effectively undertake the requisite auditing, documentation, and analysis; and (3) sufficient autonomy from management, such as direct access to the board of directors or [to] the board's audit committee?"[73]

In analyzing a compliance and ethics program's autonomy and resources, prosecutors also look to its (i) structure, including where it is housed, and what its lines of reporting are; (ii) the seniority of its staff and the program's stature within the company; (iii) the experience and qualifications of its personnel; (iv) the program's funding and resources; (v) its access to data; (vi) its autonomy and guarantees of independence; and (vii) how much the company may have outsourced its compliance functions to other firms or entities.[74]

To continue their evaluation of whether a corporation's compliance program is adequately resourced and empowered to function effectively, prosecutors examine its (c) incentives and disciplinary measures.[75] They look for whether, and to what extent, "the company's communications convey to its employees that unethical conduct will not be tolerated and will bring swift consequences, regardless of the position or the title of the employee who engages in the conduct."[76] Subparts to this analysis involve the company's human resources process ("Who participates in making disciplinary decisions, including for the type of misconduct at issue?"), whether the program is fairly and consistently applied across the organization, and the impact of the company's incentive system—especially "the implications of its incentives and rewards on compliance."[77]

Fundamental question three: Does the corporation's compliance program work in practice?

The DOJ's final guidance umbrella question is whether "the corporation's compliance system work[s] in practice."[78] The DOJ's separate Principles of Federal Prosecution of Business Organizations requires prosecutors to assess both "the adequacy and effectiveness of the corporation's compliance program *at the time of the offense*, as well as at the time of a charging decision."[79] The same document in context looks to, among other things, (1) "the nature and seriousness of the [company's] offense, including the risk of harm to the public, and applicable policies and priorities, if any governing the prosecution of corporations for particular categories of crime;" (2) "the pervasiveness of wrongdoing within the corporation, including the complicity in, or the condoning of, the wrong-doing by corporate management;" (3) the corporation's history of similar misconduct, including prior criminal, civil, and reg-ulatory enforcement actions against it;" (4) "the corporation's willingness to cooperate, including as to potential wrong-doing by its agents;" (5) "the adequacy and effectiveness of the corporation's compliance program at the time of the of-fense, as well as at the time of the charging decision;" (6) "the corporation's timely and voluntary disclosure of wrongdoing;" (7) "the corporation's remedial actions, including, but not lim-ited to, any efforts to implement an adequate and effective cor-porate compliance program[,] or to improve an existing one, to replace responsible management, to discipline or terminate wrongdoers, or to pay restitution."[80]

In seeking to answer fundamental question three—whether the corporation's compliance and ethics program works in practice—the DOJ combines these principles to consider how the company has responded and adapted to its problems. Has, for example, the company undertaken "an adequate and honest root analysis to understand both what contributed to the misconduct[,] and the degree of remediation needed to prevent similar events in the future?"[81]

DOJ's guidance to prosecutors further inquires whether the company has engaged in (a) "continuous improvement, periodic testing, and review," (b) a thorough and effective in-vestigation of the misconduct; and (c) a thoughtful root-cause analysis to remediate the underlying misconduct.[82]

To evaluate the quality of a company's (a) "continuous im-provement, periodic testing, and review" of its program, the DOJ considers the quality of the company's internal program audits, how control testing is performed, whether the com-pany continually evolves its updates, and how it measures the effectiveness of its attempts to create a "culture of compli-ance."[83] Returning to a renewed emphasis on the participation of middle management, as well as top management, the DOJ asks whether the company "seek[s] input from all levels of employees to determine whether they perceive senior and middle management's commitment to compliance."[84] Then, "[w]hat steps has the company taken in response to its measurement of the compliance culture?"[85]

In determining whether a company (b) conducts thorough and effective investigations of misconduct, the DOJ wants to know there is "a well-functioning and appropriately funded mechanism for the timely and thorough investigations of any allegations or suspicious misconduct by the company, its employees, or agents."[86] Moreover, such an "effective investigations structure will also have an established means of documenting the company's response, including any disciplinary or remediation measures taken."[87] Finally, the DOJ wants to know "[h]ow high up in the company do investigative findings go?"[88]

Finally, in examining a company's analysis for (c) its thoughtfulness and its effectiveness in remediating underlying misconduct, prosecutors ask about the strength of the company's reflections and changes based on its (i) root-cause analysis; (ii) remediation of prior weaknesses; (iii) improvement of payment systems; (iv) quality of vendor management; (v) what prior indications of misconduct there may have been, and why they may have been missed; (vi) what specific remedial measures the company took to reduce the risk of misconduct reoccurring; and (vii) how it imposed accountability.[89]

In that last category of accountability, prosecutors ask "[w]hat disciplinary actions did the company take in response to the misconduct[,] and were they timely?"[90] Specifically, "[w]ere managers held accountable for misconduct that occurred under their supervision?"[91]

What is the value of the DOJ's approach?

In sum, the breadth and scope of the DOJ's structural analysis should give businesses and businesspeople a better picture of what compliance and ethics programs should do, and how they should operate. It should also give businesses and businesspeople ideas about how to organize, evaluate, and improve their existing programs. Our next sections additionally discuss the principles and practices of high-quality compliance and ethics programs, why such programs need to be *institutionalized*, what some best practices are, and why they work.

What are other principles and practices to create high-quality compliance and ethics programs?

Some of the best information on how to create successful, high-quality compliance and ethics programs comes from the Ethics & Compliance Initiative (ECI), a group interested in best practices that brings together compliance and ethics practitioners with academics to further compliance and ethics.[92] According to ECI, "[e]volving legal and professional standards are raising the bar for compliance programs; there is a growing expectation that they must do more than prevent and detect misconduct—they must positively incentivize ethical conduct."[93] Companies establishing such programs must first set realistic goals, they should consider using structural incentives such as nudges to reach these goals, and they should articulate a code of conduct or ethics, as discussed below.

How does a company set realistic goals for its compliance and ethics program?

We will discuss setting goals and designing systems further in this chapter, but a word here first about the phenomenon of "Goals Gone Wild" as it applies to compliance and ethics.[94] In thinking about setting realistic goals that will help engage company leaders, management, and other members of an organization down to its lowest-level employees, we need to ensure that the setting of goals is realistic and includes everyone. As research warns, "[d]espite their potential benefits, incentive programs can pose risks to consumers, especially when they create an unrealistic culture of high-pressure targets."[95] Unachievable goals "generate pressure, fraud, and other misconduct."[96] Meanwhile, "communicated correctly," stretch objectives "can succeed in getting teams to achieve what even they did not believe [that] they could."[97]

In setting goals for a company, think about:

1. Are the goals too specific?
2. Are the goals too challenging?
3. Who sets the goals?
4. Is the time horizon appropriate?
5. How might these goals influence risk taking?
6. How might the goals, in fact, motivative unethical behavior? (Remember that the mis-framing and implementation of goals can backfire, and *create* more unethical behavior. (See more in Chapter 4 on science, and Chapter 10 on leadership.).)
7. Can the goals be idiosyncratically tailored for individual abilities and circumstances while preserving fairness?
8. How will the goals influence our organization's culture?
9. Are individuals within our organization intrinsically motivated? How so? Are we harnessing or interfering with their best motivations? and
10. What are the most appropriate forms for goals (such as performance goals or learning-based goals) to reach where we want to be as an organization?[98]

In setting goals and a vision for the company, we are both outright directing, as well as "nudging" human behavior. Goals inform people within our organizations to what behavior they should aspire, as well as what behavior they should expect of others. To have a massive disconnect between a program's words and actions, meanwhile, is actually to create more damage to an organization's culture than not to have attempted to create the program at all. Employees are highly sensitive to hypocrisy. If the program is not "lived" within the company, the employees will know it, and behave accordingly.

So think about articulating a broad, sweeping, and inspiring vision for your company. But then also do the hard work of figuring out how you're going to stand by it, and make it a lived reality for all involved.

As now-classic research suggests,[99] some additional things to remember in how goals are lived should be that:

- A goal should function as "a compass, not a GPS,"[100] meaning that we have to allow employees flexibility in making course corrections as they proceed, in order to arrive where we've asked them to go. In addition, goals can act as "mental blinders that keep us from evaluating the ethicality of our behavior."[101] We may find ourselves "acting in unethical ways" without even consciously knowing it, unless the goal gives us space and permission to consider its ethical implications.[102]
- Do not "punish employees for not meeting goals."[103] If you set reaching goals to be the end-all and be-all, you are inviting people to cheat to get to them. Remember that the goal also may not be realistic, and that the company may have to take steps to invest in more training, or other components of success, to reach the goal. In addition, especially when financial incentives, or threats of job loss, are on the line, people will engage in riskier and riskier behavior. (This point is closely related to the endowment effect—see generally Chapters 2 and 4—which holds that we will incur far more risks to avoid a loss than to achieve a gain.) Risky behavior, and especially repeated risky behavior, can often result in ethical violations.

- "Monitor both the 'what' and the 'how.'"[104] Goals should include expectations that employees are following ethical *processes*, not solely being judged by numerical results. Moreover, as discussed in Chapters 3, 4, and 10, ethical thinking takes time, and space, as well as mental and emotional energy. Thus, we are more likely to engage in ethical mistakes when we are tired, hungry, pressed for time, or otherwise depleted. When we single-mindedly strive to reach a goal, we may be putting pressure on our cognitive and other resources in a way that can make ethical violations more likely unless we are on the lookout for them as well.
- Do not merely "manage by numbers."[105] Remember that you are managing human beings. Numbers may not be able to capture much of what is most valuable about human contributions until they are gone, such as employee loyalty, ethical engagement, respect, morale, creativity, team cohesion, and even pleasure in work.
- Tap into employees' intrinsic motivations. Positive methods of self-motivating employees include excitement about, and commitment to, the purpose of their work, making their work "more enjoyable," as well as "offering opportunities for task improvement and advancement in the organization."[106]

A genuine, well-designed compliance and ethics systems pays dividends.[107] It can translate directly into profit, productivity, and prestige. Why does this matter? First, a company can live or die by its brand. Second, investing in ethics creates long-term, value-added benefits for shareholders and other stakeholders more broadly. (See Chapter 7 for definitions of an organization's stakeholders.) In a study comparing company data from 1984 to 2011, such companies beat both their peers' long-run stock returns, as well as their industry's benchmarks for employee satisfaction, by 2.3% to 3.8%.[108] Those numbers generate interest from the investment community too, as evidenced by its emphasis on good corporate governance, as well as other expressions of ethical standards. (See Chapter 7 for more statistics on the growth of this market, and emphasis on these qualities.)

How do companies reach these numbers? They use their compliance and ethics programs in specific ways with specific goals. They draw distinctions between achieving a baseline of compliance, and really aspiring to ethical behavior. As explained by Ethical Systems, an academic and practitioner cooperative out of New York University's Stern School of Business, with ethics "you will get compliance[,] but with compliance you may not get ethics."[109] Don't envision your compliance system as merely asking people to "follow the rules."[110] If you take the approach of encouraging people instead to find ways to do what is *right*, instead of merely what they can get away with, your company will be far stronger, and you will achieve much more robust results.

Similarly, use your investment in compliance and ethics to promote a long-term perspective. Short-term thinking yields short-term results, with potentially destructive long-term consequences. For example, research demonstrates that focusing a company on short-term profits for shareholders initially boosts financial performance, but it then damages a firm's goodwill with customers and employees—the parties who you need to stick around, both to make profits year after year, and to grow. One of this book's authors has elsewhere described this short-term approach as "fishing with dynamite."[111] Sure, you yield a lot of fish the first time that you do it, but then you destroy the fishing grounds, the local economy, and the entire environment upon which you are dependent for resources and to live.

Invest in the process of creating and implementing your compliance and ethics program, and show your work.[112] Investing in efforts to promote ethics, and highlighting those investments to both internal and external audiences, demonstrates to members of your organization and others that you value the program. This further helps employees and others to understand that the program is to be taken seriously, to engage with it, and to reinforce the company's culture of abiding by it.

Think about the composition, placement, and dedication of your compliance and ethics team. As we have talked about above, the DOJ will look to these indicators of how seriously the company takes its commitment to compliance and ethics. But so will your employees and others. There should be a dedicated compliance and ethics team (or teams) that cut across the entire company, and foster collaboration at all levels to influence its culture. That team, or teams, needs to be sufficiently well-resourced, independent, and well-respected to do its job effectively. Not only is the DOJ looking to see whether the program is a "paper program," but all the members of your organization are too. Show them with both words and actions that it has real meaning and power.

How should companies use structural behavioral incentives such as nudges?

The smartest programs harness nudges in addition to other structural incentives to enforce compliance and ethics. A "nudge" is "a small change in [the] environment that has meaningful impact on the decisions [that] we make."[113] To nudge as a concept was popularized by behavioral economist Richard Thaler and legal scholar Cass Sunstein in their book by the same name,[114] and nudges are consciously incorporated into programs either to encourage or discourage certain behaviors. The key to keeping a nudge from becoming coercive is that it must continue to preserve individuals' meaningful freedom of choice.[115] But its power is that individuals may not always be aware of how, and when, nudges are being used; to them, changes in the program's construction can be seamless, presenting the obvious choice to do the right thing, in the right way, at the right time. If you can make that user and corporate experience a reality, you have created a powerfully effective and internalized compliance and ethics program.

Why do nudges matter and work so well, especially in the implementation of compliance and ethics programs? As discussed in earlier chapters, behavioral science shows that we tend to make unethical decisions particularly (1) when we fall prey to cognitive biases; (2) when we lack the self-control to do what we know that we should do (and we are particularly adept as a species at rationalizing and self-justifying our actions, even when we know that they are wrong); and (3) when we allow the wrong type of destructive social norms to influence our decisions. (See Chapter 4 on behavioral science, Chapter 9 on common ethical traps in business, and Chapter 10 on leadership for more on these topics.)

Because no amount of formal compliance and ethics training can truly dislodge these human behavioral tendencies, we need to use other tools also to influence behavior. Good designers and administrators of compliance and ethics programs will think about nudging as "choice architects" to help people make their way through systems, and to tweak users' experience with those environments. The end result is to "increase [a] decision-maker's odds of doing the right thing" in spite of the influence of our other, perhaps negative, behavioral tendencies.[116]

How do we use nudges effectively in compliance and ethics programs? Here, we need to know (1) when to nudge; (2) how to nudge; and (3) how to combine nudges with other incentives. First, when should we nudge?

Nudges can be most effective when people have "trouble identifying that they are facing an ethical dilemma or [in] applying guiding principles learned through training, practice, and experience."[117] Nudges can also fill in for us when we have a hard time doing what's right, even when we know what that should be. For example, human beings are "especially tempted by any decisions that offer[] immediate benefits and delayed costs."[118] If we can intervene in those moments to keep people on-track to do the right thing, we will have won much of the default battle for ethical behavior.

Second, in terms of how to nudge, the best nudges can illuminate the path of least resistance in triggering our psychology—and make sure that path is the ethical one. For example, research has shown that how we frame issues deeply affects the results that we achieve. Thus, if we ask participants to sign at the top of a form *before they fill it out* that they will answer all the following questions truthfully, we receive far more truthful answers than if we wait for such a signature at the bottom of the form. Expanding this concept further, if we trigger people to think of problems in the moment as ethical problems *first*, rather than merely as matters of business necessity or cost-benefit analysis to unknown persons, we achieve far more ethical results. (See Chapters 3 and 4 for more on posing moral questions and ethical framing.)

In combining nudges with other incentives, we need to think about whether existing incentives complement—or are at cross-purposes—with how we are trying to nudge behavior toward ethical outcomes. Important questions to ask here include:

- Will individuals or departments receive bonuses or other rewards for results despite engaging in unethical behavior? As we will see later in the data collected by the ECI, this has a large statistical impact on employee behavior throughout the company, including whether employees believe that it is safe to report wrongdoing.
- Are your employees under other pressures to reach results regardless of whether they need to bend the rules to do so? This is another factor that seems to bear directly on whether employees witness, and then report, unethical behavior within the company. (See more about pressure and incentive effects in Chapters 4, 9, and 10.) The fact that the company's incentive system is perceived as putting pressure on employees to bend the rules can be interpreted by employees as the company condoning, if not actively encouraging, wrongdoing.

In addition, remember in changing the incentives within a company that such changes may grant other factors more power, sometimes with unintended consequences. The systems you create have to work together as an integrated whole. As Ethical Systems concludes, "[d]on't just quietly implement a new system; make sure [that] employees have a clear understanding of how an incentive affects them, and consider nudges that can be integrated to steer [their] decision making" and improve your system.[119]

Another important factor to consider in designing compliance and ethics systems is encouraging a self-reinforcing "speak-up culture." This discussion is so important that we dedicate an entire later section of this chapter to what it means and how to implement it.

What should an effective code of conduct or ethics include?

We turn next to the more nuts-and-bolts details of how to institute an effective compliance and ethics program. First, your organization should have an organizational code of conduct, which is sometimes also called a code of ethics. Many organizations may be legally mandated to have such a code of conduct (or the equivalent if you are a public company), but every organization *should* have one. It helps the organization to articulate and crystalize its thinking on ethical issues. As ECI notes, such a code "has value as both an internal guideline and an external statement of corporate values and commitments."[120]

Internally, well-considered, well-written, and properly-invested-in codes of conduct clarify an organization's missions, values, and principles. They define appropriate and expected standards of conduct. They become central guides and references for employees to consult in day-to-day decision-making. Such codes can also serve as benchmarks against which the company's behavior can be evaluated, and toward which it can be adjusted.

Externally, codes serve legal compliance, marketing, and risk-management purposes. Legislation such as the Sarbanes–Oxley Act of 2002 requires companies to adopt codes of conduct, or to explain and justify why they have not.[121] In terms of marketing, codes can become the public face of the company, and define what it stands for relative to its competitors.[122] For risk-management purposes, as noted more extensively above, the DOJ looks to a company's code to see what the company says about itself, and then whether it has instituted an effective compliance program to keep its behavior in line with its legal obligations and values.

What topics do codes of conduct cover? The ECI provides common code topics grouped by general subject matter. Typically, they discuss compliance, integrity, and anti-corruption; conflicts of interest; employee, client, and vendor information; employment practices; environmental issues; ethics and compliance resources; Internet, social networking, and social media use; and relationships with third parties, including procurement and negotiating contracts.[123]

Under compliance, integrity, and anti-corruption, codes often address the "[a]ccuracy of corporate finances and financial reporting," the keeping of "[e]mployee records and expense reports," prohibitions against bribes, and the terms of political contributions.[124] The conflicts of interest topics may include gifts and gratuities, political activity, outside employment, relationships with family members, and the disclosure of financial interests.

Possibly the largest number of code topics involve employment practices, in which companies often address prohibitions against workplace harassment; the need for equal opportunities, diversity, and the fair treatment of staff; work–life balance; measures against discrimination; the following of fair-labor practices; intolerance for drug or alcohol abuse; what constitutes the appropriate use of organizational property and resources; the proper exercise of authority to make decisions; what roles there are for employee volunteer activities; rules around romantic relationships with co-workers, supervisors, or subordinates; and how the organization's incentive and recognition systems operate.

Specifically under ethics and compliance resources, codes of conduct often describe the availability of an ethics advice helpline; what reporting procedures are in place; whether the company has an anonymous or confidential reporting hotline; how investigations are to be conducted; the company's anti-retaliation policy and protections for employees and others who report; and well as the company's commitment to accountability and to disciplining violators of its policies.

Simply to address this issue now, some organizations are reluctant to enforce the boundaries of interpersonal relationships in their compliance and ethics programs. As one Chief Ethics Officer explains, these can seem like "messy" issues of "less importance" than primarily "issues of integrity such as fraud or corruption." But, as the data show, this attitude is both "inappropriate and a mistake: how a company respects individuals[,] and addresses these types of [interpersonal] issues," such as discrimination, harassment, and bullying, "often has a major impact on the overall ethical climate. Sincerity and courage are key."[125]

As we shall see throughout the following discussions in this chapter, these "messy" issues are often intertwined with—and key indicators for—other compliance and ethics problems within the organization. They also have a large psychological impact on employees' well-being and commitment to the company. Employees' concerns about a respectful workplace in which they want to invest, and in which they will trust their employer to report wrongdoing internally first, revolve around the prevention of harassment and bullying, as well as the issues we will talk about a couple of segments below: promoting a "speak-up" culture and preventing retaliation against employees who report.[126]

What other elements should a comprehensive compliance and ethics program contain?

According to the ECI, in addition to a code of conduct or its equivalent, a comprehensive compliance and ethics program should include six basic elements. These elements are (1) "written standards of ethical workplace conduct" that flesh out the code of conduct; (2) "training on the standards;" (3) "company resources that provide advice about ethics issues," such as an ethics advice helpline mentioned above; (4) "a means to report potential violations confidentially or anonymously," which could mean the same hotline; (5) "performance evaluations of ethical conduct;" and (6) appropriate "systems to discipline violations."[127]

An *effective* compliance and ethics program will include all of the above, as well as an emphasis, as the DOJ has been looking for, on making sure that the program's standards are lived. The ECI defines an effective program as a "vital, living part[] of [the] company's ethos and way of doing business that ensures [that] ethical conduct is rewarded and that employees know how to[,] and feel supported in their efforts to[,] uphold ethic[al] standards in their work" and the life of the company.[128] To gauge the health of a compliance and ethics program, ECI measures (1) the freedom of employees at all levels to "question management without fear;" (2) what rewards exist within the company "for following ethic[al] standards;" (3) whether the company is careful not to reward "questionable practices, even if they produce good [short-term] results for the company;" (4) whether and how the company is providing "positive feedback for ethical conduct;" (5) how prepared (and willing) employees are to address misconduct; and (6) how willing employees are to seek ethical advice on a regular basis, and, we would add, recognize when they need it.[129]

Ultimately, as we have discussed before, and to which we will return, companies are trying to create an ethical culture. Once an ethical culture is in place, the company experiences far fewer violations, greater profitability and commitment from employees, and its effects are easier to maintain. The ECI defines the success of an ethical culture as the "extent to which employees at all levels are committed to doing what is right[,] and successfully upholding values and standards." Permeating every level of the company, an established ethical culture "includes ethical leadership (tone at the top)[,] supervisor reinforcement of ethical behavior[,] and peer commitment to support" doing what is right.[130]

What are the practices of the most effective compliance and ethics programs?

In 2016, the ECI published a blue-ribbon panel report entitled "Principles and Practices of High-Quality Ethics and Compliance Programs."[131] Since then, the ECI and its various working groups have attempted to dial in the measurement of these principles and practices to evaluate the health of programs within organizations.

The ECI has consistently found five hallmarks of high-quality compliance and ethics practices that it articulates as "principles." The five principles are:

- **Principle 1: Strategy.** These organizations make compliance and ethics "central to business strategy."[132]
- **Principle 2: Risk Management.** The organizations "identif[y], own[], manage[,] and mitigate[]" their compliance and ethics risks.[133]
- **Principle 3: Culture.** "Leaders at all levels across the organization build and sustain a culture of integrity."[134]
- **Principle 4: Speaking Up.** The "organization encourages, protects[,] and values the reporting of concerns and suspected wrongdoing."[135]
- **Principle 5: Accountability.** The "organization takes [appropriate] action[s] and holds itself accountable when wrongdoing occurs."[136]

The implementation of each of these principles breaks down into five levels, from "underdeveloped," through "adapting," "defining," "managing," and finally, "optimizing."[137]

Applying Principle 1, compliance and ethics programs central to business strategy are "optimizing" when they follow best practices and lead the field externally. What does this look like? It looks a lot like the updated DOJ guidance, but it adds the condition that the company is proud enough of its compliance and ethics program to market itself as a leader in its field on this effort for other organizations. According to the ECI, (a) these programs are "integrated with business and strategic objectives;" (b) they have "the resources and access needed to ensure proper integration" into all of a company's operations, and "an independent voice" to reach the company's leaders; (c) they are "consistent participant[s]" in the company's "key strategic discussions;" (d) they are "continuously improved through leadership, innovation[,] and feedback loops;" (e) the boards of their organizations are knowledgeable about the programs, and "actively monitor" their implementation; and (f) their organizations share their "learning externally to positively influence other organizations toward responsible practices and a commitment to integrity."[138]

Under Principle 2, what do the best compliance and ethics programs look like that identify, own, manage, and mitigate risk? Here they look almost entirely like the description of best qualities from the DOJ. That's not a surprise: the major risks that these programs are trying to manage and mitigate come from the DOJ, and similar sources of law enforcement. These best programs are (a) "calibrated to key risk areas identified through a robust, continuous risk assessment process;" (b) the leaders across their organizations "are assigned responsibility for the ongoing identification and mitigation of risks that are endemic to their operations;" (c) their organizations "recognize[] and reward[] self-assessment, early issue[-]spotting[,] and prompt remediation of compliance gaps;" (d) the health of these programs, as well as the overall health of compliance and ethics within the organization, "are regularly monitored as risk areas;" (e) within their organizations, employees are given "guidance and support for handling key risks" as appropriate for their positions; and (f) their organizations maintain "rigorous third-party due diligence processes that screen for integrity."[139]

Under Principle 3, what do the best programs look like that build and sustain a culture of integrity? Here there is an emphasis on how broadly and pervasively the program is understood, adopted, endorsed, and acted upon at all levels of the company. At the top, (a) "[l]eaders are expected and incentivized to personally act with integrity[,] and are held accountable when they are not."[140] Across these organizations, leaders at all levels (b) "own and are accountable for building a strong ethical culture."[141] These organizations' (c) "[v]alues and standards are communicated effectively through many channels."[142] And employees throughout these organizations are (d) "supported and expected to act in line with organizational values[,] and are held accountable if they are not."[143]

Under Principle 4, programs in organizations that encourage, protect, and value the reporting of concerns and suspected wrongdoing have six main features. These primarily focus on helping employees feel able and empowered to report wrongdoing around them without fearing consequences. Such organizations' leaders (a) "create an environment where employees are prepared and empowered to raise concerns," and they provide "resources . . . to support employees in ethical decision-making."[144] These organizations demonstrate that they (b) "respect[] all employees' rights to report to governmental authorities;" (c) they "provide[] a broad and varied number of reporting avenues, each with effective tracking for escalation and response of significant matters;" (d) they "treat[] all reporters the same—with consistency and fairness—throughout the entire process;" and (e) they "communicate[] directly with individual reporters[,] and more broadly with all employees[,] when cases are closed."[145]

These organizations also develop and maintain (f) "proactive process[es] . . . to prevent retaliation, including awareness training for leaders, monitoring of employee reporters[,] and demonstrated consequences for conduct that is inconsistent with the organization's values, code of conduct and/ or policies."[146]

It is also now standard practice for almost all organizations to allow individuals who report observed misconduct to remain "anonymous if they so desire, or they may choose to self-identify, upon which they are provided confidentiality to the fullest extent possible."[147] Employees are far more comfortable reporting if they can remain anonymous, and when they can trust the program to protect their identities.

Under Principle 5, what do the best programs look like in organizations that take action and hold themselves accountable when wrongdoing occurs? Here programs are evaluated for the consistency of their investigative processes, whether there is good communication about investigations, and whether the organizations properly report verified misconduct externally to governmental and other authorities. In these organizations, (a) the organizations "regularly communicate[] that individuals who violate[] organizational standards or the law will be disciplined;" and (b) "disciplinary action is consistently taken when violations are substantiated."[148] Also, (c) they "maintain[] investigative excellence;" (d) their "[s]ystems for escalation and response are well developed and regularly tested, [as well as their] leaders . . . held accountable for compliance;" and (e) they make their appropriate disclosures to "regulatory or other government authorities."[149]

Why does institutionalizing ethical practices matter?

Institutionalizing ethical practices matters because you cannot be everywhere at all times. You are needed to set and enforce the tone, but you ultimately want the conduct you desire to be self-reinforcing. Think of this as similar to the problem of people speeding on the freeway—there will never be enough police officers to catch and ticket everyone who speeds. So there have to be basic expectations, and a cultural norm, around speed limits and acceptable behavior when acting in social environments, such as when you hold other people's lives in your hands by driving a car.

"Culture" is "the pattern of basic assumptions that a group has invented, discovered, or developed to cope with its problems of external adaptions or internal integration that have worked well[,] and are taught to new members as the way to perceive, think, feel, and behave."[150] Companies, as distinct groups, create their own cultures both to adapt to external forces (social expectations, regulations, etc.), and to enable internal integration (a sense of belonging, a common purpose among employees, etc.). Culture helps us define who we are, and decide what we stand for, and what we do not. You are witnessing culture in those everyday moments, large and small, from when employees refuse to laugh at an inappropriate joke told at the water cooler, to whether an employee calls a whistleblower hotline (internal or external) about behavior that he or she witnesses from his or her boss.

As the leader of a company, you want to know about these things. But you also need each member of your company to react in the right way when such situations happen. Allowing problems to fester because there is poor management (often accompanied by unethical behavior—see, for example, Chapters 9 (major ethical traps in modern business) and 12 (why people are sometimes pushed to whistleblowing options)) means that your company could take an unexpected hit of many millions of dollars. Moreover, employees who are busy dealing with problem bosses (the number-one reason why people leave their jobs—see Chapter 10), are not investing their time, energy, and best creative potential in growing your business, and in paving the way for your future to commercialize their innovations and investments.

The rot of a company starts from the inside. And the lack of affirmative, positive ethical culture allows that rot to spread. Institutionalizing ethical practices puts something far more healthy into the structure of the organization instead. Culture will exist whether or not you manage it. Managing it to affirmatively institute positive ethical practices provides you and your company a competitive advantage in harnessing your best resources, and in incurring the fewest self-imposed losses.

It would be spectacularly short-sighted not to harness the number-one influencer of human behavior and decisions—culture—to your benefit.[151] We insist that the culture be one of positive ethics because, among many other reasons, this approach works so much better than mere intimidation. As we will see from further examples of best practices toward the end of this chapter, companies that issue (and enforce!) explicit, comprehensive policies declaring company *values*, that instruct employees on how to properly handle suspected ethical violations, and assure non-retaliation for reporting, have the best results.[152] These steps help businesses both to reduce their overall number of ethical violations, and to have an easier time dealing with ethical issues when they do arise.

Moreover, once institutionalized, positive ethical practices help steer a company to a positive ethical reputation, which pays its own dividends in the long run. (See Chapter 2 on the benefits of acting ethically.) Not only will such a company be easier to manage (not veering from one internal crisis to the next), but employees, regulators, customers, and others are far more likely to trust you, and to give you the benefit of the doubt when you do mess up. (See Chapters 2 (reputational benefits for ethical behavior), 8 (reputational penalties for unethical behavior), and 15 (cooperating with authorities and receiving the benefits of having a strong compliance and ethics system in place).)

Statistics from the ECI's quantitative surveys bear out this approach.[153] Globally, the rates of observed misconduct by employees in organizations by type of misconduct are

27% observing conflicts of interest; 25% observing abusive behaviors; 24% observing violations of health and/or safety regulations; 19% observing corruptions; 16% observing discrimination; and 13% observing sexual harassment.[154]

The definitions of these types of misconduct are fairly intuitive. In "conflicts of interest," "decisions or actions . . . benefit the employee/friends/family over the interests" of the organization.[155] "Abusive behaviors" are behaviors that are "abusive, intimidating, or [that] create[] a hostile work environment."[156] "Violations of health and/or safety regulations" are self-explanatory. "Corruption" is the "abuse of entrusted power for private gain."[157] "Discrimination" results from "actions against employees based on race, sex, age, religion, sexual orientation, or similar categories."[158] "Sexual harassment" includes "unwelcome sexual advances, requests for sexual favors, other verbal or physical harassment of a sexual nature and/or offensive remarks about the person's sex."[159]

Across the globe, according to 2019 numbers, 45% of employees observed misconduct and 34% of them did not report it.[160] Interestingly, although 43% of Europeans observed misconduct, 41% of them did not report it.[161] Fifty percent of North-American employees observed misconduct, and 31% of them did not report it.[162] In Africa & the Middle East, as well as in South America, 60% of employees observed misconduct.[163] In Africa & the Middle East, 23% of them did not report it.[164] In South America, 31% of them did not report it.[165]

When companies invest properly in their organizational ethical cultural commitments, results follow to lower these numbers and increase reporting rates. In companies with the most effective compliance and ethics programs, more than 8 in 10 (84%) workers report misconduct, versus merely 33% in organizations with weak or non-existent programs.[166]

Specifically, misconduct across problem areas is more likely to be reported in organizations in which employees perceive the business to have a strong commitment to organizational values and leadership. Again, remember that we want misconduct, when it occurs, to be *reported* so that compliance and ethics programs can address it, and management knows to reduce the underlying misconduct being reported.

In Asia, where there were strong organizational ethical commitments, only 16% of abusive behaviors, 16% of health and/or safety violations, and 25% of conflicts of interest were not reported; versus where organizational commitment was weak, 68% of abusive behaviors, 59% of health and/or safety violations, and 66% of conflicts of interest were not reported.[167] These are increases in raw percentages of 52%, 43%, and 41% respectively, solely from this change in perception of ethical commitment inside the organization. In North America, where there was strong organizational ethical commitment, 26% of abusive behavior, 28% of health and/or safety violations, and 36% of conflicts of interest were not reported; versus where organizational commitment was weak, 59% of abusive behavior, 54% of health and/or safety violations, and 74% of conflicts of interest were not reported.[168] These are increases in raw reporting percentages of 33%, 26%, and 38% respectively.

Not only are employees in companies with a strong compliance and ethics culture more likely to report the misconduct that they observe, but the misconduct itself is less likely to occur. In strong organizational ethical cultures versus weak cultures, for example, employees are 38% less likely to observe Foreign Corrupt Practices Act (FCPA) violations, 76% less likely to observe Federal Claims Act (FCA) violations, and 65% less likely to observe other white collar crimes.[169]

If company cultures change not to pressure employees to bend rules, the results are similarly dramatic. Globally, one in five employees feels pressure from his or her organization to compromise ethical standards.[170] As such pressure increases, misconduct rises. Brazilian employees report the most such pressure at 47%.[171] They are followed by employees in India (40%); Turkey (38%); the U.A.E. and Russia (both 33%); France (30%); Indonesia (28%); Italy (24%); the U.K., U.S., Germany, and South Korea (each at 22%); then China and South Africa (both at 20%).[172] The best countries in terms of organizations not pressuring employees to bend rules are Spain (10%), then Mexico (13%), Japan (15%), and Argentina (18%).[173]

Unsurprisingly, employees who feel pressure to compromise ethical standards are twice as likely also to report that they have witnessed their organizations reward, rather than punish, unethical business practices (38% versus 17%).[174] They are also more likely to have been through at least one major recent organizational change, in which the company's compliance and ethics systems presumably became weaker (32% versus 14%).[175] (See Chapter 14 for more on the impact of frequent organizational changes.)

The stronger a company's compliance and ethics program, the less that employees report that they feel pressure to bend the rules. In 2019, when their company had a strong program, only 19% of employees around the globe reported that they felt pressure to compromise their organization's ethical standards, policies, or the law, versus 50% when the program was weak.[176]

Why are reporting rates so key? First, remember that having employees report internally allows companies to better uncover and address wrongdoing in its earliest stages, before employees feel forced to go to outside authorities and further repercussions result. (See also Chapter 12 on whistleblowing.) Second, reporting rates, and employees' belief that the company *will do the right thing when they report* (a closely related indicator that feeds into reporting rates), both say a lot about the health of a company's culture and its organizational system. Third, companies need an accurate look at this data to improve their compliance and ethics systems, and, as noted above, to receive cooperation credit under the DOJ Guidelines.

Finally, as mentioned above, companies with strong compliance and ethics systems are easier to run. In programs with the most effective compliance and ethics programs, when workers do not report after observing misconduct, it is usually "because the problem has already been taken care of either by themselves or another employee."[177] Thus, in companies with the strongest compliance and ethics programs, 97% of observed misconduct is either reported to the program, or taken care of by employees, which leaves the organization with much smaller potential exposure to merely 3% of probable misconduct.[178]

Moreover, with a strong compliance and ethics program, you are significantly more likely to have employees who want to work at the organization and feel committed to it. When asked whether they wanted to stay at their organizations five years or longer, around the globe, 64% of employees wanted to stay when their organizations had a strong commitment to ethics, versus 38% of employees when the organization's commitment was weak.[179] (See Chapters 2, 4, 8, and 10 on why employees want to work for ethical companies, and also how much of a pay cut they will take to work there.)

In the following chapter, we will explore how companies can use their compliance and ethics programs to improve the overall ethical culture within their organizations.

14

DESIGNING AN ETHICAL CULTURE

Why does creating a "speak-up culture" matter?

Companies benefit in a host of ways by establishing strong compliance and ethics programs. Across the world, the trend in compliance and ethics programs is a shift from "rules-based" messaging to "a focus on 'ethical decision-making'" and creating a "speak-up" culture.[1] Frankly, people do not always follow rules well, and rules can be exploited for loopholes. Once guidance from a code of conduct is in place, what we want from people at every level of an organization is ethical investment in those values, including helping to correct issues by speaking up early when things go wrong.

Of all the Ethics & Compliance Initiative (ECI) interactive principles discussed in the previous chapter, arguably the most important indicator of the health of a company's compliance and ethics program is whether the organization has a "speak-up" culture. A speak-up culture is an indicator for other concerns about what it feels like to work within the company, and what employees truly understand their organization's expectations to be.

As Ethical Systems, the working group of ethics researchers also discussed in the previous chapter has described, in a "speak-up" culture, employees will "speak up when they observe misconduct," which helps "organizations reduce risk."[2] Under ECI's definition of "speaking up," organizations with positive speak-up cultures "encourage[], protect[], and value[] the reporting of concerns and suspected wrongdoing."[3] Research demonstrates that organizations that have this advantage "thrive by identifying issues[,] and providing opportunities to adapt, innovate, and avoid costly mistakes."[4] In addition, the more quickly that employees are willing to "speak up" about potential misconduct, "the sooner the organization can take action to prevent potential issues from developing into major scandals and damaging headlines."[5]

Why does creating a culture in which employees will speak up this way matter? It matters because most employees in organizations do not speak up when they observe unethical behavior. In many organizations, "[t]op-down hierarchies" tend to "encourage[] [employees] to remain silent."[6]

Employees at the bottom of these hierarchies name two main reasons for not speaking up to report the wrongdoing that they witness: fear and futility.

Regarding fear, employees believe that they will face retaliation and hostility for reporting. They worry about upsetting their managers, and being perceived as betraying a co-worker. More generally, employees fear that "their career opportunities will deeply suffer if they voice their concerns" about wrongdoing in the workplace.[7]

Regarding futility, employees may further believe that it will be futile to take the risk of reporting if the company will not support and protect them in doing so. They describe feeling as though they have "too little influence" within the organization to ensure that the behavior will change.[8] Additionally, if "those with [the] power [to make such changes] do not want to hear about the problem[,]" incurring the risk of reporting is "not worth the effort."[9]

Fear and futility can take different expressions depending on cultural context. According to the ECI's 2019 global survey, the seven most common reasons why employees do not report misconduct are:

1. "I did not believe [that] corrective action would be taken"—the most common reason in nine of the 18 countries surveyed, and about futility, here a lack of faith in organizations and their commitments to ethical results;
2. "I did not trust [that] my report would be kept confidential"—the most common reason in Brazil, China, and Indonesia, and about fear, revealing concern about the integrity of organizations' processes;
3. "I did not want someone to get in trouble"—the primary factor in France and the U.A.E., and about fear, in feeling conflicted social messages and loyalty;
4. "I did not want to be seen as a snitch"—the most common reason in Russia, and also about fear, here a concern about the expectations of the organization;
5. "I feared retaliation"—the most common reason in Mexico, and an overt expression of fear, in a sign of how common negative consequences for reporting can be (see Chapter 12 on whistleblowing); and
6. "in our culture, we do not tell on each other"—the most common reason in Korea, and about fear of breaking social norms, in a comment on the larger social context in which organizations operate.[10]

Finally, the least-common reason why employees do not report wrongdoing is actually a positive one, and a sign of a functional compliance system. This reason is because (7) "[t]he issue had already been addressed."[11] In the global survey, this was the most common reason in India, and a hopeful sign.[12] As we have noted, in the most effective compliance and ethics programs, 97% of observed misconduct is "either reported or taken care of by employees."[13] Employees themselves are able to solve all but 3% of reports.

What can be done to better create and reinforce a "speak-up culture"?

There are four basic ways that we can better create and reinforce a "speak-up" culture inside organizations.

First, organizations that foster healthy speak-up cultures solicit feedback from their employees.[14] They are "proactive about engaging employees."[15] They ask employees consistently to "voice their concerns," and they show that they are "open to receiving [genuine] feedback."[16] As a suggestion, "[f]ormally petition teams and make airing opinions an integral part of the evaluation process of project development."[17] Then "[m]ake sure to follow up" with the people who gave the feedback about "what has changed in response to their feedback."[18]

In soliciting such feedback—and especially in receiving it—supervisors, and leaders at all levels, must take ownership of the results. There are warning signs for companies in which employees report that a "supervisor only cares about meeting targets," and not about how employees achieve those targets; that their "supervisor blames others when things go wrong;" and that, in a related measure, "[t]op management blames others when things go wrong."[19] More ethical (lower) scores on these three factors, grouped together as an "'accountability' composite," can cut the amount of observed misconduct within an organization by roughly two-thirds (from 49% to 17%).[20] Meanwhile, failure to manage this accountability composite has consequences. Within organizations with strong accountability, 17% of employees observe misconduct, as opposed to 31% in organizations with some accountability, and nearly half (49%) in organizations with no accountability.[21]

Second, organizations with successful "speak-up" cultures engage in open discussions, and they set examples around positive and negative ethical issues.[22] Talking so openly about ethics—both about what a company is doing right, as well as owning and correcting what it is doing wrong—emphasizes that ethics are a priority for the organization, and "that you want to hear about [ethical issues] when they arise."[23]

In fact, it seems particularly important to talk openly about the things that a company does wrong in order for it to be able to do better. Only half of U.S. employees, however, perceive their leaders as willing to talk about their company's ethical failings.[24] In those companies, 82% of employees reported observed wrongdoing, versus 50% in companies in which employees described their organizations as not talking about such failings.[25]

There are definite differences by industries in these statistics. For example, only 36% of employees in the automotive sector, and 41% of employees in the arts, entertainment, & recreation sector, describe their companies as willing to talk openly about ethical failings.[26] By contrast, 65% of employees in the tech sector describe their companies as having these conversations.[27] Similarly, 62% of employees in the construction sector describe their companies as talking about ethical failings—possibly because physical safety has become a large priority for many of these organizations, and safety reviews tend to force companies to analyze and acknowledge what they have done wrong.[28]

Third, successful "speak-up" cultures make employee reviews ongoing. For example, "[d]on't make the formal, yearly review the only time [that] you provide feedback [to] employees."[29] Feedback should be a part of the organization's regular communications processes, and employees should be encouraged also to "provide feedback to you and to their peers."[30] This is not an excuse for allowing sabotage and inviting the pressure of constant culling. (See Chapter 2, 4, 9, and 10 on the dangers of that decision.) Rather, "[a]n open culture is one that facilitates" respectful, helpful, and enabling exchanges among "colleagues who are up, down, and across the organizational hierarchy."[31]

Moreover, as a practical matter, if employees know, or have a relationship of some type with their boss's boss, or others higher up in the company, and have talked to them before, they are more likely to give that person a heads-up about bad behavior when there is an opening, and such information seems like it might be well-received. These connections can take the form, among other things, of "skip" reviews, in which higher-level managers reach out to establish regular meetings, for example, every month or every other month, to get to know their subordinates' subordinates in one-on-one exchanges. Meeting individually with an open agenda either in person, or over Zoom or other platform, makes these sessions a particularly easy and enjoyable way to build rapport.

Having these conversations, and developing these relationships, can enable a greater level of trust within organizations. There is an entire literature on the value of trust within organizations for both profitability and the retention of the organization's best employees. Here, we simply mention in the reporting context that, according to 2018 numbers, merely one in four employees who observe misconduct reports it.[32] The primary reasons that they give for not reporting observed misconduct were discussed more above, but revolve also around their level of trust in their organizations. Without trust, they are concerned about the integrity of reporting processes, and the effectiveness of anti-retaliation measures. Fifty-eight percent of employees who chose not to report did so because they "do not believe that corrective action" will be taken.[33] Forty-nine percent of employees who chose not to report "do not trust" that their report would remain confidential.[34] Forty-four percent of employees "do not want to be seen as a snitch" and be subject to potential retaliation, including its social consequences.[35]

It further breaks trust with employees to apply pressure on them to "bend the rules." Employees who experience this pressure are more likely to psychologically withdraw, and to leave organizations.[36] (See Chapter 8 on how costly it is to organizations to replace workers.) They are at increased risk of "anxiety, burnout, and depression."[37] And they typically want out. Of employees who plan to stay less than a year within the organization, 35% report having experienced such pressure.[38] Of employees who plan to follow them within the next two years, 30% report having had this experience.[39] By contrast, of employees who plan to retire at the company, only 15% report having been subject to such unethical pressure.[40]

Fourth, and particularly importantly, "never tolerate retaliation."[41] This element is easier to say than to do, especially when, in the aftermath of a report, emotions among all parties may run high, and it may be human nature to lash out. In May 2018, for example, the CEO of Barclays Bank was fined the equivalent of U.S. $1.5 million for attempting to unmask the whistleblower who had reported on another member of the company, who was a friend of his.[42] At one point, it appeared that the CEO was going to lose his job over his reaction. In the end, he had to repeatedly, and publicly, apologize and to answer critics why he should not have been punished even more harshly for his reaction.

What should have been done inside Barclays not to tolerate retaliation? Any reports of retaliation by current employees or supervisors should have been dealt with immediately and reported to the board.[43] The CEO's subordinates certainly should not have helped him. Moreover, when there is retaliation, "the offending individuals should be quickly reprimanded,"[44] even if they are the CEO of the company. Finally, the process of disciplining anyone—even the CEO of the company—for retaliation, should be communicated to the rest of the company to show the organization's genuine "commitment to anti-retaliation efforts."[45]

Preventing retaliation is so important that the next section of this chapter expands on this discussion.

Why does it matter to prevent retaliation against employees who
report, and what are some ways to do this?

The healthiest compliance and ethics programs take advantage both of higher internal reporting rates when employees
observe misconduct, as well as lower retaliation rates to encourage such reports, and to keep them coming. The combination of higher reporting rates and lower rates of retaliation
"create[s] a virtuous cycle that reduces future misconduct and
organizational risk."[46] In such a virtuous cycle, the organization saves money, it averts major scandals and crises, it is able
to invest more energy and resources in positive outcomes and
profitable growth, plus it keeps its best employees happy and
committed to the company.

Unfortunately, repeated global ethics surveys have shown
that the median rate of retaliation against employees who
report ethical misconduct has not improved much in recent
years. The 2016 global median rate of employees experiencing
retaliation after reporting was 37%.[47] In 2019, it was 38%.[48]

The most common reporting subjects after which
employees suffer retaliation tend to be the personal ones. For
example, globally, almost one-half of employees (46%) who
report sexual harassment are retaliated against.[49] The largest
percentage is in Africa & the Middle East (72%), followed
by Asia Pacific (60%), but Europe and North America are
both around 50% (Europe is 51%; North America is 50%).[50]
Globally, reporting personal corruption resulted in retaliation 44% of the time; and reporting interpersonal discrimination resulted in retaliation 43% of the time.[51] Retaliation
for reporting other types of wrongdoing was closer to 30-
36%, with reporting conflicts of interest resulting in retaliation 36% of the time, abusive behaviors 34% of the time,
and violations of health and/or safety standards 30% of the
time.[52]

The attitude and reaction of supervisors has a huge impact on these numbers. When supervisors "very frequently

overlook questionable employee behavior," 77% of reporting employees faced retaliation.[53] By contrast, when, according to employees, "supervisors never overlook questionable employee behavior," only 15% of such employees faced retaliation.[54] Fifteen percent is still not great for illegal behavior, but that number is four-tenths of the global median (38%).

In addition, when employees do report, more than half of employees globally (51%) report observed misconduct to their direct supervisors.[55] These numbers are fairly consistent across the globe. The highest number (54%) is in South America; Europe and North America are around 50% (North America at 51%, Europe is at 49%); while Asia Pacific is 46%; and Africa & the Middle East is 41%.[56]

The next-most-common place for employees to report observed misconduct is to higher management within their organizations. Compared to the percentage of employees reporting to direct supervisors, this number is much smaller: 17% globally (18% in Africa & the Middle East, 22% in Asia Pacific, 20% in Europe, 18% in North America, and 14% in South America).[57] After that, the numbers tail off to 8% to the organization's human resources department, 6% to a helpline or hotline, 5% to a workplace ethics officer, 4% to the organization's legal department, 2% to another organization, and 1% to another person outside the organization.[58] *Only 1% of employees globally who report observed misconduct actually reported that misconduct to governmental or other regulatory authorities first.*[59]

Because front-line managers are so predominately the individuals to whom employees initially report, training on ethics—and what the proper thing is to do when someone reports—needs to have permeated the organization to their level. These front-line managers need to encourage reports, and supervisors whose employees report need to react properly once the employee has reported. Reacting properly to reports, without retaliation, protects both the employee and the organization, as well as keeps reports coming. Organizations need these reports to keep coming in order to be on top of wrongdoing, and to catch it in its early stages, before it grows and inflicts greater harm on the company.

What does retaliation look like within a company after an employee reports? For more on this topic, see Chapter 12 on adverse actions that can draw legal liability. But continuing with the ECI's 2019 global survey data, the most common form of retaliation against an employee who reports is that "other employees ignored me" (62%).[60] Second-most common was that "I was given an unfavorable work assignment" (54%), followed by "I was not given promotions or raises" (52%).[61] Employees are retaliated against when they are improperly "accused of doing something wrong" (52%), they feel that they could lose their jobs (51%), and "[m]y direct supervisor or management excluded me from decisions and work activity" (47%).[62]

An underlying cultural problem in retaliation cases is that employees who speak up can be perceived as "traitors," or as "not team players" inside the organization.[63] But even the vast majority of formal external whistleblowers—nearly 90%—report internally within their organizations before reporting externally,[64] even if that legally does not always best protect their rights. (For more on the whistleblowing system, see Chapter 12.) In 2019, according to the U.S. Securities and Exchange Commission (SEC), even 83% of successful whistleblowers in agency actions—those *most* potentially motivated by the agency's monetary awards and who have the least to gain legally from reporting internally—still reported internally first, at both significant risk and cost to themselves.[65]

Why would whistleblowers do this? Repeated studies of whistleblowers have found that most whistleblowers are motivated not by money, but by moral concerns. These individuals are often some of a company's most principled, ethical, committed, and valuable employees. A study in the *New England Journal of Medicine*, for example, found that not a single whistleblower filing a *qui tam* suit (see Chapter 12 for more on these suits) was originally motivated by financial reward.[66] Instead, the whistleblowers cited reasons from "integrity, altruism or public safety, [and] justice, [to] self-preservation."[67] Additional research continues to confirm that whistleblowers are primarily motivated by "fairness and justice" in their decisions to blow the whistle.[68] In a 2019 study of over 42,000 U.S. federal employees, among whistleblowers, "moral concerns about fairness outweigh[ed] pragmatic concerns (e.g., personal benefits) in guiding decisions to report wrongdoing."[69] In fact, that study found that "[c]oncern for [o]thers" was statistically the factor most closely associated with employees likely to report observed wrongdoing.[70]

Understanding that, for employees who report, reporting is a moral issue helps explain why so many whistleblowers go to extraordinary lengths to convey the information that they have to others, and they want to see it acted upon. By the time employees are upset enough to report, they want to see corrective action taken. Thus, employees reporting wrongdoing are largely going to report the wrongdoing either internally or externally. The largest factors in encouraging their reports to be first internal (versus initially external to regulators and other agencies) are, most of all, the employees' perception of their company's "[o]rganizational fairness," followed by how much employees know about their company's internal reporting procedures.[71]

Specifically, employees' confidence in what management will do, and how managers will react to reports, appear to be key factors in whether they will report internally. Within the U.S., when employees believe that top management is committed to ethics, they report observed misconduct 71% of the time.[72] When employees perceive that at least their direct supervisor is committed to ethics, they report 69% of the time.[73] By contrast, when employees believe that ethics are a lower priority for leaders, they report 56% of the time.[74]

As makes sense from these numbers, employees are also the most hesitant to report observed misconduct when it involves those within the company with more authority. When someone who is not a manager is the primary offender, for example, 67% of employees report the misconduct that they observe, whereas when top or middle managers are the primary offenders, 57% of employees report.[75]

As also makes sense from these numbers, the more pervasive employees perceive the misconduct to be within an organization—in other words, how much managers have already allowed the situation to escape them, they have not emphasized their commitment to ethics, and they have failed to enforce ethical commitment throughout the company—the less likely employees are to report observed misconduct. U.S. reporting rates are 65% when the misconduct appears to be an isolated incident, and 66% when it involves a single person.[76] By contrast, these reporting rates decline to 57% when misconduct appears to be organizationally wider, and 59% when it appears to be ongoing.[77] (It must be said that those are still fairly high numbers, and very brave employees.)

Of course, whistleblowing can come from outside a company too. (See Chapter 12 on whistleblowing.) So potential internal whistleblowers are particularly valuable to a company as early-warning signs because information on wrongdoing may escalate by other means to enforcement agencies. In the SEC's case, 69% of its tips came from employees or former employees.[78] But that leaves another 31% of tips to have come from other places, including customers, suppliers, third parties, and market-watchers.

Employees whose concerns are not appropriately addressed internally, or who are retaliated against, are particularly likely to file with outside regulators for protection, and sometimes for the availability of bounties. According to one such outside agency, the SEC, in 2019 it received over 5,200 whistleblower tips.[79] Its tips originated from individuals in 70 countries outside the United States, in addition to from within every state in the United States.[80] The tips related to a broad range of topics within the agency's jurisdiction, including a large increase in tips about cryptocurrencies.[81]

What are the consequences of not addressing internal reports appropriately, and preventing retaliation?

The answer is potentially costly legal battles and enforcement actions. Taking the SEC as an example, by 2019, based on information from meritorious whistleblowers over the program's short eight-year history, the agency had extracted "over [U.S.] $2 billion in total monetary sanctions, including more than [U.S.] $1 billion in disgorgement of ill-gotten gains and interest."[82] Meanwhile, a company now in trouble with the government has lost the goodwill of its employee, who may end up working against the company for the government to receive an award. Since the beginning of its whistleblower program, the SEC alone has paid out approximately U.S. $387 million in bounties to whistleblowers.[83]

What are some specific, helpful ways to reduce retaliation within organizations?

Values-based compliance training can increase the likelihood of internal employee reporting by 61%.[84] The same values-based programs can decrease retaliation against employees who do report by 93%.[85] The most effective U.S. compliance and ethics programs can reduce retaliation rates down to 4%.[86] Without an effective compliance and ethics program, however, 53% of employees who report observed wrongdoing experience retaliation.[87]

Many of the same actions that create an effective "speak-up" culture mentioned above can also help prevent retaliation. The actions that most decrease retaliation rates are when senior leaders (1) share credit with others, (2) are perceived as doing the right thing, and (3) treat all employees well. There obviously need to be (4) established non-retaliation policies, and other measures that encourage employees to speak up about the misconduct that they observe. Managers need to be (5) trained in these programs, and (6) held accountable for the organization's compliance and ethics programs at all levels, including its anti-retaliation commitments.

When senior leaders share credit with others, are perceived to be doing the right thing, and treat all employees well, retaliation rates nose-dive. In such organizations, only about one in 20 employees who report observed wrongdoing suffer retaliation.[88] By contrast, when senior leaders fail to exhibit these behaviors, U.S. retaliation rates climb to nearly 50%.[89]

Specifically, whether managers are perceived to be held accountable for compliance and ethics is key to whether retaliation occurs. When managers are held accountable, the average retaliation rate is 16%.[90] When they are not held accountable, the rate of retaliation against employees who report observed wrongdoing jumps to 40%.[91]

In terms of additional practical steps, the ECI recommends that organizations affirmatively follow-up with individuals who have reported, ask them whether they have experienced any form of retaliation, and actively monitor their treatment "to ensure there is no change in performance evaluation or job status that might be in retaliation" for their reports.[92]

What are some problems that larger companies and supply-side companies face?

Some compliance and ethics problems appear in other contexts, but seem to be particularly acute for large corporations and supply-side companies. The very size of a large corporation (the ECI's metric is employing 90,000 or more people) removes many of its leaders from meaningful, regular contact with large numbers of employees. This remoteness creates information-flow problems and challenges in setting ethical culture for such a large group of people. The position of supply-side companies in selling products and soliciting business from a sometimes-narrow base of customers exposes them more often to potentially unethical pressures.

Problem one: What ethical challenges do large corporations face when their leaders are removed from front-line employees?

The good news about compliance and ethics programs in large companies is that, when they work and are effective, they are very effective. As the ECI has found, "[n]early nine [in] ten employees" (87%) "who observe violations at large companies with effective programs report those violations," as opposed to merely 32% of employees reporting when programs in large companies are not as good.[93] Rates of actual, observed misconduct went down as well. One-third (33%) of employees observed misconduct in large companies with effective compliance and ethics programs, as opposed to more than half (almost 51%) inside large companies generally, and almost two-thirds (62%) inside large companies that did not have effective programs.[94]

The best news is that pressure to bend the rules, and retaliation against employees who do report observed misconduct, can fall particularly dramatically in large companies with effective compliance and ethics programs: down to an attention-grabbing 3% and 4% respectively.[95] Those would be wonderful numbers for any company to have, and large companies can be especially good at getting themselves to those levels.

The bad news is that leaders in large companies can be more easily misguided about the effectiveness of their compliance and ethics program, and the health of ethics within the company overall, unless they take affirmative steps to measure, invest in, and protect those assets. (See also Chapter 10 on the special ethical challenges of leadership.) We know that "[l]eaders have a 'rosier' view of the state of workplace integrity, and often have more positive beliefs than employees further down the chain of command."[96] Inside organizations globally, it may shock top executives to discover that 39% of employees describe their leaders as not having a strong commitment to organizational values, and 58% as not having a strong commitment to ethical leadership.[97] (As we have covered elsewhere in this chapter, there are direct links between being perceived as having a strong commitment to organizational values and ethical leadership, and having better ethical outcomes; conversely, weak commitments to organizational values and ethical leadership result in worse ethical outcomes.)

Repeatedly, "non-management employees are far less likely to give top managers high marks for ethical leadership than top managers give themselves."[98] Managers also seem to develop more-and-more-divorced-from-reality (rosier and rosier) views of their own ethical leadership as they advance through the company hierarchy. (See also the psychology of this phenomenon in Chapter 10 on the challenges of leadership.) For example, in the U.S., 94% of top management would agree that their supervisor displays ethical leadership, whereas only 67% of middle managers would agree, and 63% of first-line managers would agree.[99] Merely 61% of non-managers would agree with that statement about leadership ethics.[100]

Meanwhile, pressure to commit misconduct and corresponding levels of observed misconduct seem to rise as we go up through the ranks of organizations. There are synergies at work in a large corporation that make it a particularly likely place in which to experience such pressure to "bend the rules." The higher an individual is located within the management of an organization, the more likely he or she is to feel pressure to bend the rules. Top management are almost twice as likely as employees who are not in management to experience such pressure.[101] This pressure increases steadily as managers move up through the ranks of the organization: whereas 17% of non-managers report such pressure, 22% of first-line supervisors with direct reports experience it, 25% of middle managers, and 30% of top managers.[102]

In thinking about why ethical pressure increases when rising up an organization, there could be several factors at play, the impacts of each may be greater in a larger corporation.

First, the higher that an individual rises within an organization, the more likely that his or her compensation is tied to performance results. As illustrated in previous data, the more there is pressure for results within an organization without concern for methods, the more pressure there will be to "bend the rules" to achieve those results. (See also earlier in this chapter for a discussion of how to set realistic goals and ethically enforce them.)

Top managers may also be the most experienced in navigating the organization's pattern of incentives. For example, top managers often actually know whether the organization rewards—or does not care—about ethical behavior through information about its promotions, bonuses, or raises. Knowing this information changes the gamble of engaging in unethical conduct for top managers; of employees who agree that their organization rewards ethical conduct through its promotions, bonuses, or raises, 80% would be surprised if their organization did not discipline reported misconduct.[103] Meanwhile, of employees who do not think that their organization rewards ethical conduct through its promotions, bonuses, or raises, only 46% would be surprised if the organization failed to discipline a violator for misconduct—meaning that 64% think that someone (themselves?) could get away with misconduct within the company even if it were reported.[104]

Top managers may also have been engaged in their pattern of wrongdoing for a long time. When allowed to be promoted despite unethical behavior, top managers may engage in more and more egregious conduct. (See discussion of the ethical side and other phenomena in Chapters 4, 9, and 10.) In the case of interpersonal misconduct (such as sexual harassment, abusive behavior, and discrimination), 62% of employees who observed such misconduct noted that the behavior was one of several incidents or was part of an on-going pattern.[105] Sixty-one percent of employees who observed such interpersonal misconduct described it as serious or very serious.[106] Stories of repeated sexual harassment and sexual assault, such as the behavior of Harvey Weinstein at the Weinstein Company, Roger Ailes and Bill O'Reilly at Fox News, Matt Lauer at NBC, and many others are examples of unethical and harmful behavior on the part of people in power who were protected too long from consequences.

Second, the higher a manager rises in the organization, the closer he or she is to the board of directors (to which almost 20% of compliance and ethics programs report).[107] This level of access and status can have ethical downsides. Familiarity with the board of directors may make a top manager feel as though members of the board would protect him or her if his or her misconduct were reported. In addition, top managers are at the apex of the company, and employees are more reluctant to report violations the more highly placed a violator is within the hierarchy (see earlier in this chapter for statistics).

Third, the more highly placed an individual is within an organization, and especially a large organization, the more power and resources he or she controls. His or her control of those resources not only means that other people—who want things from him or her—are willing to overlook, or even initiate, problematic ethical transactions, but also that the manager has multiple ingredients of the Fraud Diamond: opportunity and access ("capability"). We describe Fraud Diamond Theory next.

Problem two: What ethical challenges arise from high-level employees' opportunity and capability to commit fraud?

In order to design a compliance and ethics system, especially for large corporations, we have to recognize that certain situations contain additional potential for unethical decision-making. Scandals and ethical violations, especially those that cost a lot of time, money, and company resources, are not mere random occurrences. Under Fraud Triangle Theory and its successor, Fraud Diamond Theory, situations that create a high risk of unethical behavior typically involve an actor's (1) opportunity, (2) motivation, (3) rationalization, and, as an additional factor under Fraud Diamond Theory, (4) capability.[108]

"Opportunity" is present when a person thinks that he or she can engage in fraudulent behavior without facing serious repercussions. With a weak compliance and ethics system, and poor cultural reinforcement, violators may see an opportunity to take shortcuts for personal gain.[109] Even where paper controls are in place, violators who know the system may believe that others will not take their violations seriously—perhaps based on poor "tone at the top," or failure to meaningfully enforce the company's code of conduct. We touched on some of these points in Chapter 13.

"Motivation" is defined as "forces within or external to a person that affect his or her direction, intensity, and persistence of behavior."[110] Similar to opportunity, for violators, it is only their perception of pressure incentives that matters. As we touched on in the previous chapter regarding "Goals Gone Wild," motivation to commit fraud often arises when an employee's compensation or job security are directly tied to performance goals. For example, in the Wells Fargo banking scandal, employees were under pressure to sell at least eight products to every customer, which prompted some to open hundreds of fake accounts to meet this quota.[111]

Ninety-five percent of fraud cases are influenced by some sort of financial pressure, whether generated by the company, or the circumstances of the individual.[112] (We describe the types of financial pressures that companies can put on their workplaces in Chapters 4 (science), 9 (major ethical traps), and 10 (leadership).) Individuals sufficiently motivated to trigger personal unethical behavior toward the company can exhibit warning signs such as living beyond their means, having large personal debts, suffering from gambling or drug addictions, or be experiencing a health problem within their family (which, depending on a country's healthcare system can lead to financial pressure to pay for healthcare, and accompanying debt).[113] A person who feels that his or her needs or goals are unattainable by ethical means may resort to misconduct.[114]

The third prong in Fraud Triangle Theory is rationalization, which occurs when the actor self-justifies his or her unethical behavior. Not surprisingly, most people who commit fraud will not allow themselves to believe that they are doing anything wrong. (See more in Chapter 4 on science and Chapter 9 on major ethical traps in business.) This may be one of the reasons that explains why, according to the Association of Certified Fraud Examiners (ACFE), over 88% of people convicted of occupational fraud are first-time offenders.[115] A person confronted with both the opportunity and motivation to commit wrongdoing may try to euphemize his or her actions ("I was only borrowing the money"), provide a moral justification ("I have to do this to feed my family"), or diffuse responsibility ("everyone does this").[116] (See Chapters 4, 8, and 10 for additional discussion of rationalizations.)

Fraud Diamond Theory adds one more piece to this puzzle: capability. To commit more serious types of fraud may require an actor to exhibit capabilities in the form of his or her position, abilities, and influence. Top managers in large companies have exceptional access to information, people, skills, and power. One study found that CEOs were implicated in 70% of public-company accounting fraud cases.[117] The ACFE has also found a direct correlation between seniority (age, education, and experience at the company), and the magnitude of the loss caused by an employee's fraud.[118] More expertise further allows a violator to keep track of his or her lies, and to maintain a consistent narrative to avoid or deflect suspicion and consequences.

Problem three: What ethical challenges do supply-side companies face?

Finally, we mention a few things about the particular pressures under which supply-side companies find themselves when it comes to ethical conduct. Supply-side misconduct is not a merely a problem for supply-side companies—it is a problem for the entire supply chain. "Time and again, news reports about bribery, sweatshop factories[,] or accidents caused by unsafe work conditions have shone a negative light on a high-profile company that contracted for work but failed to perform essential due diligence and/or intervene with a supplier to set matters right again."[119]

Employees in supply-side firms are more likely than employees in non-supplier firms to have observed misconduct. Inside the two types of companies, these global numbers were 42% versus 28%.[120] Supply-side firm employees are also almost twice as likely to have felt pressure to compromise ethical standards (31%), as employees of other firms (18%).[121] In an interesting mix of news, although supply-side firm employees are far more likely to report the misconduct that they observe (68%) than non-supplier employees (51%), they were also more likely to be retaliated against for their reports (45% in supply-side firms vs. 28% in non-suppliers).[122] One speculation here is that employees in these firms may be younger, and lower-level employees may leave before the retaliation against them has a pervasive effect on new recruits acculturating to the company.[123]

According to reports of observed misconduct, supply-side firms tend to experience many of the same types of compliance and ethics violations as other companies, but at far higher rates.[124] A particular example seems to be "inappropriate alteration, falsification, and/or misrepresentation of your organization's documents or records."[125] Twenty percent of supply-side firm employees globally observed this form of misconduct (33% in Germany, 31% in India, and 30% in the U.S.), whereas these numbers were only 8% among non-suppliers.[126]

Across supply-side firm patterns, the "misconduct [that] suppliers observe is frequently ongoing, involves multiple people[,] and is often perpetrated by managers."[127] These facts may, in part, be due to so many more people in supply-side firms being elevated quickly into management (65% vs. 42%).[128] With promotion to management, in combination with the opportunity and capacity for corruption (among other ethical issues), the scale and coordination of wrongdoing through management across the firm can be greater.[129]

Given the work that supply-side firms do in providing goods and services to other organizations, they tend to operate within specific networks of repeat relationships.[130] Because they are so tightly attuned to the needs of their customers, supply-side firms tend to experience far more organizational changes, and on a more frequent basis. At all types of organizations, frequent organizational changes are linked to increased risk of unethical conduct. For example, according to 2020 global data, "employees working in organizations with four to seven significant changes in 12 months" were twice as likely "to say [that] they observed misconduct than employees working in an organization without any significant changes."[131] Thirty-three percent of employees in companies with no organizational changes had observed misconduct, as opposed to 75% of employees working in companies experiencing many (4-7) organizational changes.[132] One theory here is that investment in compliance and ethics programs may take a backseat during major organizational changes, and, even if resources for the programs did not suffer, the prominence of messaging and communication about the programs and the company's expectations, as well as the processing of reports, may have.

What are some ideas for these organizations and others in crisis?

When things get hard, and there are more ethical challenges, it is important to remember that your employees are watching, and that such moments—especially crises—can define an organization's relationship with its employees for many years to come. One of this book's authors has written about this phenomenon during the 2020–21 COVID-19 pandemic.[133] Crises make business ethics *more* important, not less.

As the ECI notes, "[b]e particularly mindful of not just talking about the importance of workplace integrity, but also providing a good example—especially when things go wrong."[134] Leaders' "hypocrisy can fuel employees' cynicism;" and "times of crisis are particularly critical for shaping employees' beliefs about top managers."[135] Internationally, 68% of employees report that, when things go wrong, top management blames others.[136]

That behavior becomes a serious problem, not only for the ethical health of the organization, but for retaining talent. In nearly every country surveyed around the world, "employees who believe[d that] top management blames others" when things go wrong "are more likely to intend to leave the organization imminently, i.e., in the next 12 months or less."[137] Conversely, "employees in 11 of [the] 13 countries" surveyed who believed that "top management does not blame others" were "more likely to plan on staying for the long haul—at least five years or until retirement."[138]

Next, given what we know about the disconnect between what top managers know about the compliance and ethics resources available to them, versus what lower-level employees believe, "[o]vercommunicate to employees" about the compliance and ethics resources "available to them," and affirmatively "explore where resources are underutilized, ineffective, or lacking."[139] For example, in the U.S., although 53% of top managers were aware of all their company's compliance and ethics programs, only 39% of middle managers were, and merely 35% of non-managers.[140] The fact that a company may be going through organizational changes, and may be in crisis, means that education about its compliance and ethics programs needs to be repeatedly emphasized, even more so than in standard times.

Finally, be particularly proactive about combatting retaliation. In times of crisis, rates of retaliation can rise, and when leaders are increasingly distant from employee front lines, they are even more in need of reports and honest communication about ethical issues. Please see the earlier sections of this chapter on how to create a stronger speak-up culture and to prevent retaliation.

What are some of the best compliance and ethics programs in businesses today?

It is always risky to highlight compliance and ethics programs for specific mention, because those are sometimes the companies that have been trading on their reputations for a long time, may no longer be investing in their compliance programs, and are ripe for a fall.

Boeing is a perfect example of a company in this category: the company for years was held up as an example of a highly profitable company that had a strong code of conduct with cultural enforcement of its Code. As the DOJ's guidance discussed in the previous chapter flags, many of the company's attitude changes occurred as a result of its merger with McDonnell Douglas (MDD). Despite Boeing officially retaining many of its strongly worded statements about the importance of ethics,[141] the company appears to have significantly changed course with the decisions of "CEO Phil Condit and [former MDD, and subsequent Boeing CEO] . . . Harry Stonecipher, [who] . . . decided it was time to put some distance between themselves and the people actually making the company's planes."[142] (See above in this chapter for ethical problems such remoteness from employees can create.) Mr. Stonecipher described his contribution as, "[w]hen people say I changed the culture of Boeing, that was the intent, so that it's run like a business rather than a great engineering firm."[143] In documents released after crashes of Boeing 737-MAX aircraft, Boeing employees describe how unreasonable and distant management had become, how little it knew about the business, and how hard it drove the company to achieve short-term profits at the price of safety concerns.[144] As discussed in this chapter above and in Chapters 8, 9, and 10, all of these factors are warning signs.

With the caveat in place that we do not know the current state of the following companies' investment in their compliance and ethics programs, here are some companies as of 2021 that are well known for both being profitable, and trying to stay on the right side of law and ethics.

Costco Wholesale Corporation (Costco)

Costco, a warehouse club that operates on memberships, has a particularly strong and unusual culture. Like Southwest Airlines under its co-founder, Herb Kelleher, Costco co-founder James (Jim) Sinegal put his unique stamp on the company and the way it has made decisions from its beginning. Costco grew quickly from its founding in 1983 to become, by 2015, the second-largest retailer in the world behind Walmart.[145]

Costco employees can recite the company's Code of Ethics by heart. Although the company's stated mission is "[t]o continually provide our members with quality goods and services at the lowest possible prices," its Code is divided into five principles that address different constituencies in a core section of 38 words.[146] The first four principles of "Our Code of Ethics" are:

1. "Obey the law."
2. "Take care of our members."
3. "Take care of our employees."
4. "Respect our suppliers."[147]

According to the rest of the section, "[i]f we do these four things throughout our organization, then we will achieve our ultimate goal, which is to: 5. Reward our shareholders."[148]

Costco's Code fleshes out what each of these principles means. The first principle of its Code places Costco in the context of its communities in being a law-abiding citizen. The second principle relates to the company's obligations, by 2019, to its over 100 million members, and it pledges to support employee volunteerism and make charitable contributions.[149] The third principle about employees starts with the assertion that "[o]ur employees are our most important asset." In 2020, the company employed 275,000 people.[150] Costco states "[w]e believe we have the very best employees in the warehouse club industry, and we are committed to providing them with rewarding challenges and ample opportunities for personal and career growth."[151] The Code also highlights the company's preference for "home grown" managers, which may be a key component of inculcating new people into the company's culture and perpetuating it.

The fourth principle about respecting suppliers seems to acknowledge that supply-side company relationships can be particularly fraught with ethical dilemmas. (See also the discussion above in this chapter highlighting special issues in supply-side companies.) As Costco's Code continues, "[a]t the core of our philosophy as a company is the implicit understanding that all of us, employees and management alike, must conduct ourselves in an honest and ethical manner every day. Dishonest conduct will not be tolerated."[152] Its Code then appeals to a values-based judgment of right and wrong, rather than rule-based guidance: "If you are ever in doubt as to what course of action to take on a business matter that is open to varying ethical interpretations, TAKE THE HIGH ROAD AND DO WHAT IS RIGHT."[153] (All caps in the original.)

The company's fifth principle of rewarding shareholders utilizes muted language to describe the influence of shareholders on the company's decisions. Shareholders are "our business partners," the company is an "investment," and the relationship "involves the element of trust" through the company's ups and downs.[154] (See also discussion in Chapter 7 on CSR and the place of shareholders.)

Costco's Code of Ethics ends with the question "What do Costco's Mission Statement and Code of Ethics have to do with you?"[155] The company's short answer is displayed in bold, all caps with an explanation mark: "EVERYTHING!"[156] The company then explains: "By always choosing to do the right thing, you will build your own self-esteem, increase your chances for success and make Costco more successful, too."[157] This foundation of "each of us working together and contributing our best," is what "makes Costco the great company it is today and lays the groundwork for what we will be tomorrow."[158]

Costco has made other interesting cultural choices too. The company imposes ethical constraints on its own behavior that are unusual in a world often driven by making the most profits possible. Costco pledges not to mark up any standard item more than 14% over its wholesale cost, and no signature-series item more than 15% over cost. In a story often retold that self-defines the company, Costco, after selling out a shipment of jeans, was able to receive a second shipment at a lower cost. The company could have continued to sell the new shipment of jeans at the previous price, but instead marked them down to continue making no more than 14% over its own cost.

When Jim Sinegal retired as CEO in 2012, that story was the lead in the company's history of itself, and it sets the standard for corporate expectations and behavior into the future.[159] As Mr. Sinegal explained in another interview: "Our reputation for pricing [authenticity] is an example [of how we built the company]. We have sweated over this for years. Why would we sacrifice that just to make a quarterly target? It wouldn't make sense—sacrificing everything, risking our whole reputation. We believe our strategy will maximize shareholder value over the long term."[160]

Similarly, on the importance of culture and self-sustaining ethics, Mr. Sinegal believed that:

Good leaders make the determination how to run the company and then communicate it to everyone in the company so that they all understand it. Honesty and doing the right thing cannot be the responsibility of management alone. Every level of the company should understand what the rules are and every employee in the company should be mortified if the company and its people don't do what they are supposed to do. The attitude has got to be pervasive throughout the organization: "We don't do that kind of stuff around here! Period!"[161]

A major challenge for Costco will be what happens when its co-founders, and the people who knew them (such as the 2020 CEO who began working at the company in 1984), are no longer around to guide its culture and insist on such actions. It remains to be seen whether the next generations of Costco's leadership continue to steward the company in the same manner.

The Hershey Company (Hershey's)

Hershey's is an interesting contrast with Costco and other recently founder-run companies built around a strong personality. Founded in 1894, Hershey's has been in existence for over 125 years. The company has had time to digest lessons learned about not only establishing, but also passing on, its culture.

Hershey's has a short, well-organized, and easy-to-digest Code of Conduct.[162] The company sets itself apart by outlining for employees a streamlined, three-step process to handle ethically questionable situations. If an employee is not sure what to do, then Hershey's encourages him or her to ask: (1) "[D]oes [the action I want to take] reflect our values? (2) Is it good for Hershey and for my coworkers? (3) Would I feel okay if everyone knew about it?"[163] If the answers to all three questions are "yes," then Hershey's says the action is probably permissible. However, if any of the answers to those three questions is "no" or "not sure," then Hershey's encourages the employee to reconsider the action. In every case, Hershey's directs employees to ask for help if they are not sure about their ethical obligations.

Each rule in Hershey's Code is accompanied by a hypothetical "what if" section explaining what employees should do in various situations.[164] This format aids in digesting and understanding the Code obligations, and in answering common concerns that employees may have.

Finally, Hershey's corporate anti-retaliation policy is noteworthy because it states that it applies whether a violation is reported internally or externally. Although Hershey's does not explicitly list government reporting channels, it clarifies that its Code does not prohibit reporting to the government and, importantly, that "the Code does not require you to notify the Company of any such communications."[165]

Lockheed Martin

Lockheed Martin (LM) is an interesting contrast with both Costco and Hershey's because it was a company that got itself into deep trouble, and then had to find another way to operate in order to survive. After years of defense-contractor scandals in the 1980s, the industry pledged, under threat of regulation, to enhance its compliance and ethics programs. LM is an example of a company that turned itself around and has stayed out of major scandals since.

LM begins its Code of Conduct with a message from the CEO, Ms. Marillyn Hewson.[166] She articulates LM's three main values: (1) do what's right, (2) respect others, and (3) perform with excellence. She also encourages LM employees to report unethical behavior, and to ask managers, ethics and compliance personnel, and human resources if they ever have questions about ethics.

LM helps establish its company's ethical cultural message in several ways throughout its Code. LM begins the first section of its Code by reiterating LM's values, and then stating LM's vision: "Be the global leader in supporting our customers' missions, strengthening security and advancing scientific discovery."[167]

For each rule, LM has a "why we do it" section explaining its importance and rationale. Through its language, LM not only sets clear expectations, but it encourages adoption by explaining why employees should follow each rule. LM's requirement to report all violations, for example, contains the following "why we do it" explanations that speak to who LM collectively wants to be:

- "We are committed to the highest standards of ethical conduct in our dealings with our constituencies."[168]
- "Violations of the Code may result in disciplinary action up to and including termination. Failure to report may itself violate the Code."[169]

LM's framing seeks to involve employees in the relevance and application of the company's goals as applied to themselves and their behavior. Each rule is explained in terms of "we" as opposed to "you"—for example, "*We* report violations" versus "*You* are required to report violations."[170] Additionally, LM personalizes and formalizes the seriousness of its Code by having each employee sign a certification pledging to uphold the Code and report all violations.

Finally, LM makes its anti-retaliation policy clear. It has two pages dedicated to its zero-tolerance for retaliation, listing various departments to which employees may internally report.[171] Further, LM lists an anonymous ethics hotline, email, address, and fax by which employees may report violations.[172] One weakness of LM's Code, however, is that it does not touch on methods to report ethics violations to government agencies. Such notification is not currently legally required in the U.S., but its inclusion would enhance the accountability power of the company's Code.

What are the lessons that businesses and individuals should learn from our discussion of compliance and ethics?

We hope that the extensive discussion of compliance and ethics over the last two chapters has provided a lot to think about in creating or evaluating your own program. But, most of all, we encourage you to make your program *yours*: own it, adopt it, reflect it, and live it. That is how you will achieve the best results.

15

HOW TO RESPOND TO INVESTIGATIONS AND PROTECT YOUR REPUTATION

How much benefit is there to the company from having a compliance and ethics program in place before an investigation?

Corporate compliance and ethics programs offer benefits to companies extending beyond the satisfaction of legal obligations and the creation of an ethical corporate culture.[1] Companies with effective compliance programs in place are more likely to avoid criminal prosecution altogether.[2] (See Chapters 13 and 14 for more on compliance and ethics programs.)

Because prosecutors want to know whether the company's compliance and ethics program was put in place "in good faith," it is valuable for a company (which we will refer to generally as a corporation) to have an effective program in place *before* issues arise.[3] The United States Department of Justice's ("DOJ") U.S. Attorneys' Manual instructs federal prosecutors to evaluate "the adequacy of the corporation's compliance program and its management's commitment to the compliance program" in determining whether to prosecute.[4] Prosecutors may weigh the steps taken by the corporation to "implement the personnel, operation[al], and organization[al] changes necessary to establish an awareness among employees that criminal conduct will not be tolerated" when deciding "whether or not to prosecute a corporation."[5] Federal prosecutors are also instructed to consider "lenience" and non-prosecution when a corporation has a "compliance or audit program" that "includes sufficient measures to identify and prevent future noncompliance."[6]

Should a government investigation lead to criminal charges, the corporation is still better off having a compliance and ethics program in place.[7] Even should the corporation be found guilty of a crime, the corporation may have its sentence reduced if it had an effective program in place. This reduction in punishment can have a dramatic effect.[8] In 2017, the average fine levied against an organization by the federal government was in excess of U.S. $67 million.[9] A corporation may see up to a 95% reduction in its fines, however, if it "self-reports, cooperates with the government, and has an effective compliance and ethics program" in place.[10] A corporation with such programs may also avoid additional penalties such as being debarred (banned) from receiving federal contracts.

Corporations with effective compliance and ethics programs also enjoy more preferential outcomes in the prosecutorial process because such programs generally improve the ethical culture, economic performance, and reputation of the corporation.[11] (See Chapter 14 on institutionalizing compliance and ethics programs, as well as developing a "speak-up" culture and preventing retaliation.) Even when criminal activity within the corporation is found and charged, a corporation that has developed a reputation for sincerely valuing ethical business conduct may enjoy leniency and "the benefit of the doubt" from prosecutors.[12]

Understanding the narrative: Why does a prosecution's "theory of the case" matter?

In preparing cases, prosecutors seek to understand how the alleged criminal conduct occurred. This becomes their story or "narrative" of the case. A prosecution's "theory of the case" may evolve with the information that the government receives over time, and it may be shaped, especially early on, by new information.

Every story has some version of bad guys, innocent bystanders, and victims.[13] As potential criminal defendants, businesses and individuals need to find out which of these characters the prosecutor believes that you are. For individual defendants in particular, when corporations turn over the results of their internal investigations (see later in this chapter, and Chapters 13 and 14), you will need to know as which of these characters the company, and other potential co-defendants, want to frame you. As we will discuss in this chapter, by making certain decisions, such as to cooperate with the prosecution, you may give yourself the opportunity to reframe for the prosecution which character you are before other potential defendants have the opportunity to make you a scapegoat or otherwise to misrepresent your role.[14] (See also Chapter 12 for whistleblowing advice and strategy.)

When there is a federal investigation of a corporation, prosecutions of individuals often follow. Between 2001 and 2014, connected to the 306 cases against corporations in which companies received a deferred or non-prosecution agreement (DPA or NPA) (see Chapter 13), 414 individuals were prosecuted. Of these individuals prosecuted, most of them were middle managers or lower-level employees.

The DOJ's policy on which individuals to prosecute has changed over time. Under the 2015 Yates Memorandum, the DOJ instructed prosecutors to identify, and attempt to prosecute, all individuals responsible for, or involved in, the underlying misconduct.[15] Under the 2018 Rosenstein policy changes, they were to identify every individual "substantially" involved or responsible for the criminal conduct.[16] As of 2017, in just under half (45.8%) of prosecutions in which the DOJ convicted an organizational defendant, at least one individual defendant was also charged and pleaded guilty.[17]

In other words, if you are painted as one of the "bad guys" in the prosecution's narrative, you are likely to incur repercussions, including being prosecuted individually.[18]

Moreover, the importance of a prosecution's theory of the case doesn't end at the investigation stage. How the narrative of the case is shaped and presented at trial becomes significant. In a criminal case, the prosecutor has the opportunity to deliver opening arguments, and to present his or her case, before the defense does.[19] As a result, the finder of fact—who is typically a jury—is exposed to the prosecutor's theory of the case, and the prosecutor's characterization of the corporation and its employees, before learning any other facts or hearing any alternative narrative of events.

The prosecution's opportunity to present its theory of the case to the jury first is powerful. Prosecutors have a primary opportunity to shape the jurors' opinions.[20] Jurors, like most human beings in general, are affected by cognitive bias. One form of such bias is confirmation bias.

Once we form a theory of something—like a theory of what happened in a criminal case—we tend to discount information that challenges the accuracy of our theory. We may overvalue, even to the point of mischaracterizing, evidence that supports our theory of events. Moreover, when we are faced with new information, we are unlikely to abandon or significantly alter our original theory.

Confirmation bias even affects how we remember old information. Research suggests that, once we have developed a theory to understand events in the world, we tend to remember previous information as being more supportive of that theory than it actually is.[21]

The prosecution's theory of the case may also tie into biases held by jurors toward corporations. Although 86% of national survey respondents indicate that they hold generally favorable views of business, the public and juries are sensitive to issues of corporate abuse.[22] Over half of Americans believe that "white collar crimes to make a profit" occur "very often" in business.[23]

Eighty percent of respondents believe that "executives of big companies often try to cover up the harm [that] they do," and around half of respondents generally feel that "business and industry have too much power."[24]

A corporation's ethical reputation matters to juries. Both the corporation's overall public reputation and the perceived "social utility" of its products appear to influence jury judgments.[25] In a study of employment discrimination lawsuits against 826 companies, companies with better public reputations were 14% less likely to be held liable by juries in lawsuits than companies with worse reputations.[26]

Respondents seem to hold particularly negative opinions of corporations when they are portrayed as large and deep-pocketed.[27] People acting as jurors in experiments used a "different, and higher, standard in evaluating corporate wrongdoing" based on what they assumed to be the "resource superiority of corporations."[28]

Prosecutors aware of these biases may attempt to paint corporate defendants as being "large and deep-pocketed" when presenting their theory of the case to a jury.[29] Corporations need to be careful of their reputations and of being perceived as too powerful to respect the law. Jurors tend to want to remedy what they see as the injustice of such a corporation not following the rules. Similarly, in order to maintain the sympathy of a jury, individual defendants often want not to appear too affluent or too removed from otherwise-relatable economic circumstances.

What does cooperating with a prosecution mean for a business?

Explicitly cooperating with a prosecution may allow defendants, and particularly businesses, to avoid criminal penalties and sometimes criminal convictions altogether.[30] In addition to plea bargains, prosecutors have begun to use NPAs and DPAs to reward and encourage corporate cooperation.[31] As described more extensively in Chapters 13 and 14, NPAs are agreements with prosecutors not to file formal charges with a court regarding a defendant's conduct, as long as the defendant abides by certain terms. DPAs are agreements with prosecutors to file charges with a court, but then to withdraw those charges against defendants for agreeing to, and abiding by, conditions for better behavior, including more often, monitoring. DPAs may also typically require a defendant to admit to some fault and potentially to pay some fines. Because the government may settle a case without requiring the corporation to plead guilty in court to its criminal misconduct, the advantage of these agreements is that corporations may avoid criminal conviction entirely.

Prosecutors are more likely to agree to a NPA or DPA when the corporation voluntarily discloses its wrongdoing and cooperates with the government's investigation. NPAs and DPAs generally consist of four elements: "an admission of facts, an agreement of cooperation, a specified duration for the agreement, and an agreement to monetary and non-monetary sanctions."[32] If the corporation fails to make the changes demanded by the prosecutor as a condition of the NPA or DPA, the corporation may be criminally charged (or have its charges reinstated) and potentially convicted.

Federal prosecutors are using NPAs and DPAs with increasing frequency.[33] Before 2003, only two federal criminal cases against corporations were settled using a NPA or DPA.[34] However, between 2007–11, 44% of cases against corporations were settled using NPAs or DPAs.[35]

As of 2020, the number of NPAs and DPAs has continued to rise. In 2018, the monetary amount recovered under these programs reached nearly U.S. $8.1 billion.[36] Many recent NPAs and DPAs involve financial companies, but there seems to be a growing emphasis on antitrust, anticorruption, and other consumer-protection measures.

Although it is difficult to quantify exactly what corporations' average reductions in liability seem to be for signing NPAs and DPAs, the terms of these agreements may be on similar footing to other plea agreements, if not contain terms more favorable toward corporations.

Standard plea agreement terms are already quite favorable to corporate defendants. Under a 2014 standard plea agreement, for example, Alcoa World Alumina LLC paid U.S. $223 million in sanctions for violating the Foreign Corrupt Practices Act instead of the U.S. $1 billion that prosecutors had estimated that it would. In order to qualify for the plea agreement, the company conducted an extensive internal investigation, disclosed relevant documents to government authorities, and made employees available for interviews.[37]

In an interesting 2020 DPA, Chipotle Mexican Grill, Inc.—a large made-to-order chain restaurant—was able to resolve potential charges stemming from allegations that it pressured employees to work when they were sick, and that its poor safety practices caused foodborne illness in more than 1,000 people.[38] Although food-poisoning claims are very rarely settled without serious penalties, and they have involved jail time for executives such as Peanut Corporation of America's Stewart Parnell,[39] Chipotle was able instead to pay U.S. $25 million over four installments, and agree to adjust its food-safety practices and to increase its internal monitoring reporting to its board.[40] The company, however, also had to sign an unusual pledge affirming that it would be directly responsible for any violation of its agreement by its employees down to the level of Field Leader. In the language of the Chipotle DPA, the company agreed that, should "any Chipotle officer or employee at or senior to the rank of Field Leader (or functional equivalent) . . . knowingly violate[] or fail[] to perform any of [the company's] obligations under this agreement[,] . . . the Government may declare this [DPA] agreement breached" and potential prosecution may follow.[41]

A new prosecutorial tool to resolve cases may have emerged as well, but remains relatively rare: declinations with disgorgement.[42] In declinations with disgorgement, the prosecution declines to bring charges when the company both cooperates and pays back the full amount of its ill-gotten profits. These resolutions, however, appear to be reserved for companies with particularly good records and that have been especially cooperative with the government.

How, in brief, do businesses conduct internal investigations?

The DOJ seeks to encourage internal investigations, and it often rewards corporations that conduct them well when determining whether to prosecute.[43] The message for corporations is that, as soon as its officers become aware of potential wrongdoing, they should conduct an internal investigation for the corporation to be eligible for reduced or eliminated legal penalties.[44] (For more on the role of investigations within compliance and ethics systems, see Chapters 13 and 14. For notes on what to expect as a whistleblower during an internal investigation, see Chapter 12.)

We would break the stages of most internal investigations into five basic steps:

1. Client identification and determination of scope

Once a corporation receives an allegation of wrongdoing, or otherwise discovers an irregularity, it should initiate an internal investigation by creating a document that outlines its reasons for launching the investigation and what person or entity helped trigger the investigation. Although the corporation may initially attempt to limit the investigation's scope, that scope may broaden as the corporation collects new information in the course of its process.

2. Investigation staffing

Businesses have choices in how to conduct internal investigations, and the staffing of internal investigations may vary by how serious the company considers the allegations to be, and by what the company may be trying to signal to outside authorities about its responsiveness.

Particularly serious or politically important internal investigations may be conducted by a corporation's board of directors or special committee. Corporations also turn to in-house counsel (attorneys employed by the company) or to outside legal counsel to conduct investigations. In-house counsel may be valuable in conducting internal investigations because they may know best how the company operates. Outside counsel may be valuable because they may make the investigation appear more independent to outside authorities, and they typically have more experience conducting internal investigations across different types of organizations.

3. Document collection and analysis

Whoever conducts the investigation on behalf of the company will want to collect and analyze documents related to the allegations.[45] Investigators may instruct corporate employees to follow a document-retention policy designed to save communications and materials relevant to the investigation. Investigators may also require employees to search for, and to hand over, certain documents from their records.

4. Interviewing

Investigators typically conduct interviews within a company in "bottom-up" order.[46] They start interviewing lower-level employees first, and they then work their way up to higher-level employees.

There are a few strategic reasons for starting interviews at the bottom of a company's hierarchy. Employees at the lowest level of the company may not fully understand how their behavior may have been manipulated from above, and how it may belong to a larger pattern that superiors may seek to hide. Similarly, employees spread out across the lowest levels of the company may not as easily communicate with each other to disguise patterns or to destroy evidence. They are also less likely than executives to be able to afford an outside lawyer, and to fight or refuse to cooperate with the company's investigation. Most of all, once investigators have been able to establish the consistent testimony of a large number of people about events, it becomes harder for high-level managers and executives to contradict their subordinates or suddenly to shift the narrative of events for their own purposes. (See also this chapter's earlier discussion about the power of narrative in cases.)

Prior to every interview, investigating attorneys must issue employees what are called "*Upjohn* warnings."[47] These verbal, and sometimes also written, warnings remind employees that the attorneys represent the corporation, not any given employee. Information shared in the interview is privileged, but it is the corporation that has the exclusive right to waive that privilege.[48] (See additional discussion of these interviews in Chapter 12 on whistleblowing.)

5. Reporting findings

At the conclusion of their investigation, investigators submit their report to the person or body within the corporation charged with overseeing their process.[49] Their report should include a summary of all factual information ascertained, and it may be accompanied by recommendations for company action. The report may, for example, recommend that the company fire or discipline specific employees, as well as improve its internal control policies. If the investigation is related to an impending government action or litigation, the report may also contain recommendations relevant to those proceedings.

It is the company's decision what to do with its report, but it is becoming common for companies to share the report with authorities after implementing the report's recommended changes. Sharing the report can be an important step for the company to demonstrate its cooperation with authorities, and either to convince authorities not to bring charges, or to reduce the severity of the charges and potential penalties for wrongdoing.

What does cooperating with the prosecution mean for an employee?

Employees may consider cooperating directly with an external governmental investigation as well as the company's internal one. In practical terms, an employee usually does not have much choice whether to cooperate with a company's internal investigation. As we covered more extensively in Chapter 12, although you have the right to invoke the U.S. Constitution's Fifth-Amendment protection against self-incrimination in questioning, the company also usually has the right to fire you for not cooperating, or for not telling the full truth when you do cooperate. As we discussed in Chapter 12, if you do not trust the motives of your company in this process, you will likely want your own attorney to be present during any interviews.

Employees also end up helping a governmental authority's investigation directly when the company's internal investigation has failed, either because the company may have covered up the truth, or because it may have inappropriately portrayed someone as the scapegoat for other people's actions.

Employees may report externally as whistleblowers (see Chapter 12 on whistleblowing, and Chapter 14 on the motives of whistleblowers), seek out external authorities for negotiations to contain damage to their own liability, or be contacted directly by government agents for their testimony. Depending on the employee's potential legal liability, his or her first contact with the government may not be merely a request for an interview, but a subpoena for legal testimony, or even an arrest and interrogation.

Given these options, employees who fear for their own legal liability may hire lawyers to reach out to law enforcement in advance to offer their side of the story, and help to control the narrative of the case—including the characterizations of actors and events that we discussed earlier as particularly important at many points in the case.

In evaluating his or her own potential liability, an individual has to consider how he or she fits into the government's narrative of the case. Sometimes the government properly understands how you fit into the story of the case, and sometimes its narrative feels unfair.

If you are thinking of approaching the government separately to attempt to change its narrative of the case—particularly how you fit into it or how much liability for which you should be responsible—you have to be clear-eyed about what evidence you can present for your alternative narrative, and how credible you are as a witness. Factors to think about here may include your own criminal or professional history of misconduct, if any; how much the government already knows about what you—and others about whom you have information—have done; how accurate the information is that the government has; and whether other parties plan to cooperate.

Whether an employee will want to work with his or her employer in hiring a lawyer and making this outreach is a matter of legal strategy. As we mentioned in previous chapters, the interests of an employee and the company may or may not end up aligned. However, many corporate directors and officers maintain provisions in their contracts for special insurance ("D&O" insurance) that will pay the legal fees of attorneys to defend them. These top employees may also be backstopped by indemnification (repayment of fees as incurred for their defense) from the company. (For more on D&O insurance, indemnification, and other provisions, see Chapters 5 and 6 on corporations.)

A common practical problem for directors, officers, and employees whose companies will pay for their legal fees is that the company then ends up effectively controlling their defense. These employees (and others) often have to enter into joint defense agreements (JDAs) that enable information-sharing among defendants. But JDAs may also restrict employees' ability to make a deal with the government on their own. In a related issue, indemnification from the company may not be available if you have to plead to a lesser charge in order to avoid a more serious one. These restrictions can significantly tie an individual defendant's hands in negotiations with prosecutors.

Additionally, an individual's decision to cooperate with a government investigation, and later prosecution, may depend on how much information the prosecution already has about the case.[50] It is helpful for any potential defendant who wants to cooperate to know about the existence of an investigation early, as there can end up being a race to the government's door to provide evidence and receive cooperation credit. Typically, the company's and employees' attorneys will attempt to learn in advance what criminal charges the government is considering bringing, whom the government intends to charge, what evidence of criminal wrongdoing the government already possesses, and what the government believes happened (i.e., its narrative of the case).

As mentioned in the whistleblowing chapter (Chapter 12), cooperating with a governmental investigation is not always easy or over quickly. Even whistleblowers who have nothing of which to be ashamed can find it stressful to wear a wire for secretly recording conversations and complete other tasks that the government may ask of them during an investigation.

However, white collar defendants who hesitate may be too late in cooperating once the government has fully formulated its narrative of the case, and it has been sure enough of its narrative (and has enough evidence to support that narrative) that it has filed charges. At the federal level, criminal charges are filed as indictments. Once such charges have been filed against a defendant, the defendant has been indicted.

Much of the government's formal case will be revealed in the indictment. Defendants also usually learn soon after indictment to which judge the case will be assigned. Judges develop their own reputations for ruling on motions, presiding over trials, and harshness in sentencing. Your attorney should talk to you about both the prosecutor's and judge's reputations when counseling you about your case.

If, either at the investigatory stage or once indicted, an employee wants to cooperate with the government, he or she may have to be prepared to admit criminal wrongdoing. For white collar criminals who may never have committed crimes before or who think of themselves as otherwise good citizens of their communities and trustworthy members of their families, reaching the emotional point of admitting to criminal wrongdoing (and potentially pleading guilty to it) may be painful. This stage of the process can take a surprising amount of time, and it may require peeling back layers of self-justifications and rationalizations that defendants have spent years building. (See Chapters 10 (leadership), Chapter 4 (science), and Chapter 9 (major ethical traps), regarding some of these rationalizations.)

Employees considering cooperating with the government will have their attorneys meet with the government, discuss what information they have to give, and negotiate the terms of an agreement. Ultimately, the employee and his or her attorney will decide whether to cooperate based on factors such as:

1. "The strength of the government's case against the [employee] and [the] likelihood of prosecution if the [employee] does not cooperate."[51]
2. "The agency, division, office, or section investigating the [employee]."[52] Different agencies have different powers of enforcement, and some potential penalties may be more serious than others. In addition, if the employee or his or her company are subject to multiple investigations, the cooperation agreement may require that the employee admit to additional criminal wrongdoing outside the scope of the immediate investigation.

3. "If the government has charged the [employee], the assigned judge's history of sentencing cooperators."[53] An employee may be more likely to cooperate with the government if the judge overseeing the case tends to impose more severe penalties on defendants who go to trial, or is particularly accommodating to reductions in liability through plea agreements.

4. "The [employee's] personal characteristics and resources."[54] Employees with more resources and stronger legal defenses against government allegations may be less likely to cooperate.

5. "The [employee's] likely ability to comply with all terms of the anticipated cooperation agreement."[55] The employee needs to consider how able and prepared he or she is to answer questions truthfully, no matter how broad the government's questions are.

6. "The likelihood that other parties choose to cooperate against the [employee]."[56] If other witnesses and co-workers are prepared to testify against the employee, the employee may decide that it is in his or her interest to cooperate first, or the government may not need his or her cooperation anymore. Once the government does not need an employee's cooperation, the employee is less likely to have his or her liability reduced.

7. "The amount and type of requested cooperation."[57]

8. "The charges to which the [employee] must plead guilty."[58] The employee may not want to cooperate if, even after cooperating, he or she is still required to plead guilty to crimes carrying serious penalties. Not cooperating, however, takes the gamble that the employee won't be indicted, convicted, and face more serious liability at sentencing.

Once an employee decides to cooperate with the government, he or she will likely reach one of three types of agreements: (1) a Cooperation Agreement, which requires the employee to plead guilty; (2) a Non-Prosecution Agreement

(NPA), which does not require the employee to plead guilty, but may involve the completion of corrective measures; or (3) a Deferred Prosecution Agreement (DPA), which may not require the employee ultimately to plead guilty, but is filed in court and often does require the admission of some fault, as well as the implementation of corrective measures.

Typically, in order to receive cooperation credit from the government, the employee should expect, at a minimum, to:

- meet with the government, often multiple times, depending on the complexity of the case, and the employee's role in it;
- truthfully answer repeated questions about your criminal wrongdoing, and the potentially criminal actions of others (in many prosecutor's offices, cooperation credit is not available without also helping to build the case against others);
- turn over certain documents in your possession, or that you have access to; and
- testify at a grand jury hearing to support an indictment of defendants and at trial to support the government's case for conviction. If you accept the offer of charges to a lesser crime, you will have to admit the facts of your own wrongdoing and acknowledge them in court before a judge.

You may also, as we mentioned earlier, have to speak with other people to record conversations (such as while wearing a wire) and to establish their knowledge of events and complicity in wrongdoing. The government may ask other uncomfortable things of you as well.

Once an employee decides to cooperate with the government, it is difficult to reverse that decision.[59] Cooperation agreements often require employees to provide incriminating information that would seriously weaken defenses they might otherwise have made at a trial.

Criminal penalties issued to cooperating defendants in white collar cases, however, are substantially less severe than penalties issued to those who stand trial and are convicted of crimes.[60] Defendants charged with a white collar crime who cooperate satisfactorily with the government may receive sentences that are, on average, 90% lower than the minimum sentence recommended by the federal sentencing guidelines.[61]

What are the steps of a prosecution?

There are at least six steps to a federal prosecution. It is typically in the interest of both corporations and individuals to resolve allegations early in a prosecution before being subject to potentially larger sentencing consequences at trial.

Step 1: Allegations brought to light

As opposed to other types of crimes, white collar criminal activity may not be typically observed by patrolling law-enforcement officers.[62] Rather, allegations surface in many ways, such as through private securities lawsuits, detection by the company itself, or whistleblower reports (such as from former or current employees who notify law enforcement of criminal activity). (See Chapters 12, 13, and 14 on where whistleblower tips come from, as many of them also do not originate from inside the company.) A surprising number of allegations come to the government's attention through general media reporting as well.

Step 2: Pre-trial investigation

After the government learns of potential criminal activity, it may launch a pre-trial investigation to gather facts. Often such investigations start within specialized agencies such as the Federal Bureau of Investigation (FBI), the Internal Revenue Service (IRS), or the U.S. Securities and Exchange Commission (SEC). These agencies may either then bring charges on their own (such as the SEC), or they bring their investigations to the DOJ's federal prosecutors to review the case and file charges.[63]

Step 3: Decision whether to charge

In criminal cases against corporations, a prosecutor's decision whether or not to charge a corporation may be more consequential than the actual trial.[64] Most corporations seek to avoid trial. As a legal matter (see Chapters 5 and 6), corporate criminal liability is relatively easy to establish, and corporations face many challenges in front of juries at trial. Moreover, even when a corporation successfully defends itself against charges in court, or it is able to overturn its conviction, the business costs of being criminally charged can be deeply damaging to it. In the wake of the Enron scandal, for example, the accounting firm Arthur Andersen had to dissolve due to reputational damage from its related criminal case, despite the fact that the firm was ultimately able to overturn its conviction.

Because corporations may face such serious damage from criminal charges, they often focus on convincing a prosecutor not to charge them in the first place. Skilled defense attorneys representing corporations petition prosecutors early to exercise their discretion to not bring charges against the attorneys' clients. It is an asset in this negotiation for the corporation to be able to show prosecutors that the company conducted a thorough internal investigation, and that it handled the internal resolution of the case so well that additional governmental action should not be necessary.

In cases against corporations, prosecutors also consider whether to bring criminal charges against specific employees.[65] Federal charges stemming from the criminal investigations of corporations have been brought against both upper- and lower-level management employees. For example, in the aftermath of the 2010 BP oil spill, the employees individually criminally charged were the lower-level supervisors who worked at the site of the damaged oil well.

What the DOJ's approach should be in bringing criminal charges against individuals related to organizational wrongdoing continues to be debated.[66] Generally, the DOJ is trying to charge more individuals—and especially more individuals with management oversight responsibilities—in its cases. In the wake of the BP oil spill, and similar cases, the DOJ was particularly vulnerable to criticism that it charged only low-level employees who "had no role in the development of BP's policies or its corporate culture."[67] See Chapters 13 and 14 for discussion of the extensive emphasis that the DOJ now puts on evaluating the health of a company's ethical culture and its compliance systems.

Step 4: Plea bargaining/guilty pleas

Prosecutors offer plea bargains as opportunities for defendants to receive much more reduced sentences than they might otherwise receive should they go to trial.[68] As both prosecutors and corporations seek to avoid the high costs of a trial, plea bargains, and variations of such agreements, are the most common way for criminal cases to be resolved.[69] In fact, although the use of methods to settle criminal cases against corporate defendants such as NPAs and DPAs has increased, traditional plea bargains remain the primary way that federal criminal cases against corporations are resolved.[70] In 2017, over 68% of corporate criminal cases that settled were settled through traditional plea bargains.[71]

Ultimately, the vast majority of organizations criminally charged plead guilty. In 2017, 91.6% of organizational defendants eventually pleaded guilty.[72]

Step 5: Trial

If no plea bargain is reached, the case proceeds to trial. Criminal trials are tried before juries unless the defense waives that right and requests a trial by judge. Requesting trial before a judge can make sense for some defendants, especially in complicated factual cases under difficult points of law, but it is still rarely done.

The trial itself begins with opening statements, in which the government proceeds first because it carries the burden of proof.[73] Following opening statements, the prosecutor presents his or her case-in-chief by calling witnesses whom the defense has the opportunity to cross-examine. The defense is not required to present any evidence, but after the prosecutor rests his or her case, the defense may present a case and call witnesses of its own. Following the presentation of both initial cases, the prosecution may present a brief rebuttal case, presenting evidence and witnesses that contradict any evidence presented by the defense.[74]

Each side may present closing arguments. The judge then instructs the jury on matters of law. The jury meets separately to deliberate away from the parties. When it returns with a verdict, the verdict is read aloud in the courtroom in front of both the prosecution and the defense.

Step 6: Sentencing and outcomes

Corporations and individuals who do not resolve allegations and investigations before trial are typically found guilty, and they are almost always subject to much higher penalties than had they cooperated to avoid the imposition of charges or agreed to a plea bargain to limit their liability.

The odds of going to trial against the government and being acquitted are not good. From 2011 to 2014, of the 414 people individually prosecuted related to corporate DPAs and NPAs, 266 (64.3%) pleaded guilty to some crime. Of the 12% of individuals who went to trial over these years, roughly 80% (79.2% or 42 individuals) were convicted.[75]

It is typically the best-funded and most questionable factual cases that go to trial. Of these exceptional cases, roughly 21% (20.7% or 11 individuals) were acquitted.[76] These statistics represent the end of a long, painful, expensive, and reputationally costly process. And even then it is possible that the government may open civil or other additional cases against them.

From an individual defendant's point of view, it would have been best to have been one of the people not charged, or even one of the 23% (22.9%) of individuals charged, but against whom charges were dropped—presumably because of their cooperation.

What happens to corporations and individuals who don't resolve allegations and investigations before trial?

Corporations and individuals who don't resolve allegations and investigations before trial typically face high penalties at sentencing. The data on organizational defendants helps tell this story.

As we mentioned, 68% of organizational criminal defendants settle their cases through traditional plea bargains, and 91.6% of organizational defendants criminally charged eventually plead guilty.[77] We also know that the plea bargain discount for criminal sentencing, especially individual cases, is roughly 90%.[78]

Of the rare 8.4% of indicted organizations in 2017 that did not plead guilty to criminal charges, some may have been able to convince the prosecutor to drop charges, or we do not see them show up as convictions through potential NPAs or DPAs. The remainder would have gone to trial, at considerable financial and reputational cost.

When a defendant organization or individual loses at trial, the potential consequences at sentencing can also be high.

At sentencing, the judge will review the facts of the case as determined by the jury, as well as the defendant's criminal history, standing in the community, cooperation with prosecutors, and other mitigating factors. As organizations themselves cannot be jailed (see Chapter 6 for how laws are enforced against corporations as legal "persons"), sentences against them typically involve financial penalties, in the form of fines, restitution, and other contributions.

In 2017, of the 131 organizations convicted of federal criminal offenses, 87% were ordered to pay monetary penalties in the form of fines, restitution, or both.[79] Nearly two-thirds of the organizations (62.6%) were ordered to complete probation.[80] Probation for corporations can take many forms, but it usually requires that they stay out of legal trouble for a certain period of time, pay what they owe under a judgment, and possibly fulfill other requirements such as donating a certain amount of employee time and resources to make amends to victims and the community.

Additionally, as a condition of probation, 22.1% of organizational offenders were specifically required to develop a compliance and ethics program. (See Chapters 13 and 14 for more information on compliance and ethics programs.)

Organizations are typically ordered to pay fines and restitution. There are some interesting characteristics to these penalties in the organizational context. In 2017, for example, the median amount of the fines in organizational cases was U.S. $662,500.[81] The average amount, however, was nearly U.S. $70 million ($67,180,825).[82] (As a reminder, the median amount is the fine that sits in the middle of the range of fines. The average amount is when all the fines are totaled, and then divided by the number of fines.)

Note that the median payment amount in these cases was roughly one-hundredth of the average amount. Another way to say this is that the average payment amount of these organizational fines was roughly 100 times larger (101.4x) than the median amount.

This stark contrast in the median versus average amount highlights two important things. First, it reflects the impact of so many organizational defendants pleading guilty (91.6%) and receiving lower fines. Second, it dramatizes how high the penalties were for the few organizations that either went to trial, or that engaged in extremely costly wrongdoing and paid accordingly large fines.

A similar pattern can be seen in the 2017 organizational sentencing restitution numbers. The median amount of restitution imposed on organizational defendants that year was U.S. $277,000.[83] The average amount of restitution imposed on organizational defendants, however, was over U.S. $27 million ($27,233,269).[84] The average amount of restitution was also then roughly 100 times (98.3x) the median amount of restitution. Again, the dramatic difference in these numbers highlights the importance of cooperation and settlement.

What lessons should businesses and individuals take away from this closing chapter and this book in general?

The main lesson that business and individuals should take away is that the best course of action is the ethical one from the beginning. Businesses and individuals should not want to be in the position of having to negotiate their penalties with prosecutors or contesting their case before a jury. So many other things inside the company went wrong long before they ended up in this position.

We started this book talking about what business ethics are, and how important they are to both individuals and society. We finish this book with a pragmatic discussion of penalties, but we hope that individuals and businesses steer far clear of needing these last pieces of advice.

Well-meaning businesses and individuals can avoid the common ethical traps we have described in the book, and they can invest as we have described in building ethical businesses and cultures. What everyone needs to know about business ethics is that they are a constant work in progress, but they can be something of which you, your business, the people who work with you, and the community in which you are embedded can be proud.

We close this book by focusing again on the positive power of business ethics to increase both profitability and other rewards. Choosing to be ethical in business not only avoids the stress, expense, reputational damage, incarceration, and fines that we talk about in this chapter. Ethical business is good business. It is sustainable and profitable business. Ultimately, it is a much more deeply rewarding way of life.

APPENDIX: ADDITIONAL RESOURCES AND PEOPLE YOU CAN REACH OUT TO

The following resources are presented thematically by chapter and by the potential value that they may offer to the reader. Website references were current as of when the resources were compiled.

Chapter 1: An Overview of Business Ethics

1. *What Are Business Ethics?*, CORP. FIN. INST., https://corpor atefinanceinstitute.com/resources/knowledge/other/ business-ethics/ (discussing the three basic components of business ethics).
2. *What Is Accounting Ethics*, CORP. FIN. INST., https://corpor atefinanceinstitute.com/resources/knowledge/account ing/accounting-ethics/ (discussing ethics and possible conflicts of interests in the accounting industry).
3. *Code of Ethics*, NAT'L SOC'Y PROF. ENGINEERS, https://www. nspe.org/resources/ethics/code-ethics (containing a code of ethics for engineers).
4. *Model Rules of Professional Conduct: Preamble & Scope*, A.B.A., https://www.americanbar.org/groups/professional_ responsibility/publications/model_rules_of_professio nal_conduct/model_rules_of_professional_conduct_pre

amble_scope/ (detailing Rules of Professional Conduct for attorneys, which describe ethical rules attorneys must follow and emphasize the importance of following an unwritten, personal code of ethics).

5. *Ethics Resources*, MARKKULA CENTER FOR APPLIED ETHICS AT SANTA CLARA UNIV., https://www.scu.edu/ethics/ethics-resources/ (allowing free public access to hundreds of ethics articles, case studies, podcasts, training videos, briefings, and other materials touching on ethics across a variety of fields).

6. LYNN STOUT, CULTIVATING CONSCIENCE: HOW GOOD LAWS MAKE GOOD PEOPLE (2010).

Chapter 2: The Benefits of Acting Ethically

1. *Ethics Pays: How an Investment in Ethics Translates to Profit, Productivity, & Prestige*, NOTRE DAME DELOITTE CTR. ETHICAL LEADERSHIP, https://ethicalleadership.nd.edu/assets/256012/ethics_pays.pdf (discussing how an investment in ethics in the workplace can generate higher profits and productivity).

2. Larry Alton, *How Much Do a Company's Ethics Matter in the Modern Professional Climate?*, FORBES (Sept. 12, 2017), https://www.forbes.com/sites/larryalton/2017/09/12/how-much-do-a-companys-ethics-matter-in-the-modern-professional-climate/#7dd6b2561c79 (discussing how ethical business practices are an important factor that prospective employees consider in deciding where to work).

3. Glenn Martin, *Once Again: Why Should Businesses Be Ethical?*, 17 BUS. AND PROF'L ETHICS J. 39 (1998) (discussing four reasons a business should be persuaded to act reasonably, including legal issues, public image, pragmatic concerns, and moral reasons).

4. *3 Reasons an Ethical Business Leads to Profits*, WASH. ST. UNIV. CARSON COLLEGE OF BUSINESS, https://onlinemba.wsu.edu/blog/3-reasons-an-ethical-business-leads-to-profits/ (discussing three ways that acting ethically improves a

business's bottom line, and listing additional resources for the reader).

5. Carter McNamara, *10 Benefits of Managing Ethics in the Workplace*, BLOG: BUS. ETHICS, CULTURE AND PERFORMANCE (Oct. 23, 2010), https://managementhelp.org/blogs/busin ess-ethics/2010/10/23/10-benefits-of-managing-ethics-in-the-workplace/ (discussing ten, nonmoral reasons why acting ethically in the workplace can benefit your business).

Chapter 3: Moral Philosophical Bases for Business Ethics

1. *Special Report on Business Ethics: Moral Philosophy*, WHARTON SCH. UNIV. OF PA. (2018), https://knowledge.wharton. upenn.edu/special-report/special-report-on-business-eth ics-moral-philosophy/ (exploring how to view business behavior through the lens of moral philosophy and how to use moral philosophy to make more ethical business decisions).
2. Connie S. Rosati, *Moral Motivation*, STAN. ENCYCLOPEDIA OF PHIL., https://plato.stanford.edu/archives/win2016/entr ies/moral-motivation/ (discussing how judgments of right and wrong motivate people to take certain actions, which is also known as moral motivation).
3. Raymond D. Smith, *Motivating Ethical Behavior Through Cost–Benefit Analysis*, 16 WORLD BUS. ACAD. (Jan. 2002) (discussing how critical, ethical decisions are largely impacted by the employee's work environment and how it is up to management to maximize the attractiveness of making the ethical choice).
4. *The Major Steps in a Cost–Benefit Analysis*, AUSTL. GOV'T., DEP'T OF THE PRIME MINISTER AND CABINET, https://www. pmc.gov.au/ria-mooc/extra-detail/cba/major-steps-cost-benefit-analysis (detailing nine steps required to make a cost–benefit analysis).
5. *Ethics Guide: Virtue Ethics*, BBC, http://www.bbc.co.uk/eth ics/introduction/virtue.shtml (explaining virtue ethics, its principles, types of virtues, and some pros and cons of this type of ethical thinking).

Chapter 4: What Does Science Tell Us About Ethical Behavior?

1. Ron Carucci, *Why Ethical People Make Unethical Choices*, HARV. BUS. REV. (Dec. 16, 2016), https://hbr.org/2016/12/why-ethical-people-make-unethical-choices   (discussing five ways in which employers may unknowingly encourage otherwise ethical employees to make unethical decisions).

2. Mark Alfano et al., *Experimental Moral Philosophy*, STAN. ENCYCLOPEDIA OF PHIL., https://plato.stanford.edu/archives/win2018/entries/experimental-moral/   (discussing experiments concerning the nature of moral reasoning and judgment).

3. Henry Engler & Anna Wood, *How Banks Are Using Behavioral Science to Prevent Scandals*, HARV. BUS. REV. (Apr. 28, 2020), https://hbr.org/2020/04/how-banks-are-using-behavioral-science-to-prevent-scandals (discussing behavioral risk task forces that banks have hired, their techniques, and the cost–benefits to the banks).

4. Carsten Tams, *Ethics As Freedom, Part I: Behavioral Science's Surprising Insights About Motivation Every Ethics Manager Should Know*, FORBES (Oct. 31, 2019), https://www.forbes.com/sites/carstentams/2019/10/31/ethics-as-freedom-part-i--behavioral-sciences-surprising-insights-about-motivation-every-ethics-manager-should-know/#5d9865127de7 (discussing how managers can lead their employees in a way that increases the likelihood that the employees make ethical decisions).

5. Carsten Tams, *Ethics As Freedom, Part II: How to Apply Motivational Science to Ethics Management*, FORBES (Dec. 31, 2019), https://www.forbes.com/sites/carstentams/2019/10/31/ethics-as-freedom-part-ii--how-to-apply-motivational-science-to-ethics-management/#5afbf23d17e8 (applying the behavioral science explained in the preceding article to managers and businesses).

6. Marete Wedell-Wedellsborg, *The Psychology Behind Unethical Behavior*, HARV. BUS. REV. (Apr. 12, 2019), https://hbr.

org/2019/04/the-psychology-behind-unethical-behav ior (discussing the three psychological dynamics that lead groups to act unethically).

7. Recordings: Overconfidence Bias: Concepts Unwrapped (Ethics Unwrapped), https://ethicsunwrapped.utexas. edu/video/overconfidence-bias (discussing people's tendencies to think they are more ethical than they actually are and to be overconfident in themselves to the point of making unethical decisions).

Chapter 5: Legal Foundations of Business Ethics

1. Mark Feffer, *Ethical vs. Legal Responsibilities for HR Professionals*, Soc'y Hum. Res. Mgmt., https://www.shrm. org/resourcesandtools/hr-topics/behavioral-competenc ies/ethical-practice/pages/ethical-and-legal-responsibilit ies-for-hr-professionals.aspx (discussing the tensions that human resources professionals face between their duty to the company and their personal ethical principles).

2. *The Delaware Way: Deference to the Business Judgment of Directors Who Act Loyally and Carefully*, Del. Corp. Law, https://corplaw.delaware.gov/delaware-way-business-judgment/ (discussing the business judgment rule, the duty of care, and the duty of loyalty).

3. Catherine Pastrikos Kelly, *What You Should Know About the Implied Duty of Good Faith and Fair Dealing*, A.B.A., https:// www.americanbar.org/groups/litigation/committees/ business-torts-unfair-competition/practice/2016/duty-of-good-faith-fair-dealing/ (discussing the implied duty of good faith and fair dealing as it pertains to franchise contracts).

4. *Fiduciary Duties*, Board Source, https://boardsource.org/ resources/fiduciary-responsibilities/ (discussing fiduciary duties regarding finances in the company and specific questions board members should ask themselves).

5. *Ethics, Morality, Law—What's the Difference?*, THE ETHICS CTR., https://ethics.org.au/ethics-morality-law-whats-the-difference/ (explaining the difference between personal ethics, morality, and the narrower sphere of the law).

6. FRANK M. PLACENTI, DIRECTOR'S HANDBOOK: A FIELD GUIDE TO 101 SITUATIONS COMMONLY ENCOUNTERED IN THE BOARDROOM (2019).

Chapter 6: Understanding Corporations, LLCs, and Other "Legal Persons"

1. *Federal Securities Laws*, SEC. EXCH. COMM'N, https://www.sec.gov/page/federal-securities-laws?auHash = B8gdTzu6 DrpJNvsGlS1-JY1LnXDZQqS-JgJAgaSXimg (discussing securities laws that apply to corporations).

2. Lynn S. Paine & Suraj Srinivassan, *A Guide to the Big Ideas and Debates in Corporate Governance*, HARV. BUS. REV. (Oct. 14, 2019), https://hbr.org/2019/10/a-guide-to-the-big-ideas-and-debates-in-corporate-governance (discussing the relationships between a corporation's board of directors and its shareholders).

3. Gigio Ninan, *Should You Form an LLC or an S-Corp, and What's the Difference?*, FORBES N.Y. BUS. COUNCIL, https://www.forbes.com/sites/forbesnycouncil/2018/05/29/should-you-form-an-llc-or-an-s-corp-and-whats-the-difference/#593326356f64 (breaking down the decision-making process of business owners when looking to create either an LLC or corporation).

4. Ciara Torres-Spelliscy, *Does "We The People" Include Corporations?*, 43 HUM. RTS. MAG. (Jan. 1, 2018), https://www.americanbar.org/groups/crsj/publications/human_rights_magazine_home/we-the-people/we-the-people-corporations/ (discussing who and what the Supreme Court counts as a legal person with protectable rights).

5. Nina Totenberg, *When Did Companies Become People? Excavating the Legal Evolution*, Nat'l Pub. Radio (July 28, 2014), https://www.npr.org/2014/07/28/335288388/when-did-companies-become-people-excavating-the-legal-evolution (discussing the history of corporations' rights in the United States and how it led to the concept of corporate personhood).

Chapter 7: The Corporation as an Ethical "Person" in Modern Society

1. Jeffrey Nesteruk, *Legal Persons and Moral Worlds: Ethical Choices Within the Corporate Environment*, 29 Am. Bus. L.J. 75 (1991) (explaining a corporation as a legal person and how the moral world of a corporation and its structure can impact the ethical decision making of those associated with it).
2. *United Nations Global Compact*, https://www.unglobalcompact.org/ (discussing a voluntary initiative based on CEO commitments to implement universal sustainability principles and to take steps to support UN goals).
3. *United Nations Convention Against Corruption*, https://www.unodc.org/unodc/en/corruption/uncac.html (containing a legally binding set of standards and rules that the United States and 186 other countries have ratified to strengthen their legal and regulatory regimes and fight corruption).
4. *Statement on the Purpose of a Corporation*, Business Roundtable (Aug. 19, 2019) https://opportunity.businessroundtable.org/ourcommitment/ (signed by approximately 200 CEOs, redefining the purpose of a corporation as "generating good jobs, a strong and sustainable economy, innovation, a healthy environment and economic opportunity for all").
5. International Labor Organization, https://www.ilo.org/ (explaining a specialized agency of the UN working to promote fair labor standards across the world).

6. Kenneth E. Goodpaster & John B. Matthews, Jr., *Can a Corporation Have a Conscience?*, HARV. BUS. REV. (Jan. 1982), https://hbr.org/1982/01/can-a-corporation-have-a-con science (discussing ethical actions within corporations).
7. LYNN STOUT, THE SHAREHOLDER VALUE MYTH: HOW PUTTING SHAREHOLDERS FIRST HARMS INVESTORS, CORPORATIONS, AND THE PUBLIC (2012).
8. COLIN MAYER, FIRM COMMITMENT: WHY THE CORPORATION IS FAILING US AND HOW TO RESTORE TRUST IN IT (2013).
9. R. EDWARD FREEMAN, KIRSTEN E. MARTIN, & BIDHAN L. PARMAR, THE POWER OF AND: RESPONSIBLE BUSINESS WITHOUT TRADE-OFFS (2020).

Chapter 8: The Costs of Acting Unethically

1. D. Michael Long & Spuma Rao, *The Wealth Effects of Unethical Business Behavior*, 15 J. EC. FIN. 65-73 (1995) (discussing both the short- and long-term negative wealth effects of unethical business behavior).
2. Stuart McNeill, *The Cost of Unethical Behavior*, ETHIKOS, https://assets.corporatecompliance.org/Portals/1/PDF/ Resources/ethikos/past-issues/2014/scce-2014-03-ethi kos-mcneill.pdf (discussing the financial costs associated with unethical behavior in a company or industry).
3. *Could Unethical Behavior Cost a Business Its Best Employees?*, ETHICAL ADVOC. (Aug. 29, 2018), https://www.ethicala dvocate.com/unethical-behavior-cost-business-best-employees/ (discussing how unethical behavior in a business can cause good, ethical employees to resign).
4. *The Hidden Costs of Unethical Behavior*, JOSEPHSON INST. REP., http://josephsononbusinessethics.com/wp-content/uplo ads/2017/03/ARTICLE-Hidden-Costs-0305.pdf (bulleting several ways in which unethical behavior in business negatively impacts the company).
5. Yuval Feldman, *Companies Need to Pay More Attention to Everyday Unethical Behavior*, HARV. BUS. REV. (Mar. 2019),

https://hbr.org/2019/03/companies-need-to-pay-more-attention-to-everyday-unethical-behavior (discussing big ethical scandals and the consequences that can occur from everyday unethical behavior).

6. Jeremy Blackburn et al., *Cheating in Online Games: A Social Network Perspective* (2013), http://www.cse.usf.edu/dsg/publications/papers/cheating_TOI.pdf (discussing a statistical analysis of how players are influenced to cheat in online gaming, how other gamers view cheaters, and how unethical behavior can quickly spread throughout a gaming community).

Chapter 9: Major Ethical Traps in Modern Business

1. *How to Respond to an Ethical Dilemma*, MICH. ST. UNIV., https://www.michiganstateuniversityonline.com/resour ces/leadership/how-to-respond-to-an-ethical-dilemma/ (discussing ways businesspeople can respond to ethical dilemmas in the workplace).

2. Stephanie Francis Ward, *Top 10 Ethics Traps*, A.B.A. J., https://www.abajournal.com/magazine/article/top_10_e thics_traps (discussing the top ethics traps attorneys face).

3. Jack Schafer, *The Ethical Trap*, PSYCHOL. TODAY (Apr. 16, 2011), https://www.psychologytoday.com/us/blog/let-their-words-do-the-talking/201104/the-ethical-trap (explaining what an ethical trap is and how good ethical codes in a company can help avoid one).

4. Deborah Smith, *10 Ways Practitioners Can Avoid Frequent Ethical Pitfalls*, AM. PSYCHOL. ASS'N, https://www.apa.org/monitor/jan03/10ways (discussing ten ways psychotherapists can avoid common ethical traps and violations).

5. Robert Hoyk & Paul Hersey, *The Root Cause of Unethical Behavior: Psychological Traps Everyone Falls Prey To*, GRAZIADIO BUS. REV. (Jan. 2009), https://gbr.pepperdine.edu/2010/

08/the-root-causes-of-unethical-behavior/ (discussing ethical traps businesspeople fall into everyday).
6. Michael Housman & Dylan Minor, *Toxic Workers*, HARV.
BUS. REV. (Working Paper 16-057) (Nov. 2015), https://
www.hbs.edu/faculty/Publication%20Files/16-057_d45c0
b4f-fa19-49de-8f1b-4b12fe054fea.pdf (determining that, although unethical workers have been found to be slightly
more productive than ethical workers, it is actually better
for a company's net profitability if it avoids toxic workers,
and also discussing situations that could create toxic
workers and the consequences of hiring them).
7. EUGENE SOLTES, WHY THEY DO IT: INSIDE THE MIND OF THE
WHITE-COLLAR CRIMINAL (2016).

Chapter 10: Special Issues of Ethics in Leadership

1. Stathis Gould, *Ethical Leadership and Developing a Code of
Conduct for Organizations*, INT'L FED'N ACCT. (discussing ethical leadership and how to create an ethical culture from the
top down).
2. Corporate Laws Committee, *Corporate Director's Guidebook
(6th ed.)*, 66 THE BUS. LAW. (Aug. 2011), https://www.jstor.
org/stable/23239635?seq = 1 (giving practical guidance to
corporate directors in meeting their responsibilities).
3. Jim Whitehurst, *Leaders Can Shape Company's Culture
Through Their Behaviors*, HARV. BUS. REV. (Oct. 13, 2016),
https://hbr.org/2016/10/leaders-can-shape-company-cult
ure-through-their-behaviors (discussing how behaviors of
leaders impact organizational culture in general).
4. CARNEGIE COUNCIL FOR ETHICS IN INTERNATIONAL AFFAIRS,
https://www.carnegiecouncil.org/ (non-profit organization offering non-partisan educational resources on international ethics used by professionals, journalists, educators,
students, and the greater public).
5. Lama Ataya, *How to Be an Ethical Leader*, ENTREPRENEUR
MIDDLE E. (Mar. 26, 2016), https://www.entrepreneur.

com/article/272746) (discussing ethics in leadership as well as tips for how managers can program ethics into their leadership styles).

6. Bruce Weinstein, *Seven Bold Leaders Reveal How Ethical Leadership Is a Boon to Business*, FORBES (Oct. 14, 2019) https://www.forbes.com/sites/bruceweinstein/2019/10/14/seven-bold-leaders-reveal-how-ethical-leadership-is-a-boon-to-business/#1bf19508454c (reporting on seven CEOs discussing their opinion on how ethical practices help their corporations).

7. PAUL BABIAK & ROBERT D. HARE, SNAKES IN SUITS, REVISED EDITION: UNDERSTANDING AND SURVIVING THE PSYCHOPATHS IN YOUR OFFICE (2019).

Chapter 11: Negotiations

1. *On Professional Practice: Ethics and Negotiation*, A.B.A., https://www.americanbar.org/groups/dispute_resolut ion/publications/dispute_resolution_magazine/2019/summer-2019-new-york-convention/summer-2019-on-professional-practice/ (discussing ethics in negotiations).

2. *Ethics and Negotiation: 5 Principles of Negotiation to Boost Your Bargaining Skills in Business Situations—How to Use the Principles Behind Negotiation Ethics to Create Win-Win Agreements for You and Your Bargaining Counterpart*, PROGRAM NEGOT. HARV. LAW SCH., https://www.pon.harvard.edu/daily/negotiation-training-daily/questions-of-ethics-in-negotiation/ (discussing five questions to ask yourself to make sure you are being ethical in a negotiation).

3. *Ethics in Negotiations: How to Deal with Deception at the Bargaining Table*, PROGRAM NEGOT. HARV. LAW SCH., https://www.pon.harvard.edu/daily/dealing-with-difficult-peo ple-daily/dealing-with-difficult-people-when-youre-temp ted-to-deceive/ (discussing four ways your ethics may be challenged, or become a "gray area" in negotiating).

4. Charles B. Craver, *Negotiation Ethics: How to Be Deceptive Without Being Dishonest/How to Be Assertive Without Being Offensive*, 38 S. Tex. L. Rev. 713 (1997) (discussing different ethical rules in negotiations, such as the difference between material misrepresentation and puffing).
5. Dina Gerdeman, *Why Ethical People Become Unethical Negotiators*, Harv. Bus. Sch. Working Knowledge, https://hbswk.hbs.edu/item/why-ethical-people-become-unethical-negotiators (discussing how negotiators may be deceptive without being aware of it, and where ethical blind spots typically occur in negotiations).
6. G. Richard Shell, Bargaining for Advantage: Negotiation Strategies for Reasonable People (3d ed., 2019).
7. What's Fair: Ethics for Negotiators (Carrie J. Menkel-Meadow & Michael Wheeler, eds., 2010).

Chapter 12: Specific Liability Questions and Whistleblowing Options

1. Office of the Whistleblower, Sec. Exch. Comm'n, https://www.sec.gov/whistleblower (contact page for the SEC's whistleblower services).
2. National Whistleblower Center, https://www.whistleblowers.org (providing legal assistance to whistleblowers, advocating for stronger whistleblower protection laws, educating the public about whistleblowers' critical role in protecting democracy and the rule of law, and providing whistleblowers a way to report fraud directly through the website).
3. Government Accountability Project, https://whistleblower.org/ (whistleblower protection from advocacy to litigation; roots in protecting federal employees, but has expanded since).
4. Whistleblower Aid, https://whistlebloweraid.org/ (represents whistleblowers who uncover government and

corporate lawbreaking; has tended to have a technology focus).

5. WHISTLEBLOWER PROTECTION PROGRAM, U.S. DEP'T OF LABOR https://www.whistleblowers.gov/ (whistleblower protection program, enforced by OSHA).

6. STEPHEN M. KOHN, THE NEW WHISTLEBLOWER'S HANDBOOK: A STEP-BY-STEP GUIDE TO DOING WHAT'S RIGHT AND PROTECTING YOURSELF (2011); *The Whistleblower Handbook: Law Library*, KOHN, KOHN, AND COLAPINTO, LLP, https://kkc.com/the-whistleblower-handbook/" (hard copy of book is available to buy; free version is available through link) (discussing 30 rules regarding whistleblowing law and *qui tam* litigation).

7. *Ethics Hotline (EthicsPoint)*, A.B.A., https://www.american bar.org/groups/committees/audit/ethics-hotline/ (third-party ethics hotline for attorneys, offered by the A.B.A.).

8. State bar ethics hotlines for lawyers (ethics hotlines for attorneys, organized by each state's bar association):
   - Alabama: https://www.alabar.org/office-of-general-counsel/ethics-helpline/
   - Alaska: https://alaskabar.org/ethics-discipline/ethics-guidance-attorneys/
   - Arizona: https://www.azbar.org/for-lawyers/ethics/
   - Arkansas: https://www.arkbar.com/for-attorneys/ethics-advisory
   - California: https://www.calbar.ca.gov/Attorneys/Conduct-Discipline/Ethics/Hotline
   - Colorado: https://www.cobar.org/ethics
   - Connecticut: https://www.ctbar.org/news/informal-ethics-opinions
   - Delaware: https://www.dsba.org/sections-committees/standing-committees/professional-ethics/
   - D.C.: https://www.dcbar.org/bar-resources/legal-ethics/advice.cfm
   - Florida: https://www.floridabar.org/ethics/ethotline/
   - Georgia: https://www.gabar.org/barrules/ethicsand professionalism/

- Hawaii: https://dbhawaii.org/ethics-hotline-contact/ #:~:text=Do%20not%20use%20this%20form,speak%20w ith%20an%20ODC%20lawyer.
- Idaho: https://isb.idaho.gov/barcounsel/#:~:text = Eth ics%20Advice,at%20208%2D334%2D4500.
- Illinois: https://www.isba.org/ethics
- Indiana: https://www.inbar.org/page/legal_ethics_ opinion
- Iowa: https://www.iowabar.org/group/Ethics
- Kansas: https://www.ksbar.org/members/group. aspx?id = 111707#:~:text = Topeka%2C%20KS%2066612-, Questions,(785)%20861%2D8836.
- Kentucky: https://www.kybar.org/page/EthicsHotline
- Louisiana: https://www.lsba.org/Members/ EthicsAdvisary.aspx
- Maine: https://www.mebaroverseers.org/attorney_ services/ethics_helpline.html
- Maryland: https://www.msba.org/for-members/re-sources/ethics-hotline-opinions/
- Massachusetts: https://www.massbbo.org/
- Michigan: https://www.michbar.org/file/barjournal/ article/documents/pdf4article333.pdf
- Minnesota: https://www.mnbar.org/resources/practice-resource-center/ebooks/legal-ethics
- Mississippi: https://www.msbar.org/ethics-discipline/ ethics-opinions.aspx
- Missouri: https://mobar.org/site/content/Lawyer-Resources/Legal_Ethics_Opinions.aspx
- Montana: https://www.montanabar.org/page/ EthicsOpinions
- Nebraska: https://supremecourt.nebraska.gov/ad-ministration/professional-ethics/attorney-discipline-ethics/counsel-discipline
- Nevada: https://www.nvbar.org/member-services-3895/ethics-discipline/ethics-hotline/

- New Hampshire: https://www.nhbar.org/ethics-helpl ine#:~:text = To%20register%20complaints%20of%20vio lations,(603)%20224%2D5828.
- New Jersey: https://www.njcourts.gov/attorneys/ oaehelp.html
- New Mexico: https://www.nmbar.org/Nmstatebar/ About_Us/General_Counsel.aspx
- New York: (look to county bar association, no unified ethics hotline for the state)
  - New York City: https://www.nycbar.org/member-and-career-services/ethics/hotline#:~:text = of%20P rofessional%20Conduct-,Ethics%20Hotline,(the%20 %22Committee%22).
- North Carolina: https://www.ncbar.gov/for-lawyers/ ethics/#:~:text = After%20consulting%20the%20Ru les%20of,emailing%20ethicsadvice%40ncbar.gov.
- North Dakota: https://www.sband.org/page/ethics_ opinions
- Ohio: https://www.ohiobar.org/public-resources/about-attorneys/lawyer-ethics--discipline/
- Oklahoma: https://www.okbar.org/ec/
- Oregon: https://www.osbar.org/ethics/
- Pennsylvania: https://www.pabar.org/public/ Membership/ethics.asp
- Rhode Island: https://www.courts.ri.gov/ AttorneyResources/ethicsadvisorypanel/Pages/ Ethics%20Advisory%20Panel%20Opinions.aspx
- South Carolina: https://www.scbar.org/lawyers/ member-benefits-assistance/ethics-hotline/
- South Dakota: http://www.statebarofsouthdakota.com/ page/lawyer-discipline
- Tennessee: https://www.tbpr.org/for-legal-profession als/informal-ethicsinquiries#:~:text = ETHICS%20OPIN ION%20SERVICE%3A&text = Attorneys%20may%20c omplete%20the%20form,with%20the%20Board's%20Eth ics%20Counsel.

- Texas: https://www.texasbar.com/Content/Navigation Menu/ForLawyers/GrievanceandEthics/Toll_Free_ Ethics_Helpline_for_Lawyers/default.htm
- Utah: https://www.utahbar.org/ethics-hotline/
- Vermont: https://www.vtbar.org/FOR%20ATTORNEYS/ Advisory%20Ethics%20Opinion.aspx
- Virginia: https://www.vsb.org/site/regulation/ethics
- Washington: https://www.wsba.org/for-legal-professionals/ethics/ethics-line
- West Virginia: http://www.wvodc.org/
- Wisconsin: https://www.wisbar.org/formembers/ ethics/pages/ethics-advice.aspx
- Wyoming: https://www.wyomingbar.org/for-lawyers/ lawyer-resources/ethics-help/

Chapter 13: How to Institute Best Practices

1. BUSINESS ETHICS RESOURCE CENTER, https://berc.center forethicsinpractice.org (offering solutions to common ethics and compliance issues faced by small- and medium-sized businesses, throughout all industries).
2. INTERNATIONAL BUSINESS ETHICS INSTITUTE, https:// business-ethics.org/ (offering professional services to both individuals and organizations, including ethics assessments; codes of ethics, both in the creation and review of existing codes; ethics mentoring; ethics training; and many other services).
3. INSTITUTE OF BUSINESS ETHICS, https://www.ibe.org.uk/ (providing online tools on ethics issues and bespoke advice that is specific to the individual business; businesses can seek out their services when an ethical issue arises, or the Institute can help the business identify specific areas where they are weak and need support).
4. *Five Keys to Reducing Ethics and Compliance Risk*, ETHICS AND COMPLIANCE INITIATIVE https://www.ethics.org/resour ces/free-toolkit/reducing-risk/ (discussing, in depth, five

key steps to reduce ethical and compliance risks in a company and how to take those steps).

5. Catherine Bailey & Amanda Schultz, *Building a Strong Ethical Organization*, MIT SLOAN BUS. REV. (Jul. 17, 2018) (discussing recent ethical standards, how to avoid common ethical traps, and how to develop a culture of ethics both in an organization and in individual employees).

Chapter 14: Designing an Ethical Culture

1. *A Framework for Ethical Decision Making*, MARKKULA CENTER FOR APPLIED ETHICS AT SANTA CLARA UNIV., https://www.scu.edu/ethics/ethics-resources/ethical-decision-making/a-framework-for-ethical-decision-making/ (discussing the basics of ethics and ethical decision making, as well as a step-by-step framework people can follow to identify ethical issues and make ethical decisions).

2. *Shaping an Ethical Workplace Culture*, SOC'Y HUM. RES. MGMT., https://www.shrm.org/hr-today/trends-and-fore casting/special-reports-and-expert-views/Documents/Ethical-Workplace-Culture.pdf (discussing guidelines for organizations to follow to shape an overall ethical culture within their organization).

3. MARY C. GENTILE, GIVING VOICE TO VALUES: HOW TO SPEAK YOUR MIND WHEN YOU KNOW WHAT'S RIGHT (2012); Videos: Giving Voice to Values (Ethics Unwrapped 2018), https://ethicsunwrapped.utexas.edu/series/giving-voice-to-values (discussing how to align personal ethics with professional pressures).

Chapter 15: How to Respond to Investigations and Protect Your Reputation

1. *How to Respond to an Ethics Investigation*, AM. INST. CERTIFIED PUB. ACCT., https://www.aicpa.org/interestareas/pro

fessionalethics/resources/ethicsenforcement/resinv.html (containing guidelines on how CPAs should respond to an ethics investigation).

2. Meric Craig Bloch, *Guide to Conducting Workplace Investigations*, Soc'y of Corp. Compliance & Ethics (2008), https://assets.corporatecompliance.org/Portals/1/Users/169/29/60329/Workplace_Investigations_Guide.pdf (discussing a step-by-step procedure and guidelines to follow when conducting an internal investigation in a company).

3. *A Code of Ethics for Workplace Investigators*, Winter Compliance (2015), https://assets.corporatecompliance.org/Portals/1/PDF/Resources/past_handouts/CEI/2015/P9_Part2_Handout1.pdf (published by the Society of Corporate Compliance and Ethics, detailing a code of ethics that investigators in a company should follow to keep the investigation honest, reliable, and ethical).

4. *HR Tools and Tech: How to Conduct an Investigation*, Soc'y Hum. Res. Mgmt., https://blog.shrm.org/workforce/hr-tools-and-tech-how-to-conduct-an-investigation (presenting a step-by-step guide on how to conduct a workplace investigation).

5. *Investigation: Questions for Witnesses*, Soc'y Hum. Res. Mgmt., https://www.shrm.org/resourcesandtools/tools-and-samples/hr-forms/pages/questionsforwitnesses.aspx (proposing sample questions to ask witnesses when conducting a workplace investigation).

NOTES

Chapter 2

1 ADAM GRANT, GIVE AND TAKE: A REVOLUTIONARY APPROACH TO SUCCESS 4–7 (2013).

2 *See* Kurt Eichenwald, *Anderson Guilty in Effort to Block Inquiry on Enron*, N.Y. TIMES, June 16, 2002, https://www.nytimes.com/2002/06/16/business/andersen-guilty-in-effort-to-block-inqu iry-on-enron.html.

3 *See* Jonathan Weil, John Emshwiller & Scott J. Paltrow, *Arthur Anderson Admits It Destroyed Documents Related to Enron Account*, WALL ST. J., Jan. 11, 2002, https://www.wsj.com/articles/SB1010 695966620300040.

4 *See* Eichenwald, *supra* note 2.

5 *See* Arthur Anderson LLP v. United States, 544 U.S. 696, 706–08 (2005).

6 *See* ALBERT PAINE, MARK TWAIN'S NOTEBOOK (2016).

7 The major difference between a psychopath and a sociopath is that a psychopath does not have a conscience, whereas a sociopath may have a weak conscience. A psychopath feels no empathy, so does not feel remorse for his or her actions.

8 Scott Highhouse, Margaret E. Brooks & Gary Gregarus, *An Organizational Impression Management Perspective on the Formation of Corporate Reputations*, 35 J. MGMT. 1481, 1489 (2009) (discussing a micro-perspective view on the formation of corporate reputations).

9 False Claims Act (FCA), 31 U.S.C. § 3730(d) (2019).

10 *See id.* § 3730(h).

11   *Office of the Whistleblower*, U.S. Sec. & Exchange Comm'n,
     https://www.sec.gov/whistleblower.

12   *See Whistleblower—Informant Award*, IRS, https://www.irs.gov/
     compliance/whistleblower-informant-award.

13   *See* Whistleblower Protection Enhancement Act, U.S. Dep't of
     Just., https://www.justice.gov/pardon/whistleblower-protect
     ion-enhancement-act.

14   Plato, The Republic (Global Classics 2017).

15   Mary Morrissey, *What Gandhi Wants You to Know About the Power
     of Positive Thinking*, Huffington Post, June 16, 2016, https://bit.
     ly/3iSzJRk.

16   *See* John F. Helliwell, *How's Life? Combining Individual and
     National Variables to Explain Subjective Well-Being*, 20 Econ.
     Modelling 331, 343 (2003) (discussing international trends and
     differences in subjective well-being over the final fifth of the
     twentieth century).

17   *See* Harvey S. James, Jr., *Is the Just Man a Happy Man? An
     Empirical Study of the Relationship Between Ethics and Subjective
     Well-Being*, 64 Kyklos 193, 208–09 (2011) (discussing whether
     ethical decision-making affects a person's happiness).

18   *See* Peggy A. Thoits & Lyndi N. Hewitt, *Volunteer Work and Well-
     Being*, 42 J. Health & Soc. Behav. 115, 118–19 (2001) (discussing
     the relationships between volunteer work in the community and
     different aspects of personal well-being).

19   *See* Sheldon Cohen et al., *Positive Emotional Style Predicts
     Resistance to Illness After Experimental Exposure to Rhinovirus
     or Influenza A Virus*, 68 Psychosomatic Med. 809, 814 (2006)
     (determining whether happiness and positivity in general are
     associated with a lower risk of developing an upper respiratory
     illness).

20   *See* Deborah D. Danner, David A. Snowdon & Wallace V. Friesen,
     *Positive Emotions in Early Life and Longevity: Findings from the Nun
     Study*, 80 J. Personality & Soc. Psychol. 804, 808–09 (2001)
     (discussing the relationship between positive emotional content
     and longevity).

21   *See* Okpara Ngozi, *Popularity v. Ethics: Mutually Exclusive Ideals
     for the Media?*, 9 Res. on Human. and Soc. Sci. 78, 78–83 (2019)
     (discussing ethics in relation to popularity).

22   *See* Kristin Layous, S. Katherine Nelson, Eva Oberle,
     Kimberly A. Schonert-Reichl, & Sonja Lyubomirsky, *Kindness*

Counts: Prompting Prosocial Behavior in Preadolescents Boosts Peer Acceptance and Well-Being, PLoS ONE, Dec. 2012, at 1–3 (discussing how popularity increases when doing the right thing for others).

23 *See* Tanna M.B. Mellings & Lynn E. Alden, *Cognitive Processes in Social Anxiety: The Effects of Self-Focus, Rumination and Anticipatory Processing*, 38 BEHAV. RES. & THERAPY 243, 254–55 (2000) (examining three cognitive processes hypothesized to contribute to biases in judgments and memory of social events).

24 *See, e.g.*, S. Katherine Nelson, Kristin Layous, Steven W. Cole & Sonja Lyubomirsky, *Do Unto Others or Treat Yourself? The Effects of Prosocial and Self-Focused Behavior on Psychological Flourishing*, 16 EMOTION 850, 850–61 (2016) (discussing how happier people treat themselves and others).

25 Jana Schaich Borg, Debra Lieberman & Kent A. Kiehl, *Infection, Incest, and Iniquity: Investigating the Neural Correlates of Disgust and Morality*, 20 J. COGNITIVE NEUROSCI. 1529, 1533–36 (2008) (investigating the biological homology of pathogen-related and moral disgust).

26 *See* MARTHA STOUT, THE SOCIOPATH NEXT DOOR (2005).

27 *Id.*

28 ELEANOR ROOSEVELT, YOU LEARN BY LIVING: ELEVEN KEYS FOR A MORE FULFILLING LIFE 96 (1960) (internal quotation marks omitted).

29 *See* Andrew E. Clark, Paul Frijters & Michael A. Shields, *Relative Income, Happiness, and Utility: An Explanation for the Easterlin Paradox and Other Puzzles*, 46 J. ECON. LITERATURE 95, 95–96 (2008) (discussing the correlation between income and subjective well-being).

30 *See* Ed Diener & Robert Biswas-Diener, *Will Money Increase Subjective Well-Being?*, 57 SOC. INDICATORS RES. 119, 161 (2002) (discussing various types of evidence related to money and subjective well-being).

31 *See* H. Roy Kaplan, *Lottery Winners: The Myth and Reality*, 3 J. GAMBLING STUD. 168 (1987).

32 Richard A. Easterlin, *Does Economic Growth Improve the Human Lot? Some Empirical Evidence*, in NATIONS AND HOUSEHOLDS IN ECONOMIC GROWTH: ESSAYS IN HONOR OF MOSES ABRAMOVITZ, 89 (Paul A. David & Melvin W. Reder, eds. 1974).

33 David G. Blanchflower & Andrew J. Oswald, *International Happiness: A New View on the Measure of Performance*, 25 ACAD. MGMT. PERSP. 6, 8 (2011) (discussing the findings from new literature on happiness and well-being).

34 *See* ROBERT H. FRANK, WHAT PRICE THE MORAL HIGH GROUND? HOW TO SUCCEED WITHOUT SELLING YOUR SOUL 90 (2004).

35 *See id.*

36 *See* Robert H. Frank, *Does Absolute Income Matter?*, *in* ECONOMICS AND HAPPINESS: FRAMING THE ANALYSIS (Luigino Bruni & Pier Luigi Porta, eds. 2005).

37 Lynn A. Stout, *Killing Conscience: The Unintended Behavioral Consequences of "Pay for Performance,"* 39 J. CORP. L. 525, 555 (2014) (discussing the drawbacks of the pay-for-performance *motivational* approach).

38 *See* Jodi Kantor & David Streitfeld, *Inside Amazon: Wrestling Big Ideas in a Bruising Workplace*, N.Y. TIMES, Aug. 15, 2015, https:// www.nytimes.com/2015/08/16/technology/inside-amazon-wrestling-big-ideas-in-a-bruising-workplace.html.

39 *See* Annalisa Quinn, *Book News: New Claims About Nixon in Posthumous Robert Bork Memoir*, NPR, Feb. 27, 2013, https:// www.npr.org/sections/thetwo-way/2013/02/26/173018916/ book-news-new-claims-about-nixon-in-posthumous-robert-bork-memoir.

40 Pat Barclay, *Reputational Benefits for Altruistic Punishment*, 27 EVOLUTION & HUM. BEHAV. 325, 341 (2006) (discussing whether punishers gain social benefits from punishing).

41 *See* Judith Rehak, *Tylenol Made a Hero of Johnson & Johnson: The Recall That Started Them All*, N.Y. TIMES, Mar. 23, 2002, https:// www.nytimes.com/2002/03/23/your-money/IHT-tylenol-made-a-hero-of-johnson-johnson-the-recall-that-started.html.

42 *See, e.g.*, Rosa Chun, *Ethical Character and Virtue of Organizations: An Empirical Assessment and Strategic Implications*, 57 J. BUS. ETHICS 269, 269–84 (2005) (discussing a virtue character scale that assesses the link between organizational level virtue and organizational performance, both financial and non-financial); *see also generally* SOC'Y FOR HUMAN RES. MGMT., *Shaping an Ethical Workplace Culture* 2 (2013), https://www.shrm.org/hr-today/tre nds-and-forecasting/special-reports-and-expert-views/Docume nts/Ethical-Workplace-Culture.pdf.

43   *See* Jody Hoffer Gittell, Kim Cameron, Sandy Lim & Victor Rivas, *Relationships, Layoffs, and Organizational Resilience: Airline Industry Responses to September 11*, 42 J. Applied Behav. Sci. 300, 323–25 (2006) (discussing why some airline companies recovered successfully after the September 11 attacks, while others struggled).

44   *See* Nathan Vardi & Antoine Gara, *Valeant Pharmaceuticals' Prescription for Disaster*, Forbes, Apr. 13, 2016, https://www.for bes.com/sites/nathanvardi/2016/04/13/valeant-pharmaceutic als-prescription-for-disaster/#220427b9206c.

45   *See Greenwash Academy Awards Announced at Earth Summit*, CorpWatch, Aug. 23, 2002, https://corpwatch.org/article/ greenwash-academy-awards-announced-earth-summit.

46   *See Green Guides: Environmentally Friendly Products*, Fed. Trade Comm'n, https://www.ftc.gov/news-events/media-resources/ truth-advertising/green-guides.

47   *See Non-Financial Reporting: EU Rules Require Large Companies to Publish Regular Reports on the Social and Environmental Impacts of Their Activities*, Eur. Commission, https://ec.europa.eu/info/ business-economy-euro/company-reporting-and-auditing/comp any-reporting/non-financial-reporting_en#information-to-be-disclosed.

48   Thomas Hobbes, Leviathan (1951).

49   Stephen Knack & Philip Keefer, *Does Social Capital Have an Economic Payoff? A Cross-Country Investigation*, 112 Q. J. Econ. 1251, 1252–54 (1997) (discussing the impact of social capital on measurable economic performance).

50   *See id.* at 1256–57, 1260.

51   *See* Yuna Liu, *The Importance of Trust Distance on Stock Market Correlation: Evidence from Emerging Economics*, 20 Borsa Istanbul Rev. 37, 37–47 (2020) (describing the effect of trust distance upon stock market correlations).

52   John Stuart Mill, Principles of Political Economy 131 (Ashley ed. 1848).

53   *See* John Hudson, *Institutional Trust and Subjective Well-Being Across the EU*, 59 Kyklos 43, 58–59 (2006) (discussing the impact of individual trust of institutions upon happiness).

54   *See* Margit Tavits, *Representation, Corruption, and Subjective Well-Being*, 41 Comp. Pol. Stud. 1607, 1625–26 (2008) (discussing the

effect of corruption and representation on people's subjective well-being).

Chapter 3

1 Michael Richardson, *As West Pushes for Democracy, Asia Leans Toward Japan*, N.Y. TIMES, Nov. 9, 1991 (quoting Lee Kuan Yew as saying that the people of Asia have "little doubt that a society with communitarian values where the interests of society take precedence over that of the individual suits them better than the individualism of America").

2 Daniel Bell, *Communitarianism*, STAN. ENCYCLOPEDIA OF PHIL. (Summer 2016ed.), https://plato.stanford.edu/archives/sum2 016/entries/communitarianism/.

3 *See, e.g.*, CAROL GILLIGAN, IN A DIFFERENT VOICE: PSYCHOLOGICAL THEORY AND WOMEN'S DEVELOPMENT (1982).

4 Bell, *supra* note 2.

5 Ray Serrano et al., *Laws on Filial Support in Four Asian Countries*, 95 BULL. WORLD HEALTH ORG. 788, 788–89 (2017) (discussing the use of filial support laws as a possible solution to the problems posed by aging populations).

6 K.-S. Chang, *The Anti-Communitarian Family? Everyday Conditions of Authoritarian Politics in South Korea*, in COMMUNITARIAN POLITICS IN ASIA (Chua Beng-Huat ed., Routledge 2004).

7 IMMANUEL KANT, GROUNDWORK OF THE METAPHYSICS OF MORALS 70 (H.J. Paton trans., Harper & Row 1964), *cited in* MANUEL G. VELASQUEZ, BUSINESS ETHICS: CONCEPTS AND CASES 78 (6th ed. 2006); *accord* Robert Johnson, *Kant's Moral Philosophy*, STAN. ENCYCLOPEDIA OF PHIL. (Spring 2019 ed.), https://plato.stanford. edu/archives/spr2019/entries/kant-moral/ (citing a translation of Kant's GROUNDWORK at 4:402).

8 Marcus Noland et al., *Is Gender Diversity Profitable? Evidence from a Global Survey*, PETERSON INST. FOR INT'L ECON. (Feb. 2016), https://www.piie.com/system/files/documents/wp16-3.pdf.

9 Leif Wenar, *John Rawls*, STAN. ENCYCLOPEDIA OF PHIL. (Spring 2017 ed.), https://plato.stanford.edu/archives/spr2017/entries/rawls/.

10 The "Golden Rule" has been formulated many ways in world religions. Professor Nicholas Epley compiled the following list for a presentation before the Ethics By Design Conference in June 2016:
   • "You shall love your neighbor as yourself." (Judaism, *Leviticus* 19:18);

- "Whatever you wish that men would do to you, do so to them." (Christianity, Matthew 7:12);
- "Not one of you is a believer until he loves for his brother what he loves for himself." (Islam, *Forty Hadith of an-Nawawi*, 13);
- "A man should wander about treating all creatures as he himself would be treated." (Jainism, *Sutrakritanga*, 1:11.33);
- "Try your best to treat others as you would wish to be treated yourself." (Confucianism, *Mencius* VII:A.4);
- "One should not behave towards others in a way which is disagreeable to oneself. This is the essence of morality." (Hinduism, *Mahabharata, Anusasana Parva* 113:8).

Nicolas Epley, Video Keynote: Four Myths About Morality and Business (June 6, 2016), http://www.ethicalsystems.org/ethicsb ydesign.

11 This list of suggestions is generated in response to the excellent behavioral scientific work done and popularized by Ann Tenbrunsel, Max Bazerman, and others. *See, e.g.*, MAX BAZERMAN & ANN TENBRUNSEL, BLIND SPOTS: WHY YOU DON'T DO WHAT IS RIGHT AND WHAT TO DO ABOUT IT (2011).

Chapter 4

1 *See* Lynn A. Stout, *The Investor Confidence Game*, 68 BROOK. L. REV. 407, 410 (2002).

2 *See* Lynn A. Stout, *Taking Conscience Seriously*, UCLA SCHOOL OF LAW, LAW-ECON RESEARCH PAPER NO. 06-20 1, 3–4 (2007).

3 Nina Mazar, On Amir & Dan Ariely, *The Dishonesty of Honest People: A Theory of Self-Concept Maintenance*, 45(6) J. MKT. RES. 633, 633 (2008).

4 Toshio Yamagashi, Yang Li, Haruto Takagishi, Yoshie Matsumoto & Toko Kiyonari, *In Search of Homo Economicus*, 25(9) ASS'N PSYCHOL. SCI. 1699, 1700–02 (2014).

5 David DeSteno, *Who Can You Trust?*, HARV. BUS. REV., Mar. 2014, https://hbr.org/2014/03/who-can-you-trust (emphasis in original).

6 Alain Cohn, Michel André Maréchal, David Tannenbaum & Christian Lukas Zünd, *Civic Honesty Around the Globe*, 365 SCI. 70, 71 (2019).

7 *See id.* at 70.

8 Merrit Kennedy, *What Dropping 17,000 Wallets Around the Globe Can Teach Us About Honesty*, NPR, June 20, 2019, https://www. npr.org/2019/06/20/734141432/what-dropping-17-000-wallets-around-the-globe-can-teach-us-about-honesty.

9   *Id.*

10 Lynn A. Stout, *Other-Regarding Preferences and Social Norms*, Geo. L. Econ. R. Paper No. 265902, at 2 (2001).

11 *See* DeSteno, *supra* note 5; *see also infra* Chapter 9 text and notes 19, 20, and 29.

12 *See infra* Chapter 8 text and note 7.

13 This is a ballpark statistic related to the authors by various behavioral scientists. For an interesting brain-based analysis of cheating and how much more susceptible cheaters versus non-cheaters are to rewards, see Sebastian P.H. Speer, Ale Smidts & Maarten A.S. Boksem, *When Honest People Cheat, and Cheaters Are Honest: Cognitive Control Processes Override Our Moral Default* 31 (Jan. 2020), https://www.researchgate.net/publication/338821758_When_honest_people_cheat_and_cheaters_are_honest_Cognitive_control_processes_override_our_moral_defa ult (paper provided in early stage). In that study of forty people, all participants cheated at least once, but three participants stood out for the least amount of cheating, whereas 5% of participants in their baseline condition "missed only one or two opportunities to cheat." *Id.* at 16, and Fig. 2. Suggesting that there may be some underlying default to moral behavior that is then mediated by environment, "whether someone is a cheater or tends to be honest most of the time" seems to be determined "not only [by] reward sensitivity[,] but also the extent to which someone engages self-referential thinking processes." *Id.* at 35.

14 *See generally* Lawrence Kohlberg, *Stages of Moral Development* (1971), http://ericmazur.net/wp-content/uploads/2018/11/Kohlberg-Moral-Development.pdf.

15 Yoshie Matsumoto et al., *Prosocial Behavior Increases With Age Across Five Economic Games*, 11 PLOS One 1, 1–3, 7 (2016).

16 Kohlberg, *supra* note 14.

17 *Id.*

18 *See* Kristen Smith-Crowe & Danielle E. Warren, *The Emotion-Evoked Collective Corruption Model: The Role of Emotion in the Spread of Corruption Within Organizations*, 25(4) Org. Sci. 1154, 1157 (2014).

19 *See* Stephen Scott, Partner, Starling Trust, Presentation to the Berle XI Symposium on Law and Corporate Culture, *Trust & Technology: A New Paradigm for Culture & Risk Management* (May 17, 2019).

20   *See* Melissa Bateson, Daniel Nettle & Gilbert Roberts, *Cues of Being Watched Enhance Cooperation in a Real-World Setting*, BIOLOGY LETT. 2 (2006).

21   *See* Azish Filabi & Robert Hurley, *The Paradox of Employee Surveillance*, BEHAVIORAL SCI. (2019), https://behavioralscientist. org/the-paradox-of-employee-surveillance/ (last visited Apr. 4, 2019); J.S. Nelson, *Management Culture and Surveillance* (Berle XI Symposium: Law and Corporate Culture) 43 SEATTLE L. REV. 2, 631 (2020).

22   *See* Matsumoto et al., *supra* note 15.

23   *See* Ronald R. Sims & Johannes Brinkmann, *Enron Ethics (Or: Culture Matters More Than Codes)*, 45(3) J. BUS. ETHICS 244, 251 (July 2003); *see also* James Heskett, *What Are the Real Lessons of the Wells Fargo Case*, HARV. BUS. SCH. (Nov. 1, 2017), https:// hbswk.hbs.edu/item/what-are-the-real-lessons-of-the-wells-fargo-case?cid=wk-rss.

24   *See* Colin F. Camerer & Ernst Fehr, *When Does "Economic Man" Dominate Social Behavior?*, 311 SCI., NEW SERIES 47, 47–48 (Jan. 6, 2006).

25   *See id.* at 47–49.

26   *See* Muel Kaptein, WHY GOOD PEOPLE SOMETIMES DO BAD THINGS? 52 REFLECTIONS ON ETHICS AT WORK 24 (July 25, 2012), https://ssrn.com/abstract=2117396.

27   *Id.* at 22.

28   *See* Max H. Bazerman et al., *Goals Gone Wild: The Systematic Side Effects of Over-Prescribing Goal Setting*, HARV. BUS. SCH. 1, 3 (2009).

29   *See id.*

30   *See id.* (discussing how goal-driven environments caused employees to act unethically at Ford and MiniScribe).

31   Mark S. Schwartz, Thomas W. Dunfee & Michael J. Kline, *Tone at the Top: An Ethics Code for Directors?*, 58 J. BUS. ETHICS 79, 86–88 (2005).

32   *Id.* at 81.

33   *Id.*

34   *See* Jeffrey S. Pickerd, Scott L. Summers & David A. Wood, *An Examination of How Entry-Level Staff Auditors Respond to Tone at the Top vis-à-vis Tone at the Bottom*, 27 BEHAV. RES. ACCT. 79, 87 (2015).

35   *See* Marianna M Jennings, *That Tone-at-the-Top Thing: Tin-Eared Executives and the Ethical Issues Lost in Translation: Part II*, 12(1) CORP. FIN. REV. 42, 46 (Sep./Oct. 2007).

36   Anna Lasakova & Anna Remisova, *On Organizational Factors That Elicit Managerial Unethical Decision-Making*, 64(4) EKONOMICKY CASOPIS BRATISLAVA 334, 347 (2007).

37   *See* Michael J. O'Fallon & Kenneth D. Butterfield, *Moral Differentiation: Exploring Boundaries of the "Monkey See, Monkey Do" Perspective*, 102 J. BUS. ETHICS 379, 380, 391–92 (2011).

38   *See* William J. Becker, Matthew S. Rodgers & Stephen J. Sauer, *The Effects of Goals and Pay Structure on Managerial Reporting Dishonesty*, J. ACCT. ETHICS & PUB. POL'Y 379 (2018).

39   *Id.*

40   In 2002, a General Motors engineer chose to use an ignition switch in vehicles that was below GM's standard specifications. The switch required less force to turn, meaning that light torque, such as a heavy keychain, could move the switch to the "accessory" or "off" position while the car was still in motion. Switching to the "off" position would instantly cause the car's speed to reduce to 0 mph as well as prevent the airbags from deploying. The result of this was at least 54 frontal-impact crashes. It took GM over 11 years to recall cars with this ignition because the company labeled the issue a "consumer convenience" issue rather than a "safety" issue. While this issue passed through the hands of GM's engineers, dealers, attorneys, and employees, not one person took action or brought the issue to the top executives of the company. *See* Anton R. Valukas, *Report to Board of Directors of General Motors Company Regarding Ignition Switch Recalls* 1–5 (May 29, 2014), https://www.aieg.com/wp-content/uploads/2014/08/Valukas-report-on-gm-redacted2.pdf; Steve Kerr, *Do Your Company's Incentives Reward Bad Behavior?*, HARV. BUS. REV., Aug. 27, 2014, https://hbr.org/2014/08/do-your-companys-incentives-reward-bad-behavior.

41   *See* Mark Egan, Gregor Matvos & Amit Seru, *The Market for Financial Advisor Misconduct*, 127 J. POL. ECON. 233, 234 (2019).

42   Alexandre Ardichvili, James A. Mitchell, & Douglas Jondle, *Characteristics of Ethical Business Cultures*, 85 J. BUS. ETHICS 445, 447 (2008).

43   *See* Press Release, Dep't of Just., *Volkswagen AG Agrees to Plead Guilty and Pay $4.3 Billion in Criminal and Civil Penalties; Six Volkswagen Executives and Employees Are Indicted in Connection with Conspiracy to Cheat U.S. Emissions Tests* (Jan. 11, 2017), https://www.justice.gov/opa/pr/volkswagen-ag-agr

ees-plead-guilty-and-pay-43-billion-criminal-and-civil-penalt
ies-six.

44 *See* Joanna Walters, Graham Ruddick & Sean Farrell, *VW
Emissions Scandal Could Snare Other Firms, Whistleblower Claims,*
GUARDIAN, Sept. 21, 2015, https://www.theguardian.com/busin
ess/2015/sep/21/volkswagen-emissions-scandal-sends-shares-
in-global-carmakers-reeling.

45 The list includes Ford, Fiat Chrysler (Jeep, Dodge, Alfa Romeo),
GM, PSA (Peugeot, Citroën), Renault-Nissan, Mitsubishi, Kia,
Subaru, Honda, Mazda, Hyundai, Volvo, BMW, Daimler AG's
Mercedes-Benz, and multiple VW brands (Volkswagen, Audi,
Porsche, Seat, Skoda, Bentley, and Lamborghini). *See, e.g.,* David
Tracy, *Subaru Employees Altered Fuel Economy and Emissions Data
During New-Car Inspections,* JALOPNIK, May 2, 2018, https://
jalopnik.com/subaru-employees-altered-fuel-economy-and-
emissions-dat-1825720983; Kartikay Mehrotra & David Welch,
Why Much of the Car Industry Is Under Scrutiny for Cheating,
BLOOMBERG, Aug. 1, 2017, https://www.bloomberg.com/news/
articles/2017-08-02/why-it-seems-like-open-season-on-car-
companies-quicktake-q-a; Miles Brignall, *Up In Smoke: The VW
Emissions "Fix" Has Left Our Car Undriveable,* GUARDIAN, Mar.
25, 2017, http://www.theguardian.com/money/2017/mar/25/
vw-volkswagen-audi-skoda-seat-emissions-fix-left-car-undrivea
ble; Hyunjoo Jin, *VW, Audi, Bentley Sales Suspended by South Korea
After Emissions Scandal,* AUTOMOTIVE NEWS, Aug. 2, 2016, http://
www.autonews.com/article/20160801/COPY/308019777/
vw-audi-bentley-sales-suspended-by-south-korea-after-emissi
ons-scandal; Charles Riley, *Mitsubishi: We've Been Cheating on Fuel
Tests for 25 Years,* CNNMONEY, Apr. 26, 2016, https://money.cnn.
com/2016/04/26/news/companies/mitsubishi-cheating-fuel-
tests-25-years/index.html; *Lamborghini and Volkswagen Raided by
Police in Wake of Emissions Scandal,* HNGN.COM (Oct. 19, 2015),
http://www.hngn.com/articles/141677/20151019/lamborgh
ini-volkswagen-raided-police-wake-emissions-scandal.htm;
Damian Carrington, *Four More Carmakers Join Diesel Emissions
Row,* GUARDIAN, Oct. 9, 2015, http://www.theguardian.com/
environment/2015/oct/09/mercedes-honda-mazda-mitsubishi-
diesel-emissions-row (listing as also emitting high levels of NOx
emissions Mercedes-Benz, Honda, Mazda, Mitsubishi, Renault,
Nissan, Hyundai, Citroen, Fiat, Volvo, and Jeep); Rishi Iyengar,

Hyundai and Kia Fined for Understating Carbon-Emission Figures, TIME, Nov. 4, 2014, http://time.com/3555696/hyundai-kia-fined-carbon-emissions/ (describing Hyundai and Kia as implicated in emissions fraud).

   In January 2019, Fiat Chrysler agreed to "pay about [U.S.] $800 million in fines and costs to settle lawsuits brought by states, car owners and the U.S. Justice Department, which said the company's diesel-powered pickups and SUVs violated clean-air rules." Ryan Beene, Kartikay Mehrotra & Gabrielle Coppola, *Fiat Chrysler Called 'Bad Actor' as U.S. Settles Emissions Suit*, BLOOMBERG, Jan. 10, 2019, https://www.bloomberg.com/news/articles/2019-01-10/fiat-chrysler-agrees-to-pay-fine-recall-vehicles-in-diesel-case. Illustrating a link through companies engaging in the same behavior, "German parts components-maker Robert Bosch GmbH, which supplied the engine control devices found to be rigged to pass emission tests" for Volkswagen as well, will also pay fines. *Id.* Bosch "will pay $27.5 million as part of the settlement with consumers . . . [and] a total of $103.7 million to 50 jurisdictions." *Id.*

46 *See* J.S. Nelson, *Disclosure-Driven Crime*, 52 U.C. DAVIS L. REV. 487, 1542–43 (2019).

47 Jack Ewing, *Volkswagen Inquiry's Focus to Include Managers Who Turned a Blind Eye*, N.Y. TIMES, Oct. 25, 2015, http://mobile.nytimes.com/2015/10/26/business/international/volkswagen-investigationfocus-to-include-managers-who-turned-a-blind-eye.html; *see also* JACK EWING, FASTER, HIGHER, FARTHER: THE VOLKSWAGEN SCANDAL (2017).

48 *Cf., e.g.*, SAMUEL W. BUELL, CAPITAL OFFENSES: BUSINESS CRIME AND PUNISHMENT IN AMERICA'S CORPORATE AGE 32 (2016).

49 Benjamin van Rooij & Adam Fine, *Toxic Corporate Culture: Addressing Organizational Process of Deviancy*, 8 ADMIN. SCI. 13, 27 (2018).

50 *Id.*

51 *Id.* at 20.

52 June Carbone, Naomi Cahn & Nancy Levit, *Women, Rule-Breaking, and the Triple Bind*, ASSOC. OF AM. LAW. SCH. ANNUAL MEETING 14 (Jan. 2019), https://am.aals.org/wp-content/uploads/sites/4/2018/12/AM19SocioEconPaperWomenRuleBreaking.pdf.

53   June Carbone & William K. Black, *The Problem with Predators*, 43
     SEATTLE U. L. REV. 441, 478 (2020).

Chapter 5

1 *See* Craig Ehrlich, *Is Business Ethics Necessary?*, 4 DEPAUL BUS. &
   COM. L.J. 55, 57–58 (2005) (suggesting that legal requirements are
   not always ethically correct, and many ethics requirements are
   not required by law).

2 *See Ethics*, DICTIONARY.COM, https://www.dictionary.com/bro
   wse/ethics (defining ethics as "values relating to human conduct,
   with respect to the rightness and wrongness of certain actions
   and to the goodness and badness of the motives and ends of such
   actions").

3 *See* Adela Cortina, *Legislation, Law, and Ethics: Introduction*, 3:1
   ETHICAL THEORY AND MORAL PRACTICE: JUSTICE IN PHILOSOPHY
   AND SOCIAL SCIENCE 3–7 (Mar. 2000) ("[T]he relationship
   between ethics and law is a long-standing one in the realm of
   philosophy.").

4 *See* Mark Murphy, *The Natural Law Tradition in Ethics*, *in*
   STANFORD ENCYCLOPEDIA OF PHILOSOPHY (revised ed. Summer
   2019), https://plato.stanford.edu/archives/win2011/entries/
   natural-law-ethics/ (discussing natural law theory and the
   grounding of legal institutions in natural ethics).

5 *See* Richard Feloni, *More Than 2,600 Companies, Like Danone and
   Patagonia, Are On Board With an Entrepreneur Who Says the Way
   We Do Business Runs Counter to Human Nature and There's Only
   One Way Forward*, BUS. INSIDER, Dec. 8, 2018, https://www.busi
   nessinsider.com/b-corporation-b-lab-movement-and1-cofoun
   der-2018-11 (describing the benefit corporation movement that
   opposes legal but socially harmful shareholder primacy laws).

6 *See* LAWRENCE KOHLBERG, I ESSAYS ON MORAL DEVELOPMENT: THE
   PHILOSOPHY OF MORAL DEVELOPMENT (1981).

7 *See, e.g.*, Feloni, *supra* note 5.

8 *See, e.g.*, McMullen v. Hoffman, 174 U.S. 639 (1899) (refusing to
   enforce an illegal contract).

9 *See Duty*, BLACK'S LAW DICTIONARY (10th ed. 2014) (defining legal
   duty as "[a] legal obligation that is owed or due to another and
   that needs to be satisfied; that which one is bound to do").

10 *See id.* (noting the legal duty of parents to support their children).

11 *See* RESTATEMENT (SECOND) OF CONTRACTS § 1 cmt. B (1981) (noting that contracts are merely promises with legal remedies).

12 *See Duty*, BLACK'S LAW DICTIONARY, *supra* note 9; Heaven v. Pender, 11 Q.B. Div. 506 (1883) (Eng.) ("That which the law requires to be done or forborne to a determinate person or the public at large.").

13 *See* RALPH NADER, UNSAFE AT ANY SPEED: THE DESIGNED-IN DANGERS OF THE AMERICAN AUTOMOBILE (1965).

14 *See* RESTATEMENT (SECOND) OF CONTRACTS § 1 cmt. B (1981) (noting that contracts are merely promises that can be legally enforced).

15 *See Duty*, BLACK'S LAW DICTIONARY, *supra* note 9 (stating that a legal duty "needs to be satisfied" and that it is "that which one is bound to do").

16 *See id.* (stating that a legal duty means that "somebody else has a corresponding right"); Heaven, 11 Q.B. Div. at 506 (holding that a legal duty creates "a vested and coextensive right in such person or the public" to whom the duty is owed).

17 *See Duty*, BLACK'S LAW DICTIONARY, *supra* note 9 ("[L]egal duty [can mean a] duty arising by contract or by operation of law; an obligation the breach of which would give a legal remedy.").

18 *See* Riddell v. Peck-Williamson Heating & Ventilating Co., 69 P. 241, 243 (Mont. 1902) ("A legal duty is an obligation arising either from the contract of the parties *or* the operation of law."); Meinhard v. Salmon, 164 N.E. 545, 546 (N.Y. 1928) (determining that a partner's duty included the duty to disclose business opportunities to the fellow partner).

19 *See Duty*, BLACK'S LAW DICTIONARY, *supra* note 9 (stating that a legal duty is "[a] legal obligation that is owed or due to another and that needs to be satisfied").

20 *See Riddell*, 69 P. at 243 ("A legal duty is an obligation arising either from the contract of the parties *or* the operation of law.").

21 *See Duty*, BLACK'S LAW DICTIONARY, *supra* note 9 ("[A] legal duty [can mean a] duty arising by contract or by operation of law."); *see also Riddell*, 69 P. at 243("A legal duty is an obligation arising either from the contract of the parties or the operation of law.").

22 *See id.* (stating that a legal duty means that "somebody else has a corresponding right"); Heaven v. Pender, 11 Q.B. Div. 506 (1883) (Eng.) (stating that a legal duty creates "a vested and coextensive right in such person or the public" to whom the duty is owed).

23   *See* RESTATEMENT (SECOND) OF CONTRACTS § 1 (1981) ("A contract
     is a promise or a set of promises . . . the performance of which the
     law in some way recognizes as a duty.").
24   *See Duty*, BLACK'S LAW DICTIONARY, *supra* note 9 (stating that
     legal duties "need[] to be satisfied;" they are "that which one is
     bound to do").
25   *See id.* (noting that a legal duty can arise merely from the
     operation of law).
26   *See, e.g.*, Meinhard v. Salmon, 164 N.E. 545, 546 (N.Y.
     1928) (noting that a duty arose because the parties had formed a
     partnership and engaged in joint ventures).
27   *See Duty*, BLACK'S LAW DICTIONARY, *supra* note 9 (noting
     examples of parties owing fiduciary duties as agents, trustees,
     lawyers, corporate officers, and partners).
28   *See* ALAN R. BROMBERG & LARRY F. RIBSTEIN, 3 BROMBERG AND
     RIBSTEIN ON PARTNERSHIP 6.07(a) (2007) ("[P]artners cannot act
     vis-à-vis each other as they can with third parties."); *Meinhard*,
     164 N.E. at 546 ("Joint adventurers, like copartners, owe to one
     another, while the enterprise continues, the duty of the finest
     loyalty. Many forms of conduct permissible in a workaday world
     for those acting at arm's length, are forbidden to those bound
     by fiduciary ties. A trustee is held to something stricter than the
     morals of the market place.").
29   *See Duty*, BLACK'S LAW DICTIONARY, *supra* note 9 (noting
     examples of parties owing fiduciary duties as agents, trustees,
     lawyers, corporate officers, and partners).
30   *See id.* at *Fiduciary* (defining fiduciary as a relationship of trust).
31   *Duty*, BLACK'S LAW DICTIONARY, *supra* note 9.
32   *See id.* (stating that a fiduciary duty means "a duty to act with the
     highest degree of honesty and loyalty toward another person and
     in the best interests of the other person").
33   *See* BROMBERG & RIBSTEIN, *supra* note 28, at 6.07(a) ("The partners
     owe fiduciary duties to each other and to the partnership,
     although they do not have such duties in all circumstances.").
34   *See id.* ("One consequence of this relationship is the duty of
     full disclosure;" "The main elements of the partners' fiduciary
     duties have been summarized as utmost good faith, fairness, and
     loyalty.").
35   *See* DAN B. DOBBS, PAUL T. HAYDEN & ELLEN M. BUBLICK, THE
     LAW OF TORTS § 127 (2d ed. 2011) ("In the latter half of the 19th

century, courts began to develop a general duty or standard of
care describing the duty of all persons to exercise ordinary care,
meaning the care of a reasonable person, for the benefit of other
persons, not merely the particular duties of, say, a veterinarian to
a farmer.").

36   *See id.* ("The duty owed by all people generally—the standard
of care—is the duty to exercise the care that would be exercised
by a reasonable and prudent person under the same or similar
circumstances to avoid or minimize risks of harm to others.").

37   *See Breach of Duty of Care,* BLACK'S LAW DICTIONARY, *supra* note
9 ("Negligence that results in a foreseeable injury that would
not have occurred but for the negligent person's actions."); *id.*
at *Duty of Care* ("A legal relationship arising from a standard of
care, the violation of which subjects the actor to liability.").

38   DOBBS ET AL., *supra* note 35, at § 292 (noting that some
relationships carry a "heightened duty").

39   *See id.* ("[Professionals] must exercise at least the skill,
knowledge, and care normally possessed and exercised by other
members of their profession'"); *id.* at § 127 ("[T]he standard
for physicians and some other professionals has widely been
regarded as a standard that differs from the reasonable person
standard.").

40   *See* Richard A. Posner, *A Theory of Negligence,* 1 J. LEGAL STUD. 29,
42 (1972) (noting that, when a company's costs for a precaution
begin to outweigh its ability to operate, its duties change).

41   *See id.* ("A company should devote resources to screening out
careless workmen just as it should devote resources to inspecting
its machinery for defects but there comes a point where a further
expenditure on supervision of employees or on inspection of
machinery would exceed the accident costs that the expenditure
would save.").

42   *See* United States v. Carroll Towing Co., 159 F.2d 169, 173 (2d
Cir. 1947) ("[T]he owner's duty, as in other similar situations,
to provide against resulting injuries is a function of three
variables: (1) The probability that she will break away; (2) the
gravity of the resulting injury, if she does; (3) the burden of
adequate precautions. Possibly it serves to bring this notion into
relief to state it in algebraic terms: if the probability be called P;
the injury, L; and the burden, B; liability depends upon whether
B is less than L multiplied by P: i.e., whether B less than PL.").

43 *See* Posner, *supra* note 40 ("A company should devote resources to screening out careless workmen just as it should devote resources to inspecting its machinery for defects but there comes a point where a further expenditure on supervision of employees or on inspection of machinery would exceed the accident costs that the expenditure would save.").

44 159 F.2d 169, 171 (2d Cir. 1947).

45 *See id.* at 173.

46 5 SAMUEL WILLISTON, WILLISTON ON CONTRACTS § 12:1 (4th ed. 1993) ("Generally, whenever the performance of an act would be either a crime or a tort, a promise or agreement to do that act would also be illegal and void or unenforceable.").

47 *See* Kaiser Steel Corp. v. Mullins, 455 U.S. 72 (1982) (holding that the illegality of a contract is a defense against the legal duty to fulfill the contract).

48 *See* 5 WILLISTON ON CONTRACTS, *supra* note 46, at § 12:1 ("Generally, whenever the performance of an act would be either a crime or a tort, a promise or agreement to do that act would also be illegal and void or unenforceable."); RESTATEMENT (SECOND) CONTRACTS § 192 (1981) (holding that a promise to commit or induce commission of tort is unenforceable on grounds of public policy); Kaiser Steel Corp. v. Mullins, 455 U.S. 72 (1982) (holding that the illegality of s contract is a defense against the legal duty to fulfill the contract).

49 *See* McMullen v. Hoffman, 174 U.S. 639 (1899) (refusing to enforce an illegal contract).

50 *See* ABA MODEL RULES OF PROF'L CONDUCT, at Preamble ("As advocate, a lawyer zealously asserts the client's position under the rules of the adversary system. As negotiator, a lawyer seeks a result advantageous to the client."); *see also id.* at R. 3.3 (2004) (describing a lawyer's duty of candor toward the tribunal). *But see id.* at R. 3.3(2004) ("A lawyer shall not knowingly . . . make a false statement of fact or law to a tribunal or fail to correct a false statement of material fact or law previously made to the tribunal by the lawyer.").

51 *See id.* at R. 1.8(e) (2004) ("A lawyer shall not provide financial assistance to a client in connection with pending or contemplated litigation.").

52 *See* Riddell v. Peck-Williamson Heating & Ventilating Co., 69 P. 241, 243 (Mont. 1902) ("Judicial tribunals should not assume

power to compel the discharge of mere ethical duties arising
from imperfect or moral obligations.").

53   *See Duty*, BLACK'S, *supra* note 9 ("[M]oral duty [is a] duty the
breach of which would be a moral wrong—also termed natural
duty.").

54   *See* RESTATEMENT (SECOND) OF CONTRACTS § 1, cmt. B (1981)
("'[C]ontract,' like 'promise,' denotes the act or acts of promising.
But, unlike the term 'promise,' 'contract' applies only to those
acts which have legal effect.").

55   *See Riddell*, 69 P. at 243 ("Without a wrong, there is no cause of
action. A wrong is the breach of a legal duty. A legal duty is an
obligation arising either from the contract of the parties or the
operation of law."); 1 WILLISTON ON CONTRACTS, *supra* note 46,
at § 1:2 ("If, by reason of other operative facts, the promise is one
which creates a legal duty, or if its breach will give rise to a right
of redress, then the promise is a contract.").

56   *See Person*, BLACK'S LAW DICTIONARY, *supra* note 9 (noting that an
artificial entity is also called "legal person"); *id.* ("[An] artificial
person [is an] entity, such as a corporation, created by law and
given certain legal rights and duties of a human being.").

57   *See id.* ("An entity is a person for purposes of the Due Process
and Equal Protection Clauses but is not a citizen for purposes of
the Privileges and Immunities Clauses in Article IV § 2 and in the
Fourteenth Amendment.").

58   *See id.* ("[A] legal person [is] given certain legal rights and duties
of a human being" and "for the purpose of legal reasoning is
treated more or less as a human being.").

59   *See* Santa Clara Cty. v. S. Pac. R. Co., 118 U.S. 394 (1886) ("The
court does not wish to hear argument on the question whether
the provision in the Fourteenth Amendment to the Constitution,
which forbids a State to deny to any person within its jurisdiction
the equal protection of the laws, applies to these corporations.
We are all of opinion that it does."). This language from *Santa
Clara*, somewhat infamously, is from the court reporter, noting
in the headnotes to the case the opinion of the justices; the actual
case did not hinge on this issue. Nonetheless, it is the Supreme
Court's first "official" treatment of corporation's as entities
with constitutional protections. *See also* Citizens United v. Fed.
Election Comm'n, 558 U.S. 310, 365 (2010) ("[T]he Government

may not suppress political speech on the basis of the speaker's corporate identity.").

60 *See* 1 WILLIAM MEADE FLETCHER ET AL., FLETCHER CYCLOPEDIA OF THE LAW OF PRIVATE CORPORATIONS § 25 (updated Sept. 2019) ("It is a practical convenience to consider the corporation as a legal personality capable of . . . possessing and owning real and personal property in its own name.").

61 *See id.* ("[T]he corporation [is] a legal personality capable of . . . carrying on business in much the same manner as a natural person acting through agents of its own selection.").

62 *See Person*, BLACK'S LAW DICTIONARY, *supra* note 9 ("[A] legal person [is] given certain legal rights and duties of a human being" and "for the purpose of legal reasoning is treated more or less as a human being.").

63 *See* 1 FLETCHER, *supra* note 60, at § 25 ("It is generally accepted that the corporation is an entity distinct.").

64 *See id.* ("The corporation and its directors and officers are . . . not the same personality.").

65 *See id.* ("[A] duly organized corporation enjoys a legal identity separate and apart from its shareholders, directors and officers.").

66 *See id.* (Corporations enjoy "rights and liabilities not the same as [shareholders, officers, or directors] individually and severally.").

67 *Id.* at § 41.10 ("[A]lter ego corporations are not of themselves illegal, the fact that an individual is the alter ego of a corporation is insufficient to state a claim against an individual.").

68 *See id. at* § 25 ("The legal fiction of a separate corporate entity was designed to serve convenience and justice.").

69 *See id.* at § 41.10 ("The alter ego theory applies when there is such unity between a corporation and an individual that the separateness of the corporation has ceased. Under the alter ego doctrine, when a corporation is the mere instrumentality or business conduit of another corporation or person, the corporate form may be disregarded. Under the doctrine, courts merely disregard the corporate entity and hold the individuals responsible for their acts knowingly and intentionally done in the name of the corporation.").

70 *See* Kinney Shoe Corp v. Polan, 939 F.2d 209, 211–12 (4th Cir. 1991) (holding that, when an owner failed to treat a corporation as a separate legal entity, he was personally liable for damages the corporation caused).

71   *See* 1 FLETCHER, *supra* note 60, at § 41.10 (noting that the alter ego
     doctrine is rarely invoked because "the fact that an individual
     is the alter ego of a corporation is insufficient to state a claim
     against an individual."); *Kinney Shoe Corp v. Polan*, 939 F.2d 209
     (4th Cir. 1991) (holding that, when an owner failed to treat a
     corporation as a separate legal entity, he was personally liable for
     damages the corporation caused).

72   *See* 3 FLETCHER, *supra* note 60, at § 837.50 ("Directors and officers
     stand in a fiduciary relationship to the corporation and its
     shareholders.").

73   *See id.* ("In Delaware, corporate officers owe fiduciary duties
     that are identical to those owed by corporate directors.");
     RESTATEMENT (THIRD) OF AGENCY §8.01, cmt. G (3d ed.
     2006) ("[A]s agents, all employees owe duties of loyalty to their
     employers.").

74   *See* 3 FLETCHER, *supra* note 60, at § 837.50 ("Directors and officers
     stand in a fiduciary relationship to the corporation and its
     shareholders.").

75   *See id.* ("Inasmuch as corporate directors and officers occupy a
     fiduciary capacity, directors and other officers must exercise the
     utmost good faith in all transactions touching their duties to the
     corporation and its property. In their dealings with and for the
     corporation, they are held to the same strict rule of honesty and
     fair dealing between themselves and their principal as other
     agents.").

76   *See, e.g.*, Kahn v. Lynch Commc'n Sys., Inc., 638 A.2d 1110, 1115
     (Del. 1994) ("A controlling or dominating shareholder standing
     on both sides of a transaction, as in a parent–subsidiary context,
     bears the burden of proving its entire fairness.").

77   *See* RESTATEMENT (THIRD) OF AGENCY §8.01, cmt. c (3d ed.
     2006) ("All who assent to act on behalf of another person
     and subject to that person's control are common-law agents
     as defined in §1.01 and are subject to the general fiduciary
     principle stated in this section. Thus, the fiduciary principle is
     applicable to gratuitous agents as well as to agents who expect
     compensation for their services, and to employees as well as to
     nonemployee professionals, intermediaries, and others who act
     as agents."); RESTATEMENT (THIRD) OF AGENCY §8.01, cmt. g (3d
     ed. 2006) ("[A]s agents, all employees owe duties of loyalty to
     their employers.").

78 *See* Rob Atkinson, *Obedience as the Foundation of Fiduciary Duty*,
    34 J. CORP. L. 43, 45 (2008) (noting that the "pillars" of fiduciary
    duty are loyalty, care, which ultimately rest on the duty of
    obedience).

79 *See* RESTATEMENT (SECOND) OF AGENCY § 385 (1958) (noting that,
    "[u]nless otherwise agreed, an agent" such as an employee "is
    subject to a duty to obey all reasonable directions in regard to
    the manner of performing a service that he has contracted to
    perform").

80 *See* Atkinson, *supra* note 78 ("Commentators, both doctrinal and
    theoretical, have come to agree that the fiduciary relationship
    rests on twin pillars, the duty of care and the duty of loyalty.
    This paper argues that a third duty, obedience, is more basic, the
    foundation on which the duties of care and loyalty ultimately
    rest."); Alan R. Palmiter, *Duty of Obedience: The Forgotten Duty*,
    55 N.Y.L. SCH. L. REV. 457, 458–59 (2010) (calling for revival
    of a "duty of obedience" in order to "advance the legitimacy
    of the corporation in society," a duty which would compel
    corporate fiduciaries "to abide by legal norms—both those of
    the corporation and of external law," and provide a "clearer
    vocabulary").

81 *See* Palmiter, *supra* note 80, at 461 n.11 (noting that Delaware
    courts seem to have rolled duty of obedience into that of care and
    good faith, as corporations and their actors are prohibited from
    disregarding norms, even when doing so may be profitable); In re
    Walt Disney Derivative Litig., 906 A.2d 27, 67 (Del. 2006) (noting
    that directors violate duty of good faith "where the fiduciary acts
    with the intent to violate applicable positive law"); Marchand
    v. Barnhill, 212 A.3d 805, 809 (Del. 2019) (noting that a board acts
    in bad faith and breaches the duty of loyalty when they fail to
    attempt to assure a reasonable information and reporting system
    exists within their corporation).

82 *See* Miller v. AT&T Co., 507 F.2d 759, 762 (3d Cir. 1974) ("Where,
    however, the decision . . . is itself alleged to have been an illegal
    act[,] . . . we are convinced that the business judgment rule
    cannot insulate the defendant directors from liability if they
    did in fact breach 18 U.S.C. § 610."); Desimone v. Barrows, 924
    A.2d 908, 934 (Del. Ch. 2007) ("[B]y consciously causing the
    corporation to violate the law, a director would be disloyal to
    the corporation and could be forced to answer for the harm

he has caused. Although directors have wide authority to take lawful action on behalf of the corporation, they have no authority knowingly to cause the corporation to become a rogue, exposing the corporation to penalties from criminal and civil regulators.").

83   *See* RESTATEMENT (THIRD) OF AGENCY §8.01, cmt. c (3d ed. 2006) ("All who assent to act on behalf of another person and subject to that person's control are common-law agents . . . and are subject to the general fiduciary principle . . . the fiduciary principle is applicable to gratuitous agents as well as to agents who expect compensation for their services.").

84   *See* RESTATEMENT (SECOND) OF AGENCY § 385 (1958) ("Unless otherwise agreed, an agent is subject to a duty to obey all reasonable directions in regard to the manner of performing a service that he has contracted to perform.").

85   *See* RESTATEMENT (THIRD) OF AGENCY §8.01, cmt. g (3d ed. 2006) ("[A]s agents, all employees owe duties of loyalty to their employers.").

86   *See* Margaret M. Blair & Lynn A. Stout, *Team Production Theory of Corporate Law*, 85 VA. L. REV. 247, 292–93 (1999) (explaining that, because the corporation is an "artificial" legal person, it can only act through agents hired to conduct business on its behalf).

87   *See id.* at 276, 291 (stating that directors, as the "ultimate decision-making authority" and managers of the corporation's business and affairs, are responsible for hiring corporate agents and directing their activities).

88   *See* 3 FLETCHER, *supra* note 60, at § 837.50 § 837.50 ("[A]s a fiduciary[,] . . . a director's or officer's first duty is to act in all things of trust wholly for the benefit of the corporation."); Marchand v. Barnhill, 212 A.3d 805, 824 (Del. 2019) ("If *Caremark* [*In re Caremark Int'l Inc. Derivative Litig.*, 698 A.2d 959 (Del. Ch. 1996)] means anything, it is that a corporate board must make a good faith effort to exercise its duty of care. A failure to make that effort constitutes a breach of the duty of loyalty.").

89   *See* Del. Code Ann. tit. 8, § 102, 109.

90   *See* Andrew S. Gold, *The New Concept of Loyalty in Corporate Law*, 43 U.C. DAVIS L. REV. 457, 476–77 (2009) ("Corporate charters only allow the corporation to act consistently with positive law.").

91   *See* William T. Allen & Reinier Kraakman, COMMENTARIES AND CASES ON THE LAW OF BUSINESS ORGANIZATION 28 (5th

ed. 2016) (stating that fiduciaries have a duty of obedience to the documents that created the relationship); Gold, *supra* note 90 ("[D]irectors are bound to comply with the terms of their corporate charter.").

92 *See id.* ("The duty to act consistently with positive law is . . . not only a duty imposed directly by that positive law, it is also a duty incorporated into the charter itself. An intentional violation of positive law is an intentional violation of a corporation's charter, given the present requirements for the content of charters. Directors have committed themselves to following their corporations' charter.").

93 *See* Restatement (Third) of Agency § 8.09 (3d ed. 2006) (describing duties of agent and instructions from the principal). The law only requires agents to comply with legal instructions provided by the principal when acting within the scope of the relationship. § 8.09 cmt. b. Agents are not required to comply with instructions to commit a crime or tortious act. § 8.09 cmt. c.

94 *See Orders of a Superior*, 2 Subst. Crim. L. § 9.7(g) (3d ed.) ("It is no defense to a crime committed by an employee that he was only carrying out his employer's unlawful orders.").

95 *See* Ford v. Wisc. Real Est. Examining Bd., 179 N.W.2d 786, 792 (Wisc. 1970) (holding that, because agents entered agreement with the understanding that they would not show real estate to African Americans, thereby agreeing to assist the principal in committing a tort, they were "liable as a joint tortfeasor for the entire damage").

96 *See* United States v. Decker, 304 F.2d 702, 703–05 (6th Cir. 1962).

97 *Id.* at 705.

98 *See Loyalty*, Dictionary.com, https://www.dictionary.com/browse/loyalty (defining loyalty as fidelity to the welfare of another).

99 *See* 3 Fletcher, *supra* note 60, at § 837.50 § 837.50 ("[A] director or officer of a corporation owes the corporation complete loyalty, honesty, and good faith.").

100 *See Duty*, Black's Law Dictionary, *supra* note 9 (stating that a duty of loyalty entails "a duty to act . . . in the best interests of the other person").

101 *See* 2 James D. Cox & Thomas Lee Hazen, Treatise on the Law of Corporations § 11:8 (3d ed. 2010) ("[D]irectors and

officers . . . cannot utilize their strategic position or their powers
and opportunities for their personal advantage to the detriment
of other corporate constituencies.").

102 See Duty, BLACK'S, supra note 9 (stating that the duty of loyalty
entails "a duty to act . . . in the best interests of the other person
. . . . For example, directors have a duty not to engage in self-
dealing to further their own personal interests rather than the
interests of the corporation").

103 See Cox & HAZEN, supra note 101, at § 10:11 ("[C]ourts uniformly
remove the actions of the board of directors from the protective
presumption of the business judgment rule [when they] fear
that the directors may be acting to protect their personal self-
interest and not serving the interests of the corporation or its
stockholders.").

104 See id. at § 11:8 ("Directors and officers as insiders cannot
utilize their strategic position for their own preferment or use
their powers and opportunities for their own advantage to the
exclusion or detriment of the interests they are to represent"); Joel
Seligman, The New Corporate Law, 59 BROOK. L. REV. 1, 3 (1993)
("The duty of loyalty . . . requires that officers and directors not
profit at the expense of their corporation, whether through self-
dealing contracts, usurpation of corporate opportunities, or other
means").

105 See Seligman, supra note 104 ("The duty of loyalty is the most
important fiduciary duty of corporate officers and directors");
Gabriel Rauterberg & Eric Talley, Contracting Out of the Fiduciary
Duty of Loyalty: An Empirical Analysis of Corporate Opportunity
Waivers, 117 COLUM. L. REV. 1075, 1075 (2017) ("For centuries, the
duty of loyalty has been the hallowed centerpiece of fiduciary
obligation, widely considered one of the few 'mandatory' rules
of corporate law."). Rauterberg and Talley note that this duty
applies to "[c]orporate fiduciaries—the officers who manage a
company's daily operations, the directors who wield ultimate
decision-making authority, and the dominant shareholders who
possess swing voting power." Id.

106 See Jane R. Bambauer, Dr. Robot, 51 U.C. DAVIS L. REV. 383, 397
(2017) ("[T]he doctor–patient relationship includes a duty of
loyalty that requires a doctor to disclose conflicts of interest.").

107 See RESTATEMENT (THIRD) OF THE LAW GOVERNING LAWYERS §
16 (2000) ("[A] lawyer must, in matters within the scope of the

representation . . . avoid impermissible conflicting interests, deal honestly with the client, and not employ advantages arising from the client-lawyer relationship in a manner adverse to the client.").

108 *See* Cox & HAZEN, *supra* note 101, at § 10:11 ("[C]ourts uniformly remove the actions of the board of directors from the protective presumption of the business judgment rule [when they] fear that the directors may be acting to protect their personal self-interest and not serving the interests of the corporation or its stockholders."), and § 10:12 ("Loans, sales of property, employment contracts, and the like clearly create a conflict-of-interest when they are between the corporation and its director or officer or between the corporation and another entity in which the corporate director or officer has a significant involvement.").

109 *See id.* ("[Conflicted] transactions are commonly referred to as 'self-dealing' and are the subject of conflict-of-interest provisions found in the state corporate statute.").

110 *See* Shapiro v. Greenfield, 764 A.2d 270, 272–73, 276–77 (2000).

111 *See* Seligman, *supra* note 104 ("The duty of loyalty . . . requires that officers and directors not . . . usurp . . . corporate opportunities.").

112 Cox & HAZEN, *supra* note 101, at § 11:8 (describing three corporate-opportunity tests).

113 *See id.* ("*Lagarde* established the 'interest or expectancy' test, whereby an officer or director is deemed to usurp a corporate opportunity only where the corporation has an existing interest in the property or an expectancy growing out of an existing right.").

114 *Id.* ("In contrast to the narrowness of the 'interest or expectancy' test is the 'line of business' test.").

115 *See id.* ("[T]he 'line of business' test . . . treats as belonging to the corporation an opportunity that is related to or is in the company's line of activities.").

116 *See id.* (stating that the line of business test applies to any "activity that the company could reasonably be expected to enter").

117 *See* Guth v. Loft, Inc., 5 A.2d 503, 503–10 (Del. 1939).

118 *See* Cox & HAZEN, *supra* note 101, at § 11:8 ("A majority of the cases determine whether the director or officer has usurped a corporate opportunity by weighing a range of factors.").

119 *See id.* (stating that noting that courts weigh the "range of
     factors" to "determine whether the director or officer has
     usurped a corporate opportunity," including: "(1) Is the
     opportunity to acquire real estate, patents, etc., of special and
     unique value, or needed for the corporate business and its
     expansion? (2) Did the discovery or information come to the
     officer by reason of his official position? (3) Was the company
     in the market, negotiating for, or seeking such opportunity or
     advantage, and, if so, has it abandoned its efforts in this regard?
     (4) Was the officer especially charged with the duty of acquiring
     such opportunities for his enterprise? (5) Did the officer use
     corporate funds or facilities in acquiring or developing it?
     (6) Does taking the opportunity place the director in an adverse
     and hostile position to his corporation? (7) Did the officer
     intend to resell the opportunity to the corporation? (8) Was the
     corporation in a favorable position to take advantage of the
     opportunity, or was it financially or otherwise unable to do so?").

120 *See* Cox & Hazen, *supra* note 101, at § 11:9 ("Directors and
     officers are fiduciary representatives and as such are not allowed
     to obtain or retain a commission, bonus, gift, or personal
     profit or advantage 'on the side' for their official action, as in
     connection with a purchase, sale, lease, loan, or contract by the
     corporation.").

121 *See, e.g.,* In re Worcester Quality Foods, Inc., 152 B.R. 394, 394
     (Bankr. D. Mass. 1993) ("[C]onsulting fees paid to directors'
     businesses, loans to businesses and directors, and payment of
     directors' personal expenses were unfair to corporation and
     constituted breach of directors' duty of loyalty to corporation.").

122 *See, e.g.,* Summers v. Cherokee Children & Family Servs., Inc.,
     112 S.W.3d 486, 526 (Tenn. Ct. App. 2002) (placing nonprofits
     into receivership when directors used the company to give
     themselves personal benefits through bonuses, real estate deals,
     and other means).

123 *See* Rauterberg & Talley, *supra* note 105, at 1077–78 ("Beginning in
     2000, Delaware dramatically departed from tradition, amending
     its statutes to enable corporations to waive a critical component
     of loyalty—the corporate opportunities doctrine—which forbids
     corporate fiduciaries from appropriating new business prospects
     for themselves without first offering them to the company. From
     that moment forward, Delaware corporations and managers

became free to contract out of a significant portion of the duty of loyalty.").

124 *See id.* ("In the ensuing years, eight other states have followed Delaware's lead, granting their own incorporated entities the statutory authority to execute corporate opportunity waivers (COWs). The Corporate Laws Committee of the American Bar Association (ABA) has also recently proposed amending the Model Business Corporation Act to permit advance waivers of corporate opportunities."); *cf. also* Blake Rohrbacher, John Mark Zeberkiewicz & Thomas A. Uebler, *Finding Safe Harbor: Clarifying the Limited Application of Section 144*, 33 Del. J. Corp. L. 719–20 (2008) ("Section 144 of the General Corporation Law of the State of Delaware was adopted for a limited purpose: to rescue certain transactions, those in which the directors and officers of a corporation have an interest, from per se voidability under the common law. That is all. Under its plain language, section 144 plays no part in validating transactions or in ensuring the business judgment rule's application.").

125 *See* Glidden Co. v. Jandernoa, 173 F.R.D. 459, 480 (W.D. Mich. 1997) ("The law imposes certain obligations upon both corporate fiduciaries and attorneys who seek to advance conflicting interests. They have the duty to make full disclosure and obtain clear and informed consent. If the transaction thereafter goes sour, theirs is the burden of proving full disclosure and the fact and scope of consent. This burden is not met by arguing that the party to whom the duty was owed had constructive knowledge of the conflict.").

126 *See* Del. Code Ann. tit. 8, §§ 102(b)(7) (allowing a corporation to indemnify corporate fiduciaries for breaches of the duty of care but *not* for breaches of the duty of loyalty), 145(a) (West) ("A corporation shall have power to indemnify any person . . . by reason of the fact that the person is or was a director, officer, employee or agent of the corporation . . . if the person acted in good faith and in a manner the person reasonably believed to be in or not opposed to the best interests of the corporation."); Smith v. Van Gorkom, 488 A.2d 858, 874 (Del. 1985) (denying disloyal and careless corporate fiduciaries indemnification from the corporation).

127 *See* Del. Code Ann. tit. 8, § 145(g) (West) ("A corporation shall have power to purchase and maintain insurance on behalf of any

person who is or was a director, officer, employee or agent of the corporation . . . against any liability asserted against such person and incurred by such person in any such capacity, or arising out of such person's status as such, whether or not the corporation would have the power to indemnify such person against such liability under this section."); Arch Ins. Co. v. Murdock, No. CVN16C01104EMDCCLD, 2018 WL 1129110, at *10 (Del. Super. Ct. Mar. 1, 2018) ("Under Delaware law, therefore, a corporation is permitted to purchase insurance against any liability asserted against an officer or director even when the corporation would not be able to otherwise indemnify that person under 8 Del. C. § 145. This would include insurance for a breach of the duty of loyalty.").

128 *See Duty*, Black's, *supra* note 9 ("[F]iduciary duty [means a] duty of utmost good faith.").

129 *See* Stone ex rel. AmSouth Bancorporation v. Ritter, 911 A.2d 362, 370 (Del. 2006) ("[T]he requirement to act in good faith is a subsidiary element[,] i.e., a condition, of the fundamental duty of loyalty.") (internal quotation marks omitted).

130 *See id.* ("[B]ecause a showing of bad faith conduct . . . is essential to establish director oversight liability, the fiduciary duty violated by that conduct is the duty of loyalty.") (internal quotation marks omitted); In re Walt Disney Co. Derivative Litig., 906 A.2d 27, 63 (Del. 2006) ("[The] definition of bad faith—a conscious and intentional disregard of responsibilities, adopting a 'we don't care about the risks' attitude . . . an intentional dereliction of duty, a conscious disregard for one's responsibilities.") (internal quotation marks and alterations omitted).

131 *See In re Walt Disney*, 906 A.2d at 36–45.

132 *Id.* at 75.

133 *See id.* at 63.

134 *See* 28 Williston on Contracts, *supra* note 46, at § 71:1 (stating that the result of a threat is that the contract becomes "voidable at the will of the victim, because it was the result of duress").

135 The Godfather (Paramount Pictures 1972).

136 *See* 28 Williston on Contracts, *supra* note 46, at § 71:1 ("[Nonviolent] duress is much more common than that which takes the form of actual physical compulsion that forces the victim to engage in conduct that he or she neither engages in voluntarily nor intends to engage in at all. With this form of

duress, the coercive party makes improper threats that induce
the victim to act in a particular way—that is, to manifest assent
to the proposal made by the coercing party, in effect bending the
victim to the latter's will.").

137 *See id.* at § 69:1 ("Perhaps the most important of the defenses [of
bad faith] is fraud.").

138 *See id.* ("One who has been fraudulently induced to enter into a
contract has not assented to the agreement since the fraudulent
conduct precludes the requisite mutual assent.").

139 *See* New York Life Ins. Co. v. Nashville Trust Co., 292 S.W.2d 749
(Tenn. 1956) ("Fraud vitiates and avoids all human transactions,
from the solemn judgment of a court to a private contract. It is
as odious and as fatal in a court of law as in a court of equity.")
(quoting *Smith v. Harrison*, 49 Tenn. 230 (1871)).

140 *See* 30 WILLISTON ON CONTRACTS, *supra* note 46, at § 77:10 ("A
promisor may be at fault when it breaches its duty to deal
in good faith with other parties or known beneficiaries to a
contract. A covenant of good faith and fair dealing is implied all
contracts.").

141 *See* DOBBS ET AL., *supra* note 35, at § 127 ("In the latter half of the
19th century, courts began to develop a general duty or standard
of care describing the duty of *all persons* to exercise ordinary care,
meaning the care of a reasonable person, for the benefit of other
persons, not merely the particular duties of, say, a veterinarian to
a farmer.") (emphasis added).

142 *See id.* (stating that the duty of care is "owed by all people
generally").

143 *See id.* (stating that the duty of care "is the duty to exercise the
care that would be exercised by a reasonable and prudent person
under the same or similar circumstances").

144 *See* Bertrand Crettez, *On the Optimality of a Duty-to-Rescue Rule
and the Cost of Wrongful Intervention*, 31 INT'L REV. L. & ECON. 263
(2011) ("In common law legal systems, there is no legal duty to
rescue persons in danger.").

145 *See* RESTATEMENT (THIRD) OF TORTS, Physical & Emotional Harm
4 Scope Note (2010) ("Strict liability is liability imposed without
regard to the defendant's negligence or intent to cause harm. In
a strict-liability case, the plaintiff need not prove the defendant's
negligence or intent, and the defendant cannot escape liability by
proving a lack of negligence or intent.").

146 *See, e.g.,* Trager v. Thor, 516 N.W.2d 69, 72 (Mich. 1994) (noting the common law tradition of strict liability for injuries caused by domestic animals); RESTATEMENT (SECOND) OF TORTS § 509 (1977) (holding domestic animal owners strictly liable as long as owners knew of animals dangerous tendencies).

147 *See* RESTATEMENT (SECOND) OF TORTS § 509 cmt. d (1977) (reasoning that dangerous animals introduce a danger not common to a community and therefore require greater precautions by owners).

148 *See* DOBBS ET AL., *supra* note 35, at § 120 ("Liability for negligence is liability for one particular kind of fault. It is contrasted with liability for intentional torts and with strict liability.").

149 *See id.* at § 124 ("In modern law, the term negligence in its primary meaning merely describes conduct. In that sense it has come to mean conduct that is unreasonably risky, such as driving a car at a high rate of speed.").

150 *See* Lewison v. Renner, 905 N.W.2d 540, 548 (Neb. 2018) (defining elements of a negligence claim); Goldstein, Garber & Salama, *LLC v. J.B.*, 797 S.E.2d 87, 89 (Ga. 2017), *reconsideration denied* (Mar. 30, 2017), (defining elements of a negligence claim).

151 *See* DOBBS ET AL., *supra* note 35, at § 292 ("[The] heightened duty is sometimes referred to as the 'professional peer' standard.").

152 *See id.* ("[T]he standard for physicians and some other professionals has widely been regarded as a standard that differs from the reasonable person standard."); *id.* ("[Professionals] must exercise at least the skill, knowledge, and care normally possessed and exercised by other members of their profession.").

153 *See id.* at § 127 (2d ed.) ("[T]he standard for physicians and some other professionals has widely been regarded as a standard that differs from the reasonable person standard.").

154 *See* 3 STUART M. SPEISER, CHARLES F. KRAUSE & ALFRED W. GANS, AMERICAN LAW OF TORTS § 14:2 (2008) ("In virtually all Anglo-American jurisdictions today, the owner or the occupier of private premises may be held liable for personal injury or property damage occasioned by the owner's or occupier's negligence in the construction, maintenance, operation, and the like of the premises.").

155 *See id.* (stating that a landlord's liability is "subject, still in some states, to various exceptions in the case of licensees or trespassers"); *Who Are Invitees,* 2 PREMISES LIABILITY 3D § 37:1

(2018ed.) ("The term 'invitee' is a legal term of art more limited than the general sense of the term 'invitation.' Sometimes it is said that an invitee is one who possesses an invitation to be upon the premises, either express or implied. But not all who are invited to enter upon an owner's land are invitees; for example, a social guest, in many jurisdictions, is not considered to be an invitee, even though he or she enters the premises in response to an express 'invitation.' Thus an invited guest may be merely a licensee.").

156 *See* 3 AMERICAN LAW OF TORTS, *supra* note 154, at § 14:2 (stating that a landlord's liability is "subject, still in some states, to various exceptions in the case of licensees or trespassers").

157 *See id.* ("Landlords, also, subject to some exceptions, may be held liable for personal injury or property damage suffered by their tenants or the latter's family, privies, invitees, etc., because of the landlords' negligence in the construction, maintenance, operation of the rented premises, or their common areas.").

158 *See* 3 FLETCHER, *supra* note 60, at § 837.50 ("Directors and officers stand in a fiduciary relationship to the corporation and its shareholders . . . directors and other officers must exercise the utmost good faith in all transactions touching their duties to the corporation and its property . . . In Delaware, corporate officers owe fiduciary duties that are identical to those owed by corporate directors"); Kahn v. Lynch Commc'n Sys., Inc., 638 A.2d 1110, 1115 (Del. 1994) ("A controlling or dominating shareholder standing on both sides of a transaction, as in a parent–subsidiary context, bears the burden of proving its entire fairness.").

159 Smith v. Van Gorkom, 488 A.2d 858, 870–74 (Del. 1985) (describing the BJR).

160 *See* Revlon, Inc. v. MacAndrews & Forbes Holdings, Inc., 506 A.2d 173, 185 (Del. 1986) ("[U]nder all the circumstances the directors allowed considerations other than the maximization of shareholder profit to affect their judgment, and followed a course that ended [in] the ultimate detriment of its shareholders. No such defensive measure can be sustained when it represents a breach of the directors' fundamental duty of care. In that context the board's action is not entitled to the deference accorded it by the business judgment rule") (internal citation omitted);

Van Gorkom, 488 A.2d at 874 (denying the BJR standard when directors failed to fulfill the duty of care).

161　488 A.2d 858, 864–69, 893 (Del. 1985).

162　*See* Garrison v. Sagepoint Fin., Inc., 345 P.3d 792, 810 (Wash. App. 2015) ("Respondeat superior, or vicarious liability, imposes liability on an employer for the torts of an employee who is acting on the employer's behalf within the scope of employment.").

163　Dobbs et al., *supra* note 35, at § 27 ("Liability insurance protects the insured against tort liability by paying the insured's tort victims.").

164　*See id.* ("Liability insurance is not health or accident insurance; it pays only when the insured is legally liable to pay because of his tort.").

165　*See id.* ("No one will understand tort law in the United States without understanding that liability insurance fuels the system, limits its capacity for compensation and deterrence, shapes the litigation, and affects the costs and choices in the system as a whole.").

166　*See Liability Insurance as Covering Accident, Damage, or Injury Due to Wanton or Willful Misconduct or Gross Negligence*, 20 A.L.R.3d 320 (1st ed. 1968) ("Most liability policies contain an exclusion of liability for injury intentionally caused by the insured.").

167　*See* Dobbs et al., *supra* note 35, at § 140 ("The term gross negligence can be used to mean what it says—a high, though unspecified degree of negligence, or as courts sometimes say, the failure to use even slight care . . . some courts also permit recovery of punitive damages when the defendant is guilty of willful or wanton misconduct.").

168　*See* 1 Williston on Contracts, *supra* note 46, at § 1:2 ("[T]he term 'promise' includes . . . the moral duty to make good the assurance by subsequent performance.").

169　*See* Upjohn Co. v. United States, 449 U.S. 383, 389 (1981) (holding that confidential communications between lawyers and their clients are protected by attorney–client privilege).

170　*See* ABA Rules of Professional Conduct R. 1.6(a) ("A lawyer shall not reveal information relating to the representation of a client unless the client gives informed consent [or] the disclosure is impliedly authorized in order to carry out the representation.").

171 *See* Abelson's Inc. v. N.J. State Bd. of Optometrists, 75 A.2d 867,
873 (N.J. 1950) (finding constitutional a statute creating a right
of action against physician for revealing confidential patient
information); Smith v. Driscoll, 162 P. 572, 573 (Wash. 1917) ("A
physician is not permitted to disclose from the witness stand
the communications of his patient made in confidence merely
because the information would be relevant and pertinent
to the issues involved."); Monica Langley Lee, *Branzburg
Revisited: Confidential Sources and First Amendment Values*, 57
Geo. Wash. L. Rev. 13, 13–14 (1988) ("*Branzburg v. Hayes* [was]
the [Supreme] Court's first and only discussion of the scope of
the constitutional protections afforded a journalist's promise
of confidentiality to a source of information . . . . [T]he Court
took a narrow view of the constitutional interests at stake and
held that journalists enjoyed no privilege to refuse to appear
before grand juries and reveal their sources of information under
the circumstances presented."); ABA Rules of Professional
Conduct R. 1.6(a) ("A lawyer shall not reveal information
relating to the representation of a client unless the client gives
informed consent [or] the disclosure is impliedly authorized in
order to carry out the representation.").

172 *See* In re Mortg. & Realty Tr., 195 B.R. 740, 750 (Bankr. C.D. Cal.
1996) ("The fiduciary duty of loyalty of a corporate director
includes a duty to preserve the confidentiality of confidential
information received from the corporation during service
as a director."); Jacqueline Smoke, *Between a Rock and a Hard
Place: Attorney As Corporate Director and Shareholder's Attorney*,
21 J. Legal Prof. 277, 278 (1996) ("As part of the duty of
loyalty, a fiduciary relationship prohibits a director's disclosure
of confidential information. Even after termination of the
relationship, the corporate director has the duty to preserve the
confidentiality of any proprietary information received during
the discharge of duties as a corporate director.").

173 *See* In re Mortg., 195 B.R. at 750; Jacqueline Smoke, *Between a Rock
and a Hard Place: Attorney As Corporate Director and Shareholder's
Attorney*, 21 J. Legal Prof. 277, 278 (1996) (stating that the duty
of confidentiality is "part of the duty of loyalty" for corporate
directors).

174 *See* United States v. O'Hagan, 521 U.S. 642, 649–50 (1997) (holding that a corporate insider who trades securities with knowledge of material, non-public information committed fraud).

175 *See* Johnson Controls, Inc. v. Guidry, 724 F. Supp. 2d 612, 625 (W.D. La. 2010) ("An agreement not to use confidential information is enforceable if the information used is, in fact, confidential.") (citing *NCH Corp. v. Broyles*, 749 F.2d 247, 253 (5th Cir.1985)).

176 *See* 1 RAYMOND T. NIMMER, INFORMATION LAW § 5:59 (1996) ("In most cases, courts enforce nondisclosure clauses in agreements between two business entities.").

177 *See* § 10:17 Particular Provisions—Nondisclosure Provisions, EMPLOYEE NONCOMPETITION LAW § 10:17 (noting that a nondisclosure provision is proper in nearly every employment contract).

178 *See* 42 C.F.R. § 2 (consisting of a federal statute prohibiting disclosure of substance abuse treatment protects medical information and encourages patients to seek medical help for addiction); Upjohn Co. v. United States, 449 U.S. 383, 389 (1981) (holding that the attorney–client privilege seeks to encourage clients to fully inform their attorneys).

179 *See* Martin Marietta Materials, Inc. v. Vulcan Materials Co., 56 A.3d 1072, 1075 (Del. Ch. May 4, 2012), *aff'd*, 45 A.3d 148 (Del. 2012), *aff'd*, 68 A.3d 1208 (Del. 2012), *as corrected* (July 12, 2012) (noting that even the fact of corporation's openness to being acquired is highly confidential information to be kept from the market).

180 *See id.* ("May one of the parties—especially the one who evinced the most concern for confidentiality and who most feared having its willingness to enter into merger discussions become public— decide that evolving market circumstances make it comfortable enough to make a hostile bid for the other and then without consequence freely use and disclose publicly all the information that it had adamantly insisted be kept confidential? In this decision, I conclude that the answer to that question is no.").

181 *See* Upjohn Co. v. United States, 449 U.S. 383, 400 (1981) (holding that the work product doctrine allows disclosure where opposing counsel shows "substantial need and inability to obtain the equivalent without undue hardship").

182 *See* ABA RULES OF PROFESSIONAL CONDUCT R. 3.3(b) ("A lawyer who represents a client in an adjudicative proceeding and who knows that a person intends to engage, is engaging or has engaged in criminal or fraudulent conduct related to the proceeding shall take reasonable remedial measures, including, if necessary, disclosure . . . even if compliance requires disclosure of information otherwise protected.").

183 *See id.* at R. 1.6(b)(5)–(6) ("A lawyer may reveal information relating to the representation of a client to the extent the lawyer reasonably believes necessary . . . to establish a claim or defense on behalf of the lawyer in a controversy between the lawyer and the client, to establish a defense to a criminal charge or civil claim against the lawyer based upon conduct in which the client was involved, or to respond to allegations in any proceeding concerning the lawyer's representation of the client; or . . . to comply with other law or a court order.").

184 19 WILLISTON ON CONTRACTS, *supra* note 46, at § 54:33 ("A court will enforce a confidentiality agreement only when the information sought to be protected is actually confidential and reasonable efforts were made to keep it confidential.").

185 *See* Sissela Bok, *Truthfulness, in* CONCISE ROUTLEDGE ENCYCLOPEDIA OF PHILOSOPHY (2000) ("All societies, as well as all major moral, religious and legal traditions have condemned forms of deceit such as bearing false witness.").

186 *See* James Edwin Mahon, *The Definition of Lying and Deception, in* STANFORD ENCYCLOPEDIA OF PHILOSOPHY (Edward N. Zalta ed., Winter 2016ed.), https://plato.stanford.edu/archives/win2016/entries/lying-definition/ ("The most widely accepted definition of lying is the following: A lie is a statement made by one who does not believe it with the intention that someone else shall be led to believe it.").

187 *See* Alan Strudler, *Incommensurable Goods, Rightful Lies, and the Wrongness of Fraud*, 146 U. PA. L. REV. 1529, 1542–43 (1998) (noting that Kantian ethics consider lies as "contemptible," and Augustinian ethics consider lies "wrong in principle").

188 *See* Bok, *supra* note 185 ("All societies, as well as all major moral, religious and legal traditions have condemned forms of deceit such as bearing false witness.").

189 *See* W.D. Ross, The Right and the Good (1930) (arguing that duty not to tell lies is a prima facie duty of fidelity, and thus prohibits self-serving falsehoods).

190 *See* Bok, *supra* note 185 ("Many [moral, religious and legal traditions] have also held that deceit can be excusable or even mandated under certain circumstances, as, for instance, to deflect enemies in war or criminals bent on doing violence to innocent victims.").

191 *See* Tim Mazur, *Lying*, 6:1 Ethics (Fall 1993) ("Though the nature of virtue ethics makes it difficult to assess the morality of individual acts, those who advocate this theory generally consider lying wrong because it opposes the virtue of honesty.").

192 *See id.* ("There is some debate whether a lie told in pursuit of another virtue (e.g., compassion: the brother's lie to his sister's drunken husband is motivated by compassion for her physical safety) is right or wrong.").

193 *See id.* ("[An] apparent conflict between virtues is managed by most ethicists through a concept called the unity of the virtues. This doctrine states that the virtuous person, the ideal person we continuously strive to be, cannot achieve one virtue without achieving them all. Therefore, when facing a seeming conflict between virtues, such as a compassionate lie, virtue ethics charges us to imagine what some ideal individual would do and act accordingly, thus making the ideal person's virtues one's own.").

194 *See* 26 Williston on Contracts, *supra* note 46, at § 69:17 ("[U]nder certain circumstances failure to disclose a material fact may be deemed a misrepresentation sufficient to void a contract, and that, regardless of the existence of a duty to disclose, a direct inquiry regarding a material fact requires a truthful answer."); Weinberger v. UOP, Inc., 457 A.2d 701, 712 (Del. 1983) (holding that a failure to disclose sources of inside information regarding an offer price constituted a breach of the duty of loyalty).

195 *See* FTC v. Freecom Commc'ns, Inc., 401 F.3d 1192, 1202–03 (10th Cir. 2005) ("[M]aterial representations likely to mislead ordinary consumers to their detriment" constitute fraud under Federal Trade Commission Act.); 26 Williston on Contracts, *supra* note 46, at § 69:17.

196 *See* 26 Williston on Contracts, *supra* note 46, at § 69:17 ("A statement in a business transaction which, while stating the truth

so far as it goes, the maker knows or believes to be materially misleading because of his failure to state qualifying matter is a fraudulent misrepresentation. Such a statement of a half-truth is as much a misrepresentation as if the facts stated were untrue.").

197 *See, e.g.*, Amgen Inc. v. Conn. Ret. Plans & Tr. Funds, 568 U.S. 455, 488 (2013) (noting that securities fraud requires a *material* omission or misleading statement).

198 *See* 26 WILLISTON ON CONTRACTS, *supra* note 46, at § 69:17 ("[S]ome courts state as a general rule that nondisclosure of a material fact may constitute fraud sufficient to invalidate a contract.").

199 *See* RESTATEMENT (SECOND) OF CONTRACTS § 162 (1981) ("A misrepresentation is material if it would be likely to induce a reasonable person to manifest his assent, or if the maker knows that it would be likely to induce the recipient to do so.").

200 *See id. at* § 162 cmt. c ("The materiality of a misrepresentation is determined from the viewpoint of the maker.").

201 *See* Largey v. Rothman, 540 A.2d 504, 508–509 (N.J. 1988) (finding a doctor liable for failing to disclose all risks regarding therapy and defining "material" as risks those which "would be deemed 'material' when a reasonable patient . . . would be likely to attach significance to the risk in deciding whether to forego the proposed therapy or to submit to it").

202 *See ALI Principles of Corporate Governance: Analysis and Recommendations*, § 5.02(a)(1) cmt. (1994) ("The Principles of Corporate Governance explain what relationship of 'trust and confidence' between a director or officer and the corporation requires of directors and officers. [Directors and officers] must do more than just avoid misleading by misstatements or omissions.").

203 *See id.* (stating that D&Os should "affirmatively disclose all known material facts and, in the event they are 'interested,' must also disclose all implications of which they are aware, but which disinterested directors are not aware").

204 *See* ABA RULES OF PROFESSIONAL CONDUCT R. 3.3(b) ("A lawyer who represents a client in an adjudicative proceeding and who knows that a person intends to engage, is engaging or has engaged in criminal or fraudulent conduct related to the proceeding shall take reasonable remedial measures, including, if necessary, disclosure.") (emphasis added).

205 *See* Stroud v. Grace, 606 A.2d 75, 84, 86 (Del. 1992) (holding that the duty of candor gives directors "fiduciary duty to disclose fully and fairly all material information within the board's control when it seeks shareholder action," and "Delaware also imposes a duty of full disclosure in assessing the adequacy of proxy materials under state law").

206 *See* Borgner v. Brooks, 284 F.3d 1204, 1210 (11th Cir. 2002) (noting that states are allowed to impose mandatory disclosures with advertising if they can demonstrate that advertising would be "misleading and harmful to consumers" without mandatory disclosures).

207 *See* Moses v. Walker, 715 So. 2d 596, 598 (La. App. 1998) ("Every sale in this state carries with it the legal warranty that the thing sold is free from hidden defects.").

208 *See id.* at 598–99 (noting the seller's failure to disclose drainage and flooding problems and permitting the rescission of a sale for failure to disclose).

209 *See* PHL Variable Ins. Co. v. Fulbright McNeill, Inc., 519 F.3d 825, 829 (8th Cir. 2008) (discussing common law doctrine of "uberrimae fidei," requiring applicants to disclose facts which render insurance application untrue if application is still under consideration by the insurance company).

210 *See* Geoffrey Parsons Miller, The Law of Governance, Risk Management, and Compliance 104 (2014) (explaining the 1933 and 1934 Acts' requirements for public companies' "disclosure controls and procedures").

211 *See* 17 C.F.R. § 240.14a-3 (2017) (requiring corporations to disclose financial information to shareholders to protect investors and facilitate capital formation).

212 *See, e.g., id.* (consisting of a federal statute requiring corporations to disclose financial information to shareholders to protect investors and facilitate capital formation).

213 Sarbanes–Oxley Act of 2002, 107 Pub. L. 204, 116 Stat. 745.

214 Dodd–Frank Wall Street Reform and Consumer Protection Act, 111 Pub. L. 203, 124 Stat. 1376 (2010).

215 *See* Nadelle Grossman, *Director Compliance with Elusive Fiduciary Duties in a Climate of Corporate Governance Reform*, 12 Fordham J. Corp. & Fin. L. 393, 416 (2007) (discussing new mandatory disclosures instituted by Sarbanes–Oxley as response to accounting crisis, including auditor's knowledge of

financials); Alexandra Foster, *Where the CCO Fits in the C-Suite: A Corporation's Moral Compass*, 6 Am. U. Bus. L. Rev. 175, 180 (2017) (discussing disclosure requirements instituted by Dodd–Frank Act).

216 *See* 21 C.F.R. § 201.1 et seq. (covering Federal Drug Administration labeling and disclosure requirements for various pharmaceuticals).

217 *See Pharmaceutical Mfr. Ass'n v. Food & Drug Admin.*, 484 F. Supp. 1179, 1186 (D. Del. 1980) ("Congress intended patients using prescription drugs, as well as those using over-the counter drugs, to receive 'facts material with respect to consequences which may result from the use . . .' When it is determined that the possible side effects of a drug when used as customarily prescribed are sufficiently serious as to be material to the patient's decision on use of the drug, [the FDA] may require disclosure of those side effects on the labeling.").

218 *See* Daniel T. Ostas, *Cooperate, Comply, or Evade? A Corporate Executive's Social Responsibilities with Regard to Law*, 41 Am. Bus. L.J. 559, 561 (2005) (suggesting that social duties go far beyond what is required by law but cannot be enforced by legal sanctions).

219 *See* Craig Ehrlich, *Is Business Ethics Necessary?*, 4 DePaul Bus. & Com. L.J. 55, 57–58 (2005) (suggesting that legal requirements are not always ethically correct, and many ethics requirements are not required by law).

220 *See id.* (noting that leading American Bar Association Task Force on Corporate Responsibility's stated that "corporate responsibility" demands more than the minimum legal requirements means a firm must do more than follow the law to satisfy ethical responsibilities).

221 *See* Ostas, *supra* note 218 (suggesting social duties go far beyond what is required by law but cannot be enforced by legal sanctions).

222 *See* Margaret M. Blair & Lynn A. Stout, *Trust, Trustworthiness, and the Behavioral Foundations of Corporate Law*, 149 U. Pa. L. Rev. 1735, 1747 (2001) (stating that the legal system lacks resources to enforce and deter).

223 *See, e.g.*, Joel Slawotsky, *Reining in Recidivist Financial Institutions*, 40 Del. J. Corp. L. 280, 284 (2015) (discussing continued misconduct by financial institutions following "historic

settlements" after financial crisis); Hillary A. Sale, *Banks: The Forgotten (?) Partners in Fraud*, 73 U. Cin. L. Rev. 139, 139–40 (Fall 2004) (examining the SEC's failure to provide required information to investors following the Enron fraud, and the complicity of banks in the Enron scandal).

224 *See* Feloni, *supra* note 5.

225 *See, e.g.*, Ford v. Wisc. Real Est. Examining Bd., 179 N.W.2d 786, 792 (Wisc. 1970) (holding that an agent following a principal's orders to enforce a racist real estate scheme made the agent "liable as a joint tortfeasor for the entire damage").

226 *See* Ostas, *supra* note 218 (suggesting that executives have a social obligation to evaluate laws and the reasons and policies behind them, then decide whether to "comply, cooperate, or evade" the law based on the social duties and morality underlying the law).

Chapter 6

1 *Artificial Person*, Black's Law Dictionary (10th ed. 2014).

2 *See* James D. Cox & Thomas L. Hazen, Business Organizations Law § 1.2 (3d ed. 2011); 18 C.J.S. *Corporations* § 6, Westlaw (database updated June 2020).

3 *Id.* at § 1.1; 18 Am. Jur. 2d *Corporations* § 2 (Westlaw, database updated May 2020).

4 *See* Cox & Hazen, *supra* note 2, at §§ 1.2, 1.5.

5 *See id.* at § 1.5 (3d ed. 2011); Corporate Counsel Guides: Corporation Law § 1.4 (A.B.A. Pub. ed. 2010).

6 *See* Lynn A. Stout, *The Corporation as Time Machine: Intergenerational Equity, Intergenerational Efficiency, and the Corporate Form*, 38 Seattle U. L. Rev. 685, 703 (2015).

7 *See* Cox & Hazen, *supra* note 2, at 5§ 1.5; Corporate Counsel Guides, *supra* note 5, at § 1.4 (A.B.A. Pub. ed. 2010).

8 *See In re* Caremark Intern. Inc. Derivative Litig., 689 A.2d 959, 967 (Del. Ch. 1996).

9 Cox & Hazen, *supra* note 2, at § 1.5; Corporate Counsel Guides, *supra* note 5, at§ 1.4.

10 *See* Alan Palmiter, Frank Partnoy & Elizabeth Pollman, Business Organizations: A Contemporary Approach (West, 3d ed. 2019).

11 *See Artificial Person*, Black's Law Dictionary, *supra* note 1.

12　*See* Cox & Hazen, *supra* note 2, at § 1.5; *see also* Del. Code Ann. tit. 8, § 122 (West 2020) (addressing specific powers of corporations).

13　*See, e.g.*, Margaret Blair, Presentation on Concentration of Public Corporations and Economic Resources, Lynn Stout Memorial Conference, New York City, NY (Feb. 1, 2019).

14　*See* Sarah Anderson & John Cavanagh, Top 200: The Rise of Global Corporate Power i, iii (Inst. for Pol'y Stud., 2000).

15　*See* Ben Chapman, *Majority of the World's Richest Entities Are Corporations, Not Governments, Figures Show*, The Independent (Oct. 17, 2018), https://www.independent.co.uk/news/busin ess/news/companies-bigger-than-governments-un-human-rig hts-council-meeting-a8588676.html.

16　*See* Milan Babic, Elke Heemskerk & Jan Fichtner, *Who Is More Powerful—States or Corporations?*, The Conversation (July 10, 2018), http://theconversation.com/who-is-more-powerful-sta tes-or-corporations-99616.

17　*See* Chapman, *supra* note 15; Parag Khanna, *These 25 Companies Are More Powerful Than Many Countries*, Foreign Policy (Mar. 15, 2016), https://foreignpolicy.com/2016/03/15/these-25-compan ies-are-more-powerful-than-many-countries-multinational- corporate-wealth-power/.

18　*See* Cox & Hazen, *supra* note 2, at § 1.6.

19　*See id.*

20　*See, e.g.*, Chris Morris, *10 Iconic Companies That Have Left America*, CNBC (Apr. 21, 2016) https://www.cnbc.com/2016/04/21/10- iconic-us-companies-that-have-moved-headquarters-abroad.html (noting popular American chains that have moved abroad).

21　*See* Cox & Hazen, *supra* note 2, at § 3.2.

22　*See id.* at § 3.4.

23　*See id.* at § 3.6

24　Del. Code Ann. tit. 8, § 101(b) (West 2020).

25　*See* Cox & Hazen, *supra* note 2, at § 3.3; *see also* Del. Code Ann. tit. 8, at § 103.

26　*See* Del. Code Ann. tit. 8, at §§ 103, 106.

27　*See* 18A Am. Jur. 2d *Corporations*, *supra* note 3, at § 178; *see also* Del. Code. Ann. tit. 8, at § 108 (describing instruments and the process for submission to the Secretary of State).

28　*See* Devin Banerjee, *Private Equity to Grow to $7 Trillion by 2020*, PwC Says, Bloomberg (June 28, 2015), https://www.bloomberg.

com/news/articles/2015-06-29/private-equity-to-grow-to-7-trill
ion-by-2020-pwc-says.

29　*See* Corporate Counsel Guides, *supra* note 5, at § 1.11.

30　*See* Cox & Hazen, *supra* note 2, at § 1.20; Franklin A. Gevurtz,
Corporation Law § 3.1.5 (1st ed. 2000).

31　*See* Corporate Counsel Guides, *supra* note 5, at § 1.11.

32　*See About Hallmark,* https://corporate.hallmark.com/about/
hallmark-cards-company/ (providing resources on Hallmark's
business mission); *see also* Corporate Counsel Guides, *supra*
note 5, at § 1.11 (providing definitions of corporation types).

33　*Mars,* https://www.forbes.com/companies/mars/?sh = 7a70e
b453bb7.

34　*See* Cox & Hazen, *supra* note 2, at § 4.03; 18 Am. Jur. 2d
Corporations, supra note 3, at § 33.

35　*See* 18 Am. Jur. 2d *Corporations, supra* note 3, at § 33.

36　*See id.* at § 35; *see generally* I.R.C. §501(c)(3) (West 2020)
(describing tax exemptions for corporations).

37　*See* 18 Am. Jur. 2d *Corporations, supra* note 3, at § 35.

38　*See State-by-State Status of Legislation,* Benefit Corporation,
https://benefitcorp.net/policymakers/state-by-state-status.

39　*See What Is a Benefit Corporation?,* Benefit Corporation, https://
benefitcorp.net/.

40　*See* 1 Treatise on the Law of Corporations § 2:14, Westlaw (3d
ed. 2010).

41　*See* Cox & Hazen, *supra* note 2, at § 1.1030.

42　*See* 1 Treatise on the Law of Corporations, *supra* note 40, at
§ 1:10.

43　*See* Gevurtz, *supra* note 30, at §1.1.2(e). Since that treatise was
written, the shareholder cap has increased to less than 100. Please
note that tax rules are always changing and that you should
check that these requirements are up to date at the time you
use them.

44　*See* Nicholas G. Karambelas, 1 Limited Liability
Companies: Law, Practice and Forms, § 4:7 Sole Proprietorship
(Dec. 2018).

45　*See* Kathryn Kobe, Small Business GDP: Update 2002–2010, 1,
17 (Small Bus. Ass'n, 2012).

46　*See* Steven C. Alberty, 1 Advising Small Businesses, § 5:1
General Partnerships in General (updated July 2019).

47 *See* Mark A. Sargent & Walter D. Schwidetzky, Limited
    Liability Company Handbook, § 3:19 Generally (Sept. 2018).

48 *See* 2 Business Organizations With Tax Planning § 33.01,
    Lexis (database updated May 2020).

49 *See* id. at §§ 33.01–33.02; Cox & Hazen, *supra* note 2, at § 1.11.

50 *See* 18 Am. Jur. 2d *Corporations, supra* note 3, at § 158.

51 *See* 1 Treatise on the Law of Corporations, *supra* note 40,
    at § 3:6.

52 *See* Cox & Hazen, *supra* note 2, at § 2.3.2

53 Del. Code Ann. tit. 8, § 101 (West 2020).

54 *See* 18 C.J.S. *Corporations, supra* note 2, at § 55, 162.

55 Gevurtz, *supra* note 30, at § 3.1.4.

56 *See* 7A William Meade Fletcher et al., Fletcher Cyclopedia
    of the Law of Private Corporations § 3399 (updated Sept.
    2019) (use of the term "ultra vires").

57 18 C.J.S. *Corporations, supra* note 2, at § 14 (Disregarding
    Corporate Entity or Piercing Corporate Veil, Generally).

58 *See* Colin Mayer, Firm Commitment: Why the Corporation
    Is Failing Us and How to Restore Trust in It (2013); Colin
    Mayer, Prosperity: Better Business Makes the Greater Good
    (2018).

59 *See* William K. Black, The Best Way to Rob a Bank Is to Own
    One: How Corporate Executives and Politicians Looted the
    S&L Industry (2013).

60 *See* Paul M. Healy & Krishna G. Paleup, *The Fall of Enron*, 17 J.
    Econ. Persp. 3, 26 (Spring 2003); *see also Natural Gas Contracts
    Section 102 Energy Trading*, Thompson Information Services
    (Aug. 2003 Supp.).

61 *See* Healy & Palepu, *supra* note 60, at 3, 9–12.

62 *See id.* at 3, 12.

63 *See* Fortune 500 Rankings, Fortune, *Enron*, https://archive.
    fortune.com/magazines/fortune/fortune500_archive/
    snapshots/2001/478.html.60

64 *See* Healy & Palepu, *supra* note 60, at 3, 12.

65 *See Enron's Plan Would Repay a Fraction of Dollars Owed*, N.Y.
    Times (July 12, 2003), https://www.nytimes.com/2003/07/
    12/business/enron-s-plan-would-repay-a-fraction-of-dollars-
    owed.html#:~:text = The%20thousands%20of%20creditors%20
    of,two%20companies%20with%20new%20names.

66   *See* David Barboza, *Officials Got a Windfall Before Enron's Collapse*, N.Y. Times (June 18, 2002), https://www.nytimes.com/2002/06/18/business/officials-got-a-windfall-before-enron-s-collapse.html

67   *See* Leslie Wayne, *Turmoil at WorldCom: Retirement Money*, N.Y. Times (June 28, 2002), https://www.nytimes.com/2002/06/28/business/turmoil-worldcom-retirement-money-irate-scandals-big-losses-pension-funds-are.html

68   *See* Steven Greenhouse, *Enron's Many Strands: Retirement Money; Public Funds Say Losses Top $1.5 Billion*, N.Y. Times (Jan. 29, 2002), https://www.nytimes.com/2002/01/29/business/enron-s-many-strands-retirement-money-public-funds-say-losses-top-1.5-billion.html.

69   *See* Kristen Hays, *Enron Employees to Get $28 Million More in Severance Pay*, Wash. Post (Aug. 29, 2002), https://www.washingtonpost.com/archive/business/2002/08/29/enron-employees-to-get-28-million-more-in-severance-pay/000fe318-9f1c-4c9f-b60c-0dd01693dad0/.

70   *See* David Teather, *Enron Paid $681 Million to Top Executives*, The Guardian (June 17, 2002), https://www.theguardian.com/business/2002/jun/18/corporatefraud.enron.

71   *See* Matt Stevens & Matthew Haag, *Jeffrey Skilling, Former Enron Chief, Released After 12 Years in Prison*, N.Y. Times (Feb. 22, 2019), https://www.nytimes.com/2019/02/22/business/enron-ceo-skilling-scandal.html.

72   *See e.g.* Milton Friedman, *The Social Responsibility of a Business is to Increase Its Profits*, N.Y. Times (Sept. 13, 1970) (discussing the social responsibility of corporations as to generate profits for their shareholders).

73   *See* Michael C. Jensen & William H. Meckling, *Theory of the Firm: Managerial Behavior, Agency Costs, and Ownership Structure*, 3 J. Fin. Econ. 305–60 (1976).

74   *See* Jia L. Yang, *Maximizing Shareholder Value: The Goal That Changed Corporate America*, Wash. Post (Aug. 26, 2013), https://www.washingtonpost.com/business/economy/maximizing-shareholder-value-the-goal-that-changed-corporate-america/2013/08/26/26e9ca8e-ed74-11e2-9008-61e94a7ea20d_story.html.

75   U.S. Dep't of Def., *Charles E. Wilson*, https://history.defense.gov/Multimedia/Biographies/Article-View/Article/571268/charles-e-wilson/.

76   *Nominations: Hearing Before the Sen. Comm. on Armed Services*, 83d
     Cong. 26 (1953) (statement of Charles E. Wilson).
77   Michael C. Jensen, *Value Maximization, Stakeholder Theory, and
     the Corporate Objective Function*, 14 J. APPLIED CORP. FIN., 3, 8–9
     (2001); Constance E. Bagley, Adam J. Sulkowski, J.S. Nelson,
     Sandra Waddock & Paul Shrivastava, *A Path to Developing More
     Insightful Business School Graduates: A Systems-Based, Experiential
     Approach to Integrating Law, Strategy, and Sustainability*, ACAD.
     MGMT. LEARNING & EDUC. (Nov. 2019).
78   Unocal Corp. v. Mesa Petroleum, 493 A.2d 946, 954–55 (Del.
     1985). *But see* Leo E. Strine, Jr., *The Dangers of Denial: The Need
     for a Clear-Eyed Understanding of the Power and Accountability
     Structure Established by the Delaware General Corporation Law*,
     50 WAKE FOREST L. REV. 761, 764–66 (2015) (cautioning that,
     although "directors are generally empowered to manage the
     corporation in a way that is not dictated by what will best
     maximize the corporation's current stock price," Delaware
     corporate law still grants enormous power to shareholders).
79   *See* R. Cammon Turner, *Shareholders vs. the World: 'Revlon Duties'
     and State Constituency Statutes*, A.B.A. SEC. BUS. L. (Jan./Feb.
     1999), https://apps.americanbar.org/buslaw/blt/8-3sharehold
     ers.html.
80   *See* 15 PA. STAT. & CONS. STAT. ANN. § 1715 (West 2020).
81   *See State by State Status of Legislation*, BENEFIT CORP., https://bene
     fitcorp.net/policymakers/state-by-state-status.
82   *See* 1 TREATISE ON THE LAW OF CORPORATIONS, *supra* note
     40, at § 2:14; *see generally* DEL. CODE ANN. tit. 8, § 362 (West
     2020) (defining a public benefit corporation) .
83   *See* Yancey Strickler et. al., *Kickstarter Is Now a Benefit Corporation*,
     THE KICKSTARTER BLOG (Sept. 21, 2015), https://www.kickstarter.
     com/blog/kickstarter-is-now-a-benefit-corporation.
84   *See Kickstarter Charter*, KICKSTARTER, https://www.kickstarter.
     com/charter.
85   *See Business Roundtable Redefines the Purpose of a Corporation to
     Promote "An Economy That Serves All Americans,"* https://www.
     businessroundtable.org/business-roundtable-redefines-the-purp
     ose-of-a-corporation-to-promote-an-economy-that-serves-all-
     americans. *Statement on the Purpose of a Corporation*, BUSINESS
     ROUNDTABLE (Aug. 19, 2019), https://opportunity.businessrou

ndtable.org/wp-content/uploads/2020/06/BRT-Statement-on-the-Purpose-of-a-Corporation-with-Signatures.pdf.

86 *See* Corporate Governance: Law and Practice § 4.01 (Steven Hass ed. 2018).

87 *See* Gevurtz, *supra* note 30, at § 3.1.2.

88 *See* Cox & Hazen, *supra* note 2, at § 9.4.

89 *See* Gevurtz, *supra* note 30, at § 3.1.2.

90 *See Director*, Black's Law Dictionary, *supra* note 1; *see also Securities Regulation—Federal*, 69A Am. Jur. 2d *Due Diligence Defense* § 1454 (updated Aug. 4, 2019) (defining inside an director as a director who is also an officer of the corporation).

91 *See* 18B Am. Jur. 2d *Corporations*, *supra* note 3, at § 1147.

92 *See Director*, Black's Law Dictionary, *supra* note 1; *see also Securities Regulation—Federal*, *supra* note 90.

93 *See* Gevurtz, *supra* note 30, at § 3.1.2.

94 *See* Will Kenton, *What Is a Hostile Takeover Bid?*, Investopedia (Jan. 13, 2018), https://www.investopedia.com/terms/h/host ile-takeover-bid.asp; Daniel B. Nunn, Jr., *The Wolf at the Door*, 83 Fla. Bus. J. 10, 11 (2009); *What Is a Staggered Board?*, Investopedia (Jan. 31, 2020), https://www.investopedia.com/ask/answers/ 05/staggeredboard.asp; Komas Papadopoulos, Robert Kalb, Angelica Valderrama & Jared Sorhaindo, *U.S. Board Study: Board Accountability Practices Review*, Inst'l Shareholder Servs. 1, 4 (2018).

95 *See* Cox & Hazen, *supra* note 2 § 9.4; 18B Am. Jur. 2d *Corporations*, *supra* note 3, at § 1264.

96 *See* Corporate Governance, *supra* note 86, at § 4.01.

97 *See* 18B Am. Jur. 2d *Corporations*, *supra* note 3, at § 1264.

98 *See id.; see also* Corporate Governance, *supra* note 86, at § 4.01.

99 *See* 19 C.J.S. *Corporations* § 552 (2020).

100 *See* Gevurtz, *supra* note 30, at § 4.2.

101 *See* 18B Am. Jur. 2d *Corporations*, *supra* note 3, at § 1264.

102 *See* Corporate Governance, *supra* note 86, at § 4.04.

103 *See* Gevurtz, *supra* note 30, at §§ 4.2.6, 4.2.7.

104 *See id.* at § 4.1.

105 *See* Corporate Governance, *supra* note 86, at § 4.03.

106 *See* 29 Am. Jur. 3d *Proof of Facts* § 9.1 (2020); 3A Fletcher, *supra* note 56, at § 1038.

107 *See* Corporate Governance, *supra* note 86, at § 4.03.

108 *See* Gevurtz, *supra* note 30, at § 4.2.4.

109 *See Corporations, supra* note 3, at § 1141.

110 *See* GEVURTZ, *supra* note 30, at § 3.1.1.

111 *See id.;* DEL. CODE ANN. tit. 8 § 142(a) (2019); *see also Corporations,* 18B AM. JUR. 2D § 1140 (2020) (describing relationship between officers, agents, and employees).

112 *See* James Chen, *C-Suite,* INVESTOPEDIA, https://www.investope dia.com/terms/c/c-suite.asp (last updated Jan. 26, 2018).

113 *See* 18B AM. JUR. 2D *Corporations, supra* note 3, at §§ 1140, 1291.

114 *See* COX & HAZEN, *supra* note 2, at § 8.2; *Corporations, supra* note 3, at § 1291.

115 *See* GEVURTZ, *supra* note 30, at § 3.1.1; RESTATEMENT (THIRD) OF AGENCY § 2.01 (A.L.I. 2006).

116 *See* 18B AM. JUR. 2D *Corporations, supra* note 3, at § 1293.

117 GEVURTZ, *supra* note 30, at §3.1.1; RESTATEMENT (THIRD) OF AGENCY § 2.02 (A.L.I. 2006).

118 *See* 1 TREATISE ON THE LAW OF CORPORATIONS, *supra* note 40, at § 8:13.

119 *See* RESTATEMENT (THIRD) OF AGENCY § 2.03 (A.L.I. 2006).

120 *See* COX & HAZEN, *supra* note 2, at § 8.5; 18B AM. JUR. 2D *Corporations, supra* note 3, at § 1304.

121 *See* GEVURTZ, *supra* note 30, at § 3.1.1.

122 *See* 2 TREATISE ON THE LAW OF CORPORATIONS, *supra* note 40, at § 13:1.

123 *See Stock,* BLACK'S LAW DICTIONARY, *supra* note 1.

124 *See* COX & HAZEN, *supra* note 2, at § 13.1; *Stock,* BLACK'S LAW DICTIONARY, *supra* note 1.

125 *See* GEVURTZ, *supra* note 30, at § 2.1.2 (1st ed. 2000).

126 *See generally* 2 TREATISE ON THE LAW OF CORPORATIONS, *supra* note 40, at § 13:1 (providing overview of shareholder rights).

127 *See* Julian Velasco, *Taking Shareholder Rights Seriously,* 41 U.C. DAVIS L. REV.. 605, 616 (2007) ("Shareholders generally have a very broad right to dispose of their shares.").

128 *See* Karl T. Muth and Andrew Leventhal, *Mutuals: An Area of Legal Climate Change,* 9 WILLIAM & MARY BUS. L. REV. 597, 599 (2018).

129 *See* Julian Velasco, *The Fundamental Rights of the Shareholder,* 40 U.C. DAVIS L. REV. 407, 409, 425 (2006) (arguing that the right to sell shares is one of the most fundamental rights of shareholders because it allows shareholders to obtain the economic benefits

from their investments and allows shareholders to exit if they become dissatisfied with management).

130 *See* Cox & Hazen, *supra* note 2, at § 13.1; 2 Treatise on the Law of Corporations, *supra* note 40, at § 13:1.

131 *See* Jeffrey W. Bullock, "Annual Report Statistics," *Delaware Division of Corporations* (2018) https://corp.delaware.gov/stats/.

132 *See* Del. Code. Ann. tit. 8, §§ 211, 242, 251, 271 (West 2020).

133 *See* 17 C.F.R. § 240.14a-8 (2018).

134 *See id.*

135 *See* 12B Fletcher, *supra* note 56, at § 5729.

136 3 Treatise on the Law of Corporations, *supra* note 40, at § 15:2.

137 *See* Gevurtz, *supra* note 30, at § 4.3.1.

138 *See* 3 Treatise on the Law of Corporations, *supra* note 40, at § 15:2.

139 *See* Gevurtz, *supra* note 30, at § 4.3.

140 *See* 2 Treatise on the Law of Corporations, *supra* note 40, at §§ 13:2, 13:3.

141 *See* Gevurtz, *supra* note 30, at § 3.1.2.

142 *See* 2 Treatise on the Law of Corporations, *supra* note 40, at § 13:35.

143 *See* Gevurtz, *supra* note 30, at § 5.1.1

144 *See id.*

145 *See Shareholder*, Black's Law Dictionary, *supra* note 1 (see definitions for majority and controlling shareholder).

146 *See* 12B Fletcher, *supra* note 56, at §§ 5810, 5811.

147 *See generally* Wilkes v. Springfield Nursing Home, Inc., 353 N.E.2d 657, 663 (Mass. 1976) (holding that a controlling majority must be able to provide a legitimate business purpose for an action).

148 *See* 12B Fletcher, *supra* note 56, at § 5811.05; *see also generally* Wilkes, 353 N.E.2d at 662 (noting various forms that a freeze-out can take).

149 *See* 12B Fletcher, *supra* note 56, at § 5763.

150 *See* Cox & Hazen, *supra* note 2, at § 11.11 (describing, e.g., Sinclair Oil Corp. v. Levien, 280 A.2d 717 (Del. 1971)).

151 *See* 18 Am. Jur. 2d *Corporations*, *supra* note 3, at § 48.

152 *See* Pan E. Expl. Co. v. Hufo Oils, 855 F.2d 1106, 1131 (5th Cir. 1988).

153 *See* 18 Am. Jur. 2d *Corporations*, *supra* note 3, at § 54.

154 *See* Principles of Corporate Governance: Analysis and Recommendations § 4.01 (2020); Unocal Corp. v. Mesa Petroleum Co., 493 A.2d 946, 954 (Del. 1985).

155 *See* 1 Corporate Governance: Law and Practice § 4.03, Lexis (database updated Dec. 2019) (describing basic duties of directors).

156 *See id.; see also* Aronson v. Lewis, 473 A.2d 805, 812 (Del. 1984) ("A court under such circumstances will not substitute its own notions of what is or is not sound business judgment.").

157 *See* Cox & Hazen, *supra* note 2, at § 10.05.

158 *See* Marchand v. Barnhill, 212 A.3d 805, 809 (Del. 2019); *In re* Caremark Intern Inc. Derviative Litig., 698 A.2d 959, 970 (Del. Ch. 1996).

159 *See* Del. Code Ann. tit. 8, § 102(b)(7) (West 2019).

160 *See id.* (describing the required components of a certificate of corporation).

161 *See id.* at § 145(a)–(b).

162 *See id.* at §145(g) (noting corporate powers to indemnify officers, directors, employees, and agents).

163 *See* Phila. Indem. Ins. Co. v. Sabal Ins. Grp., Inc., 786 F. App'x 167, 172 (11th Cir. 2019) (analyzing public policy concerns of allowing restitution of ill-gotten funds); Ranger Ins. Co. v. Bal Harbour Club, Inc., 549 So. 2d 1005, 1007 (Fla. 1989) (expressing concern over allowing insurance recovery for misconduct would encourage illegal activity).

164 *See generally* Megan Wischmeier Shaner, *Officer Accountability*, 32 Ga. St. U.L. Rev. 357, 367 (2016) (exploring the distinctions in power between officers and boards of directors).

165 Law of Corporate Officers & Directors: Rights, Duties & Liabilities § 3:16, Westlaw (database updated Oct. 2019).

166 *See id.*

167 *See* Law of Corporate Officers, *supra* note 165, at § 4:2 (providing details of Delaware's corporate opportunity test).

168 18 Am. Jur. 2d *Corporations, supra* note 3, at § 1469.

169 *See* Del. Code Ann. tit. 8, § 144 (West 2019).

170 *See What We Do*, U.S. Sec. & Exch. Comm'n, https://www.sec.gov/Article/whatwedo.html (last modified June 10, 2013).

171 *See* 15 U.S.C. § 77(a) (2020) (noting executive power to intervene to prevent unfair competition).

172 *See* 15 U.S.C. § 78(a) (2020).

173 *See* Sarbanes–Oxley Act of 2002, Pub. L. No. 107-204, 116 Stat. 745.

174 *See* 15 U.S.C.A § 78u-6 (West 2020).

175 *See* 1 Treatise on the Law of Securities Regulation § 1:22, Westlaw (database updated Nov. 2018).

176 *See id.* at § 1:23.

177 *See* 17 C.F.R. § 210.3-02 (2018).

178 *See id.* at § 249.310.

179 *See id.* at § 249.308(a).

180 *See id.* at § 249.308.

181 *See id.* at §240.14a-6.

182 *See id.* at §240.14a-5.

183 *See id.* at §240.14a-9.

184 *See The Laws that Govern the Securities Industry*, U.S. Sec. & Exch. Comm'n, https://www.sec.gov/answers/about-lawsshtml.html#secexact1934 (last modified Oct. 1, 2013) (explaining that SEC has enforcement power under the Securities Exchange Act).

185 *See* 17 C.F.R. § 240.16a-3 (2018).

186 *See What We Do*, Fed. Trade Comm'n, https://www.ftc.gov/about-ftc/what-we-do; *see also Antitrust Enforcement and the Consumer*, U.S. Dep't of Just., https://www.justice.gov/atr/file/800691/download (providing consumer resources on antitrust laws); *Antitrust Laws and You*, USDOJ Antitrust Division, https://www.justice.gov/atr/antitrust-laws-and-you (last updated Jan. 5, 2017) (explaining larger pieces of legislation involving antritrust law).

187 15 U.S.C. §§ 1–7 (2020).

188 15 U.S.C. §§ 12–27 (2020).

189 *See Antitrust Laws and You*, U.S. Dep't of Just. Antitrust Division, https://www.justice.gov/atr/antitrust-laws-and-you (last updated Jan. 5, 2017).

190 *See* 15 U.S.C. §18(a) (2020).

191 *See id.* at § 78dd-1.

192 *See* 50 U.S.C.§ 4801 (2020).

193 *See id.* at § 4811.

194 Mervyn A. King, Public Policy and the Corporation (1977) (quoting Edward, First Barron Thurlow); John C. Coffee, Jr., *"No Soul to Damn, No Body to Kick": An Unscandalized Inquiry Into the Problem of Corporate Punishment*, 79 Mich. L. Rev. 3, 386 (1981) (same).

195 *Id.*

196 *See Corporations*, 19 Am. Jur. 2d §§ 2335, 2355 (2020).

197 *See id.* at §§ 2377, 2335 (explaining state power over corporations), and 2355 (explaining state power over corporations).

198 *See id.* at § 2403.

199 *See* U.S. Dep't of Just., U.S. Atty's Manual, 9-28.000 Principles of Federal Prosecution of Business Organizations, https://www.justice.gov/archives/usam/archives/usam-9-28000-princip les-federal-prosecution-business-organizations#9-28.010 (last updated Dec. 7, 2018).

200 *See* Megan Davies & Walden Siew, *45 Percent of World's Wealth Destroyed: Blackstone CEO*, Reuters (Mar. 10, 2009), http://www.reuters.com/article/2009/03/10/us-blackstone-idUSTRE 52966Z20090310 [https://perma.cc/5W8D-BUQE] (quoting the Blackstone Group L.P. CEO Stephen Schwarzman's statement that "[b]etween 40 and 45 percent of the world's wealth has been destroyed in little less than a year and a half," which "is absolutely unprecedented in our lifetime").

201 *See id.; see also* J.S. Nelson, *Paper Dragon Thieves*, 105 Geo. L. J. 871, 873 (2017) (describing some potential reasons why no executives were prosecuted after the financial crisis).

202 *See White Collar Prosecutions Fall to Lowest in 20 Years*, TRAC Reports, http://trac.syr.edu/tracreports/crim/514/; *see also* J.S. Nelson, *Disclosure-Driven Crime*, 52 U.C. Davis L. Rev. 1487, 1500 (2019) (describing the scope of damage caused by modern white collar crime, while noting the fall in prosecutions for such crimes).

203 *See id.*

Chapter 7

1 *See* George A. Mocsary, *Freedom of Corporate Purpose*, 2016 B.Y.U. L. Rev. 1319, 1340 (2016).

2 *See* Franklin A. Gevurtz, Corporation Law § 2.1.2 (1st ed. 2000).

3 Roberta Romano, *The State as a Laboratory: Legal Innovation and State Competition for Corporate Charters*, 23 Yale J. Reg. 209, 210 (2006); *see also* Mocsary, *supra* note 1, at 1341 (citing Romano).

4 Mocsary, *supra* note 1, at 1341 (quoting Nicholas Murray Butler, President, Columbia Univ., Address at the 143rd Annual Banquet

of the Chamber of Commerce of the State of New York (Nov. 16, 1911)).

5 THOMAS DONALDSON, CORPORATIONS AND MORALITY 42 (1982); *see also* Nien-hê Hsieh, *The Social Contract Model of Corporate Purpose and Responsibility*, 25:4 BUS. ETHICS Q. 433, 433 (2015) (quoting Donaldson).

6 *See* DONALDSON, *supra* note 5, at 42; *accord* Hsieh, *supra* note 5, at 434 (citing Donaldson).

7 *See* Hsieh, *supra* note 5, at 435.

8 *See* Lynn A. Stout, *Bad and Not-So-Bad Arguments for Shareholder Primacy*, 75 S. CAL. L. REV. 1189, 1189 (2002).

9 Dodge v. Ford, 170 N.W. 668, 670–71 (Mich. 1919).

10 *Id.* at 685.

11 *See* Stout, *Bad and Not-So-Bad Arguments, supra* note 8, at 1189.

12 TIMOTHY L. FORT & CINDY A. SCHIPANI, THE ROLE OF BUSINESS IN FOSTERING PEACEFUL SOCIETIES 50 (2004).

13 *See* Tamara Belinfanti & Lynn A. Stout, *Contested Visions: The Value for Systems Theory for Corporate Law*, 166 U. PA. L. REV. 579, 589–90 (2018).

14 *See* Lynn A. Stout et al., *The Modern Corporation Statement on Company Law* (2016), http://dx.doi.org/10.2139/ssrn.2848833.

15 *See* Margaret M. Blair & Lynn A. Stout, *A Team Production Theory of Corporate Law*, 85 VA. L. REV. 247, 289 (1999).

16 *See* Lynn A. Stout, *The Troubling Question of Corporate Purpose*, 3 ACCT., ECON. & LAW 61, 65 (2013).

17 *See* BUSINESS ROUNDTABLE, STATEMENT ON THE PURPOSE OF A CORPORATION 1 (2019) https://opportunity.businessroundtable. org/ourcommitment/.

18 *See* LYNN STOUT, THE SHAREHOLDER VALUE MYTH: HOW PUTTING SHAREHOLDERS FIRST HARMS INVESTORS, CORPORATIONS, AND THE PUBLIC *passim* (2012) (arguing in detail how Delaware and other corporate law has been misunderstood and misinterpreted to create a shareholder value myth); *cf. also* Leo E. Strine, Jr., *The Dangers of Denial: The Need for a Clear-Eyed Understanding of the Power and Accountability Structure Established by the Delaware General Corporation Law*, 50 WAKE FOREST L. REV. 761, 764–66 (2015) (cautioning that, although "directors are generally empowered to manage the corporation in a way that is not dictated by what will best maximize the corporation's current

stock price," Delaware corporate law still grants enormous power to shareholders).

19 Burwell v. Hobby Lobby Stores, Inc., 573 U.S. 682, 711–12 (2014).

20 *Id.* at 711 (emphasis added).

21 A.P. Smith Mfg. Co. v. Barlow, 98 A.2d 581, 582 (N.J. 1953).

22 17 C.F.R. § 240.14a-8 (prohibiting shareholder proposals from relating to a company's "ordinary business operations").

23 *See id.* (requiring shareholders who want the corporation to take an action to submit proposals for the corporation to consider).

24 *See* Daniel J.H. Greenwood, *The Dividend Puzzle: Are Shareholders Entitled to the Residual?*, 32 J. CORP. L. 103 (2006); Mocsary, *supra* note 1, at 1324; *see also Bankruptcy: What Happens When Public Companies Go Bankrupt*, U.S. SEC. AND EXCH. COMM'N (Feb. 3, 2009) https://www.sec.gov/reportspubs/investor-publications/investorpubsbankrupthtm.html.

25 *See* U.S. Const. amend. XIII.

26 *See* Lynn A. Stout et al., *Modern Corporation Statement, supra* note 14.

27 *Id.; see also* Belinfanti & Stout, *supra* note 13, at 591.

28 *See* Einer Elhauge, *Sacrificing Corporate Profits in the Public Interest*, 80 N.Y.U. L. REV. 733, 763 (2005).

29 PRINCIPLES OF CORPORATE GOVERNANCE: ANALYSIS AND RECOMMENDATIONS § 2.01(b)(1) (AM. LAW INST. 2005).

30 *Id.* at cmt. f.

31 *See* Burwell v. Hobby Lobby Stores, Inc., 573 U.S. 682, 711–12 (2014).

32 *See* PRINCIPLES OF CORPORATE GOVERNANCE, *supra* note 2913, at § 4.01(a).

33 *See id.* at cmt. d ("There are, of course, instances when § 2.01 would permit the corporation to voluntarily forgo economic benefit—or accept economic detriment—in furtherance of stipulated public policies. This could happen, for example, when the corporation takes account of ethical considerations that are reasonably regarded as appropriate to the responsible conduct of business (see § 2.01(b)(2) and Comment h to § 2.01) or devotes resources to public welfare, humanitarian, educational, or philanthropic purposes (see § 2.01(b)(3) and Comment i to § 2.01). Such actions, even though they may be inconsistent with profit enhancement, should be considered in the best interests of

the corporation and wholly consistent with the obligations set forth in § 4.01.").

34 *What Is CSR?*, U.N. Indus. Dev. Org., www.unido.org/csr/o72054.html.

35 *See* Andrew C. Wicks et al., Business Ethics: A Managerial Approach 77 (2010).

36 Alexei Oreskovic, *Google Has Been Waiting for Years to Put Don't Be Evil Out of Its Misery*, Bus. Insider, May 18, 2018, https://www.businessinsider.com/google-downgrades-dont-be-evil-2018-5 (noting that, although Google has since revised its code, the company kept a nod to the phrase in its code of conduct).

37 *See* Adam Smith, IV The Wealth of Nations ch. II, 254 (1776) ("Every individual is continually exerting himself to find out the most advantageous employment for whatever capital he can command. It is his own advantage, indeed, and not that of the society, which he has in his view. But the study of his own advantage naturally, or rather necessarily leads him to prefer that employment which is most advantageous to the society.").

38 *Social Responsibilities of Business Corporations*, Committee on Economic Development, at 27 (1971); *accord* John R. Danley, The Role of the Modern Corporation in a Free Society 217 (1994) (quoting the Committee).

39 *See* Maria O'Brien Hylton, *"Socially Responsible" Investing: Doing Good Versus Doing Well in an Inefficient Market*, 42 Am. U. L. Rev. 1, 2 n.1 (1992).

40 *See id.* at 7.

41 *See* Online Directory, US SIF, https://www.ussif.org/AF_MemberDirectory.asp.

42 *See Sustainable Investing*, BlackRock, https://www.blackrock.com/investing/investment-ideas/sustainable-investing; *see also Sustainable and Impact Investing*, Cambridge Associates, https://www.cambridgeassociates.com/sustainable-and-impact-investing/.

43 *See* Saiful Arefeen & Koji Shimada, *Performance and Resilience of Socially Responsible Investing (SRI) and Conventional Funds During Different Shocks in 2016: Evidence from Japan*, 12(2) Sustainability 540 (2020).

44 *Social Responsibilities of Business Corporations, supra* note 38, at 11; *accord* Danley, *supra* note 38, at 211.

45 *See The Power of Principles,* U.N. GLOBAL COMPACT, https://www. unglobalcompact.org/what-is-gc/mission/principles.

46 *See The 17 Goals,* UNITED NATIONS, https://sdgs.un.org/goals.

47 *SDG Ambition: Introducing Business Benchmarks for the Decade of Action,* U.N. GLOBAL COMPACT, https://unglobalcompact.org/library/5746.

48 *See* Andrew Keay, *Stakeholder Theory in Corporate Law: Has It Got What It Takes?,* 9 RICH. J. GLOBAL L. & BUS. 249, 257 (2010).

49 Business Roundtable Institute for Corporate Ethics, *Stakeholder Theory With R. Edward Freeman: What Is Stakeholder Theory?,* https://redwardfreeman.com/video-1/.

50 Keay, *supra* note 48, at 259 (*citing* Max Clarkson, *A Risk Based Model of Stakeholder Theory,* Proceedings of the Second Toronto Conference on Stakeholder Theory, Centre for Corporate Social Performance, University of Toronto, 1994 at 5, *as quoted in* Amy Hillman & Gerald D. Klein, *Shareholder Value, Stakeholder Management and Social Issue: What's the Bottom Line?,* 22 STRATEGIC MGMT. J. 125, 126 (2001)).

51 Professor Freedman clarifies that "who your stakeholders are depends on what problem you are trying to solve." He describes himself as a "more consistent pragmatist" than perhaps he was earlier in his career. Email from Professor Freedman, Dec. 1, 2020 (on file with author).

52 *See What Is Stakeholder Theory?, supra* note 49.

53 *See* WICKS ET AL., *supra* note 35, at 74.

54 *See What Is Stakeholder Theory?, supra* note 49.

55 WICKS ET AL., *supra* note 35, at 74; *What Is Stakeholder Theory?, supra* note 49.

56 *See What Is Stakeholder Theory?, supra* note 49.

57 Keay, *supra* note 48, at 256–57.

58 *See id.; What Is Stakeholder Theory?, supra* note 49.

59 *See id.*

60 *See* William Bradford, *Beyond Good and Evil: The Commensurability of Corporate Profits and Human Rights,* 26 N.D. J.L. ETHICS & PUB. POL'Y 141, 151 (2012).

61 *See* Belinfanti & Stout, *supra* note 13, at 595; *see also generally* Oliver Hart & Luigi Zingales, *Companies Should Maximize Shareholder Welfare Not Market Value,* ECGI WORKING PAPER SERIES IN FINANCE (2017), https://papers.ssrn.com/abstract = 3004794 (arguing for a broader view of shareholder value as

serving shareholders' longer-term interests in living in an ethical society).

62   964 A.2d 106 (Del. Ch. 2009).

63   Belinfanti & Stout, *supra* note 13, at 595 (citing In Re Citigroup Inc. Shareholder Derivative Litig., 964 A.2d 106, 139 (Del. Ch. 2009)).

64   Bradford, *supra* note 60, at 151.

65   *See* Belinfanti & Stout, *supra* note 13, at 595; Wicks et al., *supra* note 35, at 74.

66   *See* Barnali Choudhury, *Serving Two Masters: Incorporating Social Responsibility into the Corporate Paradigm*, 11 U. Pa. J. Bus. L. 631, 652 (2009); *see also* Claudine Gartenberg, Andrea Prat & George Serafeim, *Corporate Purpose and Financial Performance*, 30 Org'l Science 1, 1 (2019) (finding that "firms with midlevel employees with strong beliefs in the purpose of their organization and the clarity in the path toward that purpose experience better [financial] performance"); *id.* (defining corporate purpose for the organizational study as "a concrete goal or objective for the firm that reaches beyond profit maximization") (quoting R. Henderson & E. Van den Steen, *Why Do Firms Have "Purpose"? The Firm's Role as a Carrier of Identity and Reputation*, 105 Am. Econ. Rev. 5, 327 (2015).

67   *See* Robert Frank, What Price the Moral High Ground?: How to Succeed without Selling Your Soul 60 (2004).

68   *See id.* at 60–61.

69   *See* Van Thac Dang, Ninh Nguyen & Simon Pervan, *Retailer Corporate Social Responsibility and Consumer Citizenship Behavior: The Mediating Roles of Perceived Consumer Effectiveness and Consumer Trust*, 55 J. Retailing & Consumer Servs. 8 (July 2020) (describing study conducted in China in which consumers were told the CSR policies of one store and not told the policies of another store; the participants then filled out a questionnaire regarding their perceptions of the social responsibility of the stores and how likely they were to shop there and recommend the store based on these perceptions; study concluded that CSR is positively related to consumer citizenship behavior); Yoko Shirasu & Hidetaka Kawakita, *Long Term Financial Performance of Corporate Social Responsibility*, Glob. Fin. J., Jan. 2019, at 27 (studying the links between CSR and long-term stock returns in

Japan, and finding that governance, social, and environmental CSR activities are associated with better long-term stock performance); Yeonsoo Kim, *Consumer Responses to the Food Industry's Proactive and Passive Environmental CSR, Factoring in Price as CSR Tradeoff*, 140 J. Bus. Ethics 307, 318 (2017) (finding that consumers in the food industry are willing to pay more for more responsible products and that proactive environmental CSR can compensate for high prices in terms of supportive intentions and purchase intentions; also finding that when a company practices passive CSR and provides cheaper products, respondents exhibited the weakest purchase intentions); Daniel W. Elfenbein & Brian McManus, *A Greater Price for a Greater Good? Evidence that Consumers Pay More for Charity-Linked Products*, 2 Am. Econ. J.: Econ. Pol'y 28, 54 (2010) (finding that individuals bidding in charity and non-charity auctions for the same product bid significantly higher in the charity auctions; also finding that bidders in charity auctions bid earlier than those in non-charity auctions, and charity auctions had more incremental bidding, thus driving the end price of the product up).

70 *See* Frank, *supra* note 67, at 63; Marco Bertini, Luc Wathieu & Sheena S. Iyengar, *The Discriminating Consumer: Product Proliferation and Willingness to Pay for Quality*, 49 J. Mktg. Res. 39, 43 (Feb. 2012) (describing study to ascertain whether a variety of options impact a consumers willingness to pay more money for better quality products; concluding that people were willing to pay more for better quality products in the context of a dense set of alternatives); Yahua Zhang, *Are Chinese Passengers Willing to Pay More for Better Air Services?*, 25 J. Air Transport. Mgmt. 5, 6 (2012) (describing study to find whether Chinese passengers were willing to pay more for better air services; concluding that "consumers attach high value to their time and are willing to pay large amounts to avoid schedule delay and to fly with airlines with improved punctuality, especially when travel is for business purposes"); C. Victor Spain, Daisy Freund, Heather Mohan-Gibbons, Robert G. Meadow & Laurie Beacham, *Are They Buying It? United States Consumers' Changing Attitudes toward More Humanely Raised Meat, Eggs, and Dairy*, 8 Animals 12 (July 25, 2018) (describing study to determine if American consumers were willing to pay more for certified quality animal source

foods; concluding that U.S. consumers across all demographics are willing to pay more for higher-welfare animal products).

71 *Cf. also* Stavros Gadinis & Amelia Miazad, *Corporate Law and Social Risk*, Vand. L. Rev. i (forthcoming), https://ssrn.com/abstract = 3441375 (arguing that "through their sustainability initiatives, companies are looking primarily for safeguards against downside risks, and not simply for opportunities to increase their profits;" and that engaging in sustainability may in fact be a way of better managing future risk than merely focusing on legally mandated compliance).

72 *See* Frank, *supra* note 67, at 63; *Tuna: Current Issues Affecting the U.S. Industry*, Report to the Senate Committee of Finance 3–19 (1992).

73 *See* Michael J. Hiscox & Nicholas F.B. Smyth, *Is There Consumer Demand for Fair Labor Standards?: Evidence From a Field Experiment* (Apr. 22, 2011), https://scholar.harvard.edu/files/hiscox/files/is_there_consumer_demand_fair_labor.pdf; Frank, *supra* note 67, at 65.

74 *See* Frank, *supra* note 67, at 65. As a postscript, StarKist is now being sued for lying about its practices being "dolphin-safe," making the company a potentially dramatic example of greenwashing (see Chapter 2). *See generally* Gaby Del Valle, *The 3 Biggest US Tuna Companies Use Fishing Techniques that Hurt and Kill Dolphins, New Lawsuits Claim*, Vox, May 15, 2019, https://www.vox.com/the-goods/2019/5/15/18624941/dolphin-safe-tuna-lawsuit-bumble-bee-starkist-chicken-of-the-sea. The claim also follows on the heels of price-fixing allegations across the tuna industry. *See* Alexander Gladstone & Andrew Scurria, *StarKist, Facing $100 Million Fine, Says It Can't Pay*, Wall St. J., Aug. 8, 2019, https://www.wsj.com/articles/starkist-facing-100-million-cartel-fine-says-it-cant-pay-11565297682.

75 *See Employees to Employers: We Want You to Share Our Values and Make the World a Better Place*, MetLife (Nov. 29, 2017), https://www.metlife.com/about-us/newsroom/2017/november/employees-to-employers--we-want-you-to-share-our-values-and-make/ (describing study of employees asking whether they would be willing to take a pay cut to work for a company whose values aligned with their own; it concluded that nine out of ten people, across all income brackets and ages were willing to take on average a 21% pay cut; additionally, the study found that

nearly two-thirds of all workers expect their employer to provide for their well-being and the well-being of society); *see also* FRANK, *supra* note 67, at 66.

76 *See id.*

77 *See* Daniel W. Greening & Daniel B. Turban, *Corporate Social Performance as a Competitive Advantage in Attracting a Quality Workforce*, 39 BUS. & SOC'Y 254, 276 (Sept. 2000) (describing study conducted to determine whether corporations can use corporate social performance to attract job applicants; finding that prospective job applicants are more likely to attempt to interview with firms with higher CSP, and are more likely to accept a job offer from these firms); Steve Rochlin, Richard Bliss, Stephen Jordan & Cheryl Yaffe Kiser, *Defining the Competitive and Financial Advantages of Corporate Responsibility and Sustainability*, PROJECT ROI (2015) (finding that corporate responsibility can reduce turnover rate of employees by 25–50%, saving replacement costs of 90–200% of "an employee's salary, for each position that stays"); FRANK, *supra* note 67, at 60.

78 *See* Greening & Turban, *supra* note 77, at 276 (describing study conducted to determine whether corporations can use corporate social performance to attract job applicants finds that prospective job applicants are more likely to attempt to interview with firms with higher CSP, and are more likely to accept a job offer from these firms); Rochlin et al., *supra* note 77.

79 *See* Lynn A. Stout, *The Troubling Question of Corporate Purpose*, 3(1) ACCT., ECON. & L. 61, 61 (2013).

80 *See* Claire A. Hill, *The Rhetoric of Negative Externalities*, SEATTLE U.L. REV. 517, 518 (2016).

81 *See id.* at 517.

82 *See id.* at 521–23.

83 Cynthia A. Williams, *The Securities and Exchange Commission and Corporate Social Transparency*, 112 HARV. L. REV. 1197, 1199 (1999); C.A. Harwell Wells, *The Cycles of Corporate Social Responsibility: An Historical Retrospective for the Twenty-First Century*, 51 KAN. L. REV. 77, 134 (2002) (citing Williams).

84 *See* Kevin T. Jackson, *Global Corporate Governance: Soft Law and Reputational Accountability*, 35 BROOKLYN J. INT'L L. 41, 46 (2010).

85 *See id.* at 46, 81.

86 *Id.* at 74, 76.

87 *See id.* at 70–71.

88 *See* Lynn A. Stout, *Symposium: In Praise of Procedure: An Economic and Behavior Defense of* Smith v. Van Gorkom *and the Business Judgement Rule*, 96 Nw. U.L. Rev. 675, 675 (2002).

89 *See* Aronson v. Lewis, 473 A.2d 805, 812 (Del. 1984) ("Second, to invoke the rule's protection directors have a duty to inform themselves, prior to making a business decision, of all material information reasonably available to them."); *see also* Stout, *In Praise of Procedure*, *supra* note 88, at 680 (quoting *Aronson*).

90 *See* Timothy L. Fort & Cindy A. Schipani, The Role of Business in Fostering Peaceful Societies 109 (2004).

91 *See also* Hillary A. Sale, *The Corporate Purpose of Social License* 1 (2019), https://ssrn.com/abstract = 3403706 (exploring "how the failure to account for the public nature of corporate actions, regardless of whether a 'legal' license exists, can result in the loss of 'social' license" for businesses to operate and be accepted).

92 *See generally* Bill Richards, *Nike to Increase Minimum Age in Asia for New Hirings, Improve Air Quality*, Wall St. J., May 13, 1998, at B10 ("In an effort to head off attacks on its labor practices in Asia, Nike Inc. said it plans to boost the minimum age for its new Asian workers and implement a series of other labor changes."); Williams, *supra* note 83, at 1286.

93 *See* U.S. Dep't of the Treasury, Treasury Advisory Committee on International Child Labor Enforcement, 63 Fed. Reg. 30,813 (Aug. 13, 1998) (discussing the establishment of an advisory committee on the Treasury Department's enforcement of the child labor amendment); *see also* Williams, *supra* note 83, at 1286 (discussing Congress's response to public outcry over child labor).

94 *See* Andrew Caesar-Gordon, *The Perfect Crisis Response?*, PR Week, Oct. 28, 2015, http://www.prweek.com/article/1357203; Dan Fletcher, *A Brief History of the Tylenol Poisonings*, Time, Feb. 9, 2009, http://content.time.com/time/nation/article/0,8599,1878063,00.html; Judith Rehak, *Tylenol Made a Hero of Johnson & Johnson: The Recall That Started Them All*, N.Y. Times, Mar. 23, 2002, https://www.nytimes.com/2002/03/23/your-money/IHT-tylenol-made-a-hero-of-johnson-johnson-the-recall-that-started.html; Jerry Knight, *Tylenol's Maker Shows How to Respond to Crisis*, Wash. Post, Oct. 11, 1982, https://www.washingtonpost.com/archive/business/1982/10/11/tylenols-maker-shows-how-to-respond-to-crisis/bc8df898-3fcf-443f-bc2f-e6fbd639a5a3/.

95 *See* Caesar-Gordon, *supra* note 94; Fletcher, *supra* note 94; Judith Rehak, *supra* note 94; Knight *supra* note 94.

96 *See* Caesar-Gordon, *supra* note 94; Fletcher, *supra* note 94; Judith Rehak, *supra* note 94; Knight *supra* note 94.

97 *See* Howard Markel, *How the Tylenol Murders of 1982 Changed the Way We Consume Medication*, PBS NEWSHOUR, Sept. 29, 2014, www.pbs.org/newshour/updates/tylenol-murders-1982.

98 *See id.*

99 *See* Venkata Mrudula Bhimavarapu & Shailesh Rastogi, *Valuation of Transparency—A Systematic Literature Review Paper*, 83 TEST ENGINEERING & MGMT 9092, 9097 (2020) (surveying the literature and explaining that, because "[g]ood financial accounting is important to the integrity of markets[, and provides] the most objective detailed and textured portrait of managerial performance[,] . . . [f]inancial transparency [becomes important to] capture[] the intensity and timeliness of financial disclosure."); Bartley R. Danielsen et al., *Liquidity, Accounting Transparency, and the Cost of Capital: Evidence from Real Estate Investment Trusts*, 36 J. REAL ESTATE RES. 221–52 (2014) ("[W]e find strong evidence that firms choosing to 'over-invest' in financial transparency are rewarded with enhanced liquidity, as measured by lower bid-ask spreads."); Mary E. Barth, Yaniv Konchitchki & Wayne R. Landsman, *Cost of Capital and Earnings Transparency*, 2-3 J. ACCT. & ECON. 55, 206–24 (2013) (finding that transparent companies borrow money at a lower cost of capital in a large sample of U.S. companies over 27 years); Seth Armitage & Claire Marston, *Corporate Disclosure, Cost of Capital, and Reputation: Evidence From Finance Directors*, 40 BRIT. ACCT. REV. 314, 316 (2008). *But see* Farkhondeh Beigi, Mohsen Hosseini & Siavash Qodsi, *The Effect of the Earning Transparency on Cost of Capital Common Stock Based on the Fama-French and Momentum Factors*, PROCEDIA ECON. & FIN. 244–55 (2016) (not finding this link on the Tehran Stock Exchange).

100 Bert Scholtens, *Firms in Greener Countries Pay Less to Borrow Money*, THE CONVERSATION, Apr. 26, 2016, http://theconve rsation.com/firms-in-greener-countries-pay-less-to-bor row-money-new-study-5836.

101 *See* Williams, *supra* note 83, at 1277–78.

102 *See* 8 Del. C. § 220 (2020).

103 *See* United States v. Morton Salt Co., 338 U.S. 632 (1950) ("[C]orporations can claim no equality with individuals in the enjoyment of a right to privacy."); *see also* Elizabeth Pollman, *A Corporate Right to Privacy*, 99 Minn. L. Rev. 27, 33 (2014) (citing *Morton Salt Co.*).

104 *See generally Morton Salt*, 338 U.S. at 632.

105 *See also* Stout, *In Praise of Procedure, supra* note 88, at 680.

106 *See* J.S. Nelson, *The Criminal Bug: Volkswagen's Middle Management* 8–12 (Apr. 26, 2016), https://papers.ssrn.com/sol3/papers.cfm?abstract_id = 2767255; J.S. Nelson, *Disclosure-Driven Crime*, 52 U.C. Davis L. Rev. 1489, 1490 (2019).

107 Jack Ewing & Jad Mouawad, *Directors Say Volkswagen Delayed Informing Them of Trickery*, N.Y. Times, Oct. 23, 2015, http://www.nytimes.com/2015/10/24/business/international/directors-say-volkswagen-delayed-informing-them-of-trickery.html; Press Release, U.S. Env't Prot. Agency, EPA, California Notify Volkswagen of Clean Air Act Violations (Sept. 18, 2015), http://yosemite.epa.gov/opa/admpress.nsf/6424ac1caa800aab85257359003f5337/dfc8e33b5a b162b985257ec40057813b!OpenDocument; Nelson, *Criminal Bug, supra* note 106, at 9.

108 Coral Davenport & Jack Ewing, *VW Is Said to Cheat on Diesel Emissions; U.S. to Order Big Recall*, N.Y. Times, Sept. 18, 2015, http://www.nytimes.com/2015/09/19/business/volkswagen-is-ordered-to-recall-nearly-500000-vehicles-over-emissions-software.html; Nelson, *Criminal Bug, supra* note 106, at 9.

109 *See* Ewing & Mouawad, *supra* note 107; Mark Thompson & Chris Liakos, *Volkswagen CEO Quits Over "Grave Crisis,"* CNN Money, Sept. 23, 2015, http://money.cnn.com/2015/09/23/news/companies/volkswagen-emissions-crisis; Nelson, *Criminal Bug, supra* note 106, at 9.

110 *See* William Boston, *Volkswagen CEO Resigns as Car Maker Races to Stem Emissions Scandal*, Wall St. J., Sept. 23, 2015, http://www.wsj.com/articles/volkswagen-ceo-winterkorn-resigns-1443007423; Nelson, *Criminal Bug, supra* note 106, at 9.

111 *See* Nelson, *Criminal Bug, supra* note 106, at 11; Nelson, *Disclosure-Driven Crime, supra* note 106, at 1495; Danielle Ivory & Keith Bradsher, *Regulators Investigating 2nd VW Computer Program on Emissions*, N.Y. Times, Oct. 8, 2015, http://www.nytimes.com/2015/10/09/business/international/vw-diesel-emissions-scandal-congressional-hearing.html; Jack Ewing & Graham Bowley,

VW Reveals It Misstated Emissions of Gas Cars, N.Y. Times, Nov. 3, 2015, http://mobile.nytimes.com/2015/11/04/business/vw-discloses-new-emissions-problem-involving-carbon-dioxide.html.

112 *See* Dipti Kapadia, Video, *Volkswagen Emissions Scandal in Numbers*, Wall St. J., Oct. 9, 2015, http://www.wsj.com/video/volkswagen-emissions-scandal-in-numbers/3B54B80D-4381-4813-AAED-8A5A2444F79A.html; Nelson, *Criminal Bug, supra* note 106, at 13

113 *See* Klint Finley, *Volkswagen CEO Warns Employees of Massive Cutbacks*, Wired, Oct. 6, 2015, http://www.wired.com/2015/10/vw-may-not-sell-next-years-diesel-models-us; Nelson, *Criminal Bug, supra* note 106, at 13.

114 Kapadia, *supra* note 112; Nelson, *Criminal Bug, supra* note 106, at 13.

115 Gina Iacona, *Going Green to Make Green: Necessary Changes to Promote and Implement Corporate Social Responsibility While Increasing the Bottom Line*, 26 J. Land Use & Envtl. Law 113, 133–34 (2010).

116 *Changes to Boeing's Safety Protocols Are Getting Mixed Reviews*, NPR Morning Edition 2:21 (Sept. 26, 2019) (quoting Thomas Anthony, Dir. of the Aviation Safety & Security Program, Univ. of S. Cal, on Boeing's reoccurring safety problems with the 737 MAX aircraft).

117 McKinsey Global Institute, *Measuring the Economic Impact of Short-Termism*, Feb. 2017, https://www.fcltglobal.org/docs/default-source/default-document-library/20170206_mgi-shorttermism_vfinal_public.pdf?sfvrsn = 8d88258c_0.

118 *See All Our Work*, United Nations Global Compact (2020), https://www.unglobalcompact.org/what-is-gc/our-work/all.

119 *See* United Nations, Universal Declaration of Human Rights 1 (1948), https://www.un.org/en/universal-declaration-human-rights/ ("Whereas recognition of the inherent dignity and of the equal and inalienable rights of all members of the human family is the foundation of freedom, justice and peace in the world.").

120 *See id.* at 2 ("Everyone is entitled to all the rights and freedoms set forth in this Declaration, without distinction of any kind, such as race, colour, sex, language, religion, political or other opinion, national or social origin, property, birth or other status.").

121 *See* UNITED NATIONS, INTERNATIONAL COVENANT ON ECONOMIC, SOCIAL, AND CULTURAL RIGHTS 6 (1966), https://www. ohchr.org/en/professionalinterest/pages/cescr.aspx ("The States Parties to the present Covenant undertake to submit in conformity with this part of the Covenant reports on the measures which they have adopted and the progress made in achieving the observance of the rights recognized herein.").

122 UNITED NATIONS, CONVENTION ON THE ELIMINATION OF ALL FORMS OF DISCRIMINATION AGAINST WOMEN 1 (1979), https:// www.ohchr.org/EN/ProfessionalInterest/Pages/CEDAW.aspx.

123 UNITED NATIONS, CONVENTION ON THE RIGHTS OF THE CHILD 1 (1989), https://www.ohchr.org/en/professionalinterest/pages/ crc.aspx.

124 UNITED NATIONS, CONVENTION AGAINST CORRUPTION 1 (2003), https://www.unodc.org/unodc/en/corruption/uncac.html.

125 *See* FAIR LABOR ASSOCIATION, PRINCIPLES OF FAIR LABOR AND RESPONSIBLE SOURCING AND PRODUCTION (2012), https://www. fairlabor.org/our-work/principles.

126 *See* CERES, THE CERES ROADMAP FOR SUSTAINABILITY 2–3 (2018), https://www.ceres.org/roadmap.

127 *See* GLOBAL REPORTING INITIATIVE, GRI STANDARDS (2020), https://www.globalreporting.org/standards/ gri-standards-download-center/

128 CAUX ROUND TABLE, PRINCIPLES, https://www.cauxroundtable. org/principles/.

129 BUSINESS ROUNDTABLE, *supra* note 17, at 1.

130 *Id.*

131 *See id.; see also* Business Roundtable, *Business Roundtable Redefines the Purpose of a Corporation to Promote "An Economy That Serves All Americans,"* Aug. 19, 2019, https://www.businessroundtable. org/business-roundtable-redefines-the-purpose-of-a-corporat ion-to-promote-an-economy-that-serves-all-americans (stating that 181 CEOs committed at time of press release; since 15 more have signed on). There was a similar international statement on CSR entitled "Davos Manifesto 2020: The Universal Purpose of a Company in the Fourth Industrial Revolution." Klaus Schwab, Dec. 2, 2019, https://www.weforum.org/agenda/2019/12/ davos-manifesto-2020-the-universal-purpose-of-a-company- in-the-fourth-industrial-revolution/. It was, however, signed only by the World Economic Forum's Founder and Executive

Chairman, and released as the "views . . . of the author alone and not the World Economic Forum." *Id.*

132 *See* INTERNATIONAL FINANCE CORPORATION, WHO CARES WINS— CONNECTING FINANCIAL MARKETS TO A CHANGING WORLD 3 (2004), https://www.ifc.org/wps/wcm/connect/topics_ext_ content/ifc_external_corporate_site/sustainability-at-ifc/publi cations/publications_report_whocareswins__wci__131957 9355342.

133 *See* FRESHFIELDS BRUCKHAUS DERINGER, NAVIGATING THE ESG INVESTMENT LANDSCAPE: HOW TO ACCESS NEW POOLS OF ESG CAPITAL 7–9 (2019), https://www.freshfields.com/en-us/our-thinking/campaigns/navigating-the-esg-investment-landscape/.

134 *See Secretary-General Launches "Principles for Responsible Investment" Backed by World's Largest Investors,* UNITED NATIONS, Apr. 27, 2006, https://www.un.org/press/en/2006/sg2111. doc.htm.

135 Principles for Responsible Investing, *What Is the PRI's Mission?,* https://www.unpri.org/pri/about-the-pri.

136 Principles for Responsible Investing, *What Are the Six Principles of Responsible Investment?,* https://www.unpri.org/pri/ about-the-pri.

137 *See* Principles for Responsible Investing, *How Did the PRI Start?,* https://www.unpri.org/pri/about-the-pri.

138 *See* PRINCIPLES FOR RESPONSIBLE INVESTING, PRI REPORTING FRAMEWORK 2017 1 (2017), https://www.unpri.org/Uploads/k/ w/q/2017_pri_indicator_methodology_574171.pdf.

139 *See* INITIATIVE FOR RESPONSIBLE INV., CORPORATE SOCIAL RESPONSIBILITY DISCLOSURE EFFORTS BY NATIONAL GOVERNMENTS AND STOCK EXCHANGES 2–16 (2015).

140 *See* Larry E. Ribstein, *Accountability and Responsibility in Corporate Governance,* 81 NOTRE DAME L. REV. 1431, 1459 (2006).

141 *See* Sustainable Stock Exchange Initiative, *ESG Disclosure,* https://sseinitiative.org/esg-disclosure/.

142 3BLMedia, *Corporate Responsibility Magazine's 100 Best Corporate Citizens 2018,* CORP. RESP. MAG. 3 (Summer 2018), https:// www.3blassociation.com/files/exV4MF/CR_Summer%2018_ 100%20Best_revised.pdf.

143 *See* Xerox, *2011 Report on Global Citizenship* (2011), https://www. xerox.com/corporate-citizenship/2011/community-involvem ent.html.

144 *See* TOMS, *Impact*, https://www.toms.com/impact.

145 *See* TOMS, TOMS 2019 IMPACT REPORT 35, 45 (2019), https://media01.toms.com/static/www/images/landingpages/TOMS_Impact/TOMS_2019_Global_Impact_Report.pdf.

146 *See* LS&Co. *Opens Up Its Worker Well-Being Initiative*, LEVI STRAUSS, Oct. 13, 2016, https://www.levistrauss.com/2016/10/13/lsco-opens-up-its-worker-well-being-initiative; *see also Worker Well-Being Initiative*, LEVI STRAUSS (2020), https://www.levistrauss.com/how-we-do-business/worker-well-being/.

147 *See id.*

148 *See* Sarah Nassauer, *How Dicks Sporting Goods Decided to Change Its Gun Policy*, WALL ST. J., Dec. 4, 2018, https://www.wsj.com/articles/how-dicks-sporting-goods-decided-to-change-its-gun-policy-1543955262.

149 *See Walmart Statement on Firearms Policy*, WALMART, Feb. 28, 2018, https://corporate.walmart.com/newsroom/2018/02/28/walmart-statement-on-firearms-policy; Nassauer, *supra* note 148.

150 *See* Arian Campo-Flores, *Florida Gov. Scott Signs Gun-Control, School-Safety Bill*, WALL ST. J., Mar. 9, 2018, https://www.wsj.com/articles/florida-gov-scott-signs-gun-control-school-safety-bill-1520627652.

151 *See, e.g.,* Ribstein, *supra* note 140, at 1459.

Chapter 8

1 *See* Pamela MacLean & Karen Gullo, *AU Optronics Fined $500 Million in U.S. for Price-Fixing*, BLOOMBERG, Sept. 20, 2012, http://www.bloomberg.com/news/articles/2012-09-20/au-optronics-fined-500-million-in-u-s-for-price-fixing.

2 *See* Lindsey Bever, *Former Peanut Plant Executive Faces Life Sentence for Lethal Salmonella Coverup*, WASH. POST, July 24, 2015, https://www.washingtonpost.com/news/morning-mix/wp/2015/07/24/former-peanut-plant-executive-faces-life-sentence-for-selling-salmonella-tainted-food/.

3 *See* Rich McKay, *Former Peanut Company CEO Sentenced to 28 Years for Salmonella Outbreak*, REUTERS, Sept. 21, 2015, http://www.reuters.com/article/us-usa-georgia-salmonella-idUSKCN0RL24H20150922.

4 *See, e.g.,* Jennifer Robison, *Turning Around Employee Turnover*, GALLUP, May 8, 2008, http://www.gallup.com/businessjournal/

106912/turning-around-your-turnover-problem.aspx [hereinafter *Gallup Poll*].

5   *See* Isaac H. Smith, Maryam Kouchaki & Justin Wareham, *Be Careful What You Wish For: The Performance Consequences of Unethical Requests at Work*, ACAD. OF MGMT. PROC., 2013, http://proceedings.aom.org/content/2013/1/10976.abstr act?sid = 173e9653-b0a4-4af8-ba6f-f0a0c819e6b4.

6   *See Gallup Poll*, *supra* note 4.

7   *See, e.g.*, Jeremy Blackburn, Nicolas Kourtellis, John Skvoretz, Matei Ripeanu & Adriana Iamnitchi, *Cheating in Online Games: A Social Network Perspective*, 13:3 ACM TRANS. INTERNET TECHNOL. 1, 10 (2014), https://www.cse.usf.edu/dsg/data/publications/papers/cheating_TOI.pdf.

8   *Id.* at 8; *see also id.* at 9, 14.

9   *Id.* at 10.

10 *See id.* at 11.

11 *See* Angela Haupt, *How Lying Affects Your Health*, U.S. NEWS & WORLD REP., Aug. 20, 2012, http://health.usnews.com/health-news/articles/2012/08/20/how-lying-affects-your-health.

12 *See Lying Less Linked to Better Health, New Research Finds*, AM. PSYCHOL. ASS'N, Aug. 4, 2012, http://www.apa.org/news/press/releases/2012/08/lying-less.aspx.

13 *See The Costs of a Bad Reputation: The Impacts of Corporate Reputation on Talent Acquisition*, CORP. SOC. RESP. MAG. & CIELO, Oct. 2015, at 8, http://www.thecro.com/wp-content/uploads/2015/10/Cost-of-a-Bad-Reputation-2015-Final.pdf [hereinafter *Costs*].

14 *See* 10 U.S.C. § 2408(a); 48 C.F.R. § 252.203-7001.

15 *See* 21 U.S.C. § 335a(C)(2).

16 *See id.*

17 24 C.F.R. § 24.305; 48 C.F.R. pt. 9, subpt. 9.4.

18 *See* Angela Greiling Keane, *Toyota Fined Record $17.4 Million for Not Reporting Flaws*, BLOOMBERG, Dec. 18, 2012, http://www.bloomberg.com/news/articles/2012-12-18/toyota-fined-record-17-4-million-for-failing-to-report-defects.

19 *See* Tina Susman & Jerry Hirsch, *"Fraud Can Kill," Judge Tells Toyota*, L.A. TIMES, Mar. 21, 2014, http://articles.latimes.com/2014/mar/21/business/la-fi-toyota-plea-20140321.

20 *See* Andrew Grossman, *Bridgestone Agrees to Pay $425 Million Fine in Price-Fixing Probe*, WALL ST. J., Feb. 13, 2014, http://blogs.wsj.

com/law/2014/02/13/bridgestone-agrees-to-pay-425-million-fine-in-price-fixing-probe.

21 *See Just One More Fix*, Economist, Mar. 29, 2014, http://www.economist.com/news/business/21599799-trustbusters-have-got-better-detecting-cartels-and-bolder-punishing-them-incenti ves[hereinafter *Fix*].

22 *See* Jeff Cox, *Misbehaving Banks Have Now Paid $204B in Fines*, CNBC, Oct. 30, 2015, http://www.cnbc.com/2015/10/30/misb ehaving-banks-have-now-paid-204b-in-fines.html.

23 *See 2005 Volkswagen of America Settlement*, U.S. Envtl. Prot. Agency, June 15, 2005, https://www.epa.gov/enforcement/2005-volkswagen-america-settlement.

24 *Id.*

25 *See* Geoffrey Smith & Roger Parloff, *Hoaxwagen: How the Massive Diesel Fraud Incinerated VW's Reputation—and Will Hobble the Company for Years to Come*, Fortune, Mar. 15, 2016, http://fort une.com/inside-volkswagen-emissions-scandal/?xid = for_em_ sh (see graphic).

26 *See* Dipti Kapadia, Video, *Volkswagen Emissions Scandal in Numbers*, Wall St. J., Oct. 9, 2015, http://www.wsj.com/video/volkswagen-emissions-scandal-in-numbers/3B54B80D-4381-4813-AAED-8A5A2444F79A.html [hereinafter *Scandal Numbers*]; Paul R. La Monica, *Volkswagen Has Plunged 50%. Will It Ever Recover?*, CNN Money, Sept. 25, 2015, http://money.cnn.com/2015/09/24/investing/volkswagen-vw-emissions-scandal-stock.

27 *See* Klint Finley, *Volkswagen CEO Warns Employees of Massive Cutbacks*, Wired, Oct. 6, 2015, http://www.wired.com/2015/10/vw-may-not-sell-next-years-diesel-models-us; *Scandal Numbers*, *supra* note 26.

28 *See* Alex Davies, *Volkswagen's US Sales Plummet 25 Percent as Dieselgate Rolls On*, Wired, Dec. 1, 2015, https://www.wired.com/2015/12/volkswagen-us-sales-plummet-25-as-dieselg ate-rolls-on.

29 *Scandal Numbers*, *supra* note 26.

30 Jack Ewing, *VW Presentation in '06 Showed How to Foil Emissions Tests*, N.Y. Times, Apr. 26, 2016, http://www.nytimes.com/2016/04/27/business/international/vw-presentation-in-06-showed-how-to-foil-emissions-tests.html.

31   *See* Remi Trudel & June Cotte, *Does Being Ethical Pay?*, WALL ST. J., May 2, 2008, http://www.wsj.com/articles/SB12101873549 0274425.

32   *See Will Consumers Pay More for Products From Socially Responsible Companies?*, MARKETING CHARTS (Oct. 15, 2015), http:// www.marketingcharts.com/traditional/will-consumers-pay-more-for-products-from-socially-responsible-companie-60166 (consolidating recent reports).

33   *See id.*

34   *The Sustainability Imperative*, NIELSEN.COM (Oct. 12, 2015), http:// www.nielsen.com/us/en/insights/reports/2015/the-sustainabil ity-imperative.html.

35   *See* Nielsen Global Survey of Corporate Social Responsibility and Sustainability, *Consumer-Goods' Brands That Demonstrate Commitment To Sustainability Outperform Those That Don't*, NIELSON.COM (Oct. 12, 2015), http://www.nielsen.com/us/en/ press-room/2015/consumer-goods-brands-that-demonstrate-commitment-to-sustainability-outperform.html.

36   *See Costs, supra* note 13, at 4, 6.

37   *See* Ben DiPietro, Risk and Compliance J., *Chasing the "Holy Grail": How to Measure Compliance?*, WALL ST. J., May 23, 2016, http://blogs.wsj.com/riskandcompliance/2016/05/23/chasing-the-holy-grail-how-to-measure compliance (interviewing a range of compliance professionals).

38   *See Costs, supra* note 13, at 5.

39   *See Gallup Poll, supra* note 4.

40   Emiko Terazono & Avantika Chilkoti, *Palm Oil Battle Spreads Beyond Ethical Investors*, FIN. TIMES, May 26, 2016, http://www. ft.com/intl/cms/s/0/d9c87b0e-229c-11e6-aa98-db1e01fabc0c. html#axzz49u6kCTn6 (quoting Emily Chew at financial index and data group MSCI).

41   *Id.* (quoting Jean-Francois Lambert, founding partner of Lambert Commodities and former head of commodity trade finance at HSBC).

42   *See Fix, supra* note 21.

43   *See Cheating MBA Applicants: Trick Shots*, ECONOMIST, Nov. 17, 2015, http://www.economist.com/whichmba/cheating-mba-applicants-trick-shots.

44   *See Fix, supra* note 21.

Chapter 9

1 *See* Ethics Resource Center, *2011 National Business Ethics Survey: Workplace Ethics in Transition* at 39, data available at O.C. Ferrell, John Fraedrich & Linda Ferrell, Business Ethics: Ethical Decision Making and Cases at 62 (2015).

2 Michael Housman & Dylan Minor, *Toxic Workers*, Harv. Bus. Rev. at 2 (Working Paper 16-057) (Nov. 2015), http://www.hbs.edu/faculty/Publication%20Files/16-057_d45c0b4f-fa19-49de-8f1b-4b12fe054fea.pdf.

3 *Id.* at 9, 12.

4 *See* Ethics and Compliance Initiative, *2013 National Business Ethics Survey of the U.S. Workforce: Key Findings*, https://www.ethics.org/eci/research/eci-research/nbes/nbes-reports/nbes-2013.

5 *See* Housman & Minor, *supra* note 2, at 3, 10–15, 18.

6 *See* Richard J. Wolf, HSBC North America, Inc., *Beyond Carrots and Sticks: Encouraging a Speak Up Culture* at 2 (Presentation to Ethics by Design Conference) (June 3, 2016), *available at* http://www.eth icalsystems.org/ethicsbydesign.

7 *See id.* (reporting that the amount is 51.5%).

8 Pub. L. No. 111-203, 124 Stat. 1376 (2010).

9 David T. Welsh, Lisa D. Ordóñez, Deirdre G. Snyder & Michael S. Christian, *The Slippery Slope: How Small Ethical Transgressions Pave the Way For Larger Future Transgressions*, 100 J. Applied Psychol. 1, 114–27, at 13 (page numbers refer to downloaded manuscript) (Jan. 2015) [hereinafter *Slippery Slope*].

10 *See* Jenny Anderson, *Fund Manager in London Who Dodged Train Fares Is Barred From Financial Jobs*, N.Y. Times, Dec. 15, 2014, http://dealbook.nytimes.com/2014/12/15/fund-manager-in-lon don-who-dodged-train-fare-is-barred-from-financial-jobs/; Neal Sears et al., *Outrage at High Flying City Asset Manager Who Became "Biggest Fare Dodger in History" By Avoiding £43,000 in Rail Tickets While Owning Two Country Mansions Worth £4 Million*, Daily Mail, Aug. 1, 2014, http://www.dailymail.co.uk/news/article-2713784/Unmasked-City-high-flier-Jonathan-Burrows-dodged-43-000-rail-fares-paid-3-days.html.

11 *See* Financial Conduct Authority, *Final Notice: Jonathan Paul Burrows* (Dec. 15, 2014), http://www.fca.org.uk/static/docume nts/final-notices/jonathan-paul-burrows.pdf.

12 *Cf.* Eleazar David Melendez, *Financial Crisis Cost Tops $22 Trillion, GAO Says*, HuffPost, Feb. 14, 2013, http://www.huffingtonpost.com/2013/02/14/financial-crisis-cost-gao_n_2687553.html.

13   Researchers explain the rationalization mechanism this way:
A key assumption of compensatory ethics is that individuals
recognize and appreciate the wrongness of their behavior.
Without the acknowledgment of an ethical violation, there
is no motive for morally compensatory behavior to occur.
Thus, the justification of unethicality that occurs through
moral disengagement may explain why morally disengaged
individuals do not fully appreciate the wrongness of their
actions and may continue behaving unethically.

Slippery Slope, supra note 9, at 11.

14   *Id.* at 1 (quoting Bernard Madoff); *see also* Jordan Maglich, *Madoff
Ponzi Scheme, Five Years Later*, FORBES, Dec. 9, 2013, http://www.
forbes.com/sites/jordanmaglich/2013/12/09/madoff-ponzi-sch
eme-five-years-later/#6b30726a789f.

15   *See* Assoc. Press, *Enron Sentences Will Be Tied to Investor Losses*,
NBC NEWS.COM, May 26, 2006, http://www.nbcnews.com/id/
12993408/ns/business-corporate_scandals/t/enron-sentences-
will-be-tied-investor-losses/#.V3HKQld6rzI.

16   Matti Rantanen, *Chapter 11: Reasons of Systemic Collapse in Enron*,
in SYSTEMS INTELLIGENCE IN LEADERSHIP AND EVERYDAY LIFE
180 (Raimo P. Hämäläinen & Esa Saarinen, eds., 2007) (citing
BETHANY MCLEAN & PETER ELKIND, THE SMARTEST GUYS IN THE
ROOM: THE AMAZING RISE AND SCANDALOUS FALL OF ENRON 132
(2003), at 92).

17   *Id.*

18   MCLEAN & ELKIND, *supra* note 16, at 132.

19   *See Slippery Slope, supra* note 9, at 2 (citing Mazar et al.).

20   As researchers describe this phenomenon: "[W]e posit a
magnitude range of dishonesty within which people can
cheat, but their behaviors, which they would usually consider
dishonest, do not bear negatively on their self-concept (i.e.,
they are not forced to update their self-concept [of themselves
as honest people])." Nina Mazar, On Amir & Dan Ariely, *The
Dishonesty of Honest People: A Theory of Self-Concept Maintenance*,
45:6 J. MKTG. RES. 634 (Nov. 2008).

21   *See, e.g., Slippery Slope, supra* note 9, at 12.

22   Famous Yale University psychologist Stanley Milgram conducted
a series of experiments on subjects that might not be allowed
today. In his findings, however, he demonstrated the disturbing
lengths that subjects will go to violate their own ethics when
ordered by an authority. Key to the experiments was that the

"shocks" subjects were ordered to administer gradually got larger and larger. *See* Stanley Milgram, *The Behavioral Study of Obedience*, 67 J. ABNORMAL & SOC. PSYCHOL. 4, 371–78 (1963).

23 *See In It to Win It: The Jack Abramoff Story*, Cases Unwrapped Video Series, ETHICS UNWRAPPED, http://ethicsunwrapped.ute xas.edu/series/cases-unwrapped; *Jack Abramoff: The Lobbyist's Playbook*, 60 Minutes, CBS NEWS.COM, May 30, 2012, http:// www.cbsnews.com/news/jack-abramoff-the-lobbyists-playb ook-30-05-2012.

24 *Lobbyist's Playbook, supra* note 23.

25 *Id.*

26 *See Slippery Slope, supra* note 9, at 12 (describing additional research and studies).

27 *See, e.g.*, Robert H. Tillman & Henry N. Pontell, Opinion, *Corporate Fraud Demands Criminal Time*, N.Y. TIMES, June 29, 2016, http://www.nytimes.com/2016/06/29/opinion/corporate-fraud-demands-criminal-time.html.

28 Anita Raghavan, *Law Enforcement 'Not Winning' War on White-Collar Crime*, N.Y. TIMES, Sept. 6, 2016, http://www.nytimes. com/2016/09/07/business/dealbook/law-enforcement-not-winning-war-on-white-collar-crime.html (quoting Alison Levitt of the law firm Mishcon de Reya).

29 *See* Mazar et al., *supra* note 20, at 634.

30 *Id.*

31 *See* Anita Bruzzese, *Avoid the Slippery Slope of Unethical Behavior*, THE FAST TRACK, May 29, 2012, http://quickbase.intuit.com/ blog/avoid-the-slippery-slope-of-unethical-behavior (throughout this subsection).

32 *See* Ann Tenbrunsel, *What Business Professionals Should Know About Human Nature*, Presentation to the Markkula Center for Applied Ethics (May 11, 2016); *accord* Margaret Steen, *The Behavioral Movement*, MARKKULA CTR. FOR APPLIED ETHICS (May 17, 2016), https://www.scu.edu/ethics/focus-areas/busin ess-ethics/resources/the-behavioral-movement (report on the presentation).

33 MODEL PENAL CODE § 5.03(6) (Proposed Official Draft 1962) ("Renunciation of Criminal Purpose"). This version of the Model Penal Code has become the basis for most of the criminal law across the United States, and by imitation, many other jurisdictions as well.

34 James O'Toole, *Speaking Truth to Power: A White Paper*, MARKKULA CTR. FOR APPLIED ETHICS (Oct. 15, 2015), https://www.scu.edu/ethics/focus-areas/business-ethics/resources/speaking-truth-to-power-a-white-paper/.

35 *Id.*

36 *See id.* The following list is from O'Toole's paper and references Stephen L. Carter's book, INTEGRITY (1996).

37 Gentile's foundational book is MARY C. GENTILE, GIVING VOICE TO VALUES: HOW TO SPEAK YOUR MIND WHEN YOU KNOW WHAT'S RIGHT (2010). The Voice to Values website is www.babson.edu/Academics/teaching-research/gvv/Pages/curriculum.aspx. The University of Texas hosts a series of videos about the program as well entitled "Ethics Unwrapped," which is available for free at ethicsunwrapped.utexas.edu.

38 *See* Mary C. Gentile, *An Action Framework for Giving Voice to Values "The To-Do List,"* GIVINGVOICETOVALUES.ORG, http://www.babson.edu/Academics/teaching-research/gvv/Documents/Student/An-Action-Framework-for-GVV_S.pdf.

39 Gentile's text cites RUSHWORTH M. KIDDER, MORAL COURAGE: TAKING ACTION WHEN YOUR VALUES ARE PUT TO THE TEST 47 (2005).

40 Mary C. Gentile, *Ways of Thinking About Our Values in the Workplace* 18, GIVINGVOICETOVALUES.ORG, http://www.babson.edu/Academics/teaching-research/gvv/Documents/Ways-of-Thinking-About-Our-Values.pdf.

41 Gentile cites Donna Dubinsky in Mary Gentile, Case Study, *Donna Dubinsky and Apple Computer, Inc. (A)*, Harv. Bus. Sch. Case Study #9-486-083 (1986), at 12.

42 Gentile, *Ways of Thinking About Our Values, supra* note 40, at 23.

Chapter 10

1 *See* Ethics and Compliance Initiative, *2013 National Business Ethics Survey of the U.S. Workforce: Key Findings*, https://www.ethics.org/eci/research/eci-research/nbes/nbes-reports/nbes-2013.

2 *See* Ass'n of Certified Fraud Examiners, *2016 ACFE Report to the Nations on Occupational Fraud and Abuse*, http://www.acfe.com/rttn2016/costs.aspx.

3 Delroy L. Paulhus & Kevin M. Williams, *The Dark Triad of Personality: Narcissism, Machiavellianism, and Psychopathy*, 36 J. RES. IN PERSONALITY 556, 557 (2002).

4 Adrian Furnham, Steven C. Richards & Delroy L. Paulhus, *The Dark Triad of Personality: A 10 Year Review*, 7/3 Soc. & Personality Psychol. Compass 199–216, 206 (2013).

5 *See id.* (citing Babiak, 1995; Dotlich & Cairo, 2003; Furnham, 2010; Hogan & Hogan, 2001; Kets de Vries, 2006; Lubit, 2004).

6 *See id.* (citing O'Boyle, Forsyth, Banks, & McDaniel, 2012).

7 *See id.* (citing Furnham, 2010).

8 *See* Michael Housman & Dylan Minor, *Toxic Workers*, Harv. Bus. Rev. at 3, 19 (Working Paper 16-057, Nov. 2015), http://www.hbs.edu/faculty/Publication%20Files/16-057_d45c0b4f-fa19-49de-8f1b-4b12fe054fea.pdf.

9 *See, e.g.*, Jeremy Blackburn, Nicolas Kourtellis, John Skvoretz, Matei Ripeanu & Adriana Iamnitchi, *Cheating in Online Games: A Social Network Perspective* A:7 (2013), http://www.cse.usf.edu/dsg/publications/papers/cheating_TOI.pdf.

10 *See* Robert I. Sutton, *Why Good Bosses Tune In to Their People*, McKinsey Q. (Aug. 2010), http://www.mckinsey.com/global-themes/leadership/why-good-bosses-tune-in-to-their-people (citing research by Cornell University's David Dunning).

11 *See Toxic Workers, supra* note 8, at 19.

12 Max H. Bazerman & Ann E. Tenbrunsel, Blind Spots: Why We Fail to Do What's Right and What to Do About It (2011) [hereinafter Blind Spots].

13 *See id.* at 62–66.

14 *See* Ilona Babenko, Viktar Fedaseyeu & Song Zhang, *Do CEOs Affect Employees' Political Choices?*, 33:4 Rev. Fin. Stud. 1781 (Apr. 2020).

15 *See id.* at 1782.

16 *See id.* at 1875–86; *see also* Ilona Babenko, *Do CEOs Affect Employee Political Choices?*, Harv. L. Sch. Forum on Corp. Governance and Fin. Reg. (Aug. 28, 2016), https://corpgov.law.harvard.edu/2016/08/28/do-ceos-affect-employee-political-choices (describing findings).

17 *See* Blind Spots, *supra* note 12, at 66–72.

18 Ann Tenbrunsel & David Messick, *Ethical Fading: The Role of Self-Deception in Unethical Behavior*, 17 Soc. Just. Res. 2, 223–36 (June 2004).

19 Blind Spots, *supra* note 12, at 70–71.

20 *See* Max H. Bazerman & Ann E. Tenbrunsel, *Ethical Breakdowns*, Harv. Bus. Rev. (Apr. 2011), https://hbr.org/2011/04/ethical-bre

akdowns [hereinafter *Ethical Breakdowns*] (quoting *Mother Jones* article).

21 *See* Hiroko Tabuchi, *A Cheaper Airbag, and Takata's Road to a Deadly Crisis*, N.Y. TIMES, Aug. 26, 2016, http://www.nytimes.com/2016/08/27/business/takata-airbag-recall-crisis.html.

22 *Id.*

23 Hiroko Tabuchi, *Airbag Propellant Bound for Takata Factory Detonates en Route*, N.Y. TIMES, Aug. 29, 2016, http://mobile.nytimes.com/2016/08/30/business/airbag-propellant-bound-for-takata-factory-detonates-en-route.html.

24 *See id.*

25 *See* David Shepardson, *Fiat Chrysler Recalling 1.9 Million Cars for New Air Bag Defect*, REUTERS BUSINESS, Sept. 16, 2016, http://mobile.reuters.com/article/idUSKCN11L2KI.

26 *See* Mike Spector, *Takata Air Bag-Recall More Than Doubles in the U.S.*, WALL ST. J., May 4, 2016, http://www.wsj.com/articles/takata-air-bag-recall-more-than-doubles-in-the-u-s-1462384824.

27 BLIND SPOTS, *supra* note 12, at 75.

28 *See Ethical Fading, supra* note 18, at 223.

29 *Id.* at 226–27.

30 *See id.* at 228–29.

31 *See id.* at 229–31.

32 *See Ethical Breakdowns, supra* note 20.

33 *See* Suzanne Woolley, *Next Time Your Boss Sets a Crazy Sales Goal, Show Him This*, BLOOMBERG, Sept. 14, 2016, http://www.bloomberg.com/news/articles/2016-09-14/how-sales-targets-encourage-wrongdoing-inside-america-s-companies.

34 *See* Michael Corkery, *Wells Fargo Fined $185 Million for Fraudulently Opening Accounts*, N.Y. TIMES, Sept. 8, 2016, http://www.nytimes.com/2016/09/09/business/dealbook/wells-fargo-fined-for-years-of-harm-to-customers.html.

35 *See* Peter J. Henning, *Wells Fargo Settlement Raises Questions on Disclosure*, N.Y. TIMES, Sept. 19, 2016, http://www.nytimes.com/2016/09/20/business/dealbook/wells-fargo-settlement-raises-questions-on-disclosure.html.

36 *See* Emily Glazer, *How Wells Fargo's High-Pressure Sales Culture Spiraled Out of Control*, WALL ST. J., Sept. 16, 2016, http://www.wsj.com/articles/how-wells-fargos-high-pressure-sales-culture-spiraled-out-of-control-1474053044.

37 Upton Sinclair, I, Candidate for Governor: And How I Got Licked 109 (1935, republished by U. Calif. Press, 1994).

38 *See* Oliver Staley, *Wells Fargo Just Became the Poster Child for When External and Internal Values Don't Match*, Quartz (Sept. 8, 2016), http://qz.com/777241/wells-fargos-fake-accounts-scandal-makes-it-the-perfect-poster-child-for-when-external-and-internal-values-dont-match/.

39 *See id.*

40 *See* James B. Stewart, *Wells Fargo Tests Justice Department's Get-Tough Approach*, N.Y. Times (Sept. 22, 2016), http://mobile.nytimes.com/2016/09/23/business/wells-fargo-tests-justice-departments-get-tough-approach.html; James F. Peltz, *Demand for "Clawback" of Bank Executives' Multimillion-Dollar Pay Expected at Senate Hearing*, L.A. Times (Sept. 20, 2016), http://www.latimes.com/business/la-fi-wells-fargo-clawbacks-20160920-snap-story.html.

41 Glazer, *supra* note 36.

42 *Ethical Breakdowns, supra* note 20.

43 *See, e.g.*, Susan Adams, *Apple's New Foxconn Embarrassment*, Forbes, Sept. 12, 2012, http://www.forbes.com/sites/susanadams/2012/09/12/apples-new-foxconn-embarrassment/#7ebe57758ae6.

44 Glazer, *supra* note 36.

45 *See* Matt Egan, *I Called the Wells Fargo Ethics Line and Was Fired*, CNNMoney, Sept. 21, 2016, http://money.cnn.com/2016/09/21/investing/wells-fargo-fired-workers-retaliation-fake-accounts.

46 *Id.*

47 *See id.*

48 Bill George, *Research and Ideas*: *Why Leaders Lose Their Way*, Harvard Business School Working Knowledge: Thinking That Leads (June 6, 2011), http://hbswk.hbs.edu/item/why-leaders-lose-their-way.

49 Daniel Vasella & Clifton Leaf, *"Temptation Is All Around Us": Daniel Vasella of Novartis Talks About Making the Numbers, Self-Deception, and the Danger of Craving Success*, Fortune, Nov. 18, 2002, http://archive.fortune.com/magazines/fortune/fortune_archive/2002/11/18/332268/index.htm.

50 *See* Glazer, *supra* note 36.

51 George, *supra* note 48.

52   Vasella & Leaf, *supra* note 49.

53   Sutton, *supra* note 10.

54   Jack Welch, Letter to Share Owners, Leadership, *GE 2000 Annual Report*, at 3, http://www.ge.com/annual00/letter/page3.html.

55   Adrian Furnham, Steven C. Richards & Delroy L. Paulhus, *The Dark Triad of Personality: A 10 Year Review*, 7/3 Soc. & Personality Psychol. Compass 199–216, 206 (2013) (citing Hogan, 2007).

56   *Toxic Workers, supra* note 8, at 3.

57   *See* Furnham et al., *supra* note 55 (citing Furnham, 2010; Hogan, 2007).

58   Seth M. Spain, P.D. Harms & James M. LeBreton, *The Dark Side of Personality at Work* 18, J. Org. Behav., Int'l Rev. Indus. & Org. Psych. Special Issue.

59   *Id.* at 15 (citing Lombardo & McCauley, 1994; Dotlitch & Cairo, 2003).

60   *Id.* at 14.

61   Sutton, *supra* note 10.

62   *Id.*

63   Adam Bryant, *Victor Ho of FiveStars: Take Management Advice From Interns*, N.Y. Times, Sept. 23, 2016, http://www.nytimes.com/2016/09/25/business/victor-ho-of-fivestars-take-management-advice-from-interns.html.

64   Sutton, *supra* note 10.

65   *See* Gretchen Morgenson, *In Wells Fargo's Bogus Accounts, Echoes of Foreclosure Abuses*, N.Y. Times (Sept. 21, 2016), http://mobile.nytimes.com/2016/09/22/business/in-wells-fargos-bogus-accounts-echoes-of-foreclosure-abuses.html; Michael Corkery, *Elizabeth Warren Accuses Wells Fargo Chief of "Gutless Leadership,"* N.Y. Times, Sept. 20, 2016, http://www.nytimes.com/2016/09/21/business/dealbook/wells-fargo-ceo-john-stumpf-senate-testimony.html [hereinafter *Gutless Leadership*].

66   *See* Glazer, *supra* note 36.

67   *Gutless Leadership, supra* note 65.

68   *See* Glazer, *supra* note 36.

69   Michael Corkery & Stacy Cowley, *Wells Fargo Warned Workers Against Sham Accounts, But "They Needed a Paycheck,"* N.Y. Times (Sept. 16, 2016), http://www.nytimes.com/2016/09/17/business/dealbook/wells-fargo-warned-workers-against-fake-accounts-but-they-needed-a-paycheck.html.

70   *Id.*

71   *See Gutless Leadership, supra* note 65.

72   *See* Peltz, *supra* note 40.

73   *See* William D. Cohan, *Wells Fargo Scandal May Be Sign of a Poisonous Culture*, N.Y. TIMES, Sept. 16, 2016, http://www.nyti mes.com/2016/09/17/business/dealbook/wells-fargo-scandal-may-be-sign-of-a-poisonous-culture.html.

74   *See* Emily Glazer, *Wells Fargo Claws Back Millions from CEO After Scandal*, WALL ST. J., Sept. 27, 2016, http://www.articles/wells-fargo-board-actively-considering-executive-clawbacks-147 4985652.

75   Sutton, *supra* note 10.

76   Matti Rantanen, *Chapter 11: Reasons of Systemic Collapse in Enron, in* SYSTEMS INTELLIGENCE IN LEADERSHIP AND EVERYDAY LIFE 184 (Raimo P. Hämäläinen & Esa Saarinen, eds., 2007).

77   Sutton, *supra* note 10.

78   Staley, *supra* note 38.

79   Corkery & Cowley, *supra* note 69.

80   Stewart, *supra* note 40; Emily Glazer & Christina Rexrode, *Wells Fargo CEO Defends Bank Culture, Lays Blame With Bad Employees*, WALL ST. J. (Sept. 13, 2016), http://www.wsj.com/articles/wells-fargo-ceo-defends-bank-culture-lays-blame-with-bad-employees-1473784452.

81   John G. Taft, *Want to Change Banking Culture? Stop Talking About Cross-Selling*, N.Y. TIMES, Sept. 22, 2016, http://www.nytimes.com/2016/09/23/business/dealbook/want-to-change-banking-culture-stop-talking-about-cross-selling.html.

82   *See Ethical Breakdowns, supra* note 20.

83   Woolley, *supra* note 33.

Chapter 11

1   *See* G. RICHARD SHELL, BARGAINING FOR ADVANTAGE: NEGOTIATION STRATEGIES FOR REASONABLE PEOPLE 199 (2d ed. 2006) (quoting Professor James J. White).

2   *See* Jeremy A. Yip, Maurice E. Schweitzer & Samir Nurmohamed, *Trash-Talking: Competitive Incivility Motivates Rivalry, Performance, and Unethical Behavior*, ORG. BEHAVIOR AND HUMAN DECISION PROCESSES at 43–47 (2018) (finding that, among other effects, anger induced in opponents by trash-talking may motivate them to be more competitive, but also reduces their creativity).

3 *See* SHELL, *supra* note 1, at 200.

4 *Id.*

5 RESTATEMENT (SECOND) OF TORTS §525 (AM. LAW INST.
   1977) (titled "Liability for Fraudulent Misrepresentation").

6 RESTATEMENT (SECOND) OF CONTRACTS § 159 (AM. LAW INST.
   1981) (amended Oct. 2017) (titled "Misrepresentation Defined").

7 *See id.* § 161 (titled "When Non-disclosure Is Equivalent to an
   Assertion").

8 *See id.* § 163 (titled "When a Misrepresentation Prevents
   Formation of a Contract").

9 *See id.* § 164 (titled "When a Misrepresentation Makes a Contract
   Voidable").

10 *Id.* § 162 cmt. a (titled "When a Misrepresentation Is Fraudulent
   or Material").

11 RESTATEMENT (SECOND) OF TORTS, *supra* note 5, § 526 cmt. on
   clause (b) (titled "Conditions Under Which Misrepresentation is
   Fraudulent (Scienter)").

12 RESTATEMENT (SECOND) OF CONTRACTS, *supra* note 6, § 169(b)
   (titled "When Reliance on an Assertion of Opinion Is Not
   Justified").

13 *See* RESTATEMENT (SECOND) OF TORTS, *supra* note 5, §525 cmt. h
   (titled "Liability for Fraudulent Misrepresentation").

14 *See id.* § 557A (titled "Fraudulent Misrepresentations Causing
   Physical Harm").

15 *See* RESTATEMENT (SECOND) OF CONTRACTS, *supra* note 6, § 347
   (titled "Measure of Damages in General").

16 *See id.* at ch. 7 (titled "Misrepresentation, Duress and Undue
   Influence").

17 *See* MODEL RULES OF PROF'L CONDUCT R. 4.1 cmt. 2 (1983); *accord*
   Charles B. Craver, *Negotiation Ethics for Real World Interactions*, 25
   OHIO ST. J. DISP. RESOL. 299, 306–07 (2010).

18 *Accord generally* MODEL RULES OF PROF'L CONDUCT R. 4.1 (1983).

19 *See, e.g.*, Selena Larson, *Every Single Yahoo Account Was Hacked—3
   Billion In All*, CNN TECH (Oct. 4, 2017), http://money.cnn.com/
   2017/10/03/technology/business/yahoo-breach-3-billion-accou
   nts/index.html.

20 *See* MODEL RULES OF PROF'L CONDUCT R. 4.1 (1983) (titled
   "Truthfulness in Statements to Others").

21 *See id.* at R. 4.1(b).

22 *See* Restatement (Second) of Torts, *supra* note 5, §551(1) (titled "Liability for Nondisclosure).

23 Art Hinshaw & Jess K. Alberts, *Doing the Right Thing: An Empirical Study of Attorney Negotiation Ethics*, 16 Harv. Negot. L. Rev. 95, 104–05 (2011) (describing implementation of Rule 4.1(b)).

24 *See* Shell, *supra* note 1, at 205 (citing *Kabatchnick v. Hanover-Elm Bldg. Corp.*, 103 N.E. 2d 692 (Mass. 1952)).

25 *See, e.g.*, Roger Fisher, *A Code of Negotiation Practices for Lawyers*, 1 Negot. J. 105 (1985).

26 Hinshaw & Alberts, *supra* note 23, at 100.

27 Rule 4.1 states:
In the course of representing a client, a lawyer shall not knowingly:
(a) Make a false statement of material fact or law to a third person; or
(b) Fail to disclose a material fact to a third person when disclosure is necessary to avoid assisting a criminal or fraudulent act by a client, unless disclosure is prohibited by Rule 1.6.
Model Rules of Prof'l Conduct R. 4.1 (American Bar Ass'n 1983) (titled "Truthfulness in Statements to Others").

28 Roger Fisher, *A Code of Negotiation Practices for Lawyers*, *in* What's Fair: Ethics for Negotiators (Carrie Menkel-Meadow & Michael Wheeler eds., 2004).

29 *See id.* at 26–28.

30 Deborah M. Kolb & Judith Williams, *Everyday Negotiation: Navigating the Hidden Agendas in Bargaining 264*, *in* What's Fair, *supra* note 28.

31 *See* Carrie Menkel-Meadow, *What's Fair in Negotiation? What Is Ethics in Negotiation?* XXX–XXXI, *in* What's Fair, *supra* note 28.

32 *See, e.g.*, Thomas Mussweiler, Fritz Strack & Tim Pfeiffer, *Overcoming the Inevitable Anchoring Affect: Considering the Opposite Compensates for Selective Accessibility*, 26:9 Personality & Soc. Psychol. Bull. 1142 (2000).

33 *See* Cal. Labor Code § 432.3(b) (West 2017); Del. Code Ann. tit. 19, § 709B(b)(1)–(2) (West 2017)); Massachusetts Pay Equity Act, Mass. Gen. Laws ch. 149, §105A(c)(2) (2016); Or. Rev. Stat. Ann. § 652.220(c) (West 2017); N.Y.C., N.Y., Admin Code § 8-107(25)(b) (1)–(2) (2017); Phila., Pa., Code § 9-1131(2)(a)–(c) (2017); Puerto

Rico Equal Pay Act, 2017 P.R. Laws Act 16 (2017) (prohibiting employers from seeking salary history of job applicants).

34   Rodger Buehler, Dale Griffin, & Michael Ross, *Exploring the Planning Fallacy: Why People Underestimate Their Tasks Completion Times*, 67 J. PERSONALITY & SOC. PSYCHOL. 366 (1994).

35   Cynthia M. Marlowe, Sandra L. Schneider, & Carnot E. Nelson, *Gender and Attractiveness Biases in Hiring Decisions: Are More Experienced Managers Less Biased?*, 81 J. APPLIED PSYCHOL. 1, 11–21 (1996).

36   *See* SHELL, *supra* note 1, at 223.

37   *See* Michael Wheeler, *Swimming with Saints/Praying with Sharks, in* WHAT'S FAIR, *supra* note 28.

38   *See id.* at XXXIX (citing Cialdini, 1993).

39   Art Hinshaw & Jess K. Alberts, *Doing the Right Thing: An Empirical Study of Attorney Negotiation Ethics*, 16 HARV. NEGOT. L. REV. 95, 98 (2011) (describing implementation of Rule 4.1(b)).

40   *Id.* at 161.

41   *Id.*

Chapter 12

1   *See* Lowell H. Brown, *The Corporate Director's Compliance Oversight Responsibility in the Post-Caremark Era*, 26 DEL. J. CORP. L. 1, 85, 107, 142–43 (2001).

2   *Id.*

3   *See* Susan Lorde Martin, *Compliance Officers: More Jobs, More Responsibility, More Liability*, 29 NOTRE DAME J.L. ETHICS & PUB. POL'Y. 169, 173–74 (2015) (citing Stephen L. Cohen, Assoc. Dir. of Enforcement, SEC, Remarks at SCCE's (Society of Corporate Compliance and Ethics) Annual Compliance & Ethics Institute (Oct. 7, 2013)).

4   *See id.*

5   *See id.* at 174.

6   *See* Brown, *supra* note 1, at 115–18.

7   *See* Martin, *supra* note 3, at 174.

8   *See Hearings and Appeals*, U.S. SOC. SEC. ADMIN., http://www.ssa.gov/appeals.

9   *See What We Do*, FED. COMM. COMM'N, https://www.fcc.gov/about-fcc/what-we-do.

10   *See About the FTC*, U.S. FED. TRADE COMM'N, https://www.ftc.gov/about-ftc.

11 *See What We Do*, U.S. Sec. Exch. Comm'n, https://www.sec.gov/about/what-we-do.

12 *See The Commission*, U.S. Commodity Futures Trading Comm'n, https://www.cftc.gov/About/AboutTheCommission.

13 *See Mission*, Financial Crimes Enforcement Network (FinCEN), https://www.fincen.gov/about/mission.

14 *See About Us*, Office of the Comptroller of the Currency, https://www.occ.treas.gov/about/index-about.html.

15 *See About Us*, Dep't of Labor, Wage & Hour Division, https://www.dol.gov/agencies/whd/about.

16 *See What We Do*, Nat'l Labor Relations Bd., https://www.nlrb.gov/about-nlrb/what-we-do.

17 *See Office of Foreign Assets Control- Sanctions Programs and Information*, U.S. Dep't of the Treasury, https://home.treasury.gov/policy-issues/office-of-foreign-assets-control-sanctions-programs-and-information.

18 *See Examinations and Enforcement*, Internal Revenue Serv., https://www.irs.gov/retirement-plans/examinations-and-enforcement.

19 *See About DHS*, U.S. Dep't of Homeland Sec., https://www.dhs.gov/about-dhs.

20 *See About the U.S. Department of State*, U.S. Dep't of State, https://www.state.gov/about/about-the-u-s-department-of-state/.

21 *See What We Do*, U.S. Food & Drug Admin., https://www.fda.gov/about-fda/what-we-do.

22 *See About HHS*, U.S. Dep't of Health & Human Servs., https://www.hhs.gov/about/index.html.

23 *See We're Putting Patients First*, Ctrs. for Medicare & Medicaid Servs., https://www.cms.gov/.

24 *See About VA*, U.S. Dep't of Veterans Affairs, https://www.va.gov/ABOUT_VA/index.asp.

25 *See About NHTSA*, Nat'l Highway Traffic Safety Admin., https://www.nhtsa.gov/about-nhtsa.

26 *See About NIST*, Nat'l Inst. of Standards & Tech., https://www.nist.gov/about-nist.

27 *See Office of Management and Budget*, White House, https://www.whitehouse.gov/omb/.

28 *See Office of Management and Budget: Information and Regulatory Affairs*, WHITE HOUSE, https://www.whitehouse.gov/omb/information-regulatory-affairs/.

29 *See About Us*, U.S. GEN. SERVS. ADMIN., https://www.gsa.gov/about-us.

30 *See About DLA*, DEF. LOGISTICS AGENCY, https://www.dla.mil/AboutDLA/.

31 *See About the National Science Foundation*, NAT'L SCI. FOUND., https://www.nsf.gov/about/.

32 *See What Is the MSC?*, MARINE STEWARDSHIP COUNCIL, https://www.msc.org/en-us/about-the-msc/what-is-the-msc?gclid=Cj0KCQjwuL_8BRCXARIsAGiC51ANqA3lwMkrp7HRv81wfygwlq73Wj2NiPnVg7GYJ5Gr0fomixJewsMaAlMUEALw_wcB.

33 *See The Children's Advertising Review Unit (CARU)*, BBB NAT'L PROGRAMS, https://bbbprograms.org/programs/all-programs/caru.

34 *See Self-Regulation Leadership & Support*, BBB NAT'L PROGRAMS, https://bbbprograms.org/self-regulation-leadership-and-support.

35 *See About NERC*, NORTH AMERICAN ELECTRIC RELIABILITY CORPORATION (NERC), https://www.nerc.com/AboutNERC/Pages/default.aspx.

36 *See About FINRA*, FINANCIAL INDUSTRY REGULATORY AUTHORITY, INC. (FINRA), https://www.finra.org/about.

37 *See Model Rules of Professional Conduct*, AM. BAR ASS'N (ABA), https://www.americanbar.org/groups/professional_responsibility/publications/model_rules_of_professional_conduct/.

38 *See e.g.*, William D. White, *Professional Self-Regulation in Medicine*, AMA J. ETHICS (Apr. 2014), https://journalofethics.ama-assn.org/article/professional-self-regulation-medicine/2014-04.

39 *See* Martin, *supra* note 3, at 174.

40 *See* DANIEL P. WESTMAN & NANCY M. MODESITT, WHISTLEBLOWING: THE LAW OF RETALIATORY DISCHARGE 46–47 (2004).

41 *See id.*

42 *See id.*

43 *See* 17 C.F.R. § 240.21F-17(a) (stating that no person can prevent an individual from communicating directly with the SEC about a securities law violation).

44   *See* Westman & Modesitt, *supra* note 40, at 46–47.

45   *See* Amelia T. Rudolph, *If a Whistleblower Blows In-House, Does It Still Make a Sound? Issues Regarding Internal Whistleblowers Under Dodd–Frank (Part 2)*, 62:5 Prac. Law. 22, 26 (Oct. 2016).

46   *See* Digital Realty Trust, Inc. v. Somers, 138 S. Ct. 767, 778 (U.S. 2018) (holding that individuals must report externally to SEC within 180 days under Sarbanes–Oxley protections, even if they previously reported internally to obtain whistleblower protections).

47   *See* 17 C.F.R. § 240.21F-4(c).

48   *See Environmental Whistleblowers FAQ*, Nat'l Whistleblower Ctr. (NWC), https://www.whistleblowers.org/faq/environmen tal-whistleblowers-faq/.

49   *See File a Complaint*, Occupational Safety & Health Admin. (OSHA), U.S. Dep't of Labor, https://www.osha.gov/workers/ file_complaint.html

50   *See, e.g.*, Cooney v. Bob Evans Farms, Inc., 645 F. Supp. 2d 620, 634 (E.D. Mich. 2009) (holding that an employee who threatened an employer with reporting legal violations to keep her job was not a protected whistleblower because she engaged in a protected activity for an improper purpose).

51   *See False Claims Act/ Qui Tam FAQ*, NWC, https://www.whistle blowers.org/faq/false-claims-act-qui-tam-faq/.

52   *See* 18 U.S.C. §1344; 18 U.S.C. § 3293(1) (2019).

53   *See* 15 U.S.C. 78i(e) (2019).

54   *See Top Ten Things You Should Know Before You Blow the Whistle*, Whistleblower Protection Blog, Mar. 9, 2013, https://www. whistleblowersblog.org/2011/03/articles/news/top-ten-things-you-should-know-before-you-blow-the-whistle/.

55   *See The Whistleblower Protection Programs, Statutes*, U.S. Dep't of Labor, https://www.whistleblowers.gov/statutes.

56   *See Office of the Whistleblower: Submit a Tip*, U.S. Sec. & Exch. Comm'n, https://www.sec.gov/whistleblower/submit-a-tip.

57   *See Report Fraud*, Fed. Trade Comm'n, https://reportfraud.ftc. gov/#/.

58   *See Reporting Resources: EPA Hotlines*, Envtl. Prot. Agency (EPA), https://www.epa.gov/home/epa-hotlines.

59   *See Submit a Tip*, U.S. Commodity Futures Trading Comm'n, http://www.cftc.gov/ConsumerProtection/FileaTiporCompla int/index.htm.

60 *See* Commodity Futures Trading Comm'n, www.cftc.gov.

61 *See Tax Fraud Alerts,* Internal Revenue Serv. (IRS), https://
www.irs.gov/compliance/criminal-investigation/tax-fraud-
alerts.

62 *See Complaint Form,* U.S. Dep't of Energy, https://www.energy.
gov/ig/complaint-form.

63 *See How to File a Complaint with the FEC,* Fed. Election Comm'n,
https://www.fec.gov/legal-resources/enforcement/complaints-
process/how-to-file-complaint-with-fec/.

64 *See How Consumers Can Report an Adverse Event or Serious Problem
to FDA,* U.S. Food & Drug Admin., https://www.fda.gov/saf
ety/reporting-serious-problems-fda/how-consumers-can-report-
adverse-event-or-serious-problem-fda.

65 *See Electronic Consumer Complaint Form,* U.S. Dep't of Agric.,
https://foodcomplaint.fsis.usda.gov/eCCF/.

66 *See What We Investigate,* Fed. Bureau of Investigation (FBI),
https://www.fbi.gov/investigate.

67 *See Our Investigative Mission,* U.S. Secret Serv., https://www.
secretservice.gov/investigation/.

68 *See Duties,* U.S. Marshals Serv., https://www.usmarshals.gov/
careers/duties.html.

69 *See What We Do,* Bureau of Alcohol, Tobacco, Firearms, &
Explosives, https://www.atf.gov/about/what-we-do.

70 *See Mission,* U.S. Drug Enforcement Admin., https://www.dea.
gov/mission.

71 *See Mission,* U.S. Transp. Sec. Admin., https://www.tsa.gov/
about/tsa-mission.

72 *See Report a Crime,* U.S. Dep't of Just., https://www.justice.gov/
actioncenter/report-crime.

73 *See* Ruth Ann Strickland, *Whistleblowers,* The First Amendment
Encyclopedia, https://www.mtsu.edu/first-amendment/
article/1029/whistleblowers (stating that whistleblowers can
anonymously inform the press of wrongdoing and the press can
report on it, protecting the whistleblower from retaliation).

74 *See* 31 U.S.C. § 3730(d).

75 *See* U.S. Sec. & Exch. Comm'n, 2016 Annual Report to
Congress on the Dodd–Frank Whistleblower Program, 3, 8,
https://www.sec.gov/whistleblower/reportspubs/annual-repo
rts/owb-annual-report-2016.pdf [hereinafter SEC 2016 Annual
Report].

76 *See id.*
77 *See SEC Office of the Whistleblower Hotline,* U.S. SEC. & EXCH. COMM'N, http://www.sec.gov/whistleblower (providing the phone number of (202) 551–4790).
78 *See* ASSOCIATION OF CERTIFIED FRAUD EXAMINERS, REPORT TO THE NATIONS ON OCCUPATIONAL FRAUD AND ABUSE—2016 GLOBAL FRAUD STUDY 26, https://www.acfe.com/rttn2016/docs/2016-report-to-the-nations.pdf.
79 *See* DLA PIPER, WHISTLEBLOWING—AN EMPLOYER'S GUIDE TO GLOBAL COMPLIANCE 38 (2d ed. June 23, 2015), https://www.dlapiper.com/en/us/insights/publications/2015/06/whistle blowing-law-2015/.
80 *See* Press Release, Sec. & Exch. Comm'n, SEC Adds Clarity, Efficiency and Transparency to Its Successful Whistleblower Award Program (Sept. 23, 2020), https://www.sec.gov/news/press-release/2020-219.
81 *See* Upjohn Co. v. United States 449 U.S. 383 (1981).
82 *See Sarbanes–Oxley (SOX) FAQ,* NWC, https://www.whistleblow ers.org/faq/sarbanes-oxley-sox-faq/.
83 *See id.*
84 *See* SEC 2016 ANNUAL REPORT, *supra* note 75, at 4.
85 *See* Dodd–Frank Wall Street Reform and Consumer Protection Act of 2010, H.R. REP. No. 4173-466, § 21F(b)(1) (limiting awards to between 10% and 30% of what the SEC recovers).
86 *See* Press Release, U.S. Sec. & Exch. Comm'n, SEC Announces Largest-Ever Whistleblower Award (Sept. 22, 2014), https://www.sec.gov/news/press-release/2014-206 [hereinafter 2014 Press Release].
87 *See* Geoff Schwaller, *SEC Issues $114 Million Whistleblower Award—The Largest in SEC History,* WHISTLEBLOWER NEWS NETWORK, Oct 22, 2020.
88 *See* 2014 Press Release, *supra* note 86.
89 *See* Dodd–Frank Wall Street Reform and Consumer Protection Act of 2010, H.R. REP. No. 4173-466, § 21F(b)(1) (limiting awards to between 10% and 30% of what the SEC recovers); 2014 Press Release, *supra* note 86.
90 *See, e.g.,* Adam Waytz, James Dungan & Liane Young, *The Whistleblower's Dilemma and the Fairness–Loyalty Tradeoff,* 49 J. EXPERIMENTAL SOC. PSYCHOL. 6, 1027 (2013); Aaron S. Kesselheim, David Studddart & Michelle M. Mello, *Whistleblower*

Experiences in Fraud Litigation Against Pharmaceutical Companies,
326 New Eng. J. Med. 1832 (2010).

91 Kesselheim, *supra* note 90.

92 *Id.*

93 *Id.*

94 *Id.*

95 *Id.* at 1835 tbl. 2 (quoting Relator 5) (2010).

96 *Id.* (quoting Relator 6) (2010).

97 *Id.*

98 *Id.* at 1838 tbl. 4 (quoting Relator 9).

99 *See* Eric Ben-Artz, *Opinion: We Must Protect Shareholders from
    Executive Wrongdoing,* Fin. Times, Aug. 18, 2016.

100 *Id.*

101 *Id.*

102 *Id.*

103 *See* U.S. Sec. & Exch. Comm'n, 2017 Annual Report to
    Congress: Whistleblower Program, 10, 23 (Nov. 15, 2017),
    https://www.sec.gov/files/sec-2017-annual-report-whistleblo
    wer-program.pdf [hereinafter SEC 2017 Annual Report].

104 *See id.* (assuming each of the 12 individuals were counted for
    one tip).

105 *See generally id.*

106 *See generally id.*; *Office of the Whistleblower: Claim an Award, Notice
    of Covered Actions,* U.S. Sec. & Exch. Comm'n, https://www.sec.
    gov/whistleblower/claim-award

107 *See* SEC 2017 Annual Report, *supra* note 103, at 13–15.

108 17 C.F.R. § 240.21F-4(a) (2021).

109 17 C.F.R. § 240.21F-4(b).

110 17 C.F.R. § 240.21F-4(c).

111 *See* 17 C.F.R. § 240.21F-4(b)(4)(iii)(B).

112 *See* 17 C.F.R. § 240.21F-4(b)(4)(iii)(A).

113 *See* Patricia Patrick, *Be Prepared Before You Blow the Whistle,*
    Oct. 2010, http://www.acfe.com/article.aspx?id = 4294968
    656&terms=(fraud + prevention).

114 Richard Moberly, *Sarbanes–Oxley's Whistleblower Provisions: Ten
    Years Later,* 64 S.C. L. Rev. 1, 19–20, n.116 (2012).

115 *See* Patrick, *supra* note 113.

116 Elisa Batista, *Dubinsky's 15 Lessons for Success,*
    Wired, Nov. 13, 2001, www.wired.com/2001/11/
    dubinskys-15-lessons-for-success.

117 *Id.*
118 *Id.*
119 *See* DavisPolk, Recent Developments in Whistleblower Protections: Legal Analysis and Practical Implications 14 (June 9, 2014), https://www.davispolk.com/files/06.09.14.Rec ent.Developments.in_.Whistleblower.Protections.pdf.
120 *See, e.g.*, Press Release, U.S. Dep't of Labor, OSHA News Release—Region 4, U.S. Labor Department Orders Tennessee Commerce Bank to Reinstate Whistleblower and Pay More Than $1 Million in Back Wages and Other Relief (Mar. 18, 2010), https://www.osha.gov/news/newsreleases/region4/03182010.
121 *See OSHA Fact Sheet: OSHA's Whistleblower Protection Program,* Occupational Safety & Health Admin., https://www.osha. gov/Publications/OSHA3638.pdf.
122 *See* Westman & Modesitt, *supra* note 40, at 231 (citing 18 U.S.C. § 1514(a)).
123 *See id.* at 249 (2004); DavisPolk, *supra* note 119.
124 *See, e.g.*, U.S. ex rel. Brown v. Aramark Corp., 591 F. Supp. 2d 68, 77 (D.D.C. 2008) (holding that an employer cannot possess retaliatory intent if they did not know employee was investigating fraud).
125 *See, e.g.*, U.S. ex rel. Yesudian v. Howard University, 153 F.3d 731, 743 (D.C. Cir. 1998).
126 Paul H. Tobias, Whistleblower Protection Statutes, LITWDCS §2:106.
127 *OSHA Fact Sheet: Your Rights As a Whistleblower*, Occupational Health & Safety Admin. (OSHA), 1, https://www.osha.gov/ OshDoc/data_General_Facts/whistleblower_rights.pdf.
128 *Id.*
129 *See OSHA Fact Sheet: Your Rights As a Whistleblower, supra* note 127.
130 *See* Westman & Modesitt, *supra* note 40, at 232.
131 *See* Ethics & Compliance Initiative (ECI), 2016 Global Business Ethics Survey: Measuring Risk and Promoting Workplace Integrity 2, https://www.ethics.org/wp-content/ uploads/2018/09/GBESFinal-1.pdf.
132 *See* Westman & Modesitt, *supra* note 40, at 232.
133 *In re* Davis v. United Airlines, Inc., 2001-AIR-5, at 4 (ARB Apr. 25, 2002); Westman & Modesitt, *supra* note 40, at 232 (quoting *In re*

Davis v. United Airlines, Inc., 2001-AIR-5, at 4 (ARB Apr. 25, 2002)) (other internal citations omitted).

134   *In re Davis*, 2001-AIR-5, at 4; Westman & Modesitt, *supra* note 40, at 232 (quoting *In re Davis*) (other internal citations omitted).

135   *In re Davis*, 2001-AIR-5, at 4; Westman & Modesitt, *supra* note 40, at 232 (quoting *In re Davis*) (other internal citations omitted).

136   *See OSHA FactSheet: OSHA's Whistleblower Protection Program*, *supra* note 121.

137   *See* Moberly, *supra* note 114, at 8–9.

138   *See* Mount Healthy City Sch. Dist. Bd. of Educ. v. Doyle, 429 U.S. 275, 281–82, 287 (1977).

139   *See* N.L.R.B. v. Local 1229, Int'l Bhd. of Elec. Workers, 346 U.S. 464, 471, 475 (1953) (holding that protestors disparaging business practices and products are not protected from firing).

140   Moberly, *supra* note 114, at 8–9.

141   *See* DavisPolk, *supra* note 119, at 11.

142   *See, e.g.*, U.S. ex rel. Ruhe v. Masimo Corp., 929 F. Supp. 2d 1033, 1039 (C.D. Cal. 2012) (holding that strong public policy considerations demand protection of whistleblowers' contractual liability for violating nondisclosure agreement when they report fraud); U.S. v. Mount Sinai Hospital, 2015 WL 7076092, at *6 (S.D.N.Y. Nov. 9, 2015).

143   *See* State Farm Fire & Cas. Co. v. U.S. ex rel. Rigsby, 137 S. Ct. 436 (U.S. 2016); *Huge Win for Whistleblowers With Unanimous Supreme Court Decision*, NWC, Dec. 6, 2016, https://www.whistleblowers. org/component/content/article/88-general/1714-huge-win-for-whistleblowers-with-unanimous-supreme-court-decision-.

144   *See* Exchange Act Rule 21F-17(a)(2019) ("No person may take any action to impede an individual from communicating directly with the Commission staff about a possible securities law violation, including enforcing, or threating to enforce, a confidentiality agreement . . . with respect to such communications."); *see also* Amelia T. Rudolph, *If a Whistle Blows In-House, Does It Still Make A Sound? Issues Regarding Internal Whistleblowers Under Dodd–Frank (Part 2)*, 62 No. 5 Prac. Law. 22, 30 (Oct. 2016).

145   *See* Amelia T. Rudolph, *If a Whistle Blows In-House, Does It Still Make A Sound? Issues Regarding Internal Whistleblowers Under Dodd–Frank (Part 2)*, 62:5 Prac. Law. 22, 30 (Oct. 2016).

146 *See* DLA Piper, A Study by DLA Piper's Employment
     Group. Whistleblowing –An Employer's Guide to Global
     Compliance 39 (2d ed. 2015), https://www.dlapiper.com/~/
     media/Files/.../Whistleblowing_Law_Report_2015.pdf.

147 *See* Rudolph, *supra* note 145, at 34.

148 *See id.* at 30; DLA Piper, *supra* note 146.

149 *See* Jeffrey R. Boles, Leora F. Eisenstadt & Jennifer M. Pacella,
     Whistleblowing in the Compliance Era, 55 Ga. L. Rev. 147 *passim*
     (2020) (describing the difficult job landscape for whistleblowers
     going forward, and proposing modest legal solutions).

150 *See* Joyce Russell, *Career Coach: Advice for Whistleblowers and Job
     Seekers*, Wash. Post, Aug. 26, 2012, https://www.washingtonp
     ost.com/business/capitalbusiness/career-coach-advice-for-whi
     stleblowers-and-job-seekers/2012/08/24/ad770d7e-ecb6-11e1-
     b09d-07d971dee30a_story.html?utm_term=.ce1e6fa722d4.

151 *See also* Karen L. Soeken, *A Survey of Whistleblowers: Their Stressor
     and Coping Strategies*, Integrity Int'l, https://www.whistleblo
     wer-net.de/pdf/Soeken.pdf.

152 *See* NWC, www.whistleblowers.org.

153 *See Find a Whistleblower Attorney*, NWC, https://www.whistle
     blowers.org/find-a-whisteblower-attorney/.

154 *See Choosing a Whistleblower Lawyer*, Phillips & Cohen LLP,
     https://www.phillipsandcohen.com/whistleblower-resources/
     tips-for-choosing-whistleblower-lawyer/.

155 *Top Ten Things You Should Know Before You Blow the Whistle*,
     Whistleblower Protection Blog, Mar. 9, 2011, https://www.
     whistleblowersblog.org/2011/03/articles/news/top-ten-things-
     you-should-know-before-you-blow-the-whistle/.

156 *See, e.g.*, J.S. Nelson, *Disclosure-Driven Crime*, 52 U.C. Davis
     L. Rev. 1487, 1544–45 (2019) (describing the compliance system
     inside Volkswagen); *see also* Matt Egan, *More Wells Fargo Workers
     Allege Retaliation for Whistleblowing*, CNN Money, Nov. 7, 2017
     (noting a "common thread at Wells Fargo where scandals are
     often accompanied by worker retaliation claims"); Matt Egan,
     Wells Fargo Admits to Signs of Worker Retaliation, CNN Money, Jan.
     24, 2017 (describing retaliation at Wells Fargo after employees
     identified themselves through the company's ethics hotline).

157 *See Top Ten Things You Should Know*, *supra* note 155.

Chapter 13

1   *See Workers Prefer Ethical Company to Higher Pay*, WORKSPAN MAG.,
    Mar. 2007, https://www.worldatwork.org/workspan/Pubs/
    News_and_Notes-Employees_Prefer_Ethical_Company_to_Hig
    her_Pay.pdf.

2   *See Report to the Nations on Occupational Fraud and Abuse—2016
    Global Fraud Study*, ASSOCIATION OF CERTIFIED FRAUD EXAMINERS
    at 4 (2016), https://www.acfe.com/rttn2016/docs/2016-report-
    to-the-nations.pdf (hereinafter "ACFE Report").

3   *See Leading Corporate Integrity: Defining the Role of the Chief Ethics
    & Compliance Officer (CECO)*, ETHICS RESOURCE CENTER (2007),
    http://www.corporate-ethics.org/pdf/Leading_Corporate_I
    ntegrity_Report.pdf.

4   U.S. SENT'G COMM'N, U.S. SENT'G GUIDELINES MANUAL § 8B2.1
    (2018).

5   *Id.* at § 8B2.1(a).

6   *Id.*

7   *Id.*

8   *Id.* at § 8B2.1(b)(2)(B) (emphasis added).

9   *Id.* at § 8B2.1(b)(2)(C).

10 *Id.*

11 *Id.* at Application Notes, 1. Definitions.

12 *Id.* at § 8B2.1(b)(4)(A).

13 *Id.* at § 8B2.1(b)(5)(A).

14 *Id.* at § 8B2.1(b)(5)(B).

15 *Id.* at § 8B2.1(b)(5)(C).

16 *Id.* at § 8B2.1(b)(6).

17 *Id.* at § 8B2.1(b)(7).

18 *Id.* at § 8B2.1(c).

19 *Id.* at Commentary, 2. Factors to Consider in Meeting
    Requirements of this Guideline at (D).

20 *Id.* at § 8B2.1 Commentary 2. Factors to Consider in Meeting
    Requirements of this Guideline at (B).

21 *Id.* at § 8B2.1 Commentary 2. Factors to Consider in Meeting
    Requirements of this Guideline at (C)(ii).

22 *Id.*

23 *Id.*

24 *Id.*

25 *Id.*

26 *Id.*

27 *Id.*

28 *Id.*

29 *See* U.S. Dep't of Just., *Evaluation of Compliance Programs*, June 1, 2020, https://www.justice.gov/criminal-fraud/page/file/937 501/download.

30 *See generally*, Aisling O'Shea, Nicholas Bourtin & Anthony Lewis, *DOJ Updates Guidance on the Evaluation of Corporate Compliance Programs*, Harv. L. Sch. Forum on Corp. Gov't, June 20, 2020.

31 *Evaluation of Compliance Programs*, *supra* note 29, at 2 (emphasis added).

32 *Id.*

33 *Id.*

34 *Id. passim.*

35 *Id.* at 3.

36 *Id.*

37 *Id.*

38 *Id.*

39 *Id.*

40 *Id.*

41 *Id.* at 4.

42 *See id.*

43 *Id.*

44 *Id.* at 4–5.

45 *Id.* at 5.

46 *Id.*

47 *Id.* at 5–6.

48 *Id.* at 6.

49 *Id.*

50 *Id.*

51 *Id.*

52 *Id.*

53 *Id.*

54 *Id.* at 7.

55 *See id.* at 6–7.

56 *Id.* at 7.

57 *Id.* at 8.

58 *Id.*

59 *See id.*

60 *Id.* at 9.

61 *Id.*

62   *Id.* at 9–14.

63   *Id.* at 9.

64   *Id.*

65   *Id.* at 10.

66   *Id.*

67   *Id.*

68   *Id.*

69   *Id.*

70   *Id.*

71   *Id.*

72   *Id.* at 11.

73   *Id.*

74   *See id.* at 12–13.

75   *See id.* at 13.

76   *Id.*

77   *Id.* at 14.

78   *Id.*

79   *Id.* (quoting Justice Manual (JM) 9-28.300) (emphasis added);
      accord U.S. Dep't of Just., Principles of Federal Prosecution
      of Business Organizations (Justice Manual) § 9-28.300
      (updated July 2020), https://www.justice.gov/jm/jm-9-28000-
      principles-federal-prosecution-business-organizations.

80   Principles of Federal Prosecution of Business
      Organizations§ 9-28.300, *supra* note 79.

81   *Evaluation of Compliance Programs, supra* note 29, at 14.

82   *Id.* at 15–18.

83   *Id.* at 15–16.

84   *Id.* at 16.

85   *Id.*

86   *Id.*

87   *Id..*

88   *Id.*

89   *See id.* at 17–18.

90   *Id.* at 18.

91   *Id.*

92   *See About ECI,* Ethics and Compliance Initiative, https://
      www.ethics.org/about/.

93   Ethics & Compliance Initiative, *Best Practices Series: Using
      Your Organization's Performance Evaluation System to Drive Ethical
      Conduct* 10 (2018).

94 *Id.* at 15.

95 *Id.* at 14.

96 *Id.* (describing the research findings of Professor Lisa Ordóñez and her colleagues' 2009 Harvard Business Review Working Paper).

97 *Id.*

98 *See id.* at 15 (paraphrasing Professor Lisa Ordóñez and her colleagues' work).

99 *See* Lisa D. Ordóñez et al., *Goals Gone Wild: The Systematic Side Effects of Overprescribing Goal Setting*, 23 ACAD. OF MGMT. PERSPECTIVES 6–16 (2009).

100 *Goals Gone Wild: How Aggressive Goal Setting Can Lead to Unethical Behavior*, ETHICAL SYSTEMS, https://www.ethicalsystems.org/goals-gone-wild/ (making even more accessible Professor Lisa Ordóñez and her colleagues' work).

101 *Id.*

102 *Id.*

103 *Id.*

104 *Id.*

105 *Id.*

106 *Id.*

107 *See Ethics Pays: How an Investment in Ethics Translates to Profit, Productivity, & Prestige*, ETHICAL SYSTEMS, https://www.ethicalsystems.org/ethics-pays-2/.

108 *See id.*

109 *Id.*

110 *Id.*

111 LYNN A. STOUT, THE SHAREHOLDER VALUE MYTH: HOW PUTTING SHAREHOLDERS FIRST HARMS INVESTORS, CORPORATIONS, AND THE PUBLIC (2012).

112 *See Ethics Pays, supra* note 107.

113 *Nudging for Ethics: Applying Small Changes to Promote Ethical Outcomes*, ETHICAL SYSTEMS, https://www.ethicalsystems.org/nudging-for-ethics/.

114 *See* RICHARD H. THALER & CASS R. SUNSTEIN, NUDGE: IMPROVING DECISIONS ABOUT HEALTH, WEALTH, AND HAPPINESS (2008).

115 *See Nudging for Ethics, supra* note 113.

116 *Id.*

117 *Id.*

118 *Id.*

119 *Id.*

120 *Why Have a Code of Conduct*, Ethics and Compliance Initiative, https://www.ethics.org/resources/free-toolkit/code-of-conduct/.

121 *See* Sarbanes–Oxley Act of 2002, Pub. L. 107–204, 116 Stat. 745, § 406; *see also Final Rule: Disclosure Required by Sections 406 and 407 of the Sarbanes–Oxley Act of 2002; Rel. No. 33-8177, File No. S7-40-02*, U.S. Sec. & Exch. Comm'n II.B.1.c, https://www.sec.gov/rules/final/33-8177a.htm ("The final rules require a company to disclose whether it has adopted a code of ethics that applies to the registrant's principal executive officer, principal financial officer, principal accounting officer or controller, or persons performing similar functions. If the company has not adopted such a code of ethics, it must explain why it has not done so.").

122 *See Why Have a Code of Conduct, supra* note 120.

123 *See Common Code Provisions*, Ethics and Compliance Initiative, https://www.ethics.org/resources/free-toolkit/code-provisions/; *see also generally Final Rule: Disclosure, supra* note 121 ("The final rule defines the term 'code of ethics' as written standards that are reasonably designed to deter wrongdoing and to promote:

• Honest and ethical conduct, including the ethical handling of actual or apparent conflicts of interest between personal and professional relationships;

• Full, fair, accurate, timely, and understandable disclosure in reports and documents that a registrant files with, or submits to, the Commission and in other public communications made by the registrant;

• Compliance with applicable governmental laws, rules, and regulations;

• The prompt internal reporting to an appropriate person or persons identified in the code of violations of the code; and

• Accountability for adherence to the code.") (internal citations omitted).

124 *Common Code Provisions, supra* note 123.

125 *2018 Global Business Ethics Survey*, Ethics & Compliance Initiative, https://www.ethics.org/knowledge-center/2018-gbes-2/ (quoting Emmanuel Lulin, SVP & Chief Ethics Officer, L'Oréal).

126 *See generally, e.g.*, Ethics & Compliance Initiative, ECI Working Group Paper: Respectful Workplace (2018) (describing these topics as central to a respectful workplace).

127 *Definition of Values*, Ethics and Compliance Initiative, https://www.ethics.org/resources/free-toolkit/definition-values/ (definition of "Comprehensive Ethics and Compliance Program").

128 *Id.* (definition of "Effective (or Well-Implemented) Ethics and Compliance Program").

129 *Id.*

130 *Id.* (definition of "Ethics Culture").

131 Ethics & Compliance Initiative, Principles and Practices of High-Quality Ethics and Compliance Programs (2016).

132 Ethics & Compliance Initiative, High-Quality Ethics & Compliance Program Measurement Framework 3 (2018).

133 *Id.*

134 *Id.*

135 *Id.*

136 *Id.*

137 *Id.* at iii.

138 *Id.*

139 *Id.* at 7.

140 *Id.* at 9.

141 *Id.*

142 *Id.*

143 *Id.*

144 *Id.* at 11.

145 *Id.* The authors of this text have changed the order of the ECI's list, but we retain its original items and meaning.

146 *Id.*

147 Ethics & Compliance Initiative, ECI Working Group Paper: Hotlines and Investigations 15 (2019).

148 High-Quality Ethics, *supra* note 132, at 13. Again, the authors of this text have changed the order of the ECI's list, but we retain its original items and meaning.

149 *Id.* at 13 (same).

150 E.H. Schein, Organizational Culture and Leadership (1992); Ethics & Compliance Initiative, Report of ECI's Blue Ribbon Panel 11, Dec. 2, 2015, https://higherlogicdownload.s3.amazon

aws.com/THEECOA/1651fdd3-e31c-4ac8-a93d-9b99f9e75727/
UploadedImages/certification/finalBRPReport.pdf.

151 *See* SCHEIN, *supra* note 150 (1992); REPORT OF ECI's BLUE RIBBON
     PANEL, *supra note* 150, at 6.

152 *See* REPORT OF ECI's BLUE RIBBON PANEL *supra* note 150, at 11.

153 *See* ETHICS & COMPLIANCE INITIATIVE, THE IMPACT OF
     ORGANIZATIONAL VALUES AND ETHICAL LEADERSHIP ON
     MISCONDUCT: A GLOBAL LOOK, 2019 GLOBAL BUSINESS ETHICS
     SURVEY 7 (2019).

154 *See* ETHICS & COMPLIANCE INITIATIVE, WORKPLACE MISCONDUCT
     AND REPORTING: A GLOBAL LOOK, 2019 GLOBAL BUSINESS ETHICS
     SURVEY 4 (2019).

155 *Id.* at 3.

156 *Id.*

157 *Id.*

158 *Id.*

159 *Id.*

160 *See id.* at 5.

161 *See id.*

162 *See id.*

163 *See id.*

164 *See id.*

165 *See id.*

166 *See* ETHICS & COMPLIANCE INITIATIVE, INCREASING REPORTING
     FREE FROM RETALIATION (2013) www.ethics.org/knowledge-
     center/increasing-employee-reporting-free-from-retaliation/.

167 *See* WORKPLACE MISCONDUCT AND REPORTING, *supra* note
     154, at 7.

168 *See id.*

169 *See Stronger Cultures Reduce Risks*, ETHICS & COMPLIANCE
     INITIATIVE, July 2018, https://www.ethics.org/knowledge-cen
     ter/ethicsstat/.

170 *See Pressure to Bend Rules?*, ETHICS & COMPLIANCE INITIATIVE,
     Apr. 2019, https://www.ethics.org/knowledge-center/eth
     icsstat/.

171 *See id.*

172 *See id.*

173 *See id.*

174 *See id.*

175 *See id.*

176 *See* IMPACT OF ORGANIZATIONAL VALUES, *supra* note 153, at 6.

177 *Id.* at 5.

178 *See id.*

179 *See id* at 7.

Chapter 14

1 *What Do E&C Departments Communicate?*, ETHICS & COMPLIANCE INITIATIVE, Feb. 2018, https://www.ethics.org/knowledge-center/ethicsstat/.

2 *Speak Up Culture: Designing Organizational Cultures that Encourage Employee Voice*, ETHICAL SYSTEMS, https://www.ethicalsystems.org/speak-up-culture/.

3 ETHICS & COMPLIANCE INITIATIVE, GLOBAL DIFFERENCES IN EMPLOYEES' VIEWS OF E&C PROGRAM MATURITY: 2019 GLOBAL BUSINESS ETHICS SURVEY 5 (2019).

4 *Speak Up Culture, supra* note 2.

5 *Id.*

6 *Id.*

7 *Id.*

8 *Id.*

9 *Id.*

10 *Id.* (describing finding of the organization's 2019 Global Ethics Survey).

11 *Id.*

12 *See id.*

13 *Increasing Employee Reporting Free from Retaliation: A Research Report from the National Business Ethics Survey*, ETHICS & COMPLIANCE INITIATIVE, https://www.ethics.org/knowledge-center/increasing-employee-reporting-free-from-retaliation/.

14 *See Speak Up Culture, supra* note 2.

15 *Id.*

16 *Id.*

17 *Id.*

18 *Id.*

19 *Are You An Accountable Leader?*, ETHICS & COMPLIANCE INITIATIVE, Feb. 2019, https://www.ethics.org/knowledge-center/ethicsstat/. As an aside, employees who "believe top management blames others are [also] more likely to leave the organization imminently, i.e., in the next 12 months or less." ETHICS & COMPLIANCE INITIATIVE, ETHICAL LEADERSHIP AROUND

THE WORLD—AND WHY IT MATTERS: A RESEARCH REPORT FROM ECI's GLOBAL BUSINESS ETHICS SURVEY 14 (2017).

20 *Are You An Accountable Leader?*, *supra* note 19. The numbers by factor are that, among employees who agree that their "supervisor only cares about meeting targets[,] and not how they got there," 41% observe misconduct within their organizations, versus 18% who do not witness this behavior in their supervisors. *Id.* Among employees who agree that their "supervisor blames others when things go wrong," 45% observe misconduct within their organizations, versus 17% who do not witness this behavior in their supervisors. *Id.* Among employees who agree that "[t]op management blames others when things go wrong," 42% observe misconduct within their organizations, versus 17% who do not witness this behavior in their supervisors. *Id.*

21 *See id.*

22 *See Speak Up Culture, supra* note 2.

23 *Id.*

24 *See Does Your Company Discuss Its Mistakes?*, ETHICS & COMPLIANCE INITIATIVE, Jan. 2019, https://www.ethics.org/knowledge-center/ethicsstat/.

25 *See id.*

26 *See id.*

27 *See id.*

28 *See id.*

29 *Speak Up Culture, supra* note 2.

30 *Id.*

31 *Id.*

32 *See Why Don't Employees Speak Up About Misconduct?*, ETHICS & COMPLIANCE INITIATIVE, Dec. 2018, https://www.ethics.org/knowledge-center/ethicsstat/.

33 *See id.*

34 *See id.*

35 *Id.*

36 *See Want Employees to Stay with Your Organization Longer?*, ETHICS & COMPLIANCE INITIATIVE, June 2020, https://www.ethics.org/knowledge-center/ethicsstat/.

37 *Id.*

38 *See id.*

39 *See id.*

40 *See id.*

41 *Speak Up Culture, supra* note 2.

42 *See* Lawrence White & Huw Jones, *Barclays CEO Fined $1.5 Million for Trying to Unmask Whistleblower*, Reuters, May 11, 2018, https://www.reuters.com/article/us-barclays-ceo-idUSKB N1IC119.

43 *See Speak Up Culture, supra* note 2.

44 White & Jones, *supra* note 42.

45 *Id.*

46 *Retaliation in the Workplace*, Ethics & Compliance Initiative, https://www.ethics.org/knowledge-center/ethicsstat/.

47 *See id.*

48 *See id.*

49 *See* Ethics & Compliance Initiative, Workplace Misconduct and Reporting: A Global Look, 2019 Global Business Ethics Survey 7 (2019).

50 *See id.*

51 *See id.*

52 *See id.*

53 *Retaliation in the Workplace, supra* note 46.

54 *See id.*

55 *See* Workplace Misconduct and Reporting, *supra* note 49, at 6.

56 *See id.*

57 *See id.*

58 *See id.* (the last 2% of reporting is to "other").

59 *See id.*

60 *Retaliation in the Workplace, supra* note 46.

61 *Id.*

62 *Id.*

63 Jeremy Willinger, *Internal Reporting*, Ethical Systems, https://www.ethicalsystems.org/internal-reporting/.

64 *See* Nat'l Whistleblower Ctr., Impact of Qui Tam Laws on Internal Compliance: A Report to the Securities Exchange Commission 5 (2010), https://www.whistleblowers.org/storage/documents/DoddFrank/nwcreporttosecfinal.pdf (describing study of federal qui tam plaintiffs filing between 2007 and 2010).

65 *See* U.S. Sec. & Exch. Comm'n, 2019 Annual Report to Congress: Whistleblowing 18 (2019), https://www.sec.gov/files/sec-2019-annual-report-whistleblower-program.pdf.

66   *See* Aaron S. Kesselheim, David M. Studdert & Michelle M. Mello, *Whistle-Blowers' Experiences in Fraud Litigation Against Pharmaceutical Companies*, 362 New Eng. J. Med. 1832–39 (2010).

67   *Id.* (text and tbl. 2).

68   Adam Waytz, James Dungan & Liane Young, *The Whistleblower's Dilemma and the Fairness–Loyalty Tradeoff*, 49 J. of Experimental Soc. Psychol. 1027–33 (2013).

69   Adam Waytz, *Whistleblowers are Motivated by Moral Reasons Above Monetary Ones*, Pro Market, Aug. 30, 2016, https://promarket.org/2016/08/30/whistleblowers-motivated-moral-reasons-monetary-ones/ (describing early findings of the study then-in-progress, which follows next).

70   James A. Dungan, Liane Young & Adam Waytz, *The Power of Moral Concerns in Predicting Whistleblowing Decisions*, 85 J. Experimental Soc. Psychol. 103848 (2019).

71   *Id.*

72   *See Increasing Employee Reporting, supra* note 13.

73   *See id.*

74   *See id.*

75   *See id.*

76   *See id.*

77   *See id.*

78   *See* U.S. Sec. & Exch. Comm'n, *supra* note 65, at 18.

79   *See id.* at 2.

80   *See id.*

81   *See id.*

82   *Id.* at 1, 3.

83   *See id.* at 1.

84   *See Increasing Employee Reporting, supra* note 13.

85   *See id.*

86   *See id.*

87   *See id.*

88   *See id.*

89   *See id.*

90   *See id.*

91   *See id.*

92   Ethics & Compliance Initiative, ECI Working Group Paper: Respectful Workplace 12 (2018).

93 *State of Ethics in Large Companies*, ETHICS & COMPLIANCE INITIATIVE, https://www.ethics.org/knowledge-center/state-of-ethics-in-large-companies/.

94 *See id.*

95 *See id.*

96 *Ethical Leadership Around the World—and Why It Matters*, ETHICS & COMPLIANCE INITIATIVE, https://www.ethics.org/knowledge-center/ethical-leadership-around-the-world-and-why-it-matters/.

97 *See* ETHICS & COMPLIANCE INITIATIVE, THE IMPACT OF ORGANIZATIONAL VALUES AND ETHICAL LEADERSHIP ON MISCONDUCT: A GLOBAL LOOK, 2019 GLOBAL BUSINESS ETHICS SURVEY 5 (2019).

98 *Id.* at ii. It is interesting to note here that, "[i]n addition to being less positive about the ethical leadership of their top managers and supervisors, non-management employees are also a) less aware of the ethics and compliance resources available[,] and b) less likely to find their organization's . . . programs valuable and effective." *Id.*

99 *See* ETHICAL LEADERSHIP AROUND THE WORLD, *supra* note 19 at 25 (App. G: Employee Level of Beliefs About Supervisors).

100 *See id.* at 25, App. G: Employee Level of Beliefs About Supervisors.

101 *See* ETHICS & COMPLIANCE INITIATIVE, PRESSURE IN THE WORKPLACE: POSSIBLE RISK FACTORS AND THOSE AT RISK, A GLOBAL LOOK, 2020 REPORT #1 GLOBAL BUSINESS ETHICS SURVEY 10 (2020).

102 *See id.* at 10.

103 *See The Impact of Recognizing Ethical Conduct*, ETHICS & COMPLIANCE INITIATIVE, July 2019, https://www.ethics.org/knowledge-center/ethicsstat/.

104 *See id.*

105 *See Is Your Workplace at Risk of Interpersonal Misconduct?*, ETHICS & COMPLIANCE INITIATIVE, Oct. 2018, https://www.ethics.org/knowledge-center/ethicsstat/.

106 *See id.*

107 *See* ETHICS & COMPLIANCE INITIATIVE, ECI WORKING GROUP PAPER: HOTLINES AND INVESTIGATIONS 18 (2019).

108 *See* Chad Albrecht et al., *The Role of Power in Financial Statement Fraud Schemes* (2014), DOI: 10.1007/s10551-013-2019-1; Rabi'u

Abdullahi et al., *Fraud Triangle Theory and Fraud Diamond Theory: Understanding the Convergent and Divergent for Future Research*, Eur. J. Bus. & Mgmt., Vol.7, No.28, (2015), http://www.iiste.org/Journals/index.php/EJBM/article/viewFile/26274/26919.

109 *See* Abdullahi, *supra* note 108, at 33.

110 Albrecht, *supra* note 108, at 2.

111 *See* Maggie McGrath, *How the Wells Fargo Phony Account Scandal Sunk John Stumpf*, Forbes, Sept. 23, 2016, https://www.forbes.com/sites/maggiemcgrath/2016/09/23/the-9-most-important-things-you-need-to-know-about-the-well-fargo-fiasco/#5f14c df93bdc.

112 *See* Abdullahi, *supra* note 108, at 32.

113 *See id.; see also* Assoc. of Cert. Fraud Examiners, Report to the Nations on Occupational Fraud and Abuse—2016 Global Fraud Study 68 (2016), https://www.acfe.com/rttn2016/docs/2016-report-to-the-nations.pdf (hereinafter "ACFE Report") (finding living beyond means to be a red flag in 45.8% of fraud cases, and large expenses or debts to be a warning sign in 30% of cases).

114 *See* Abdullahi, *supra* note 108, at 32.

115 *See* ACFE Report, *supra* note 108, at 66.

116 *See* Abdullahi, *supra* note 108, at 33.

117 *See id.* at 35.

118 *See* ACFE Report, *supra* note 2, at 49–61.

119 Ethics & Compliance Initiative, Ethics & Compliance Risk in the Supply Chain: 2016 Global Business Ethics Survey 1 (2016).

120 *See id.* at ii.

121 *See id.*

122 *See id.*

123 The personal characteristics of supply-side firm employees in the survey, however, do not seem to bear this out strongly. Although supply-side employees seem to be younger (23% vs. 19% ages 18–29; and 38% vs. 36% ages 30–44), and significantly more male (64% vs. 56% male; 36% vs. 44% female), their average tenure with the organization seems only slightly shorter and more grouped in the mid-term ranges (more in the 3–5 year range: 28% vs. 23%; the 6–10 year range: 26% vs. 22%; and much less in the 11 + year range: 25% vs. 32%). *See id.* at 3. It must be noted,

though, that far more supplier employees were in management (where misconduct was more commonly observed) than not in management relative to other companies (35% of employees in suppliers were non-management vs. 58% of non-suppliers). *See id.* at 3. This may be because unethical employees were more likely to be promoted, and to be promoted earlier, than in non-supply-side firms.

124 *See* Ethics & Compliance Risk in the Supply Chain, *supra* note 119, at ii.

125 *Id.* at 6.

126 *See id.*

127 *Id.* at ii.

128 *See id.* at 3.

129 One of the authors has written about the place of middle-management, in particular, in wide-spread corporate wrongdoing. *See, e.g.,* J.S. Nelson, *The Criminal Bug: Volkswagen's Middle Management,* https://hq.ssrn.com/submissions/Classif_Distrib_Info.cfm?AbstractID = 2767255&AuthorID = 2290306; J.S. Nelson, *Disclosure-Driven Crime,* 52 U.C. Davis L. Rev. 1487 (2019).

130 *See* Ethics & Compliance Risk in the Supply Chain, *supra* note 119, at ii.

131 *Id.* at 5.

132 *See id.*

133 *See, e.g.,* J.S. Nelson, *Opinion: 5 Ethical Challenges Employers Will Face As They Reopen,* HR Dive, June 17, 2020, https://www.hrd ive.com/news/5-ethical-challenges-employers-will-face-as-they-reopen/579989/; J.S. Nelson, *5 Ethical Challenges During COVID-19 That Businesses Need to Meet,* Ethical Systems, June 3, 2020, https://www.ethicalsystems.org/5-ethical-challenges-during-covid-19-that-businesses-need-to-meet/.

134 Ethics & Compliance Risk in the Supply Chain, *supra* note 119, at iii.

135 *Id.* at 11.

136 *See id.* at 14.

137 *Id.*

138 *Id.*

139 *Id.* at iii.

140 *See id.* at 26 (App. H: Employee Level of Awareness and E&C Resources).

141   *See, e.g., Boeing: Ethics & Compliance*, BOEING, https://www.boe ing.com/principles/ethics-and-compliance.page ("At Boeing, ethical business conduct isn't just a part of what we do—it's at the very core of how we operate. Doing the right thing for our employees, customers, stakeholders and communities has helped us earn trust and build partnerships that will drive us forward in our next century, and beyond.").

142   Jerry Useem, *How Boeing Lost Its Bearings*, THE ATLANTIC, 2019, https://www.theatlantic.com/ideas/archive/2019/11/how-boe ing-lost-its-bearings/602188/.

143   *Id.*

144   *See, e.g.,* Joseph Holt, *How Boeing Lost Its Way*, FORBES, Feb. 3, 2020, https://www.forbes.com/sites/josephholt/2020/02/03/ how-boeing-lost-its-way/.

145   *See* COSTCO WHOLESALE CORP., *Historical Highlights—Costco Investor Relations* 1, 3 (Jan. 21, 2020), https://investor.costco.com/ static-files/b5294947-8164-432c-b5c6-5e122a0f5c29.

146   COSTCO WHOLESALE CORP., *Mission Statement and Code of Ethics* (updated Mar. 2010), https://investor.costco.com/static-files/ 1a1a8efe-73a8-4079-a8eb-25fcb41316b2.

147   *Id.* at 1.

148   *Id.*

149   *See* COSTCO WHOLESALE CORP., *Historical Highlights, supra* note 145, at 3.

150   *See* Costco Wholesale Corporation, *Corporate Profile*, 2020, https://investor.costco.com/corporate-profile-2/.

151   *Id.*

152   *Id.* at 3.

153   *Id.*

154   *Id.*

155   *Id.* at 4.

156   *See id.*

157   *Id.*

158   *Id.*

159   *See The Empire Built on Values*, COSTCO CONNECTION 24, Jan. 2012, https://www.costcoconnection.com/connection/201201?article_ id = 1240935&lm = 1528989234000.

160   James D. Sinegal: A Long-Term Business Perspective in a Short-Term World, ETHIX, Apr. 1, 2003, https://ethix.org/2003/04/01/ a-long-term-business-perspective-in-a-short-term-world.

161 *Id.*

162 *See generally Hershey Code of Conduct,* https://www.thehershey
company.com/content/dam/corporate-us/documents/invest
ors/code-of-conduct.pdf.

163 *Id.*

164 *E.g., id.* at 6.

165 *Id.* at 6.

166 *See Code of Ethics and Business Conduct,* LOCKHEED MARTIN at ii,
https://www.lockheedmartin.com/content/dam/lockheed-mar
tin/eo/documents/ethics/code-of-conduct.pdf.

167 *Id.* at 1.

168 *Id.*

169 *Id.*

170 *E.g., id.* at 7.

171 *See id.*

172 *See id.* at 8.

Chapter 15

1 *See Corporate Ethics and Sarbanes–Oxley,* FINDLAW, http://corpor
ate.findlaw.com/law-library/corporate-ethics-andsarbanes-
oxlye.html ("The creation and enforcement of an effective ethics
program may offer substantial benefits to companies in terms of
both legal and performance measurements . . . . Apart from legal
requirements, at least two academic studies have suggested that a
commitment by corporate management to follow an ethical code
of conduct confers a variety of benefits.").

2 *See* U.S. DEPT. OF JUSTICE U.S. ATTORNEYS' MANUAL: TITLE 9
CRIMINAL § 9-28.900 (2015), http://www.justice.gov/usam/
united-states-attorneys-manual [hereinafter U.S. ATTORNEYS'
MANUAL].

3 *Factors in Decisions on Criminal Prosecutions,* U.S. DEPT. OF JUSTICE
2, July 1, 1991, last updated Apr. 15, 2015, https://www.justice.
gov/enrd/selected-publications/factors-decisions-criminal-
prosecutions.

4 U.S. ATTORNEYS' MANUAL, *supra* note 2, at § 9-28.900.

5 *See id.* at § 9-28.1000.

6 *Factors in Decisions on Criminal Prosecutions, supra* note 3, at 2.

7 *See* Phillip A. Wellner, *Effective Compliance Programs and Corporate
Criminal Prosecutions,* 27 CARDOZO L. REV. 497, 497 (2005).

8 *See* JOSEPH E. MURPHY, A COMPLIANCE & ETHICS PROGRAM ON
   A DOLLAR A DAY: HOW SMALL COMPANIES CAN HAVE EFFECTIVE
   PROGRAMS 1, 4 (Society of Corporate Compliance and Ethics ed.,
   2010), https://www.corporatecompliance.org/Portals/1/PDF/
   Resources/CEProgramDollarADay-Murphy.pdf ("[A] company
   that is convicted of federal crime will face extraordinarily large
   fines.").

9 *See Quick Facts on Organizational Offenders*, U.S. SENTENCING
   COMMISSION ORGANIZATIONAL DATAFILES, July 2018, https://
   www.ussc.gov/sites/default/files/pdf/research-and-publicati
   ons/quick-facts/Organizational-Offenders_FY17.pdf.

10 MURPHY, *supra* note 8, at 1, 4.

11 *See Corporate Ethics and Sarbanes–Oxley*, FINDLAW, http://corpor
   ate.findlaw.com/law-library/corporate-ethics-andsarbanes-
   oxlye.html.

12 *See id.* ("Organizations that emphasize ethical business
   conduct are often given greater deference by regulators and
   law enforcement authorities. In many cases, ethically-oriented
   organizations have positive reputations with law enforcement
   and regulators and enjoy the 'benefit of the doubt.'").

13 *See* Case Theory, Indiana Law (https://www.law.indiana.edu/
   instruction/tanford/b584/CaseTheory.pdf).

14 *See* Brandon L. Garrett, *The Corporate Criminal as Scapegoat*, 101
   VA. L. REV. 1789, 1795 (2015).

15 *See* Memorandum from Sally Q. Yates, Deputy Att'y Gen ,
   U.S. Dep't of Just., to All Component Heads and United States
   Attorneys, *Individual Accountability for Corporate Wrongdoing* 3,
   Sept. 9, 2015, https://www.justice.gov/dag/file/769036/downl
   oad (commonly known as the Yates Memorandum).

16 *See* Remarks of Rod J. Rosenstein, Deputy Att'y Gen., U.S. Dep't
   of Just., Remarks at the American Conference Institute's 35th
   International Conference on the Foreign Corrupt Practices Act,
   Nov. 29, 2018, https://www.justice.gov/opa/speech/deputy-
   attorney-general-rod-j-rosenstein-delivers-remarks-american-con
   ference-institute-0.

17 *See Quick Facts on Organizational Offenders, supra* note 9, at 177.

18 *See generally* Garrett, *supra* note 14, at 1802.

19 *See Your Day in Court*, JUDICIAL LEARNING CENTER (2019),
   https://judiciallearningcenter.org/your-day-in-court/.

20 *See* Alafair S. Burke, *Improving Prosecutorial Decision Making: Some Lessons of Cognitive Science*, 47 WM. & MARY L. REV. 1587, 1593–94 (2006).

21 *See id.* at 1595–96.

22 *See* Valerie P. Hans, *The Jury's Response to Business and Corporate Wrongdoing*, 52 L. & CONTEMP. PROB. 177, 192 (1989).

23 *See id.* at 193.

24 VALERIE P. HANS, BUSINESS ON TRIAL: THE CIVIL JURY AND CORPORATE RESPONSIBILITY (2000).

25 *See* Hans, *Jury's Response, supra* note 22, at 192.

26 *See* Brayden King & Mary Hunter-McDonnell, *Juries Treat Prestigious Companies Differently in Employment Discrimination Suits*, KELLOGGINSIGHT, Mar. 1, 2018, https://insight.kellogg. northwestern.edu/article/how-prestige-can-benefit-companies-in-court; *see also* Brayden King & Mary Hunter-McDonnell, *Order in the Court: How Firm Status and Reputation Shape the Outcomes of Employment Discrimination Suits*, 83 AM. SOC. REV. 61–87 (Jan. 2018).

27 *See* Hans, *Jury's Response, supra* note 22, at 192.

28 *Id.* at 197–98.

29 *Id.* at 192.

30 *See* SEARLE CIVIL JUST. INST., TRENDS IN THE USE OF NON-PROSECUTION, DEFERRED PROSECUTION, AND PLEA AGREEMENTS IN THE SETTLEMENT OF ALLEGED CORPORATE CRIMINAL WRONGDOING 1–2 (2015), https://masonlec.org/site/rte_uplo ads/files/Full%20Report%20-%20SCJI%20NPA-DPA%2C%20Ap ril%202015%281%29.pdf; *see also* Memorandum from Gary G. Grindler, Acting Deputy Att'y Gen., U.S. Dep't of Just., *Additional Guidance On the Use of Monitors in Deferred Prosecution Agreements and Non-Prosecution Agreements With Corporations*, May 25, 2010, https://www.justice.gov/archives/usam/ criminal-resource-manual-166-additional-guidance-use-monitors-dpas-and-npas (commonly known as the Grinder Memorandum); Memorandum from Craig S. Morford, Acting Deputy Att'y Gen., U.S. Dep't of Just., to Heads of Department Components, *Selection and Use of Monitors in Deferred Prosecution Agreements and Non-Prosecution Agreements With Corporations*, Mar. 7, 2008, https://www.justice.gov/archives/jm/criminal-resource-manual-163-selection-and-use-monitors (commonly known as the Morford Memorandum); Memorandum from

Brian A. Benczkowski, Ass't Att'y Gen., U.S. Dep't of Just., to All Criminal Division Personnel, *Selection of Monitors in Criminal Division Matters*, Oct. 11, 2018, https://www.justice.gov/opa/speech/file/1100531/download (commonly known as the Benczkowski Memorandum).

31   *See* SEARLE CIVIL JUST. INST., *supra* note 30, at 102.

32   *Id.* at 2.

33   *See id.* at 31.

34   *See id.*

35   *See id.*

36   *See 2018 Year-End Update on Corporate Non-Prosecution Agreements and Deferred Prosecution Agreements,* GIBSON DUNN, Jan. 10, 2019, https://www.gibsondunn.com/2018-year-end-npa-dpa-update/.

37   *See* Plea Agreement, U.S. v. Alcoa World Alumina LLC, No. 14-7 (W.D. Pa. Jan. 8, 2014), https://www.justice.gov/sites/default/files/criminal-fraud/legacy/2014/01/15/01-09-2014plea-agreem ent.pdf; Leslie R. Caldwell, Ass't Att'y Gen. for the Criminal Division, U.S. Att'y's Office, N.D. Cal., Remarks at the 22nd Annual Ethics and Compliance Conference (Jan. 26, 2017).

38   *See* Deferred Prosecution Agreement for Defendant Chipotle Mexican Grill, Inc., U.S. v. Chipotle Mexican Grill, Inc., Case No. 2:20-cr-00188-TJH (C.D. Cal. Apr. 21, 2020); *see also* Press Release, *Chipotle Mexican Grill Agrees to Pay $25 Million Fine and Enter a Deferred Prosecution Agreement to Resolve Charges Related to Foodborne Illness Outbreaks,* U.S. DEP'T OF Just., Apr. 21, 2020, https://www.justice.gov/opa/pr/chipotle-mexican-grill-agrees-pay-25-million-fine-and-enter-deferred-prosecution-agreement.

39   *See, e.g.,* Dan Flynn, *Parnell Brothers Finally in Prison for Deadly Peanut Butter Outbreak,* FOOD SAFETY NEWS, Feb. 17, 2016, https://www.foodsafetynews.com/2016/02/123674/ (describing the former CEO Stewart Parnell's prison sentence of 28 years).

40   *See* Deferred Prosecution Agreement for Defendant Chipotle Mexican Grill, *supra* note 38.30

41   *Id.*

42   *See Corporate Enforcement Policy: Declinations,* U.S. DEP'T OF Just., https://www.justice.gov/criminal-fraud/corporate-enforcem ent-policy/declinations; *see also* Nicole Sprinzen & Kara Kapp, *Emerging Trends Under the DOJ's Corporate Enforcement Policy,*

CORPORATE COMPLIANCE INSIGHTS, Feb. 20, 2020, https://www.
corporatecomplianceinsights.com/emerging-trends-doj-corpor
ate-enforcement-policy (describing how declinations with
disgorgement have been used recently to enforce the Foreign
Corrupt Practices Act).

43 *See* U.S. ATTORNEYS' MANUAL, *supra* note 2, at § 9-28.900.

44 *See* Michael J. Missal, Stavroula E. Lambrakopoulos & Curtis
S. Kowalk, *Conducting Criminal Investigations,* K&L GATES LLP,
http://www.klgates.com/files/Publication/9c8c688d-f33b-4e00-
befd-067ccd918740/Presentation/PublicationAttachment/08668
f67-5813-4c92-ac28-121554cc82a2/Conducting_Internal_tInvesti
gations.pdf.

45 *See id.* at 13–14.

46 *See id.* at 14–15.

47 Upjohn Co. v. United States, 449 U.S. 383 (1981). *Upjohn* warnings
are also sometimes referred to as "corporate *Miranda* warnings"
for their similarity to the even more famous *Miranda v. Arizona*
case, 384 U.S. 436 (1966).

48 *See Upjohn Co.,* 449 U.S. at 389–90; Missal et al., *supra* note 44,
at 14–15.

49 *See* Missal et al., *supra* note 44, at 18–19.

50 *See* Nicole L. Buseman & Brian Jacobs, *Navigating the Cooperation
Process in a Federal White Collar Criminal Investigation,* WESTLAW-
PRACTICAL LAW, w-002-8193 (2019).

51 *Id.*

52 *Id.*

53 *Id.*

54 *Id.*

55 *Id.*

56 *Id.*

57 *Id.*

58 *Id.*

59 *See* Nicole L. Buseman & Brian Jacobs, *Evaluating Whether an
Individual or Entity Should Cooperate in a Federal White Collar
Criminal Investigation 3,* WESTLAW-PRACTICAL LAW, w-005-4565
(2019) .

60 *See* Jillian Hewitt, *Fifty Shades of Gray: Sentencing Trends in Major
White-Collar Cases,* 125 YALE L.J. 1018, 1053 (2016).

61 *See id.*

62 *See* Solomon L. Wisenberg, *White-Collar Crime: The Crash Course,*
WISENBERG L., https://www.wisenberglaw.com/Articles/White-
Collar-Crime-The-Crash-Course-page-2.shtml.

63 *See id.*

64 *See* Elkan Abramowitz & Jonathan Sack, *Recent Developments
in the Prosecution of Corporations,* N.Y. L.J., Jan. 4, 2018, https://
www.maglaw.com/publications/articles/2018-01-04-recent-
developments-in-the-prosecution-of-corporations/_res/id = Atta
chments/index = 0/Abramowitz%20Sack%201.4.18.pdf.

65 *See* David M. Uhlmann, *The Pendulum Swings: Reconsidering
Corporate Criminal Prosecution,* 49 U.C. DAVIS L. REV. 1235, 1275–
78 (2016).

66 *See* J.S. Nelson, *Disclosure-Driven Crime,* 52 U.C. DAVIS L. REV.
1487, 1512 (2019); Yates Memorandum, *supra* note 15, at 2.

67 Uhlmann, *supra* note 65, at 1277.

68 *See* Offices of the United States Attorneys, *Plea Bargaining,* U.S.
DEPT. OF JUSTICE, https://www.justice.gov/usao/justice-101/ple
abargaining.

69 *See* SEARLE CIVIL JUST. INST., *supra* note 30, at xi.

70 *See id.* at 27–31.

71 *See id.* at 31.

72 *See Quick Facts on Organizational Offenders, supra* note 9.

73 *See* Offices of the United States Attorneys, *Trial,* U.S. DEPT. OF
JUSTICE, https://www.justice.gov/usao/justice-101/trial.

74 *What Are Some Common Steps of a Criminal Investigation and
Prosecution?* LEWIS AND CLARK LAW SCHOOL, NATIONAL CRIME
VICTIM LAW INST., https://law.lclark.edu/live/news/5498.

75 Brandon L. Garrett, *The Corporate Criminal as Scapegoat,* 101 VA.
L. REV. 1789, 1806 (2015).

76 *See id.*

77 *See Quick Facts on Organizational Offenders, supra* note 9.

78 *See* Hewitt, *supra* note 60, at 1053.

79 *See Quick Facts on Organizational Offenders, supra* note 9.

80 *See id.*

81 *See id.*

82 *See id.*

83 *See id.*

84 *See id.*

INDEX

For the benefit of digital users, indexed terms that span two pages (e.g., 52–53) may, on occasion, appear on only one of those pages.

rational maximization
  development of ethical
    capacity, 47–49
  environmental pressures, 51–53
  general discussion, 44–47, 372n.13
  incentive plans, 54–55
  influence of others, 54
  pressures to act unethically, 49–51
  resources, 350, 351
  tone at the top, 53–54, 350
Rawls, John
  Rawlsianism, 31, 40–42
  veil of ignorance, 31, 41
Reagan, Ronald, 21–22
regulatory agencies
  corporate transparency, 143–44
  discovery of unethical
    behavior, 167–69
  fines and penalties, 158–60, 224
  general discussion, 222–28
  information sharing, 164
  monitoring systems, 163–64, 167
relationships
  ECI recommendations, 277–79,
    459n.121, 459n.123
  general discussion, 11, 61
  negotiations, 216–17
  unethical behavior effects, 156–57
religious persons, 32, 171–72
Renault (Groupe Renault), 56–57,
    375–76n.45
reporting ethical violations. See
    also speak-up culture;
    whistleblowers
  attorney representation, 238–39,
    242, 254–55
  benefit entitlements, 240–45
  employees, 221, 228–33
  enforcement entities, 222–28
  internal mitigating
    activities, 218–21
  international whistleblowing, 255
  military whistleblowing, 255
  outside of organization, 233–38

possible consequences and other
    matters, 252–55, 454n.149
  protections, 245–52
  reporting period, 231–34,
    448n.46, 448n.50
  reporting to authorities, 238–40
  resources, 358–62
  state bar ethics hotlines, 359–62
Republic, The (Plato), 16–17
reputation
  compliance programs, 322–23,
    470n.1, 471n.12
  ethical organizations, 22–24
  general discussion, 14–16, 22
  internal investigations
    conducting interviews,
      330–31, 364
    determining scope, 329
    document collection and
      analysis, 330
    investigation staff, 329–30
    overview, 329
    reporting findings, 331–32
  prosecution and
    business cooperation, 326–29
    employee cooperation, 332–38
    steps taken by, 338–42
    theory of the case, 323–26
  trial consequences
    of unresolved
      investigations, 342–44
  unethical behavior
    consequences to
      individuals, 154–56
    consequences to
      organizations, 160–63
    overview, 13
reputational penalties
  Apple, 193
  Arthur Andersen, 339
  individual, 154–56
  negotiation puffery, 207–8
  organizational, 13, 160–63
  resources, 354–55